W9-AZJ-076

1972

THE
NEW BOOK
OF
KNOWLEDGE
ANNUAL

THE YOUNG PEOPLES
BOOK OF THE YEAR

A REVIEW OF THE EVENTS OF 1971

Grolier
INCORPORATED
NEW YORK

ISBN 0-7172-0603-3
The Library of Congress Catalog Card Number: 40-3092

COPYRIGHT © 1972 BY  Grolier
INCORPORATED
NEW YORK

Copyright © in Canada 1972 BY GROLIER LIMITED

PRINTED
IN
U. S. A.

No part of this book may be reproduced without
special permission in writing from the publishers

STAFF

William E. Shapiro
Editor in Chief

Russell J. Sully
Art Director

Fern L. Mamberg
Associate Editor

Allen Reuben
Picture Editor

Wallace S. Murray
Vice-President and Editorial Director, Grolier Incorporated

Martha Glauber Shapp
Director, Young People's Publications

Lowell A. Martin
Editorial Consultant

EDITORIAL AND ART

Editors:	Jay Bennett	**Style Editors:**	J. M. A. Raikes
	Patricia Ellsworth		Eleanor C. Wood
	Eleanor Felder		
	Wayne Jones	**Production Editor:**	Harriet L. Spiegel
	Henry Kurtz		
	Sylvia Rosenthal	**Production Assistant:**	Susan Rubin
	Leo Schneider		
	Janet Stone	**Indexers:**	Kathleen Leerburger
			Myrna Movtady
Researchers:	Eileen M. Farrell		
	Jo Ann Hauck	**Staff Assistants:**	Janet H. Ramlow
			Ruth E. Northlane
Art Assistant:	Margaret Alessi		Gloria James

MANUFACTURING

| **Director:** | Edward C. McKenna | **Assistant Director:** | Walter Schenone |

CONTENTS

CONTRIBUTORS

Laulicht, David
Editor, Reuter Focus Desk, Reuters News Service
West Europe   page 204

MacVane, John, B.A., B.Litt.
United Nations Correspondent, American Broadcasting Company
United Nations   page 358

Manoogian, Haig P., B.S., M.F.A.
Professor, Institute of Film and Television, New York University
Motion Pictures   page 172

Martin, Wilbur
Managing Editor, *Nation's Business*
Economy   page 146

May, Charles Paul, M.A.
Author, *Box Turtle Lives in Armor, Stranger in the Storm, The Early Indians, Natural and Imaginary Worlds*
Literature for Young People
page 246

Mishler, Clifford
Editor, *Coins* magazine and *Numismatic News*
Coins   page 216

Newbauer, John, B.A.
Editor in Chief, *Astronautics & Aeronautics*
Space Exploration   page 316

Psomiades, Harry J., Ph.D.
Professor of Political Science, Queens College, The City University of New York; Author, *The Eastern Question: The Last Phase*
Middle East   page 262

Reuwee, A. Daniel, M.A.
Director of Information, Future Farmers of America
Future Farmers of America
page 392

Rudin, Jacob Philip, B.A., M.H.L., D.D.
Former President, Central Conference of American Rabbis and Synagogue Council of America
Jews and Judaism   page 302

Schwartz, Harry, Ph.D.
Specialist in Soviet Affairs; Editorial Board Member, *The New York Times*
Soviet Union and East Europe
page 210

Segal, Jo Ahern, B.S.
Former Fashion Editor, *Look* magazine
Fashion   page 276

Shaw, Arnold, M.A.
Author, *The Rock Revolution, The World of Soul, The Street That Never Slept*
Popular Music   page 179

Singell, Larry D., Ph.D.
Associate Professor of Economics, University of Colorado
Consumerism   page 26

Stapleton, E. J.
Director, Public Information, Boys' Clubs of America
Boys' Clubs   page 388

Stasio, Marilyn, M.A.
Drama Critic, *Cue* magazine; Author, *Broadway's Beautiful Losers*
Theater   page 168

Tapp, E. J., M.A.
Former Associate Professor of History, The University of New England, New South Wales, Australia; Author, *Early New Zealand*
Australia, New Zealand, and the Pacific Islands   page 124

Taylor, Robert, A.B.
Art Editor, *The Boston Globe;* Lecturer, Wheaton College
Painting   page 92
Sculpture   page 100

Topping, Audrey
Free Lance Photographer and Writer
Chinese Acupuncture   page 260

Vaughan, E. Dean, Ph.D.
Director, 4-H and Youth Development Division, Federal Extension Service, U.S. Department of Agriculture
4-H Clubs   page 393

Verter, Leslie
Public Relations Coordinator, Camp Fire Girls
Camp Fire Girls   page 389

Vestal, David
Former Editor, *U.S. Camera Annual*; Instructor, School of Visual Arts
Photography   page 102

Wagner, Walter F., Jr., S.M., A.I.A.
Editor, *Architectural Record*
Architecture   page 106

Wilson, Kenneth L., Litt.D.
Editor and Publisher, *Christian Herald* magazine
Protestantism   page 298

THE REOPENING OF CHINA

By TILLMAN DURDIN

The New York Times

THROUGHOUT its long history, China has, more often than not, kept to itself. Rarely did it have any contact with the outside world, and when it did, it was only for relatively short stretches of time. But in 1971, after a long period of aloofness, China suddenly reopened its doors. Americans and visitors from other nations were let into the huge country.

Suddenly a vast territory and a huge population came into clear focus. China, the unknown, the mysterious, became a country of real people, of visible cities, farms, plains, and mountains. China emerged into the world's view as a land whose people had problems, hopes, fears, and urgent demands. In a word, the People's Republic of China became a living reality.

▶ PING-PONG DIPLOMACY

The reopening came suddenly and unexpectedly in April of 1971. It came just after the completion of a world table-tennis tournament in Japan. At this tournament a team from mainland China competed after six years of abstention from Ping-Pong play outside its borders. Sung Chung, secretary of the Chinese team, suggested casually, almost tentatively, to Graham Steenhoven, manager of the American team, that the Americans make a tour of the People's Republic.

Members of the American Ping-Pong team pose on the Great Wall of China. Right: A statue of Chairman Mao Tse-tung, leader of Communist China.

After a quick consultation with the officials of the United States Embassy in Tokyo, Mr. Steenhoven accepted the Chinese invitation. With this agreement the influx of foreigners into Asia's largest communist state was under way.

The table-tennis team from the United States blazed a trail that has since been followed by many other visitors. Along with the American players, the Chinese admitted a U.S. television team and several journalists. Mr. Steenhoven's Ping-Pong squad and the other travelers visited Peking, Shanghai, Canton, and their surrounding areas. They played matches, went sight-seeing, and attended a number of banquets. They visited farms and factories and talked with farmers, workers, teachers, and officials. Everywhere they were greeted with warmth and cordiality. One of the highlights of the tour was a meeting and a talk with Premier Chou En-lai.

The journalists, the television group, and even the Ping-Pong players reported about their experiences in China. They revealed a China that most people the world over had never heard of or seen. For millions of TV viewers and readers, the Chinese scene and its people suddenly came alive.

In the weeks that followed, a small but steady flow of foreign journalists, study groups, and trade delegations continued to enter the People's Republic. These visitors came from countries whose people had been barred entry up to that time. The Chinese Government focused upon *The New York Times* as the channel for presenting its views abroad. In April, it permitted Tillman Durdin, the *Times* Hongkong correspondent, to visit China for a three-week stay. He was the first American special correspondent to be admitted into China in many years. He was followed by Seymour Topping, the paper's assistant managing editor, and then in July and August by James Reston, the noted columnist of *The New York Times*. Mr. Reston was granted a five-hour taped interview with Premier Chou En-lai, one of the top communist leaders. In this interview, Premier Chou gave a detailed presentation of Chinese Communist views and attitudes on a number of major issues. These were issues involving China in its relations with the United States and other countries.

In answer to the Chinese initiative, the Americans invited a table-tennis team from the People's Republic to tour the United States. The U.S. Government ensured visas for Chinese journalists accompanying the team.

But the climax of the new China thaw came in July. After a secret visit to Peking by Henry Kissinger, special assistant to President Nixon, an important announcement was made. Peking and Washington jointly declared that the American President would visit the Chinese capital. There he would discuss important problems with Chinese Communist Party Chairman Mao Tse-tung and Premier Chou En-lai.

A factory on Shanghai Harbor.

A farmer in Fancheng, central China.

On a second trip to Peking, in late October, Kissinger worked out the details and dates: President and Mrs. Nixon would visit China February 21–28, 1972.

The visitors who entered China in 1971 found a fairly stable country. It was a country that was making progress in almost every important sphere. This was remarkable when one considers the last few years of Chinese history. For they were years that were marked by sporadic fighting and much disruption. From 1966 through 1969, China went through what Peking calls the Great Proletarian Cultural Revolution.

This was a movement launched by Mao Tse-tung. It purged tens of thousands of entrenched bureaucrats, including chief of state and longtime Communist Liu Shao-chi. It reshaped the structure and changed the personnel of the Communist Party and of the government. This was done to reverse what Mr. Mao regarded as a drift into a "revisionist" conservatism on the Soviet pattern. During the Great Proletarian Revolution, China turned its back on the world and virtually suspended relations with almost all foreign countries.

The visitors to China discovered a growing industrial base. Factories were busy turning out a great variety of light and heavy products. Shops had ample stocks of consumer goods. The collective farms were neat and attractive, with crops that were flourishing. The millions upon millions of Chinese people were energetically going about their tasks. They appeared to be in a relaxed and easygoing mood. This mood seemed to reflect a general acceptance, if not always a happy one, of the authoritarian and disciplined regime under which they lived.

The educational system had been severely disrupted by the Cultural Revolution. But now the system was beginning to function again. Students spent time not only in the classrooms but also in factories and in the fields, doing hard physical work. There were

THE PEOPLE OF CHINA

With nearly 800,000,000 people, China is the most populous nation in the world. Most of the people—more than 80 per cent—live and work on farms. Although peasants earn somewhat less than city workers, everyone benefits from low rents, free medical care, and very low prices for necessities such as food and clothing. Further, there is no unemployment in China; nor does anyone pay an income tax.

A May Day rally.

Mother and child in Yenan.

Farmer on a commune.

Student at technical school in Peking.

14

Shepherd in Yenan.

Traffic policeman in Sian.

Factory worker in Anshan.

other signs that the country was once again on the march in social and economic spheres—after years of suffering and turbulence.

▶CHINESE GOVERNMENT

The visitors found that China had a new governing structure, though still incomplete in some respects. It was made up of revolutionary committees for the provinces and the cities and of commissions at the national level. The extreme Leftists who had surged into prominence during the Cultural Revolution had, for the most part, been eliminated from important positions. Instead a new leadership had taken control of the country. This was a leadership made up of many military men. Yet it must be pointed out that it shared power with many old and with some new civilian officials.

There was a major shake-up in the country's leadership in 1971. Defense Minister Lin Piao, who had been Chairman Mao's political heir, disappeared. It was thought that he had been engaged in a power struggle with Mao—and had lost. Huang Yung-sheng, armed-forces chief of staff, also disappeared. Premier Chou En-lai was elevated to the number two position in the political hierarchy. Mao's wife, Chiang Ching, was third in importance.

Mao Tse-tung
Mao Tse-tung was born in Hunan Province in 1893. Chairman of the Chinese Communist Party since 1931, he is leader of the world's most populous nation. His writings have been published as "The Thoughts of Mao Tse-tung." These little red books are distributed free all over China. Mao has great appeal to his country's youth, who, as the Red Guards, helped purge China of anti-Maoist influences.

Chou En-lai
Communist China's premier since 1949, Chou En-lai is his country's chief spokesman to the outside world. His role in national affairs has made him nearly as important as Mao Tse-tung. Following Lin Piao's removal from power in 1971, Chou moved into the second most important political position. Chou was born in 1898 in Kiangsu Province. He was one of the chief organizers of the Chinese Communist Army.

Lin Piao
In late 1971 it was reported that Lin Piao had been ousted. As defense minister since 1959 and the chosen successor of Chairman Mao Tse-tung since 1969, Lin had wielded great power. He played an important role in the Cultural Revolution and launched the Red Guard student movement. Lin joined the Communist Party in 1927 and became known as a brilliant strategist of guerrilla warfare.

▶LIFE IN CHINA TODAY

Visitors found that the people of China were still poor. Urban salaries ranged from $10 to $15 a month up to $70 or $80. Rural cash incomes were $50 and $60 a year in addition to the food and housing that go with peasant living. But by all accounts, there seemed to be enough food for everyone. Clothing, while often faded and patched, appeared adequate. There was employment for all; stable and slowly decreasing prices for consumer goods. There were medical, old-age, and other welfare services for everyone.

Though teeming with bustle and activity, the cities looked drab. The people, men and women alike, were dressed in dull blue and gray trousers and jackets. There was very little private-automobile traffic. Yet the streets surged with pedestrians, public buses, and swarms of bicycle riders. The buildings of the downtown areas of the cities were often aged, grim, and gray. Shops, restaurants, and even the large stores were plain and almost unattractive. The bright lights, the advertising signs, the great differences that are evident in the housing of the rich and poor in cities of many other countries and of old China—all this was missing from these cities of the new China.

Chinese propaganda posters (left to right, top to bottom): "The people's militia is the key to victory," "Follow Chairman Mao's guidance to resolutely progress forward," "Raise high our vigilance; protect the fatherland," and "Follow the Communist Party to make revolution always."

兵民是胜利之本

沿着毛主席指引的方向奋勇前进

提高警惕 保卫祖国

跟着共产党 永远闹革命

The cities were drab but they were clean. Slums had been done away with. Parks and housing complexes were built in suburban areas. The main decorative feature in the cities was the abundance of political slogans. Often the sayings of Mao were seen painted on almost every wall, fence, and vehicle. They were also shown, along with colorful Mao portraits, on billboards, banners, and placards. However, as more and more people traveled to China, many Mao portraits were removed from prominent positions in major cities.

The campaign to exalt Mao and the ideals of the regime is not confined to slogans and portraits. Almost every public place has a loudspeaker which relays messages from Mao of work to be done, of theory to be put into practice, and of the aims and standards of the government. Compulsory political sessions are held quite regularly. At these meetings, the people are told to follow the regime's communist aims, and to devote themselves to the needs of the society and the state. These needs are to be put above all other needs. The propaganda effort has been an all-out one. It seems to have produced a sober, conformist, and community-centered people. There is very little crime. Antisocial behavior of any kind draws not only official but also neighborhood censure.

Below: Peking shopping center, and youngsters with their grandfathers. (The carriages are made of wood.) Right: Shanghai, China's most important port.

Acrobatic performers in Yenan. Acrobatic and gymnastic shows are popular in China.

The visitors saw a society short on what might be called fun and games. Means of amusement were limited to sports for a few, to public performances of a few politically-approved theatrical works, to gymnastic shows, and to the marching, singing, and slogan-shouting that went along with public ceremonies. However, it was not a dour society. Youth groups went singing and marching through the streets to their schools and to work. Adults seemed to find life not too grim.

The People's Republic is proud of its cultural and historical treasures. The visitors were taken to see a magnificent sweep of the Great Wall north of Peking. They saw the excavated tomb of the Ming Emperor Wan Li, which was outside the capital of the country. One of the key moments of their visit was the tour of the Forbidden City, one of two old walled towns situated within Peking. The Forbidden City was the old Imperial-Palace quarter, which, since the beginning of the Cultural Revolution, had been barred to all sightseers.

Some travelers were able to travel far into the interior of the vast country. They came to Sian, Wuhan, and to Changsha. It was there, during the civil war with the Kuomintang (the Nationalist Chinese forces led by Chiang Kai-shek), that the communist leaders held out for years. Then they finally started the surge that carried them to national power in 1949.

▶CHINA'S PROBLEMS

These recent visitors to China found settled conditions and signs of busy progress. It seemed that the country had recovered from the near-chaos of the Cultural Revolution. Yet it was clear to any perceptive visitor in 1971 that the People's Republic still faced mammoth problems. For example, China has a population that has been estimated to be about 800,000,000. The government has made great efforts to curb population growth. Yet with all that was done with birth control, it is clear that it was not enough and will not be enough. The economic development is just barely able to keep pace with the continuing increase of the population.

The regime has a policy of self-reliance without foreign assistance. It wants to raise the living standards of the people and to transform the country into a first-rank economic power. Yet the country's resources and technological skills are just not enough to do that great task.

Factionalism among the leadership still exists. There are millions of surly youth and other dissatisfied Chinese who were banished to frontiers and rural areas. These were the ones who had spearheaded social and political change during the Cultural Revolution. It is estimated that these people are a grave source of discontent and of potential trouble. It must also be considered that in 1971, Mao Tse-tung was 78 and in failing health. His death could create problems of succession among leaders, some as old as he is.

The question often asked is this: How long will the Chinese people perform effectively without getting more material rewards,

Performers in a revolutionary play.

THE YOUTH OF CHINA

In many ways the lives and experiences of the young people of China are different from those of their Western counterparts. The youth of China, for example, seem to have a greater sense of contributing to their society. But perhaps because of this their lives are more regimented. On the other hand, the youth of both China and the West enjoy many of the same things, including sports, the arts, and reading. Despite cultural and political differences, young people the world over are very much the same.

Young actors in a revolutionary play.

Marching with a portrait of Mao Tse-tung.

Playing soccer, a popular sport.

A concert in Nanking; the instrument is a Chinese violin.

Reciting lessons in an elementary school.

Playground in Peking.

Children's showcase bookstore in Shanghai.

more individual liberty, and more democratic rights? For it remains to be seen whether China's new flexibility in foreign relations will go hand in hand with more internal political and cultural relaxation.

▶FOREIGN RELATIONS

The logic behind Peking's move toward a bettering of foreign relations in general, and toward the United States in particular was not, in 1971, hard to see. Hostility between China and Russia had deepened. This was so because of sharp disputes over frontier territories. There was a rivalry for world power, and differing conceptions of communism. During the Cultural Revolution, anti-Soviet agitation inside China grew tremendously. Both countries marshaled forces for possible war.

Russia deployed a million men along the 6,000-mile border between China and itself, and between China and the Soviet ally, the Mongolian People's Republic. China's suspicion and hostility had already been heightened by the Russian occupation of Czechoslovakia in 1968. Nor did the Soviet statement following the occupation help things much. It declared that the Russians reserved the right to intervene in any communist country judged to be departing from Moscow policies and doctrine.

The tensions between the two countries were somewhat eased when they began talks on the border problems. But no real progress was made toward a settlement. Faced with the menace of a Soviet state much more powerful than China, the Chinese leadership moved to meet the situation. Internally, they brought to a halt the turbulent and destructive phase of the Cultural Revolution. They restored domestic equilibrium. Defense production was speeded up

Chinese soldiers welcome Rumanian leader Nicolae Ceausescu to Peking. Rumania has - been China's most important ally in Europe.

and increased. More nuclear weapons and missiles were developed.

On the international front, the Chinese noted President Nixon's doctrine of U.S. military disengagement in Asia, and his plans for settling the Vietnam war. A decision was made to ease China's relations with one of the world's great powers. This way they would be better able to confront the other great power.

Peking decided to cultivate improved and useful contacts with countries that formerly had been shunned. It saw the possibility of weakening U.S. and other opposition to the point that Peking could take a seat in the United Nations. This was the seat that was occupied so long by the small, rival China Nationalist Government on Taiwan. (On October 25, the General Assembly of the United Nations voted to admit Communist China and to expel the Chinese National Government. The Communist Chinese delegates arrived in New York City in November and were admitted to the Security Council, the General Assembly, and other UN bodies.)

At the same time, the People's Republic saw the chance of easing the danger it believed coming from Japan. It saw Japan's economic might and interest in Taiwan and Korea being transformed into military power and into a grave military threat.

In the light of all of these considerations, the new phase of Peking's foreign policy was launched. The results have already been far-reaching and complex.

Moscow has clearly become worried. A situation has been created whereby three big powers can jockey within the scope of their mutual hostilities and attractions. The People's Republic has made new approaches for trade and, in some cases, diplomatic relations with countries formerly on Peking's blacklist. Many new nations have switched their representation from the Taiwan Government to that of Peking.

To American visitors, communist officials have made plain that there is little to yield on points at issue with the United States. They declare that the United States must give up its protection of the Nationalists on Taiwan, signalized by a mutual-defense treaty. The United States, they say, must permit the islands to come under Communist China's control.

Peking says that the United States must accept demands of the communist regimes in Indochina that the Americans withdraw completely from that area and leave its future to be settled by the Indochinese peoples. The United States must withdraw its military forces from South Korea, Thailand, and the Philippines.

If a climate of understanding develops with the United States, then it is possible that these hard demands may be softened. But propaganda from Peking continued even after the visits, with the familiar denunciations of "U.S. imperialism" and "U.S. capitalist exploitation." So there were plenty of indications that things ahead for the two big powers, the United States and the People's Republic, would not be easy going.

CONSUMERISM

By **LARRY D. SINGELL**
University of Colorado

DURING the middle decades of the twentieth century, most of the countries of the world underwent enormous changes. Many of these changes came about as the result of major new industrial advances. In most countries the technological revolution of the fifties led to generally improved working conditions, increased employment opportunities, and rising income levels. The widely heralded technological advances and fantastic industrial progress of the earlier decades also spurred the creation of enormous numbers of new items and services every year.

The advantages of increased incomes and higher standards of living are, however, not without their problems. Buying is becoming a more complicated process, and the problems of consumer choice in the marketplace are growing increasingly difficult. The average consumer often lacks the knowledge to compare the qualities of goods available and to make intelligent choices.

Greater technical and material success has given rise to a new wave of concern about consumer problems that is known as "consumerism." Consumerism's main goal is to assert the rights of the consumer to be safe, to be informed, and to choose wisely.

Grocery stores in the early 1900's (below) carried small supplies of necessary items. Today's supermarkets (right) stock such an abundance of items that shopping has become a complicated process.

▶WHO IS A CONSUMER?

A consumer is anyone who buys or uses any kind of product or service. Consumers buy things that are produced—automobiles, refrigerators, furniture, clothing, and food, for example. They also make use of the skills of other people—plumbers, mechanics, teachers, secretaries, and doctors—all of whom provide the consumer with important services. These people receive payment for their services, and they in turn become consumers.

In the most highly industrialized nations, consumers are offered the widest variety of goods and services. In the developing countries where industry and technology are slowly growing, consumers are offered a smaller variety of goods and services. Where the per capita, or individual, income is the highest, consumer goods are both more numerous and more complex. Where the per capita income is the lowest, consumer goods are simpler and fewer.

▶THE AMERICAN CONSUMER

The United States is the richest country in the world. In 1970 the money value of all the goods and services produced in the United States (clothes, food, automobiles, defense, medical services, and so on) amounted to about $980,000,000,000. About

A large part of the consumer's dollar goes to buy necessities, such as food. . . .

$225,000,000,000 of this total was purchased by the government for national defense, education, highways, and other services. Another $140,000,000,000 was used by businessmen to build new factories and buy machinery and other equipment for producing more consumer goods in the future. The remaining $665,000,000,-000, about two thirds of the total, was available to American householders as consumer goods and services.

The median family income in the United States in 1970 was $9,400. This means that half of all families received more income than this, and half received less. The income received by American families is either saved, paid out in taxes, or used to buy consumer goods.

A large part of the consumer's dollar goes to buy food, drink, housing, and clothing. But this proportion is changing. In 1929 more than half of every dollar the consumer spent was for these essential items. By 1969 less than half of every dollar went for these items. This means that as families become richer, they have more money to spend on luxuries. In recent years Americans have been spending more on such things as travel and recreation. Other services, like those provided by doctors, dentists, lawyers, and accountants, have also grown very rapidly.

. . . .housing. . . . . . . .and clothing.

▶CONSUMERS' PROBLEMS

The high standard of living of the average American has relieved him of the fear of poverty and hunger. But the same material success has brought with it a new set of problems.

A good illustration of how consumers' problems increase can be seen in the simple example of the growth of the corner grocery store. Grocery stores in the early 1900's carried small stocks of necessary items. In 1950 the average supermarket carried about 1,500 items, and in 1970 the same store stocked about 8,000 items. In the earlier store the manager was available to help the customer make his selection. The modern supermarket, on the other hand, is almost completely self-service and impersonal. Today the consumer not only has more choices, but also less assistance in making them. He is forced to rely largely on advertising campaigns.

But the problems of today's consumer do not end when he has made his purchase. When he buys a modern appliance, he needs the skill of a highly trained mechanic to keep it in working order. The old icebox, for example, or the Model T Ford, required simple servicing compared with the modern refrigerator or the latest deluxe-model automobile with all its gadgets.

Other problems of consumerism in an industrialized society involve the poor. The poor frequently have the least information for making wise choices in the marketplace, even though their need for information is great. And because of such devices as installment buying, people in low-income brackets often have to pay high prices for their purchases.

"When a consumer buys a modern appliance, he needs the skill of a highly trained mechanic to keep it in working order."

Today's consumer is faced with additional problems of which he was unaware as recently as a decade ago. He is gradually learning that he must be more concerned about the effects of the products he buys on the environment in which he lives. In an effort to

A popular toy was plastic "clackety-clack balls." However, a warning was issued about its dangers, such as shattering.

In 1970, N.Y. Representative Richard Ottinger criticized toy manufacturers for making harmful playthings for children.

protect the natural world around him he must weigh the dangers as well as the merits of detergents and insecticides and packaging materials. He must be aware that he can no longer buy a product because advertisers have told him that it will make his wash whiter or kill more insects. He must also take into account the effect of modern washing products on his rivers and streams, and the effect of insecticides on the birds of his woods and fields.

There is almost no area of modern life that is not affected by a person's role as a consumer. When he buys food for his family he must make certain that the contents of canned goods are not contaminated, and that the lamb his butcher sells him is really lamb and not a less expensive sort of meat. He wants to know that the scales on which his purchases are weighed are in balance, and that the produce is fresh. When his doctor prescribes a medicine, the patient must be sure that the prescription is made up according to strict government standards and that it contains no harmful ingredients. It is important that children's toys be free of poisonous dyes and paints, and that they are neither highly flammable nor explosive.

The quality of the services a consumer seeks is just as important as that of the goods he buys. When a consumer wishes to buy an insurance policy he has to make certain that he is getting all he can for his money. Similarly, when he buys a house and borrows money to do so, he must be sure that the rates he is paying for this service are not too high. And when he moves into his new home, he must have the assurance of knowing that the prices the mover charges will not be excessive.

These are just a few of the problems a consumer faces in his daily life. The greater his dependence on goods and services, the more complicated the difficulties become. The modern consumer, if he is to get the most for his money, must be a well-informed buyer.

Ida Tarbell

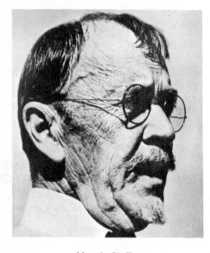

Lincoln Steffens

Upton Sinclair

▶HISTORY OF CONSUMERISM

Each period of concern about consumer problems occurs at a time of unusually rapid social change. In every period new laws to protect the consumer come only after the public has become aroused and insistent on government action. To understand the present wave of consumerism, it should be studied in relation to past periods.

The 1800's saw a period of rapid changes in the economy and society generally. Output of goods and services increased fivefold. The population doubled, and at the same time many people migrated from the farms to the cities. A nationwide network of railroads was completed. New mass-circulation magazines and newspapers began to advertise increasing numbers of products. The rapidly growing urban and industrial society produced a variety of new and difficult consumer problems, and social pressures began to mount.

By the 1870's the Federal Government and some of the states began to enact a few laws to deal with abuses. But the Supreme Court as well as the lower courts was relatively slow to make decisions regulating business practices. "Let the buyer beware" (Caveat Emptor) was still the accepted policy.

In the early part of the 20th century a group of journalists began to write works that stimulated public concern. These men and women were given the name "muckrakers" because they exposed the unfair practices of powerful businessmen. The writings of such people as Ida Tarbell, Lincoln Steffens, Charles Russell, and Upton Sinclair were the spearheads of the movement. Their work aroused public concern, and soon the government was forced from its position of inaction. Eventually, more and more consumer protection laws were passed. For example, the Meat Inspection Act (1906), the Food and Drug Act (1906), and the Federal Trade Commission Act (1914) all served to improve consumer protection. In addition, the courts were gradually forced to alter their "let the buyer beware" policy to one of "let the seller beware" (Caveat Venditor).

The 1930's saw the second wave of concern regarding consumer problems. During this period a great number of new kinds of large appliances were produced. Problems of misleading advertising, along with the social and economic difficulties of the Great Depression, led to the rise of a new group of muckrakers. Books like *Your Money's Worth* by Chase and Schlink and *100,000,000 Guinea Pigs* by Kallet and Schlink brought these issues to the attention of the public, and the government was forced to act. The National Industrial Recovery Act (1933), for example, provided for labor and consumer advisory boards to be set up. In addition, private groups like Consumers Union (1936) were established.

The wave of modern consumerism began in the 1950's. During the middle decades of the 20th century, the average worker earned

Rachel Carson (above) warned in her book "Silent Spring" against the use of pesticides. Her words seem to have been prophetic as one witnesses the booming sales of organic foods today.

more money than ever before, and a larger proportion of his income was spent on luxuries and nonessentials. Businesses turned their efforts toward trying to "manage the market" by manufacturing a product and then creating a desire for it. This sort of marketing very often means stressing qualities like styling and appearance rather than, for example, safety and durability.

Public opinion in the new wave of consumerism has once again been stimulated by the writings of a group of concerned consumer advocates. People like Rachel Carson, Vance Packard, David Caplovitz, and Ralph Nader have aroused consumers and alerted them to the dangers faced by an uninformed public.

▶ THE ROLE OF THE GOVERNMENT

Government action has been increasing in the modern wave of concern about consumer problems. On March 14, 1962, President John F. Kennedy sent to Congress a special message on protecting consumer interests. As a result, a Consumer Advisory Council was formed under the jurisdiction of the Council of Economic Advisers. In 1964, President Lyndon B. Johnson set up the President's Committee on Consumer Interests. In 1971, President Nixon created the Office of Consumer Affairs to coordinate all Federal consumer activities. In addition, a consumer-education office has been instituted. The chief function of this office is to plan a set of guidelines for consumer education in the schools.

Congress has enacted legislation to deal with consumer complaints. The Fair Labeling and Packaging Act (truth in packaging) in 1966 and the Credit Disclosure Act (truth in lending) in 1968 are attempts to protect consumer interests in these fields. Other important legislation has affected poultry and meat inspection, pipeline safety, land sales, and appliances.

People such as Vance Packard (above) and Ralph Nader (below) are modern-day muckrakers, alerting the public to consumer dangers. Their writings have spurred a new wave of consumerism. Packard's books include "The Hidden Persuaders." Nader rose to national prominence when he came out with "Unsafe at Any Speed" in 1965.

Since 1969, when President Nixon recommended a consumer unit within the Justice Department, concerned congressmen and other consumer advocates have been trying to obtain passage of a bill that would create an independent Consumer Protection Agency. The agency would have important powers. As originally conceived it would sponsor tests of consumer products, conduct investigations, and issue reports. In short, it would serve as an action agency to protect the rights of the consumer.

The most important consumer agencies of the Government operate within the Department of Agriculture, the Federal Trade Commission, and the Department of Health, Education, and Welfare. A division of the Department of Agriculture seeks to prevent diseased meat from reaching the country's markets. The department's Bureau of Human Nutrition and Home Economics grades a wide variety of products and informs the public about which foods are the most economical.

The Federal Trade Commission guards against false claims in advertising. It makes sure that labels are accurate, and that no highly flammable fabrics are sold. The Federal Communications Commission monitors broadcasting practices.

Two offices within the Department of Health, Education, and Welfare offer valuable aids. The Office of Education develops consumer programs in the schools. The Food and Drug Administration regulates the safety of foods, drugs, cosmetics, and chemical additives.

▶ THE ROLE OF TODAY'S CONSUMER

At a time when people's lives are so vitally affected by the purchases they make and the services they employ, it is no longer pos-

In 1971 President Nixon created the Office of Consumer Affairs, with Mrs. Virginia H. Knauer (above) as its director. Its purpose is to "give every American consumer a permanent voice in the White House."

sible for them to rely on government agencies to solve their problems. Consumers are gradually coming to understand that they themselves must accept a large measure of responsibility.

The consumer is becoming more and more aware of what is involved in the purchasing process, and developing some understanding of what causes him to buy. Does he really need the product? Will it improve his standard of living or add to his pleasure? Is he buying it not so much out of necessity but rather because of the persuasiveness of an advertising campaign? Will it live up to the manufacturer's claims?

Concerted consumer action has brought about encouraging results in many fields. For example, consumers led the movement against the practice of misleading labeling. One of the results of their efforts was to force action on "unit pricing." Unit pricing gives the buyer the exact cost per pound, pint, or piece of every item, and the manufacturer's claim that the "Giant Economy Size" is really more economical can be easily verified.

Independent consumer groups have grown enormously in the past decade. The largest of these is the International Organization of Consumers Unions, which was formed in 1960. The IOCU has more than 50 member organizations in 31 countries. Its purpose is to share ideas on a wide range of subjects of interest to the consumer, from product testing to drug control.

Many groups operate on a national level. Consumers Union in the United States is primarily a testing agency. Its magazine, *Consumer Reports,* has over 2,000,000 subscribers. There are similar organizations in Japan, Canada, Belgium, and West Germany.

Independent troubleshooting groups like Nader's Raiders have emerged, and consumers are lending support to special-interest organizations such as Public Citizen and Common Cause. The circulation of magazines that specialize in product evaluation has grown at an enormous rate.

The basic question, of course, is whether these efforts are adequate in dealing with the problems of the modern consumer. The answer is that there is clearly more work to be done. Achieving the solution to the consumer's dilemma will require a great deal of effort. A wider consumer-education program will have to be developed. Businessmen will have to provide better information. Manufacturers will have to guard against pollution. And the government will have to set rigid standards.

Many of the current consumer problems arise from the great economic success that has produced a high standard of living and a knowledgeable buying public. This success is seriously threatened if we do not learn to deal with the human and environmental problems that have been created in the process. The very quality of life will suffer considerably unless the productive system can be modified in some way to meet the ever-growing needs and demands of the consumer.

THE YOUTHFUL CONSUMER

By MARYLIN BENDER

THE word youth is an elastic term. Like beauty, youth can be said to lie in the eye of the beholder. But, for business, youth usually means all or any part of the population between the ages of one day and 25 years. Teen-agers, or those between junior-high-school and voting age, for the most part are a group that has spendable income (through allowances and earnings) and little or no financial responsibility for anyone but themselves. From a seller's standpoint, they are an ideal target—or used to be. The younger group—children rather than teen-agers—may also have money to spend, but the sums are smaller.

Young people love to travel, and spend a great deal of money doing so. In 1971 airlines courted youth with such drastically low fares that it was hard for any teen-ager to resist.

It is the American teen-ager, however, that has become a major sales target during the last twenty years. All through the 1950's, teens were studied, analyzed, and cultivated. Teen-agers developed a culture of their own, and through the mid-sixties it was almost totally a consumer culture. Youth took the lead away from adults in numerous industries, from fashion to movies and recordings. They started a retailing revolution through the boutiques that they patronized because larger stores didn't sell the clothing they wanted. The miniskirt, which was a symbol of youthful independence and freedom, was taken up by mothers and grandmothers who also let their hair grow into Alice in Wonderland manes.

▶HOW DO ISSUES INFLUENCE BUYING?

In the drive to open a new market—that of youth—American business created a new specialist. The youth expert was a market researcher. By regularly polling young people about their whims and preferences, he was supposed to guide business clients toward the youth moneymaking machine.

Today market researchers have started asking more basic questions of youth than they used to. Instead of concentrating on "which product do you prefer," they are trying to find out how youth feel about everything from the world at large and their place in it, to specific issues such as pollution and drugs.

The 1960's myth about the rich, recklessly spending young has given way to a business fear of a turned-off generation that keeps its money in its faded jeans. Young people are displaying a new attitude toward money and the consumption of goods. It ranges from a personal awareness of inflation (rising costs of books and college tuition, and the increasing unemployment of white-collar and professional as well as blue-collar parents) to "new poor" or "antimaterialistic" expressions that mean it's bad taste to look rich or showy.

For today's antimaterialistic youth, blue jeans have become the all-purpose "uniform."

Traditional stores lost business when teen-agers turned to boutiques and sidewalk vendors for their clothing.

Seventeen magazine produced a study—its first social-attitudes study on teen-age boys as well as girls. Called "The World I Live In," the report shows that teen-age consumers are vitally interested in such matters as ecology and poverty and that they are saying (although not all adults believe them) that happiness means more to them than material possessions. "Social change might have a greater effect on youth consumption than economic change," said Aaron Cohen, research director of *Seventeen*. "If they turn off a product, it's hard for that product to come back again." He was referring to detergents with a high pollution factor, leaded gasoline, and perhaps even those auto companies that fail to produce an emission-free engine.

▶WHERE IS THE YOUTHFUL CONSUMER HEADED?

No one is saying that this shift in social values has touched every person under twenty, but it does seem to have noticeably affected youthful buying habits. Some businessmen are overjoyed, others panicky, and still others perplexed.

Merchants of traditional clothing are worried by an obvious tendency of young people to dress down and to reject their brand of fashion and the stores in which it is sold.

"It was as if somebody drew a curtain in the fall of 1969," says Collette Touey, youth merchandise manager of Bergdorf Goodman. Mothers used to try to curb their daughters' reckless shopping impulses. But ever since that autumn of antiwar moratoriums, followed by a spring of campus unrest, they have had to plead with them to buy a proper dress or coat. "Clothes are way down on kids' list of priorities," added Miss Touey.

It was no surprise to any merchant or parent who has observed blue jeans becoming youth's all-purpose uniform that Levi Strauss had sales of over $250,000,000 in 1970, up from $196,000,000 the year before. Or that in the last 5 years it has more than doubled its blue-jeans sales, to 120,000,000 a year.

Nine out of ten teen-age girls own sunglasses.

Another youth trend that perceptive merchants are trying to follow is the creative or do-it-yourself kick. The home sewing industry is a $3,000,000,000 industry and growing. Some stores have hired demonstrators for knitting, crocheting, and leatherworking kits, a surefire magnet to attract young girls back into traditional stores.

The youthful consumers' fondness for shopping in boutiques, or small shops that sell the kind of casual, impudent clothing they want, has ignited the spark for a merchandising and manufacturing revolution. Such stores, and even traditional stores that are trying to copy the boutique formula, are buying their merchandise from unorthodox manufacturers such as hippie communes or teen-age students working out of their own homes.

The cosmetic industry, too, has cause to smile about the youth market. *Seventeen*'s surveys show that 13,000,000 teen-age girls spend $500,000,000 a year on cosmetics and toiletries. Nine out of 10 teen girls own sunglasses.

Any survey of youthful consumer priorities invariably puts music and travel at the top of the list. Music means records, which they mostly buy for themselves. Columbia Records is the company that guessed best on the youth trend toward rock and country music. Where rock had been 15 per cent of Columbia's output in 1967, in 1970 it was over 50 per cent. Within those 3 years, Columbia doubled its share of the record market to 22 per cent.

Music is at the top of the list for the youthful consumer. And music means records, tapes, cassettes, and expensive audio equipment.

Mobility means that youth is on the move by various means of transportation. In the fall of 1970, bicycles suddenly were nestling next to Camaros and Mustangs in some high-school parking lots. The cyclists are "having fun and doing their ecology thing," said one high-school senior who bicycled five miles to school without polluting the suburban air on a $95 English racer she bought in London with her summer job earnings.

When it comes to cars, young drivers are influenced, and in turn influence the market, by price, compact size, and function. The companies with the largest share of the youth market in the fall of 1970 (just before the new American subcompacts were coming out) were Volkswagen, Ford (Maverick), Datsun, Renault, and Toyota.

Most airlines are now courting the young with youth fares. And Pan Am is introducing a student credit card (based on a C plus grade average), adding a menu choice of soul food, spreading the word of education bargains abroad, and stressing the theme, "you can't improve a world you haven't seen."

The fads and fancies that will engage the youthful consumer in the near future are no easier to predict than the course of inflation, unemployment, or any other factors in the business climate.

What is clear is that youth cannot be treated as gullible consumers. The values and perceptions of the young will continue to affect their purchasing. And insofar as these sensibilities indicate changing social currents, they will anticipate as well as reflect the buying behavior of older consumers.

For young people, bicycles have become a popular, and inexpensive, way of getting around.

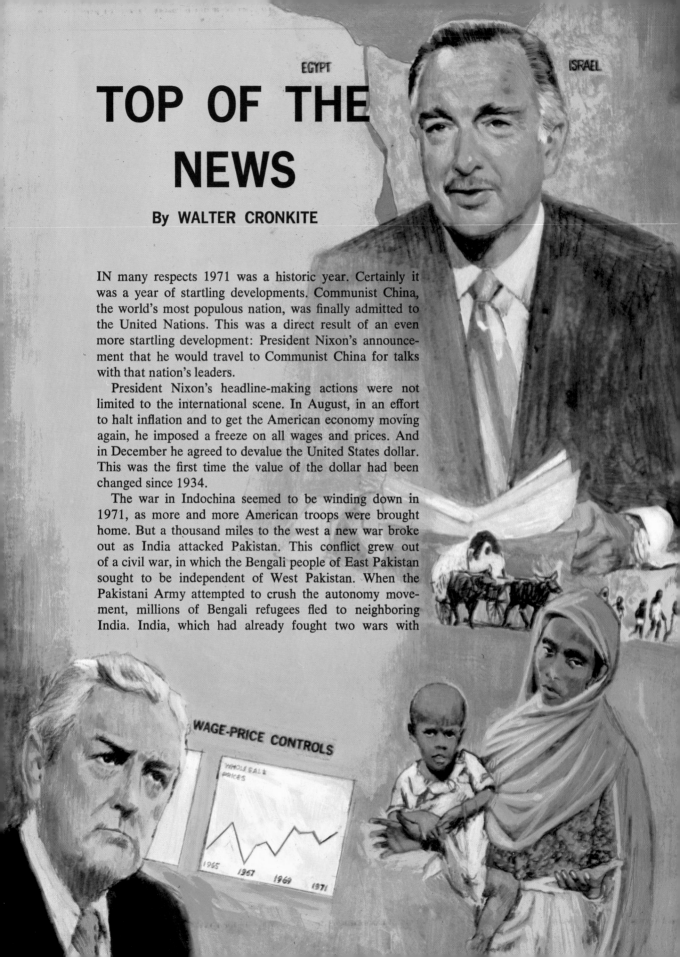

TOP OF THE NEWS

By WALTER CRONKITE

IN many respects 1971 was a historic year. Certainly it was a year of startling developments. Communist China, the world's most populous nation, was finally admitted to the United Nations. This was a direct result of an even more startling development: President Nixon's announcement that he would travel to Communist China for talks with that nation's leaders.

President Nixon's headline-making actions were not limited to the international scene. In August, in an effort to halt inflation and to get the American economy moving again, he imposed a freeze on all wages and prices. And in December he agreed to devalue the United States dollar. This was the first time the value of the dollar had been changed since 1934.

The war in Indochina seemed to be winding down in 1971, as more and more American troops were brought home. But a thousand miles to the west a new war broke out as India attacked Pakistan. This conflict grew out of a civil war, in which the Bengali people of East Pakistan sought to be independent of West Pakistan. When the Pakistani Army attempted to crush the autonomy movement, millions of Bengali refugees fled to neighboring India. India, which had already fought two wars with

Pakistan, invaded East Pakistan, and in two weeks brought an end to West Pakistani rule. Out of this brief war a new nation—Bangladesh—was born.

Three other nations—Bahrain, Qatar, and the Union of Arab Emirates—were born in 1971, though in a more peaceful manner. These three small nations are located in the Persian Gulf area of the Middle East. Elsewhere in the Middle East there was great political instability. But another major war between Israel and its Arab neighbors was avoided.

The major development in Europe was agreement on terms for acceptance of Great Britain into the European Economic Community. If this powerful economic union leads, eventually, to political union, Europe will become the world's fourth superpower, taking its place with the United States, the Soviet Union, and Communist China.

PENTAGON PAPERS

Dr Daniel Ellsberg at news after he surrendered himself in Boston with his wife after he stopped Washington Post from publishing material from the

JANUARY

					1	2
3	4	5	6	7	8	9
10	11	12	13	14	15	16
17	18	19	20	21	22	23
24	25	26	27	28	29	30
31						

2. A crowd barrier collapsed after a soccer match in Glasgow, Scotland, killing 66 persons. It was the worst tragedy in the history of British soccer. . . . John W. McCormack, Democrat from Massachusetts, retired after serving 42 years as a member of the U.S. House of Representatives and 9 years as Speaker of the House.

5. Chile became the second Latin-American country to recognize Communist China. (Cuba had been the first.)

8. The British Ambassador to Uruguay, Geoffrey Jackson, was kidnaped by Tupamaro guerrillas in Montevideo.

15. The Aswan High Dam, a billion-dollar project to provide Egypt with more electricity and cropland, was dedicated by U.A.R. President Anwar el-Sadat and Soviet chief of state Nikolai V. Podgorny.

16. The Swiss Ambassador to Brazil, Giovanni Enrico Bucher, was released by the Leftist guerrillas who had kidnaped him on December 7, 1970.

25. Milton Obote, Uganda's head of government since 1962, was ousted by a military coup; Major General Idi Amin became leader of the new Government.

President Nixon delivers his State of the Union Message to Congress.

STATE OF THE UNION. President Richard Nixon delivered his State of the Union Message to a joint session of Congress on January 22. The President called for a $16,000,000,000 sharing of Federal revenues with state and local governments. He also asked Congress to pass a welfare-reform bill and to approve a major health program, which would include funds for a fight against cancer.

JEWISH DEFENSE LEAGUE. Continuing tactics they had begun late in 1970, members of the militant Jewish Defense League harassed Soviet officials in New York City. Soviet diplomats were threatened, and a bottle was thrown through the window of the Soviet UN Mission. In Washington, D.C., a bomb was exploded outside a Soviet cultural building.

Members of the Jewish Defense League stage a demonstration near the Soviet UN Mission in New York.

	1	2	3	4	5	6
7	8	9	10	11	12	13
14	15	16	17	18	19	20
21	22	23	24	25	26	27
28						

2. The Organization of American States ended a nine-day special meeting in Washington, D.C., with the adoption of a convention condemning the political kidnaping of diplomats.

7. A constitutional amendment was passed in Switzerland giving women the right to vote in federal elections. The only independent countries that do not permit women to vote are Liechtenstein, Saudi Arabia, Jordan, Kuwait, and Yemen.

10. Cambodia's Deputy Premier, Sisowath Sirik Matak, was put in charge of the Government after Premier Lon Nol suffered a stroke two days earlier.

11. The United States, the Soviet Union, Great Britain, and 64 other nations signed a treaty barring nuclear weapons from the ocean floor. The pact will take effect when it is ratified by at least 22 countries.

15. Great Britain converted its currency to the decimal system, ending the old currency system which had been used for more than a thousand years.

21. A series of tornadoes struck Mississippi, Louisiana, and Tennessee, killing about one hundred people and leaving thousands more homeless.

Buildings lie in ruins following the February 9 Los Angeles earthquake.

LOS ANGELES EARTHQUAKE. At 6 A.M. on February 9 a powerful earthquake struck the Los Angeles area. Sixty-four people were killed and hundreds injured. Property damage was put at more than one billion dollars.

APOLLO 14. On February 5, Apollo 14 astronauts Alan B. Shepard and Edgar D. Mitchell became the 5th and 6th men to walk on the moon. The two astronauts stayed on the lunar surface for 33½ hours. They set up the nuclear-powered ALSEP—Apollo Lunar Scientific Experiment Package—and collected rock and lunar-dust samples before rejoining Stuart A. Roosa in the command module. The trip home was uneventful: they splashed down in the Pacific on February 9.

LAOS INVASION. On February 7–8, South Vietnamese Rangers and Army troops invaded Laos. The stated purpose of the invasion was to destroy communist supply lines and to deprive the Vietcong of sanctuaries in Laos. The South Vietnamese were supported by United States air power.

The Apollo 14 Launch Control Center at Kennedy Space Center, Florida.

U.S. troops rest near Khesan, South Vietnam, not far from the Laotian border.

MARCH

2. U.S. agronomist Claude L. Fly, held captive by Uruguay's Tupamaro guerrillas since August 7, 1970, was released.

10. John G. Gorton, Australia's prime minister since 1968, was ousted as leader of the Liberal Party. William McMahon was elected party leader and thus became prime minister.

15. The United States ended its ban on travel by Americans to Communist China.

17. Trygve M. Bratteli succeeded Per Borten, who had resigned in the midst of a political scandal, as prime minister of Norway.

19. Nihat Erim was named premier of Turkey after the military had forced the resignation of Premier Suleyman Demirel.

23. In Northern Ireland, Brian Faulkner became prime minister, succeeding James D. Chichester-Clark, who had resigned.

26. Lt. Gen. Alejandro Lanusse became president of Argentina after a military junta had ousted President Roberto Levingston.

29. An Army court found 1st Lt. William L. Calley, Jr., guilty of the premeditated murder of at least 22 South Vietnamese civilians at Mylai in 1968.

ELECTIONS IN INDIA. In March national elections, Prime Minister Indira Gandhi's ruling New Congress Party won 350 of 518 seats in the lower house of the Indian Parliament. The elections had been marked by a great deal of violence, especially in West Bengal State, where more than forty people were killed. On March 17, Mrs. Gandhi was reelected leader of the New Congress Party.

Election posters in Old Delhi, India, showing Prime Minister Indira Gandhi. Mrs. Gandhi's ruling New Congress Party won a majority of seats in the lower house of Parliament.

CIVIL WAR IN PAKISTAN. Civil war broke out in East Pakistan on March 26 after talks between Pakistani President Agha Mohammad Yahya Khan and Awami League leader Sheik Mujibur Rahman had failed. The Awami League, the chief political party in East Pakistan, had won a majority of seats in the National Assembly in December 1970 elections. Sheik Mujibur then tried to negotiate autonomy for East Pakistan. When this failed, civil war erupted. The Sheik was arrested and jailed.

Above: Followers of Sheik Mujibur Rahman prepare to fight the Pakistani Army. Below: Bengali refugees in India use drainage pipes as temporary homes.

			1	2	3
4	5	6	7	8	9	10
11	12	13	14	15	16	17
18	19	20	21	22	23	24
25	26	27	28	29	30

3. President Nixon announced that he would personally review the case of 1st Lt. William L. Calley, Jr., "before any final sentence is carried out." (Calley had been found guilty by a court-martial of murdering at least 22 South Vietnamese civilians at Mylai.)

17. Egypt, Libya, and Syria signed an accord to form a union of the three countries with "one president, one flag, one anthem, and one federal capital," and a strong anti-Israel position.

19. The West African country of Sierra Leone was proclaimed a republic.

22. Jean-Claude Duvalier became president of Haiti upon the death of his father, François Duvalier (Papa Doc), dictator of Haiti for 13½ years.

24. Nearly half a million marchers massed in Washington, D.C., and San Francisco, peaceably demonstrating against the war in Indochina.

25. Soyuz 10, with three cosmonauts aboard, returned safely to the Soviet Union, ending a 48-hour mission. During the flight the Soyuz docked with an unmanned orbital laboratory, called Salyut, that had been launched several days earlier.

PING-PONG DIPLOMACY. During April an American Ping-Pong team visited Communist China. Chinese Premier Chou En-lai stated that the visit had "opened a new page in the relations of the Chinese and American people." During the same month, President Nixon relaxed a U.S. embargo on trade with China. These events heralded a dramatic change in the 20-year history of U.S.-Communist Chinese relations.

Chinese Premier Chou En-lai (front row, second from right) poses for pictures with members of the United States and other visiting Ping-Pong teams in Peking, capital of China.

Many businessmen joined students in Washington, D.C., for a mass demonstration against the Vietnam war. Another large demonstration was held in San Francisco.

						1
2	3	4	5	6	7	8
9	10	11	12	13	14	15
16	17	18	19	20	21	22
23	24	25	26	27	28	29
30	31					

3. East German Communist Party leader Walter Ulbricht resigned; Erich Honecker was named to succeed him. . . . During anti-war protests designed to close down Washington, D.C., over 7,000 people were arrested, the largest mass arrest in a single day in United States history.

19. During a 12-day visit to the Soviet Union, Canadian Prime Minister Pierre Trudeau signed an agreement with Premier Aleksei Kosygin calling for regular high-level talks to encourage greater cooperation between the two countries.

20. In the Soviet Union, a Leningrad court found 9 Soviet Jews guilty of organized anti-Soviet activity. They were sentenced to prison-camp terms ranging from 1 to 10 years.

22. An earthquake ravaged parts of eastern Turkey, leaving nearly 1,000 people dead.

23. In Turkey, the Israeli Consul General Ephraim Elrom was found murdered. He had been kidnaped on May 17 by Leftist terrorists who demanded the release of "all revolutionary guerrillas under detention."

27. Austria and Communist China agreed to establish diplomatic relations.

WORLD CURRENCY CRISIS. The stability of the world monetary system was shaken during May. The U.S. dollar, backed by gold, is the key currency in the Western world. In recent years, however, the United States has experienced deficits in its international balance of payments. This has weakened the dollar. At the same time, other currencies have grown stronger. As a result, in May, five European currencies were allowed to "float" relative to the dollar or were revalued upward. This, in effect, devalued the dollar.

SOVIET-EGYPTIAN TREATY On May 27 the Soviet Union and Egypt signed a 15-year friendship treaty. This signified that the Soviets would continue to give military aid to Egypt. Earlier in the month, the Soviets had been angered because Egypt had purged pro-Soviet officials from the Government. The officials were accused of having plotted to oust President Anwar el-Sadat.

In Washington, D.C., soldiers arrest anti-Vietnam-war demonstrators.

Because of the money crisis, many American tourists were unable to exchange U.S. dollars for local currencies.

		1	2	3	4	5
6	7	8	9	10	11	12
13	14	15	16	17	18	19
20	21	22	23	24	25	26
27	28	29	30			

10. The United States ended its 21-year embargo on trade with Communist China, authorizing the U.S. export of many non-strategic items and lifting controls from all imports.

17. The United States signed a treaty with Japan providing for the return of Okinawa to Japanese sovereignty. U.S. troops had captured the Japanese island during World War II. (The treaty must be ratified by the U.S. Senate and the Japanese Diet before it goes into effect.) . . . Dom Mintoff became prime minister of the Mediterranean island of Malta after his Labor Party won in parliamentary elections.

21. The International Court of Justice ruled 13–2 that South Africa's administration of the territory of South-West Africa (Namibia) was illegal.

23. Britain and the six-nation European Economic Community (Common Market) agreed on the entry terms for Britain to become a member of the trade bloc.

30. The 26th Amendment to the U.S. Constitution was ratified when Ohio became the 38th state to approve it. The Amendment provides for the lowering of the minimum voting age from 21 to 18 years in Federal, state, and local elections.

SOVIET COSMONAUTS KILLED. On June 30, three Soviet cosmonauts were found dead in their Soyuz II spacecraft when it returned to earth. Georgi T. Dobrovolsky, Vladislav N. Volkov, and Viktor I. Patsayev had stayed in space for a record-breaking 24 days. Experts believed that they had failed to properly secure the hatch of their spacecraft.

PENTAGON PAPERS. Starting June 13 *The New York Times* published documents and articles detailing United States involvement in the Vietnam war. The so-called Pentagon Papers had been given to the *Times* and other newspapers by Daniel Ellsberg, who had helped prepare the secret study. The U.S. Department of Justice tried to halt publication of the documents. The Supreme Court, however, ruled that the newspapers could continue publishing them. The Government ordered the arrest of Ellsberg; he was charged with the theft of Government property and violation of the Espionage Act.

Workers in "The New York Times" composing room applaud after hearing that the U.S. Supreme Court had ruled that the "Times" could publish the Pentagon Papers.

Daniel Ellsberg talks to reporters and supporters outside the Boston Federal Court. He had been arrested—and released on bond—after he admitted giving the Pentagon Papers to the press.

			1	2	3	
4	5	6	7	8	9	10
11	12	13	14	15	16	17
18	19	20	21	22	23	24
25	26	27	28	29	30	31

1. The United States Postal Service, an independent government corporation with non-cabinet status, assumed control of the nation's mail system. The new agency replaced the 182-year-old Post Office Department.

12. The Soviet Union announced that the deaths of the three cosmonauts aboard Soyuz 11 resulted from a rapid change in the air pressure in their capsule shortly before they returned to earth on June 30.

14. Olafur Johannesson was sworn in as prime minister of a new Leftist coalition Government in Iceland.

28. President Nixon named career diplomat William J. Porter to succeed David K. E. Bruce as chief delegate to the Paris peace talks on Vietnam. . . . U.S. Vice-President Spiro Agnew returned to Washington, ending a 32-day diplomatic tour of Asia, Africa, and Europe. He visited South Korea, Singapore, Kuwait, Saudi Arabia, Ethiopia, Kenya, Congo (Kinshasa), Spain, Morocco, and Portugal.

30. A Japanese jet airliner collided with a Japanese Air Force jet fighter over the Japanese Alps; 162 persons were killed in the worst disaster in aviation history.

NIXON ANNOUNCES CHINA VISIT. On July 15 President Nixon announced that he would visit Communist China sometime before May 1972 for talks with Chinese leader Mao Tse-tung and Chinese Premier Chou En-lai. Arrangements for the trip had been made by presidential adviser Henry Kissinger.

TURMOIL IN MOROCCO AND SUDAN. Two northern African nations experienced attempted coups in July. In Morocco a coup by rebellious Army officers was crushed. King Hassan II narrowly escaped assassination. In Sudan, Leftist officers ousted General Gaafar al-Nimeiry on July 19. Three days later, with the aid of Egypt and Libya, forces loyal to al-Nimeiry regained control of the country.

Morocco's King Hassan with General Mohammad Medbouh, in an early photo. Medbouh, thought to have led the attempted military coup in July, was killed in the fighting.

In Athens, U.S. Vice-President Spiro T. Agnew poses with a Greek child (above) and with Mrs. Agnew in front of the Parthenon on the Acropolis (below). The Vice-President also visited several other countries in Europe and the Middle East.

AUGUST

1	2	3	4	5	6	7
8	9	10	11	12	13	14
15	16	17	18	19	20	21
22	23	24	25	26	27	28
29	30	31				

2. The United States announced it would support the seating of Communist China in the United Nations, but was opposed to the expulsion of Nationalist China from the organization.

9. The Soviet Union and India signed a 20-year friendship treaty pledging support if either country was attacked by an outside aggressor.

11. New York Mayor John V. Lindsay formally switched from the Republican Party to the Democratic Party.

14. Bahrain, a Persian Gulf island group that had been a British protectorate, became an independent nation.

21. Red Cross officials from North and South Korea met to try to solve the problem of families divided by the Korean war. It was the first direct contact between the two countries since the war (1950–53). . . . George Jackson, one of the three black convicts known as the "Soledad Brothers," was killed as he attempted to escape from San Quentin in California.

22. Hugo Banzer Suarez assumed the presidency in Bolivia after an anticommunist coup toppled the Government of Juan Jose Torres Gonzales.

WAGE-PRICE FREEZE. On August 15 President Nixon announced that he was placing a 90-day freeze on all wages, prices, and rents. He also said that he was ending the traditional convertibility of the U.S. dollar into gold. A 10 per cent surcharge was put on foreign goods imported into the United States. The President said that he took these steps to halt inflation, growing unemployment, and international speculation against the dollar.

NORTHERN IRELAND. In early August the Government of Northern Ireland began arresting and jailing suspected Catholic terrorists. On August 9, heavy fighting broke out in Belfast, Londonderry, and other cities. Buildings were burned and British troops fired upon. By the end of the month, more than thirty persons had been killed.

APOLLO 15. In the United States' most successful manned spaceflight, Apollo 15 astronauts David R. Scott and James B. Irwin stayed on the moon for three days. They explored the lunar surface in a special lunar rover and collected large amounts of lunar material. The lunar module liftoff from the moon was televised. A safe splashdown was made on August 7. Space officials felt there were no harmful germs on the moon, and the Apollo 15 astronauts were the first not required to undergo quarantine.

Apollo 15 astronauts (left to right): James Irwin, Alfred Worden, David Scott.

A British soldier with a young boy in Belfast, Northern Ireland.

Many houses were burned down during Belfast riots.

A wary British soldier watches a side street. He is all but ignored by Irish Catholic shoppers.

SEPTEMBER

1. The Persian Gulf sheikdom of Qatar, a British protectorate since 1916, became an independent nation. . . . The Federation of Arab Republics, a union of Egypt, Syria, and Libya, was overwhelmingly approved in referendums in the three countries.

9. Geoffrey Jackson, the British ambassador to Uruguay, was released by Uruguay's Tupamaro guerrillas who had held him hostage for eight months.

16. Because of loss of revenue, and other poor economic factors, *Look*, one of the last U.S. mass-circulation picture and text magazines, announced it would cease publication with its issue dated October 19.

17. Hugo L. Black, associate justice of the U.S. Supreme Court since 1937, retired.

23. John M. Harlan, associate justice of the U.S. Supreme Court since 1955, retired.

24. Great Britain expelled 105 Soviet representatives from the country because of espionage activities.

26. President Richard Nixon met Emperor Hirohito in Alaska. It was the first time in history a U.S. president met with a Japanese emperor.

ATTICA PRISON REVOLT. On September 9, at Attica Correctional Facility in New York, more than 1,000 convicts seized 32 prison guards and civilian workers and held them as hostages. They issued a list of demands that included amnesty for their part in the revolt. State authorities refused. On September 13 some 1,500 law officers stormed the prison, killing or fatally wounding more than 40 prisoners and hostages. An investigation of the tragedy was ordered.

Rebellious prisoners at Attica Correctional Facility in upstate New York.

N.Y. Governor Nelson Rockefeller: criticized for not joining negotiations with prisoners.

New York State Correction Commissioner Russell Oswald ordered the Attica revolt put down. More than forty hostages and prisoners were killed.

Eight days after authorities regained control of Attica, the prison yard was still strewn with rubble.

OCTOBER

1. The retirement of Dr. Ralph J. Bunche, United Nations under-secretary-general for special political affairs, was announced.

8. The Soviet Union expelled or denied re-entry to 18 British citizens on charges of spying, and canceled several high-level meetings to have been held by the two countries.

10. Austria's Socialist Party, headed by Chancellor Bruno Kreisky, became the first party to win more than 50 per cent of the vote in postwar Parliamentary elections.

11. Jens Otto Krag became premier of Denmark.

12. President Richard Nixon announced that he would visit the Soviet Union in May 1972.

17. Starting an 8-day trip, Aleksei N. Kosygin became the first Soviet head of government to visit Canada.

20. National Security Adviser Henry A. Kissinger began a 5-day visit to Peking to arrange the details of Nixon's planned trip to Communist China.

28. Great Britain's House of Commons voted 356 to 244 for British membership in the Common Market.

Huang Hua, Communist China's permanent representative to the United Nations, prepares to take his seat in the Security Council.

COMMUNIST CHINA ADMITTED TO UN. On October 25, the United Nations General Assembly voted 76–35, with 17 abstentions, to seat Communist China and to oust Nationalist China. Communist China's admission had been expected ever since President Nixon announced in July that he would visit that country early in 1972. Still, the vote was a defeat for the United States, for it wanted to keep Nationalist China (Taiwan) in the world organization.

SOUTH VIETNAM ELECTIONS. In October 3 elections, South Vietnamese President Nguyen Van Thieu was re-elected for another four-year term. Thieu ran unopposed and received more than 90 per cent of the vote. His two major opponents had withdrawn from the race. Vice-President Nguyen Cao Ky and Duong Van Minh, a popular general, had withdrawn on August 20, after accusing Thieu of rigging the elections. During the campaign, there were widespread disturbances by anti-Thieu forces, especially Army veterans.

President Thieu at a press conference after his re-election.

Vice-President Nguyen Cao Ky withdrew from the election.

Soldiers guard against anti-Thieu demonstrations.

A South Vietnamese woman casts her vote.

NOVEMBER

	1	2	3	4	5	6
7	8	9	10	11	12	13
14	15	16	17	18	19	20
21	22	23	24	25	26	27
28	29	30				

5. As the first step in an expansion of trade with the Soviet Union, the U.S. announced a commercial sale of $136,000,-000 worth of livestock feed grains to the Soviet Union.

10. Cuba's Premier Fidel Castro began a 3½-week visit to Chile, his first trip to South America in 11 years.

11. Secretary of Agriculture Clifford M. Hardin resigned, and Earl L. Butz was nominated to succeed him.

12. President Nixon announced that 45,000 more American soldiers would be withdrawn from South Vietnam by February 1, 1972, leaving a force of 139,000 men.

24. Great Britain and Rhodesia signed a compromise agreement ending the discord that began in 1965 when Rhodesia declared itself unilaterally independent of Great Britain. The agreement provided greater political rights for black Africans.

28. Premier Wasfi Tal of Jordan was assassinated by Palestinian guerrillas in Egypt.

29. It was announced that President and Mrs. Nixon would begin their visit to Communist China on February 21, 1972.

PHASE 2. Phase 2 of President Nixon's economic-stabilization program began on November 14. Phase I—the total freeze on wages, prices, and rents—was ended and replaced with a system of restraints. Wage increases would be limited to an average 5.5 per cent, and price increases to an average 2.5 per cent. Earlier, President Nixon had announced that Phase I, which had been in effect for ninety days, had been successful—that inflation had been slowed considerably.

AMCHITKA NUCLEAR TEST. On November 6, on the island of Amchitka in the Aleutians, the United States exploded underground a 5-megaton H-bomb. The purpose of this test was to develop a warhead for the Spartan missile. The test came after a four-month legal battle by environmentalists who feared that the blast would start a tidal wave and harm the environment in other ways. The case had gone to the Supreme Court, which denied appeals to halt the test.

In Toronto: a protest against the Amchitka nuclear test.

At a news conference Secretary of the Treasury John Connally explains how Phase 2 of President Nixon's economic-stabilization program will work.

Prison guards and state police wait outside the New Jersey State Prison at Rahway. A prisoner revolt was ended without violence after N.J. Governor Cahill agreed to review prisoner demands.

DECEMBER

			1	2	3	4
5	6	7	8	9	10	11
12	13	14	15	16	17	18
19	20	21	22	23	24	25
26	27	28	29	30	31	

2. The Union of Arab Emirates, formed of 6 Persian Gulf sheik-doms, proclaimed independence.

10. The U.S. Senate confirmed the nomination of William H. Rehnquist to the Supreme Court. Four days earlier, Lewis F. Powell, Jr., had been confirmed.

13. Communist China released two Americans held prisoner since 1952 and 1968. . . . The UN General Assembly passed a resolution calling on Israel to withdraw from occupied Egyptian territory.

17. Col. Oran K. Henderson, the last person to be tried for having been involved in the 1968 Mylai killings, was acquitted of charges that he had covered up the massacre.

21. Kurt Waldheim of Austria was chosen by the Security Council to succeed U Thant as UN secretary-general.

28. President Nixon met with West German Chancellor Willy Brandt. (Earlier in December Nixon had met individually with Israeli Prime Minister Golda Meir, Canadian Prime Minister Pierre Trudeau, French President Georges Pompidou, and British Prime Minister Edward Heath.)

29. Giovanni Leone became president of Italy.

WORLD CURRENCY AGREEMENT. President Nixon announced on December 18 that the ten leading Western industrial nations had agreed to realign world currency exchange rates. The U.S. dollar was devalued by what amounted to a 12 per cent depreciation against gold, the official price of which went to $38 an ounce from $35. The President also removed the 10 per cent surtax on imported goods.

INDIA-PAKISTAN WAR. On December 3, Indian forces attacked East Pakistan, and in two weeks of bitter fighting defeated the Pakistani forces. Nearly 100,000 Pakistani soldiers were captured. This brief war severed East Pakistan from West Pakistan, and a Bengali state—Bangladesh—was established. In West Pakistan the disastrous war forced President Agha Mohammad Yahya Khan to resign. He was replaced by Foreign Minister Zulfikar Ali Bhutto. Still under arrest in West Pakistan was Sheik Mujibur Rahman, who had been named president of the newly proclaimed nation of Bangladesh. It was expected that Bhutto would release him.

A Russian-built Indian helicopter inside East Pakistan.

On December 16, Pakistani General A. A. K. Niazi (right) surrenders to Indian Army General Jagjit Singh Aurora.

Sheik Mujibur Rahman, president of Bangladesh. This photo was taken in March, before his arrest and imprisonment.

THE YEAR IN

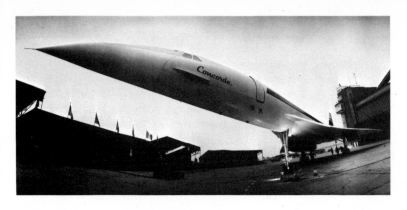

REVIEW

WE FIGHT INFLATION • WE SUPPORT THE U.S. ECONOMIC PROGRAM

APOLLO 15

SCOTT WORDEN IRWIN

1971

AFRICA

DURING 1971 there were several coups and attempted coups on this vast continent. In Uganda, President Milton Obote was ousted, and Major General Idi Amin took control of the country. In Sudan, Major General Gaafar al-Nimeiry was for a brief moment out of power, but then returned to crush the opposition and execute its leaders. A coup in Chad was put down, and an alleged attempt at a coup was smothered in Somalia.

In addition to political instability, many nations of sub-Saharan Africa faced another major problem: how to stimulate their economies and food production. These are not keeping pace with a rapidly growing population. In February, the severity of this problem was pointed out by the United Nations Economic Commission for Africa. It reported that Africa's population increases by 9,000,000 to 10,000,000 every year. The report estimated that by the year 2000 the population of Africa will be a staggering 650,-000,000. In response to the growing urgency of the situation, an African conference on population was scheduled.

Chadian youngsters drink milk supplied by the United Nations International Children's Emergency Fund. Lack of adequate food is a major problem in many parts of Africa.

There was much political instability in Africa during 1971. General Gaafar al-Nimeiry (right) was ousted as leader of Sudan, but he regained power a few days later. General Idi Amin is sworn in as president of Uganda (below) after the military seized power.

WEST AFRICA

William S. Tubman, who was for 28 years the president of Liberia, died in London after an operation. Vice-President William R. Tolbert became the 19th president of Liberia. Tolbert, 58, is a wealthy rubber planter and has long been a member of what Liberians call the Establishment.

In neighboring Sierra Leone, in March, a coup was attempted but it failed. There was also a plot to kill Prime Minister Siaka Stevens. But this, like the coup, was unsuccessful. The following month, Sierra Leone was proclaimed a republic. Siaka Stevens became the first president of the country.

On June 29 four Army officers were executed for their part in the abortive coup.

An important event of 1971 was the visit of French President Georges Pompidou. He toured five countries which in the past had been French colonies. President Pompidou received an extremely warm welcome in Mauritania, Senegal, Ivory Coast, Cameroon, and Gabon. It was evident that the ties between these African lands and France were still quite secure.

Pompidou made a number of speeches during his travels in western Africa, and in these speeches he emphasized some key points. He promised that the French Government would under no circumstances reduce its aid to these countries. On the contrary, French aid would be increased in the near future. Pompidou also promised that his Government would encourage French private investment. He was aware that up to that time French businessmen had invested very little in West Africa. President Pompidou emphasized that his country and the West African countries should draw closer to each other in friendship and in trade.

Nigeria, too, sought friendly ties with other countries on the continent. On October 11, it was announced that Nigeria would exchange ambassadors with Ivory Coast, Tanzania, and Zambia. During its civil war with Biafra, Nigeria had severed relations with Ivory Coast, Tanzania, and Zambia because of their support for the seceding region.

In 1971 Guinea reacted to the abortive invasion of late 1970. According to a United Nations fact-finding mission, Portuguese officers, coming from neighboring Portuguese Guinea, had led a 350-man invading force. In 1971 the people of Guinea supported President Sékou Touré and his program of

making the country strong, and secure from any further attack. Roadblocks were set up in many sections of the nation. The Government launched a purge, and made plans to give military training to thousands of the nation's men and women.

To drum up the militant spirit of the people of Guinea, political rallies and meetings were held fairly regularly. Patriotic slogans and signs were placed in many areas of the country.

The general mood of the country became somewhat anti-Western. In 1966 the Peace Corps had been asked to leave Guinea. But a few short years later, the Government's policy changed, and the Peace Corps was invited back. In 1971, however, the policy changed again, and the Peace Corps was once more out of favor with Guinea's lead-

French President Georges Pompidou is welcomed by the people of Abidjan during his visit to Ivory Coast.

A food market in Nigeria, which is recovering from its costly civil war.

Even during the abortive coup against General Gaafar al-Nimeiry, rebels in southern Sudan continued their fight against the Arab-dominated Government of the north.

ers. Accordingly, the last volunteer left the country in August.

By all accounts, President Touré seemed to be firmly in power. Kwame Nkrumah, the former leader of Ghana, still was living in Guinea under the protection of Touré's Government.

▶ **CENTRAL AND EAST AFRICA**

The six-year rebellion in Chad continued during 1971. The insurrection has been carried out by Muslim tribesmen of the north, central, and eastern parts of the sparsely populated former French colony. These Muslim tribesmen have long resented the domination of the country by the people of the south. It is the people of the south, the Sara, who are in control of the Government in Chad.

For a while in 1971 it seemed that the rebellion was coming to an end. Most of the French troops that had been called in three years earlier, under the terms of a mutual defense pact between Chad and France, left the country. Many signs pointed to a period of peace and stability for this troubled nation. But suddenly, in August, a group of northerners attempted to overthrow the Government of President Tombalbaye.

The coup was crushed. But the Government angrily termed the attempt a "foreign-directed" coup. Chad broke diplomatic relations with neighboring Libya. Foreign Minister Baba Hassane accused Libya of "openly trying to interfere with the internal affairs of our young republic. . . ."

The month of July was a turbulent one for the people of Sudan. The events of that month aroused much discussion and controversy in many countries. Sudan had a coup and then a countercoup. On the night of July 19, Major General Gaafar al-Nimeiry was ousted, and power was seized by a group of Leftist Army officers. Two of the men who were expected to take leading posts

in the new Leftist regime were in London, where they had gone for medical treatment. A few days after the take-over, the two men boarded a plane for Khartoum, to assume the leadership of the country. But the British airliner which carried them was forced down in Libya. The Libyan Government was opposed to the overthrow of Nimeiry.

The seizure of both men was undoubtedly a factor in the collapse of the coup. On July 22, Nimeiry was able to regain power. Though the British Government strongly protested to Libya over the seizure of the men and the violation of air law, the revolutionists were turned over to General Nimeiry.

In the violent days that followed, a number of people were killed, and more than a thousand people were arrested. Among those

In Uganda, crowds cheer Major General Idi Amin as he drives his jeep through the streets of Kampala. General Amin had ousted President Milton Obote.

Milton Obote, president of Uganda since 1966, was ousted in 1971. He went into exile in neighboring Tanzania.

executed was Abdul Khalek Mahgourb, secretary-general of the Sudanese Communist Party. His death caused a storm of protests from the socialist countries. The Soviet Union threatened to sever relations with Sudan.

The country remained stable in the months that followed, and Nimeiry consolidated his position of strength. In a two-week national referendum that ended October 1, General Nimeiry received 98.6 per cent of the total vote. He was the only candidate for president. On October 12, Nimeiry took the oath of office as the first elected president of Sudan. He announced the formation of a 26-man Cabinet and the establishment of a single political party, the Sudanese Socialist Union.

On October 27, the Democratic Republic of the Congo (Kinshasa) announced that the country would now be known as the Republic of Zaire. The new name was taken from the original name of the Congo River. Where this enormous river runs through the territory of Zaire, it will be called the Zaire River.

Late in the year, the Ethiopian ruler, Emperor Haile Selassie, went on a trip to Peking, the capital of Communist China. There he met and talked with China's leader, Mao Tse-tung. The trip was evidently a fruitful one for Ethiopia, for it was announced that the country would receive a loan of $84,000,000 from Communist China. The loan, a virtually interest-free one, will be used to buy agricultural equipment.

Another African leader went on a trip in 1971, but this one turned out to be quite disastrous for him. President Milton Obote left Uganda to attend a conference of Commonwealth leaders in Singapore. While he was there, he lost the presidency. Major General Idi Amin led a successful coup which deposed the absent Obote.

Obote returned to Africa and took refuge in Tanzania. The Amin Government offered a reward of $139,000 for the return of Milton Obote alive. Relations between Uganda and Tanzania worsened. Amin threatened to

Dr. Hastings Banda, president of Malawi.

shoot down any aircraft approaching from Tanzania and claimed that pro-Obote guerrillas had entered Uganda from Tanzania. The effect of this bitter dispute on the East African Community was uncertain. The EAC is a customs and economic union which links Kenya, Uganda, and Tanzania. However, in November tensions eased when Amin reopened the border with Tanzania and restored direct travel and communications.

▶**SOUTHERN AFRICA**

On August 20, President Hastings Banda of Malawi completed an official state visit to South Africa. He was the first black African head of state to travel to that country. In a sense this was a diplomatic victory for South Africa, which is trying to bring about a dialogue with the black countries of Africa.

South Africa practices a policy of apartheid—or separation of the races—which is opposed by all black African nations.

The controversy over holding a dialogue with South Africa is a bitter one. The issue was debated with much heat at the full session of the Organization of African Unity in June. After a split vote, it was decided that no black African nation should open a dialogue with South Africa.

When asked whether he thought his visit would have an influence on apartheid, Banda said, "I do not like the system of apartheid. But I prefer to talk."

In a step considered to be an alternative to outright apartheid, Britain and Rhodesia signed an agreement on November 24 ending their 6-year dispute. In 1965 Rhodesia had declared itself independent of Britain rather than prepare itself for eventual rule by the country's black majority. Subsequently, Britain, as well as other member nations of the UN, imposed economic sanctions against Rhodesia. Under the terms of the new agreement, power remains in the hands of the country's 250,000 whites. But the 5,000,000 black Africans are offered guarantees against discrimination, and the hope of eventual political control.

JAY BENNETT
Africa Editor
Lands and Peoples Encyclopedia

AFRICA'S YOUTH

Falasha boys of the Ethiopian Jewish community learn to read Hebrew.

An Ewe boy in Ghana.

Above: In northern Nigeria, a young religious student studies verses (in Arabic) from the Koran, the holy book of Islam. Below: In Niger a nun teaches first-graders how to read French.

Pupils at the Hospital Hill School in Nairobi—the first Kenyan elementary school to be integrated.

A Hausa girl from Niger.

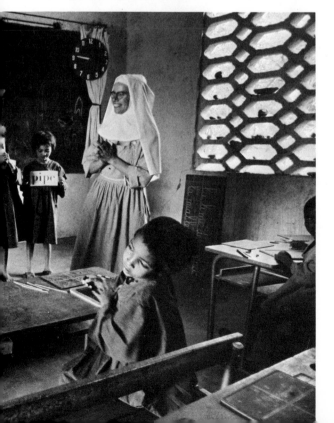

In Cameroon, a member of the Bamileke tribe rides to market on a home-made bicycle. The entire bicycle, including the wheels, is made of wood.

A boy poles a canoe along the Niger River.

A young Masai herdsman in Tanzania.

At an experimental school in Niger, pupils work on an assignment, and get instruction by television.

AGRICULTURE AND FOOD

FARMERS began 1971 fearing a crop shortage from drought and blight. They turned on their full productive power and finished the year with the biggest grain harvest ever. The result was lower prices for wheat and feed grains. Lower prices left farmers with almost no gain in net incomes after paying higher business costs.

Yet farmers took pride in their production. They took special pride since President Richard M. Nixon's new economic program focused on the need for greater output per man-hour of work. In fact, the President honored farmers with a Salute to Agriculture day at the White House in May. Agriculture was the only industry so honored. There were several reasons for the honor:

One American farmer produces more than 7 times as much food and fiber with an hour's work as an American farmer did 50 years ago. From 1960 to 1970, farm production shot up about 70 per cent—twice the rate of United States nonfarm industry.

Food prices have risen just about 7.8 per cent in 20 years. Almost all of this increase comes from higher processing and labor costs after food leaves the farm.

Food is so abundant that aid can be given to about 15,000,000 people through food-stamp programs and direct food distribution. School-lunch programs cut the cost of hot lunches almost in half for some 25,000,000 students.

Farms produce enough food for each American to eat a yearly average of 231 pounds of meat, chicken, and turkey; 190 pounds of fruit; 366 pounds of vegetables; and 586 pounds of milk and dairy products.

In 1971 farmers harvested a wheat crop of 1,600,000,000 bushels.

Late in 1971 Earl L. Butz, left, was named secretary of agriculture. He replaced Clifford M. Hardin, shown below-right with President Nixon and Norman E. Borlaug at the Salute to Agriculture Day at the White House. Dr. Borlaug, director of the International Maize and Wheat Improvement Center in Mexico, won the 1970 Nobel Peace Prize for developing improved strains of wheat and rice.

5,500,000,000 bushels of corn were harvested in 1971.

▶CROPS

In early spring farmers in much of the Corn Belt had a major worry. How much of the corn crop would be lost to Southern leaf blight? The disease had destroyed about 15 per cent of the 1970 crop and would surely be back. Crop-disease experts set up a blight-watch reporting system. Farmers planted all the blight-resistant seed available. Because a corn shortage was expected, prices shot up, and the drama was on.

Unexpectedly, farmers planted 7,000,000 acres more corn, rather than playing it safe with other crops. Weather for planting was near-perfect. Corn sprouted earlier than usual, and by midsummer lush, deep emerald fields promised a huge harvest.

August brought drier, cooler weather than usual. This slowed the spread of the blight spores. Then people slowly realized that a record 5,500,000,000 bushels of corn would descend on the market—35 per cent more than a year before. Spring prices of $1.60 a bushel dived to below $1.00 as the yellow grain poured from combines in September and October. As a result, the huge 1971 crop had almost the same total dollar value as the 1970 crop, which was ¼ smaller.

Southwest and Great Plains farmers harvested a record 880,000,000 bushels of grain sorghum, another livestock feed. The crop was 26 per cent more than the preceding year's. One of the worst droughts on record had scorched Texas and New Mexico, where half the grain-sorghum crop grows. However, much of the Texas crop is irrigated. And farmers beyond the drought area in Kansas, Nebraska, and Colorado boosted their output considerably.

Wheatgrowers harvested 18 per cent more than in 1970. The crop was a price-crushing 1,600,000,000 bushels.

There was also a record crop of soybeans (1,200,000,000 bushels). But even the record crop wasn't enough to keep up with growing demand for this high-protein, high-oil wonder crop. The demand is a sign that people in the United States and other nations are improving their diets by switching to higher-protein foods.

A new device developed by the Agricultural Research Service may prove to be of great importance to soybean growers. The device makes use of a beam of infrared light, and measures instantly the quantity of oil and protein in a powdered sample of soybeans. (Present chemical tests are slow and fairly expensive.) High-oil, high-protein beans could mean higher prices to farmers.

Drought in western Texas.

▶EXPORTS

Farmers wound up the trade year with record sales abroad: $7,800,000,000. United States farmers exported the equivalent of about one acre in four. They could have sold more, except for limits on imports abroad, dock strikes at home, and early reactions to President Nixon's international currency-revaluation policy.

The biggest overseas customer for United States farm products is the European Economic Community (EEC). However, it fences out many American products by placing high tariffs on them. When Great Britain formally enters the EEC, that nation will also be behind EEC's tariff walls.

Japan is a major customer for American feed grains and soybeans. The country was slow to renew its purchases after the announcement of the Nixon program.

▶LIVESTOCK

About 60 per cent of all farm income comes from sales of livestock. The big crop of corn and other feed grains meant cheaper feed costs for farmers. Hog prices tumbled; beef prices held fairly steady; and milk prices rose a little. On the whole, livestock producers had a fair year.

At Duluth, Minnesota, a Greek freighter is loaded with grain that is being exported to Europe.

A Limousin bull, a European breed being imported by American beef breeders.

The demand among beef breeders for exotic breeds of cattle grew. The demand was mostly for European kinds that will be used for crossbreeding. Promoters brought in cattle or semen from about a dozen European breeds, including Simmental, Chianina, Limousin, and Maine-Anjou. For years to come, breeders will be judging which bloodlines give the faster growth and meat tenderness United States consumers want.

▶ LABOR UNIONS

Labor unions have used collective bargaining for years to win better wages and benefits. But collective bargaining by farmers has made headway very slowly. Their chief bargaining agent is the National Farmers Organization, which is believed to have about 8 per cent of United States farmers as members. (Enrollment totals are secret.)

Three new bills waited in Congress. They would give farmers more bargaining machinery under Federal approval. But none seemed likely to be enacted immediately. Meanwhile, the National Farmers Organization, acting under the older Capper-Volstead farm bargaining act, extended its collection and delivery system for farm products. Its aim is to build a network of members who can block together large amounts of each product and deliver them to buyers at an agreed price.

Dairymen joined together their huge cooperatives for this same purpose. For years dairymen have been nearly powerless in dealing with supermarket giants and big milk processors. Toward the end of the year, the merger of three big co-ops seemed about to take place. The merger would link one-sixth of the nation's dairymen into one bargaining group. One of the three co-ops, Associated Milk Producers, staged an indoor meeting in Chicago attended by 40,000 dairymen, their families, and officials, including President Nixon.

▶ OF INTEREST TO CONSUMERS

Meat marketers made fresh progress toward an old cost-saving idea that could help hold retail meat prices down. The idea is the sale of frozen retail meat cuts. Meat cutting could be done with assembly-line methods,

and packers could ship ready-to-sell cuts straight to the store. One retail test in New Jersey found a surprising level of acceptance of bright, well-packaged frozen beef. An Indiana experiment proved that pork, sharp-frozen at sub-zero temperatures, keeps its fresh look.

Worry rose among consumer groups about medicines and growth stimulants farmers use in livestock feed. The fear was that some of the chemicals would remain in the product when it reached the retail counter. An estimated 80 per cent of all United States animal protein comes from animals that have received some kind of medicated feed during their lives.

Five or six scattered instances of milk and poultry contamination occurred. Use of the chemicals, known as PCB compounds, with which the products were contaminated, is being discontinued.

Two cases of botulism, a severe form of food poisoning, were traced to contaminated canned soup. Rare as these cases were, they made dramatic news. Farmers recognized the dangers from both real mistakes and strong public reaction to them. As a result, farmers started voluntary programs to ensure safe use of animal-health products. In one program, producers state in writing before selling livestock that they have followed all rules about drugs.

▶ HEALTH

Long-term health studies have been carried out on a group of people in the Framingham, Massachusetts, Diet Study Group. Results thus far have failed to prove a solid relationship between what people eat and their levels of blood cholesterol. (Cholesterol, a chemical found in animal tissues and fluids, is being studied for its possible link to heart disease.) One heart expert, Dr. Bernard Lown of Boston, said, "There is not one shred of real evidence that changes in diet relieve or decrease coronary attacks."

However, the Federally funded Intersociety Commission for Heart Disease Resources recommended a large government effort to change American diets. The commission recommends cutting in half the amount of animal fat, which is high in cholesterol, in people's diets. And in fact, Americans are switching steadily toward more high-protein foods, fruits, and vegetables, and away from starchy and fatty foods, as they improve their diets.

During the summer the health of horses in southern states became a major concern. About 1,000 horses died in Texas from a disease called Venezuelan equine encephalomyelitis (VEE). The disease is carried by mosquitoes. Veterinarians warned of the disease as it spread from Mexico. A vaccine was available to protect Mexican horses and check the spread of the disease. But action came too late.

When horses began dying in Texas, the United States Department of Agriculture (USDA) began a mass vaccination program. USDA paid veterinarians $4.00 per horse to vaccinate more than 2,000,000 horses in 11 southern states. USDA also started the biggest aerial-spray program in its history to kill VEE-carrying mosquitoes. Late in the year it looked as though every horse in the United States would have to be vaccinated against VEE.

▶ENVIRONMENT

United States farmers spend millions of dollars each year on conservation and pollution control. Measures include building terraces to reduce soil erosion on sloping land, planting trees, and building ponds for water control and recreation.

A 4-H'er in Nueces County, Texas, examines a horse that caught Venezuelan equine encephalomyelitis (VEE) and recovered. VEE killed thousands of horses in the Southwest.

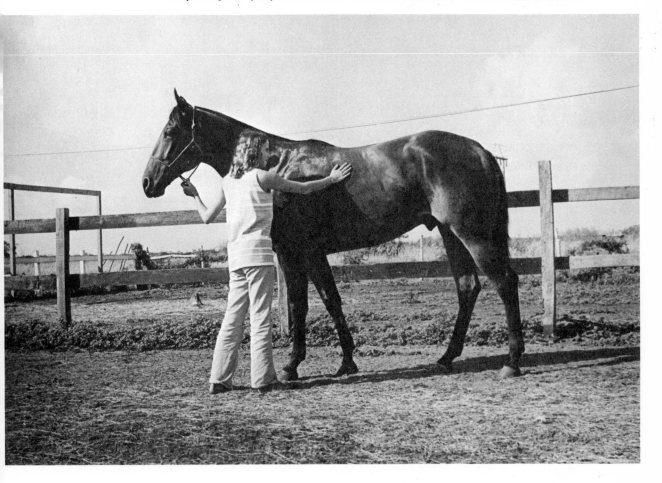

In 1971 more and more farmers produced "organically grown" foods—fruits and vegetables, for example, that are grown without the use of artificial fertilizers or chemicals.

Farmers are also shifting toward a balance between biological and chemical insect controls. Farmers use smaller quantities of chemicals, and they are singling out the particular pests among one hundred or so insect enemies they face.

New England states learned what a serious pest outbreak can do as gypsy-moth larvae stripped foliage from thousands of acres. Some communities used DDT sprays which they had earlier banned. Later in the summer a Federal study commission reported there is no pressing need to outlaw DDT.

Late in the year Congress moved toward passage of a new pesticide-control law. It will legally divide all weed- and insect-killing chemicals into two groups: unrestricted ones that are so safe anyone may buy and use them, and restricted types. Only a licensed buyer can buy and apply these because they are more poisonous.

Each state will set up its own licensing procedure. An applicant may have to prove, for example, that he can read and understand label instructions, and has basic knowledge of safety procedures.

New chemicals go through a tough government-approval process to make sure of their safety in the environment when they are used properly. But until now, anyone could use them in most states without personal requirements. The new law will help protect the environment, yet give responsible people the right to use chemicals that are important for weed and insect control.

Those concerned with the environment, such as Barry Commoner, stepped up the argument over a question basic to our food supply: How much of nitrate and phosphate fertilizers finds its way into streams, and where does it enter the streams?

First results of a carefully designed fertilizer-runoff study were released during the summer by the Tennessee Valley Authority. It was found that adding commercial fertilizer at normal crop-growing rates did not increase in an important way the fertilizer runoff.

In most cases where ponds, wells, or streams are found to have dangerously high nitrate content, the cause has been organic wastes from nearby animal feed yards.

Top-level scientists gathered in dozens of study sessions to puzzle over control of animal wastes. Waste-disposal problems mount as farmers gather together in one place thousands of cattle, hundreds of cows, and hundreds of thousands of chickens and other poultry. Thus far, there has been no agreement on disposal systems.

A growing number of farmers stopped using any fertilizer or chemicals in order to supply the booming demand for "organically grown" foods. Many people fear their food contains traces of chemicals, and they are willing to pay more for naturally grown products. By the end of the year consumers could buy organically-grown fruit, meat, eggs, and vegetables. Most of these products came from small gardens. But big commercial farms were beginning to eye the high rewards in organic foods.

▶ YOUTH

There was a shift among 4-H clubs from a rural to a more urban focus. Only one third of all 4-H members now live on farms. A third are inner-city or suburban young people. The rest live in small towns or in nonfarm rural homes.

Communal farms kept popping up from Vermont to California, as young city-bred people looked for an ideal society or simply escape from the Establishment rat race. The farms' failure rate approached 100 per cent. The basic problem apparently is that most communes are based on sharing all things equally—including the hard work of making a living from the earth. The few who fail to do their share cripple the commune. Yet, as one commune failed, other groups started up elsewhere.

At the same time, the general farm population fell. About 5 per cent of farm families leave for cities each year.

It was a bad year for city farmers, the large-scale ventures into agriculture backed by city investors. At least five major corporate farms failed. They included Black Watch Farms of upstate New York, once the world's largest breeder of Angus cattle. Gates Rubber Company sold its irrigated-farming venture in Colorado.

▶ THE PRESIDENT'S NEW ECONOMIC PLAN

Prices of raw agricultural products were not included in the wage-price freeze announced by President Nixon on August 15. The administration felt that farm prices were not contributing to inflation.

However, the prices of processed food were frozen at the retail level, to prevent widening the spread between farm and retail prices. Already 60 cents of the consumer food dollar goes for processing and distribution.

Farmers heartily approved of the wage-price freeze. It offered them a rest from their own cost-price squeeze. Farm costs have been climbing at 4 to 5 per cent a year, while farm products have remained about the same. "The freeze will give us a chance to catch up with the rest of the economy," said one Midwest farmer.

Most observers felt that future wage-price controls would weigh lightly on agriculture.

JERRY CARLSON
Managing Editor, *Farm Journal*

THE ARTS

FOR art lovers, 1971 was a banner year. There were many wonderful exhibitions of paintings and sculptures. Several major photographers also had their works exhibited at museums and galleries. The increasing popularity of this art form was emphasized when a *Life* magazine contest drew more than 1,000,000 photographs from 100,000 contestants.

Of course, architects cannot exhibit their massive works in museums or galleries, but their creations are there for all to see. And in 1971, architects combined form and function to create a great variety of interesting buildings.

Self-portraits of Paul Gauguin (left) and Vincent van Gogh at the Detroit Institute of Arts.

"The Photography Game," a popular and practical guide to an increasingly popular art form.

"A Slave Ship and Slaves," by Larry Rivers, exhibited at the Institute for the Arts of Rice University.

The Lecture Hall at Stony Brook was designed by William Kessler.

PAINTING

During 1971 many exciting new museums and art centers opened in the United States. The Cleveland Museum unveiled its Education Wing, designed by Marcel Breuer and Hamilton Smith. The new addition increased the size of the museum by one third. A $4,800,000 Arts Center opened at the University of California, at Berkeley. The Walker Art Center in Minneapolis moved into a splendid new building designed by Edward Larrabee Barnes. And, in October, Denver's new art museum gave visitors a look at the art center of the future. The exterior of the huge six-story building is made up of nearly a million specially designed glass tiles. It is the work of Italian architect Gio Ponti and Denver's firm of James Sudler Associates.

The dedication of the Rothko Chapel in Houston, Texas, was also an important event for the art world. The chapel is named after the late Mark Rothko, the Russian-born abstract painter. The small octagonal building was designed to display 14 large canvases by Rothko. *Broken Obelisk,* an important sculpture by the late Barnett Newman, is located in a reflecting pool outside the chapel.

▶MUSEUMS IN TROUBLE

For some museums and art galleries 1971 was not a happy year. Mounting budgetary problems forced many of them to charge admission and cut back services.

The museums in New York City had many difficulties. The Metropolitan Museum of Art's expansion program was hotly attacked. Many New Yorkers did not want Central Park land to be used for the new museum wing. The Museum of Modern Art had a million-dollar deficit, despite a peak in attendance. The Brooklyn Museum and the Museum of Primitive Arts were open to the public on fewer days. And the Jewish Museum decided to discontinue all exhibitions not related to the Jewish community.

In Detroit, the Institute of Arts was forced to close about one third of its 75 galleries each day, on a rotating basis.

The Museum of Fine Arts in Boston had troubles of a different kind. They stemmed from a small portrait believed to be by the Italian Renaissance master Raphael. The portrait became the subject of a legal battle between the museum, U.S. Customs, and the Italian Government. Charges were made that the painting had been smuggled out of Italy. After months of negotiations the museum agreed to return the portrait to Italy.

"Kneeling Donor," 1506, by Albrecht Dürer, leader of the German Renaissance school of painting.

▶TRADITIONAL AND MODERN ART

During the month of May, the prints of Robert Indiana were shown in an unusual exhibition. Indiana selected one of his paintings from each year of the past decade (1960–69). He then had them translated into silk-screen prints. Twenty-seven galleries, on three continents, simultaneously displayed his ten prints. His art went on view in the United States, Canada, France, Italy, Germany, Puerto Rico, and Venezuela.

The Princeton University museum in New Jersey had a large showing of the canvases of Josef Albers, now in his eighties. Albers paints basic geometric forms, like the square. He finds fresh ideas of color in each work.

A large exhibition was a retrospective of the works of the American modernist painter John Marin. Marin's vigorous style could be seen in his sprightly oils, watercolors, drawings, and etchings. The show was organized and circulated by the Los Angeles County Museum of Art.

The National Gallery of Art's exhibition "Dürer in America: His Graphic Work"

Raphael's "Portrait of a Young Girl," smuggled out of Italy in 1969, was returned to that country in 1971.

Denver's new art museum, a six-story structure which many consider the "art center of the future."

"Parrot," by Robert Indiana.

Official portraits of President and Mrs. John F. Kennedy by Aaron Shikler. The portraits, unveiled in 1971, were commissioned by the White House Historical Association.

commemorated the 500th anniversary of the German artist's birth. The Washington showing included 36 of the 38 Dürer drawings known to exist in North America. There were also 207 engravings, etchings, and woodcuts. It was the largest Dürer graphics show ever held in the United States. Other exhibitions paying homage to Albrecht Dürer took place during the year in many cities throughout the United States and Western Europe.

A vivid circulating exhibition was devoted to the paintings of Paul Cézanne. The show comprised 83 of his paintings, watercolors, and drawings. The power of Cézanne's art was seen in the varied view of his oils. He can give the structure of an apple or pear the excitement of the structure of a cathedral.

The show was seen during 1971 at the Phillips Collection in Washington, D.C., the Chicago Art Institute, and at Boston's Museum of Fine Arts.

The Toledo, Ohio, Museum of Art's "Age of Magnificence" show consisted of 18th-century paintings from Venice, Tuscany, and Rome. Many had never been seen before in the United States. Some will probably never again leave Italy.

A panorama of the early works of the French artist Paul Gauguin was on view at the Cincinnati Art Museum. (Gauguin's later works were influenced by his life in Tahiti. There his bold colors and simplified forms found a profound echo in the tropics.) At the Worcester Art Museum in Massachusetts, there was a survey of the drawings

Environmental art: blocks
of ice on the Charles River
by David Lowry Burgess.

and prints of Toulouse-Lautrec. The exhibit was assembled from the museum's own collection.

▶ENVIRONMENTAL ART

1971 boasted many shows that went outside the traditional boundaries of art materials. Perhaps the most impressive was "Earth, Air, Fire, Water: Elements of Art," which was held at Boston's Museum of Fine Arts. The exhibition included works by many important environmental artists. Alan Sonfist erected Plexiglas columns. Inside them, chemical crystals reacted to changes of heat and light. Marvin Torffield used the sky itself as a canvas. His designs were spread across the atmosphere in a day of skywriting. David Lowry Burgess is an artist interested in the process of change in nature. He placed huge ice blocks containing crocus bulbs on the ice of the Charles River. When all the ice melted, the bulbs presumably floated to shore and took root. Thus, states of matter, temperature, and time were connected in this artwork.

▶CONCEPTUAL ART

An idea alone is enough for some artists. "Conceptual" art seeks to go beyond the reproduction or use of objects. For example, the Addison Gallery of Phillips Andover Academy in Massachusetts commissioned an artist named Larry Stark to drive coast-to-coast and spend an entire month eating at McDonald's Restaurants. The purpose of the project was not frivolous. Stark wanted to make a statement about the way in which mass production has made one place in America look like another. He returned with extensive tape-recorded interviews and film footage. His documented travels across the country became the subject of an unusual show at the gallery.

ROBERT TAYLOR
Art Editor
Boston Globe Magazine

CHILDREN'S ART FROM THE SOVIET UNION

Children are children the whole world over. Their interests and talents are rich and expressive no matter what part of the world they live in. One way for a child in any land to express his imagination and creativity is in his paintings and drawings. And the artwork of a Russian child may be surprisingly similar to that of an American, Canadian, or South American youngster.

This was readily seen at an unusual art exhibition that opened in New York City in the spring of 1971. Held at The Metropolitan Museum of Art's Junior Museum, the show consisted of works by young Soviet artists, aged 5 to 14. On view were 50 paintings, drawings, and woodcuts by children attending schools in the Leningrad area. Their art presented an interesting and varied picture of Soviet daily life. But most of the subjects of the pictures were universal ones: home, school, play, and animals.

The paintings were imaginative and delightfully colorful. Many were finely detailed and skillfully executed. And they all had one thing in common—they indicated a child's awareness of the world around him.

"It's Me," by Ira Kuzmitsheva, age 4.

Because there is much snow in Leningrad, a number of the children's works were snowscapes. Many of the pictures were outdoor scenes showing children playing. The Soviets have an active space program, and this too was reflected in one work. Any youngster is thrilled by the idea of men walking on the face of the moon. Still other pictures were realistic portraits of young people.

Like children in other countries, the young Soviet artists also found inspiration in the zoo and its fascinating animals, the circus and its comical clowns, and the enchanted world of fairy tales.

But what was especially appealing about the show was its attraction for children—they came, they saw, they were fascinated.

From New York, the widely praised exhibition traveled to other cities in the United States and Canada. At some of these showings, the artwork of American children was hung alongside the Russian children's pictures. U.S. or U.S.S.R.—through a child's eye, the world appears very much the same.

The entire program was sponsored by the Citizen Exchange Corps, a nonprofit, nonpolitical organization devoted to educational exchanges between the United States and various countries of Eastern Europe.

An exhibition of the artwork of American schoolchildren will soon be sent to Moscow, as part of the exchange program. Soviet children will see that U.S. children work and play the same as they do.

"A Princess, a Swan," by Ylga Lintsbach, age 10.

"The Lunakhod with Cosmonauts on the Moon," by Sveta Kapitskiva, age 5.

"On the Slope," by Natasha Auverina, age 6.

"At the Zoo," by Lyndoi
Mironova, age 10.

"At the Circus," by Olga
Sinulina, age 7.

SCULPTURE

Two of the most interesting sculptural events of 1971 occurred at opposite ends of the United States. In San Francisco, James Reineking showed "sound sculpture." He used long lengths of tube, often suspended in dramatic positions. Each tube concealed a battery-operated sound unit, which droned continuously, mysteriously, and ominously. At the Massachusetts Institute of Technology, Chinese-born American artist Wen-Ying Tsai had an exhibition of delicate rods and machines. They danced and swayed whenever a spectator came into the vicinity.

An unusual exhibit was Red Grooms' *The Discount Store*. This sculptural environment was made up of comic replicas of things that might be found in a Midwestern store. It was circulated by the Walker Art Center.

▶UNUSUAL SCULPTING MATERIALS

Several interesting exhibits revealed that strange and striking artworks could be made from materials not always associated with sculpting. One show, at the Museum of Contemporary Crafts, was called simply "Furs and Feathers."

New York sculptor William King had several showings throughout the country. His exhibits consisted of witty figures made from

"The Discount Store" by Red Grooms.

aluminum sheets. They were fashioned to suggest paper-doll cutouts. And Nancy Graves distinguished herself with an abstract piece at the Whitney Museum in New York. Made of latex strips, muslin, and other materials, the piece suggested the form of a Kwakiutl Indian medicine man.

▶THE BLACK EXPERIENCE

Six black artists collaborated with Larry Rivers on the theme of black experience. The result was an exhibit called "Some American History," at the Institute for the Arts of Rice University, in Texas. It consisted, in part, of several vast wood sculptures by Rivers: a model of the hold of a slave ship, depictions of lynchings, and a reconstruction of a Harlem tenement.

Also concerned with the black experience was "The Sculpture of Black Africa: the Paul Tishman Collection." This exhibition assembled the ceremonial and household objects of several African cultures. It traveled throughout the southwest in 1971.

In Washington, D.C., the Museum of African Art was renovated and expanded and a sculpture garden was added. The museum, and its jointly operated Frederick Douglass Institute of Negro Arts and History, received a million-dollar grant from the National Endowment for the Humanities.

▶THE LITTLE 14-YEAR-OLD DANCER

A lovely bronze figure made the headlines in the art world in 1971. Edgar Degas' *La Petite Danseuse de Quatorze Ans* was sold by the Parke-Bernet Galleries for $380,000. The price set a world auction record for a sculpture. The sculpture came from the private collection of millionaire industrialist Norton Simon.

ROBERT TAYLOR
Art Editor
Boston Globe Magazine

"La Petite Danseuse de Quatorze Ans" by Edgar Degas.

PHOTOGRAPHY

More people than ever before were taking pictures in 1971. Eastman Kodak's unusually high gross earnings were due largely to the sales of Instamatic cameras. Another indication of photography's popularity was the response to *Life* magazine's 1971 photo contest for amateurs. About one million pictures were received from 100,000 contestants. (*Life* had expected about 15,000 people to enter the contest.) Because of the overwhelming response, *Life* announced plans for a new contest for 1972.

While 1971 was a successful year for amateur photographers, contests for professionals were not so well received as they had been in the past. In a competition among press photographers, the lack of entries for "Pictures of the Year" was clearly disappointing. This turn of events caused the sponsors to consider dropping the "magazine" division of the contest in 1972. In general, photographic professionals had a difficult year while the amateurs worked—or played—with renewed enthusiasm.

Photography suffered a tremendous loss in 1971 with the deaths of two distinguished photographers. Diane Arbus died in July, and in August, people throughout the world were saddened at the news of the death of Margaret Bourke-White, a pioneer woman photographer and successful war correspondent.

▶ PHOTOGRAPHY MAGAZINES

Popular Photography, Modern Photography, and *Camera 35* continued to be among the most widely read photography magazines in the United States. All three publications pay serious attention to the work of genuinely strong photographers as well as celebrities. These magazines contain

Young dancers: a black-and-white prizewinner from the "Life" photography contest.

some excellent photographs, and the reader can gain useful knowledge and gather interesting opinions from the many informative articles.

Two new photo magazines, representing very different approaches, are in the planning stage. One, *Photography Quarterly,* is described by its publisher as a "how-to magazine, but a beautiful one." The other, not yet named, is to be published monthly by Time Inc. Its editors hope to set new high standards for intelligence and taste in a photography magazine. The publication will be more concerned with pictures, understanding, and vision than with equipment or technique.

Album, edited and published in Britain, carries no advertisements and has very little material on camera equipment. Rather, it deals mainly with photographers and their pictures. Issue No. 12 of *Album* will be of interest to both amateur and professional photographers. It contains a remarkable portfolio of photographs taken by Elliott Erwitt as well as an interview with this outspoken photographer. *Album* is sold only by subscription and can be obtained by writing to: *Album,* 103 Norwich Road, Wisbech, Cambridgeshire, England.

▶**PHOTOGRAPHIC BOOKS**

One of the year's most welcome books for photographers is a newly revised edition of Ansel Adams' Basic Photo Book One, *Camera and Lens,* subtitled "The Creative Approach." It is intended mainly for photographers who do their own black-and-white developing and printing.

This book amounts to a concentrated course in photography. It is extremely thorough and accurate. Adams, unlike many "how-to" authors, is a practicing photographer and a master of his craft. *Camera and Lens* concerns itself mostly with large-format, tripod-based photography, but what it says can be applied to any format.

The Photography Game, by Arthur Goldsmith, is an entertaining and factual book aimed at beginners who are planning to become professional photographers. The book is generally well written, and very easy to understand. Mr. Goldsmith makes it clear

Cover photo from "Album" (No. 12), by Elliott Erwitt.

that professional photography takes intelligence, patience, dedication, and hard work. However, he never forgets that it's an enjoyable line of work.

André Kertesz's book *On Reading* is a beautiful surprise. It has no written text, but consists of 67 photographs taken between 1915 and 1971 that show all kinds of people reading under widely varying conditions.

Doubleday has issued a series of portfolios of reproductions of photographs-as-works-of-art. The two portfolios introduced in 1971 are *Eight Photographs: Arthur Freed* and *Eight Photographs: Edward Weston.* Freed is a young photographer who also teaches his craft; Weston is considered by many experts to be one of photography's authentic masters. Both portfolios are worth having, but may be hard to find. Booksellers tend to keep them in the back room and

Photos by Edward Weston (left) and Arthur Freed from Doubleday "Photography Portfolios."

sometimes don't know they have them in the store. To purchase one, it may be necessary to place a special order.

Walker Evans is a book of photographs by Walker Evans. It presents 106 pictures from The Museum of Modern Art's 1971 Evans exhibit. Evans is a quiet photographer whose special talent is to portray not only the appearances of the places he photographs (a house, small town, street, room, or store) but their spirit as well. The pictures make you *feel* the places.

A very different kind of book is Mark Jury's *Vietnam Photo Book*. It is a photographic report centering on the ugliness of the Vietnam war, with written commentary by the photographer. Mr. Jury has carefully let the photographs speak for themselves and maintained a more-or-less factual, unfrenzied tone in his writing.

Lustrum Press, a newly formed publishing company, released two important books by present-day photographers. *Portugal,* by Neal Slavin, is a thoughtful, many-sided look at the solemn people of Portugal, and their environment. Larry Clark's *Tulsa* gives a disturbing glimpse of the life and death of Tulsa, Oklahoma, young people who are hooked on drugs.

▶ PHOTOGRAPHIC EXHIBITIONS

One of the year's most important shows was W. Eugene Smith's show titled "Let Truth Be the Prejudice," at the Jewish Mu-

"Post Office, Sprott, Alabama, 1936" by Walker Evans.

seum in New York City. However, this extraordinary and captivating exhibition had one fault. It was much too large and complex (more than 600 pictures in all) to take in, either in one visit or in many.

The Museum of Modern Art had many photo shows in 1971. Among the most interesting were one-man shows by Berenice Abbott, Walker Evans, Manuel Alvarez-Bravo, and the early 20th-century photographer Clarence White. Following the nostalgia trend that seemed to be so prevalent in 1971, the subject matter of all these shows harked back to the past.

The George Eastman House in Rochester, New York, under its new director, Van Deren Coke, held an important exhibition in 1971. Its title was "Photo-Graphics," and it consisted of prints in other art media in which photography had been used as part of the process.

Perhaps more important than "big name" exhibitions at established galleries and museums are the hundreds of local photography shows held each year in many cities and towns in the United States and Canada. At least 16 states and Ontario have regular photography galleries, and many colleges hold at least one photo show per year. Fifteen years ago, places that regularly exhibited photographs as works of art were rare. Today, there are almost too many to keep track of. Probably the most comprehensive listing of better-known exhibitions can be found in the "Shows to See" column in each issue of *Popular Photography*.

DAVID VESTAL
Former Editor, *U.S. Camera Annual*

ARCHITECTURE

A tight-money economy in 1971 caused a slowdown in the construction industry, especially Government-financed or -insured building programs. As a result, architects in many parts of the country found themselves with much less work than before. To offset the loss of new projects, a growing number of architects busied themselves with the remodeling or rehabilitation of existing buildings.

While there was an overall decline in the construction industry, the housing field showed an upward turn. By the end of the year, new housing units were being built at a rate of two million units per year—the highest volume ever to be recorded. Roughly half the new units were in single-family houses, while the rest were in high-density apartment-house projects.

There were discussions about the use of what is known as industrialized housing—housing built in factories and then carried to a particular location by truck or railroad. However, very little such housing was actually completed in 1971. A Federal Government experiment in this type of housing—called Operation Breakthrough—has not been highly successful. It is hoped that better results will be forthcoming in the near future.

▶ **NEW CONCEPT IN CONSTRUCTION**

Possibly the most-talked-about new idea in recent months was the so-called "Fast Track" or "phased construction." Under this plan, buildings can be completed much more rapidly. The result is a two-way saving of money. For one thing, quicker construction means a reduction in costs, which continue to soar because of inflation. Secondly, the sooner a building is finished, the sooner it can be put to use earning money for its investors.

The "Fast Track" concept eliminates the usual procedure of first designing a building and then constructing it. Instead, both activities go on at the same time. As soon as the location of a building is approved, the ground is cleared. When the architect has drawn up a basic floor plan, excavation is begun and the foundations are laid. Meanwhile, the architect stays at the drawing board to work out details of the building's floor plan and superstructure. At the point when the skeleton of the structure is being built, the architect is designing the interior of the building. The idea is a bold one and still in the experimental stage. But when tried, it seems to have worked out well. Many experts believe that this new management concept will be a more important factor in lowering building costs than any new breakthrough in technology.

St. Mary's Cathedral: designed to be "comparable in scale and size to the cathedrals of the past."

The interior of St. Mary's combines traditional religious elements with modern form.

▶ IMPORTANT NEW BUILDINGS

A number of beautifully designed and executed buildings were completed in 1971.

St. Mary's Cathedral

Cathedrals are rarely built these days, and so there was considerable excitement about the completion of St. Mary's Cathedral in San Francisco. The new church was hailed for its brilliant design and for its combination of the traditional religious elements with modern form and structure. The cathedral's chief designer was the architect Pietro Belluschi, an American citizen of Italian birth. His aim was to create a building that would be "an expression of the modern age, comparable in scale and size to the cathedrals of the past."

Belluschi wanted his cathedral to have a strong structural concept, as impressive as the medieval cathedrals, with their soaring arches and great domes. To achieve his purpose, Belluschi called on the outstanding Italian structural engineer Pier Luigi Nervi to assist him. Together they worked out the plan for St. Mary's. The cathedral is dominated by a great cross-shaped cupola, which consists of great shells of cast concrete covered over in marble. The cupola rises 190 feet from the floor and encloses a nave that seats 2,500 people. The nave is a completely open area, free of columns.

Two large stained-glass windows, 6 feet wide and 130 feet long, are a feature of this new Roman Catholic cathedral. Designed by Gyorgy Kepes, these great works of art fill the spaces between the roof shells and form a colorful cross overhead. There is also a shining baldachino (canopy) of aluminum rods that hangs over the altar.

McCormick Place

The McCormick Place complex, built on the Lake Michigan waterfront in Chicago, Illinois, is another building with a spacious interior. One part of the building contains a vast exhibition hall for trade shows and conventions. The other section has a large 4,500-seat theater flanked by restaurants and meeting rooms. In addition, there are 7 auditoriums with sloped seating areas of 8,000 seats each. There is room enough for 5 football fields in the main exhibition area, which is 750 feet long, 450 feet wide, and 50 feet high. The roof extends for 74 feet beyond the building, providing shade for the glass walls and the pedestrian walk overlooking the lake. Architects for the building were C. F. Murphy Associates of Chicago.

Phillips Exeter Physical-Education Building

Phillips Exeter Academy in New Hampshire has completed a physical-education building that is both spectacular in size and unique in its arrangement. Designed by Kallmann and McKinnell of Boston, the Athletic Building seems to turn things inside out. Three-dimensional steel trusses have been placed outside on top of the building instead of inside supporting the ceiling. In effect, the roof hangs from the trusses. A multilevel spine of concrete runs along the length of the sports center. As one moves through the complex, there is an unobstructed view of various sporting areas. There are two hockey rinks, three basketball courts, a swimming pool, and dozens of squash courts and exercise rooms.

Orange County Government Center

In sharp contrast to the structural design of these three buildings is the Orange County Government Center in Goshen, New York. An unusual building, the Center has the improvised look of a Tinkertoy construction. This is a characteristic of buildings designed by Paul Rudolph, who tries to avoid both the monumental and the simple look. Rudolph prefers a design that makes use of a series of small units connected in an almost random manner. The inside creates the exciting effect of spaces flowing around each other. Costs were held down by the use of a simple concrete structural frame, and concrete blocks for the walls.

Federal Reserve Bank in Minneapolis

A truly spectacular building is the Federal Reserve Bank of Minneapolis, Minnesota, scheduled for completion in 1972. Even in its unfinished state, the building has a breathtaking appearance. For it is built in the form of a suspension bridge and spans a gap of 330 feet between two office towers. The novel structure was conceived by the architect Gunnar Birkerts. Much of the bank's facilities will be underground so that more open space will be saved for public use. "People love to take a boat under a bridge," Birkerts remarked, and strollers passing under the suspended portion of the building will have the same feeling.

▶ COMBINING FORM AND FUNCTION

In their efforts to find new ways to shape their buildings, architects must always bear in mind the most important element of all—how well the building is suited to the purpose for which it is being built. Most often a new or innovative shape grows out of the function that takes place inside.

Orange County Government Center.

Stony Brook Lecture Hall

The Lecture Hall at Stony Brook, one of the new colleges of the State University of New York, is a good example. Viewed from afar, it appears to have almost a random design. Its sloping, windowless sides make it seem scaleless. In other words, from a distance, it is hard to form an impression of how large the building is. But once inside, the visitor finds that it contains a tight-knit series of lecture halls arranged around a skylighted central area. The Stony Brook Lecture Hall was designed by William Kessler and Associates.

Two buildings honoring former presidents were dedicated in 1971. The John F. Kennedy Center for the Performing Arts (above) is on the banks of the Potomac River in Washington, D.C. The Lyndon Baines Johnson Library (below) is in Austin, Texas.

Regency Hyatt House

Chicago's Regency Hyatt House hotel, at the O'Hare airport, is a small city within a city. Its designers, John Portman and Associates, provided for every need of the hotel guests. There are restaurants, recreational facilities, and meeting rooms, as well as hundreds of guest rooms and suites. Four large corner towers, sheathed in copper-colored reflective glass, house most of the guest rooms. The centerpiece of the structure is a ten-story skylighted open court. Here are located the registration desks, cocktail lounges, and restaurants. The central square also has trees, balconies, and pedestrian bridges.

Avoriaz Ski Resort

In the case of Avoriaz, a new ski resort in the French Alps, the hotel buildings were designed to blend in with the natural surroundings of craggy mountains. Some 15,-000 people will eventually be housed in a variety of hotels, hostels, and houses, which are being built on an unusual structural system. Concrete columns or pilings have been sunk down to the base rock of the mountain. These pilings support floors made of poured concrete. Partitions between rooms, and the sloping faces of the buildings are wood-framed, with a covering of cedar shingles.

As a result of the cold climate, the wood shingles will eventually turn to a silver gray color, matching the granite rock of the surrounding mountains.

Mummers Theater

Possibly the most extreme example of allowing the function of a building to determine its appearance is the Mummers Theater in Oklahoma City, Oklahoma. A creation of the architect John M. Johansen of Connecticut, the building has won the praise of some critics and the sharp disapproval of others. Among the elements of this complex are two theaters, several rehearsal halls, and a number of offices, lounges, and other facilities. Each of the separate units is linked by what architect Johansen calls a "circuitry system" of stairs, ramps, and bridges. All of the connecting circuits follow "the shortest line between two points."

▶REGIONALISM IN ARCHITECTURE

In many areas the style of a building is determined by weather conditions, custom, the nature of the land, or the preferences of the local people. This is known as regionalism. One example is the Cape Cod house, a simple wood construction with a sharply slanted roof designed to withstand rain and snow. Centuries ago the Indians of the Southwest built thick-walled houses of adobe brick for protection against the hot sun. The shape and form of the old Pueblo adobe houses continues to influence modern architecture in that region—as illustrated by Bennie Gonzales' City Hall, in Scottsdale, Arizona. This building is part of a larger grouping that will form the Scottsdale civic and cultural center. The City Hall features heavy walls of masonry coated on the outside with white mortar. Steel trusses on the inside permit broad, open spaces. The open city council chamber is surrounded by balconies from which the public can view the proceedings.

▶SKYSCRAPER TOWERS

Because of limited space, the nation's big cities have built upward. In recent years, a soaring skyline of tall towers has sprung up in major urban areas throughout the nation. But this type of construction is now being criticized by younger architects who object to the overcrowding that results from too many such buildings. They argue that corporations should scatter their offices in smaller communities instead of cramming them into the major cities. A number of large corporations are following that advice and are leaving congested urban areas.

Typical of the new suburban office buildings is the handsome corporate headquarters of the Union Camp Corporation, in Wayne, New Jersey. Designed by architects Schofield and Colgan, the building is on a fifty-acre wooded site, and the offices overlook a small lake. The cafeteria is built over the water's edge so that the employees are provided with a splendid view of the lake and nearby woodlands. Because it is isolated from the crowded city center, employees have ample parking space and do not have to fight rush-hour traffic.

Two steel-and-glass towers form the Toronto-Dominion Centre in Canada's second-largest city. In addition to offices, the Centre houses shops, a movie house, restaurants, and underground garages.

In contrast to this quiet setting, the tall city towers result in a host of problems for the worker—including commuter delays, lack of parking space, and general overcrowding. Nevertheless, many corporations still want to be located in the heart of large cities. So the tall towers continue to be built, and often admired for their giant scale and beauty.

The Toronto-Dominion Centre is the most imposing tower built in the past year. It is the last great work of the late Mies van der Rohe, who designed the famous Seagram Building in New York. Two steel and glass towers—one 56 stories and the other 46—form the complex. Each of the towers shows the incredibly careful, almost machinelike precision that was the trademark of Van der Rohe's work. Although often criticized for his conservatism, Van der Rohe continued to use the simple classic design common to all of his buildings.

▶IMPORTANT NAMES IN ARCHITECTURE

Louis I. Kahn, the distinguished Philadelphia architect, received the Gold Medal of the American Institute of Architects. This is the highest award granted by the A.I.A. and the most prestigious an American architect can win.

Architect George White of Cleveland was appointed to the post of Architect of the Capitol. In this capacity, Mr. White will be responsible for the development and maintenance of all Government buildings in Washington, D.C., including the Capitol—which recent studies have shown may be dangerously weakened in some places. Other landmarks may also require renovation. The preceding Architect of the Capitol was an engineer, and many felt that he had made serious misjudgments in his work on national landmarks. Therefore Mr. White's appointment met with the delighted approval of most architects.

WALTER F. WAGNER, JR.
Editor, *Architectural Record*

ASIA

DEVELOPMENTS in Asia during 1971 captured headlines in newspapers throughout the world. Perhaps the most startling news concerned the People's Republic of China. In October, after more than two decades of continuous and heated debates, Communist China was finally admitted to the United Nations. Equally surprising had been President Richard Nixon's announcement in July of his scheduled visit to Peking.

All the reports from Asia in 1971 were not as hopeful. The war in Vietnam continued, but United States involvement was becoming less evident. The withdrawal of American soldiers from the war-torn country continued at a steady pace, and by the end of the year, about 157,000 troops remained in South Vietnam.

As one conflict seemed to be winding down, another broke out. In March, President Yahya Khan of Pakistan ordered his Army to crush a movement for autonomy in East Pakistan. A civil war with the people of East Pakistan followed. In December, Indian troops invaded East Pakistan, defeating the Pakistani Army. With Indian aid, the East Pakistanis set up their own Government. They named their new country Bangladesh.

In Bangladesh, former East Pakistan, a guerrilla fighter poses with his rifle.

Chinese are among the best Ping-Pong players in the world. In 1971 they used this sport to pave the way to better relations with the United States. In April an American Ping-Pong team was invited to Communist China. Three months later President Nixon made the surprise announcement that he would visit Communist China early in 1972.

© Herblock, in The Washington Post

Great Leap Forward

South Vietnamese soldiers wait to board American-built helicopters. In 1971 the Vietnamization of the Vietnam war seemed to be succeeding. South Vietnamese troops were doing more of the fighting, and American troops were heading home by the tens of thousands.

THE BENGALIS OF BANGLADESH

Bangladesh is one of the most densely populated countries in the world. The average Bengali earns only about one dollar a week. Further, in little more than a year the Bengalis have suffered through cholera epidemics, a cyclone and tidal wave, and a civil war. Their faces reflect the hardships of life in that unfortunate part of the world.

Bengali girl.

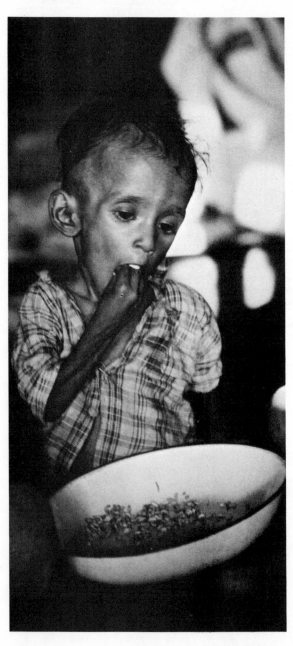

A young Bengali with too little to eat.

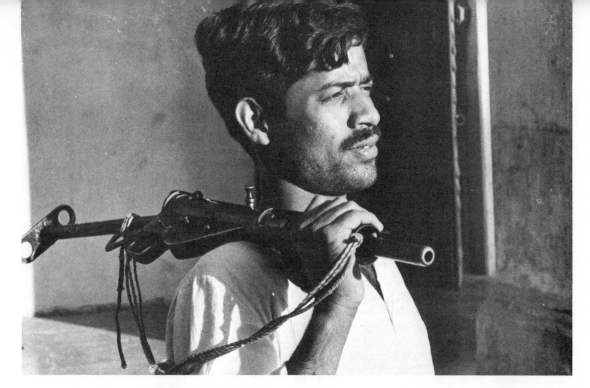

A Mukti Bahini—a Bangladesh freedom fighter—who helped Indian forces defeat Pakistan.

Bengali refugees in India. Ten million refugees started the long trek home to Bangladesh.

Communist China

In 1949, communist forces swept to power in China, the most populous nation in the world. Immediately upon taking over the reins of government, the Communists closed their borders to foreigners. A bamboo curtain was drawn around the country. Inside China, great turmoil was taking place. Reports reached the western world that hundreds of thousands of people were put into prison and many others were executed.

When the Communists gained control of the Chinese mainland, the Chinese Nationalist Government, headed by Generalissimo Chiang Kai-shek, fled to Taiwan, a large

Outside a newspaper office, Taiwanese read that their country—Nationalist China—has been expelled from the United Nations and that Communist China has been seated.

island off the China coast. The United States and many other countries considered the Nationalists on Taiwan the real Government of China and refused to recognize the communist Government in Peking.

Consequently, relations between Peking and the West, particularly the United States, were almost nonexistent for more than twenty years. During that time, the Communists, under a cloud of secrecy, made many advances in the field of technology. They developed their own atomic and hydrogen bombs and placed a satellite into orbit around the earth. This last achievement led many people to believe that China was also in the process of developing missiles.

In 1969, U.S. President Richard Nixon declared that, in the interest of peace and stability in Asia and the world, steps should be taken to improve relations with Peking. As a result, many changes took place. The United States permitted its citizens, for the first time, to buy Chinese goods without a special permit. This was followed by permission to trade with China through neutral countries. Foreign ships were allowed to stop at American seaports for fuel on voyages to and from China. The Government of the United States also encouraged members of Congress, journalists, teachers, college students, and scientists to visit mainland China. However, Peking was hesitant about opening its doors to Americans.

In June 1971, Nixon ended the trade ban imposed on China during the Korean war. In August came the announcement that the United States would no longer oppose the entry of Peking into the United Nations, where the Chinese seat was held by the Taiwan Government.

The Chinese Communists, meanwhile, began to make moves of their own. An American Ping-Pong team was invited to play in a tournament in Peking. The Chinese, who are among the world's best Ping-Pong players, easily defeated the Americans. However, the importance of this trip was not in the winning or the losing of the game, but rather in the diplomatic overture it represented. The American team was warmly received and very well treated. They were taken on sight-seeing trips and given lavish banquets, one of which was hosted by Premier Chou En-lai.

Almost immediately following this visit by the Ping-Pong team, one of the major barriers between America and China was lifted. American newspapermen were permitted inside the People's Republic and allowed to report on what they saw.

In July, at the request of President Nixon, his Assistant for National Security Affairs, Henry Kissinger, made a secret flight to mainland China. When Kissinger returned to the United States, the President announced that he would visit Peking sometime before May 1972. The news stunned the country—and the world.

In October, Kissinger returned to Peking and completed the details for the President's trip. Almost at the same time these arrangements were being settled, the crucial vote on Peking's admission to the United Nations was taken. The United States was in favor of admitting Communist China, but not at the cost of unseating the Nationalist Chinese, who held the China seat. However, in an unprecedented move, the United Nations voted to expel the Chinese Nationalists from the world body and invited Peking to take the Chinese seat in the General Assembly and on the Security Council. This came as a devastating blow to Chiang Kai-shek and the Nationalist Chinese. In the face of this defeat, they vowed to retain their important position in world affairs and to carry on their struggle to one day invade the mainland and free what they considered the oppressed Chinese people.

In the midst of these developments, there was speculation that Lin Piao, Communist China's defense minister and constitutional successor to Mao Tse-tung, had been ousted from power. Premier Chou En-lai was assumed to have moved into the second most important political position.

Korea

There were promising developments on the Korean peninsula in 1971. In April, President Chung Hee Park was re-elected to a third term as president of South Korea. In answer to many of his critics, Park declared that this would be his last election.

A first step was taken in August to ease relations with North and South Korea. The Red Cross societies of both countries entered into talks on the problems of divided families in the two Koreas. Both delegations expressed hope that their negotiations would lead to eventual reunification of North and South Korea. It was also agreed that a permanent Red Cross liaison office should be established at the Panmunjom armistice site.

As the year ended, however, South Korean President Park declared a state of national emergency. He said the changing international situation, presumably the recent events involving Communist China, and intensified war preparations in North Korea had made the action necessary. Three weeks later, on December 27, Park signed into law a highly controversial bill enabling him to censor the press, control wages, and restrict strikes. While most observers discounted the idea of North Korean war preparations, it was clear that South Korea was going through a period of difficult economic and political adjustment.

Japan

Relations between the United States and Japan deteriorated significantly during the year. One of the major problems concerned the 10 per cent surtax on imports that had been put into effect by President Nixon's new economic policy. In May, the United States asked Japan to revalue the yen to help reduce the large dollar outflow for Japanese goods. The Government of Japan refused to do so. Later in the year, it was announced that the yen would not be revalued, but it would be allowed to "float" on the international money market and find its own value. Because of this move, Japan requested the removal of the surtax.

The United States did not remove the surtax on all imported goods, but it did remove the surtax on some categories of textiles from Japan and other nations. This was part of an accord reached by Japan and the United States in October. After a three-year textile dispute, Japan agreed, under heavy pressure, to limit its exports of man-made and woolen textiles to the United States.

Then in December the ten leading Western

A textile mill in Japan.

industrial countries concluded a new monetary pact. The United States agreed to devalue the dollar and remove the import surcharge. Japan agreed to an official revaluation of the yen. This was a heavy blow to Japan's economy, for its goods will cost more overseas and people may buy less. Nevertheless, the new monetary pact was a necessary step because it ended the uncertainty over international monetary exchange rates. This will help spur world trade.

Japan was also quite disturbed over America's friendly overtures to Communist China. Many Japanese felt that their Government should have been notified of President Nixon's pending trip to Peking while it was still in the planning stages. Premier Eisaku Sato came under fire from the opposition Japanese Socialist Party. They have long favored a policy of improved relations with Peking and felt that Japan, rather than the United States, should have been the first to establish ties with China.

A treaty was signed in June committing the United States to return to Japan, sometime in 1972, the island of Okinawa and the other islands in the Ryukyu group. Control of the archipelago had been taken over by American forces during World War II.

President Nixon greeted Japanese Emperor Hirohito in Anchorage, Alaska, on September 26 during a stopover on the Emperor's flight to Denmark at the beginning of a European goodwill tour. This was the first time in history that a president of the United States met with an emperor of Japan. The occasion also marked the first time in 2,600 years—since the founding of the world's oldest surviving imperial dynasty—that a reigning Japanese monarch had left his native soil to visit a foreign land.

▶ SOUTHEAST ASIA

Indochina War

When Richard Nixon campaigned for the presidency in 1968, he promised that, if elected, he would "end American involvement in the Vietnam war." To accomplish this, Nixon put into effect a policy of Vietnamization. Under this plan, American forces would be withdrawn from Vietnam, and the South Vietnamese would gradually take over the fighting.

By the spring of 1971, more than 265,000 American soldiers had been withdrawn from the battlefield. In April it was announced that another 100,000 would be withdrawn by December. The plan appeared to be working so well that in November, Nixon announced a further withdrawal of 45,000 men by February 1, 1972, leaving only 139,000 American troops in the war-ravaged country.

Many people wondered whether South Vietnam could defend itself after the American forces had departed. Observers noted the military failures suffered by the South Vietnamese Army in 1971. The first and most significant defeat occurred early in the year. In February, thousands of South Vietnamese troops, supported by American planes, artillery, and observers, crossed the Vietnam border into Laos. Their primary objective was to attack a network of jungle roads said to be used as communist supply routes. After

A South Vietnamese soldier in Cambodia rounds up suspected communist sympathizers.

heavy fighting, the South Vietnamese army was forced to flee from Laos.

During the year, South Vietnamese forces also continued to move into neighboring Cambodia in search of communist staging areas. Although these campaigns were more successfully executed, the Communists continued to hold much of eastern Cambodia. The threat of a complete take-over by communist forces became so severe that in October, Premier Lon Nol declared Cambodia to be in a state of emergency, and suspended constitutional rule.

As the year ended, American-backed forces in Cambodia and Laos suffered crushing defeats. And new communist assaults were anticipated in South Vietnam. For these reasons, the United States began a major military offensive in December. For five days, antiaircraft installations and fuel and supply depots in North Vietnam were heavily bombed. The air attacks were the heaviest since President Johnson had suspended heavy bombing in 1968.

Fewer and fewer American GI's were being killed in Vietnam, but the desire to leave was still very strong.

South Vietnamese President Nguyen Van Thieu votes in October 3 presidential election. No one ran against Thieu; he received more than 90 per cent of the vote.

Wright—Miami News

'One Man, One Vote . . . What's More Democratic Than That?'

South Vietnam's presidential elections were held on October 3, 1971. From the very start of the campaign, charges and countercharges were exchanged by the three leading candidates—President Nguyen Van Thieu, Vice-President Nguyen Cao Ky, and General Duong Van Minh. The campaign was a long and very bitter one. General Minh, declaring that Thieu had already rigged the election, withdrew from the race. Later, Vice-President Ky, calling the election a fraud, also withdrew. President Thieu announced that, since he was the only candidate, he would consider the outcome as a test of popular support of his policies.

The outcome was as expected. President Thieu was re-elected to office, receiving 94.3 per cent of the vote. Some observers thought that the American position in South Vietnam had been badly hurt by the nature of the election.

Indonesia

Indonesia held its first Parliamentary election since 1955, and only its second since 1949 when the island republic had won its freedom from Dutch colonial rule. The voting was the first test of public support for President Suharto, who had taken power from the late President Sukarno six years earlier.

Queen Juliana of the Netherlands became the first Dutch ruling monarch to visit Indonesia. In late August, the Queen, accompanied by her husband, Prince Bernhard, traveled to this island republic, which, for centuries, had been the crown jewel of the Dutch empire.

Malaysia

Nearby Malaysia returned to rule by a parliamentary government after nearly two years of emergency rule by the National Operations Council. Although Malaysia had been somewhat free of turmoil since the Malay-Chinese rioting of 1969, signs of unrest began to appear in August. New communist-guerrilla attacks were reported to have been launched in many key sections of the country. The Government declared that Malaysian troops and police would fight until the rebel forces had been defeated.

The Philippines

The Republic of the Philippines experienced numerous and often violent clashes, with what President Ferdinand Marcos called "Marxist-Maoist forces." The most serious incident occurred in August when a grenade attack killed ten persons. As a result, President Marcos suspended constitutional rights, a move bitterly opposed by many. President Marcos later restored some of the constitutional freedoms that had been suspended.

Thailand

In Thailand a group of military and other leaders headed by Premier Thanom Kittikachorn seized full powers of the Government in November. They abolished the constitution, dissolved Parliament, disbanded the Cabinet, and declared martial law. Kittikachorn announced that these measures were necessary because of internal strife, and that the country's democratic institutions were too inefficient to control the turmoil. Thailand had been the target of communist insurrection in the north, student demonstrations, strikes, and terrorism during 1971. The new leaders pledged, however, to continue Thailand's strongly anticommunist foreign policy.

▶ SOUTH ASIA

India, Pakistan, and Bangladesh

During December 1971, India and Pakistan fought a brief but costly war. The conflict stemmed from a bloody civil war that had been raging in East Pakistan since late March.

East and West Pakistan are divided by 1,000 miles of Indian territory. Their peoples have completely different cultures. East Pakistan has 55 per cent of the nation's population. Yet West Pakistan has always dominated East Pakistan.

In December 1970, Pakistan had elected a new Parliament. The major political party in East Pakistan, under Sheik Mujibur Rahman, won a majority of seats. Within Rahman's party were voices demanding that East Pakistan declare itself independent of the rest of Pakistan. In late March 1971 a crisis was reached. Troops of the Pakistan

Agha Mohammad Yahya Khan, former president of Pakistan.

Zulfikar Ali Bhutto, the new president of Pakistan.

Indira Gandhi, Indian prime minister and foe of Pakistan.

Army (made up of soldiers from West Pakistan) launched widespread attacks in an attempt to crush East Pakistan's movement for autonomy. Heavy fighting raged throughout the major cities of East Pakistan. Sheik Mujibur was arrested, and thousands of his supporters were killed during the fighting. Millions of refugees fled into neighboring India.

Meanwhile, accusations were made that India was giving arms to the East Pakistani rebels. And relations between Pakistan and India, which had always been bad, worsened. There was a growing fear that the two nations would go to war again—for the third time since their independence in 1947.

In December these fears were realized. Clashes between the Indian and Pakistani armies grew larger and more frequent. Then, in the first week of December, India launched a full-scale attack against East Pakistan. The two countries also clashed in Kashmir, which borders northwestern India and West Pakistan. No one gained the upper hand in fighting here. In East Pakistan, however, Indian forces, aided by the Mukti Bahini, the Bengali guerrillas, quickly overcame Pakistani resistance. In two weeks the war was over. East Pakistan's Army commander surrendered on December 16, and a new nation —Bangladesh—was born.

Because of the loss of East Pakistan, Pakistani President Yahya Khan resigned. Foreign Minister Zulfikar Ali Bhutto assumed the presidency. Early in January 1972, he promised to release Sheik Mujibur Rahman

Near Jessore, East Pakistan, Indian soldiers man a large-caliber mobile gun. By mid-December, after two weeks of war, the Indians had defeated the Pakistani Army.

from prison. The Sheik had been named head of the new Bangladesh Government.

The war found the United States and Communist China on the same side: both countries supported Pakistan. The Soviet Union lent its support to India. In August the Soviet Union and India had signed a twenty-year friendship treaty.

Ceylon

Early in 1971, Ceylon, too, faced a rebellion. Radical youths, disillusioned by Ceylon's extreme unemployment problem, launched terrorist attacks on police stations, government buildings, and patrols. It was reported that thousands had been killed before the insurrection was put down. An amnesty period was granted in May, and more than a thousand rebels surrendered to Ceylonese forces. At year's end, it appeared that peace had returned to this beautiful tropical island.

ARNOLD C. BRACKMAN
Author, *The Communist Collapse in Indonesia*

AUSTRALIA, NEW ZEALAND,
AND THE PACIFIC ISLANDS

IN 1971 this vast, empty third of the world was the scene of much varied activity. The biggest stir came in the political field. On March 10, Prime Minister John G. Gorton of Australia was ousted from office and his place taken by William McMahon.

The area continued to hold much interest for peoples from other parts of the globe. Thousands of Europeans and North Americans emigrated to Australia and New Zealand. And tourists continued to travel great distances to view the unspoiled beauty of the Pacific islands. Among the thousands of visitors to this part of the world was the Duke of Edinburgh. He toured all the British territories in Oceania and also New Guinea.

In spite of some economic difficulties and new political tensions, it was a year of progress. With Britain withdrawing from the area and preparing to enter the European Economic Community (EEC), Australia and New Zealand both played more independent roles in world affairs. They also drew more closely together, especially in matters of trade and defense.

Australia's new Prime Minister, William McMahon, with his wife, Sonia, and their two children.

Left: Australian and South African rugby players fight it out on the playing field. Below: Australians opposed to South Africa's policy of apartheid demonstrate against the South African rugby team.

▶AUSTRALIA

Politically, 1971 was a year of feverish activity in the Federal Parliament in Canberra. After bitter party strife Prime Minister John Gorton was replaced in March by the deputy leader of the Liberal Party, William McMahon. Gorton lost a vote of confidence by members of his Liberal Party. A secret ballot ended in a 33–33 vote. Then John Gorton rose and declared that he no longer had the support of his followers. He then cast the deciding vote, in effect ousting himself from office.

The Liberal-Country Party Government was constantly attacked by the opposition Labor Party. Its leader, Gough Whitlam, scored some political advantage from a successful visit to Communist China.

Both political parties and the public alike warmly approved the decision of Australia and New Zealand to withdraw their combat troops from South Vietnam by the end of 1971.

The Senate, or upper house of Australia's Parliament, made history when Neville Bonner became the first aboriginal senator. While there was little major political activity in the States themselves, the Northern Territory, which at present is administered from the country's capital, Canberra, demanded statehood.

A Year of Protest

The year turned out to be a record one for protest movements. Thousands of Australians joined city marches that were organized to protest conscription, and many draft-age Australians burned their call-up cards. The visit of the South African rugby footballers stirred Australians opposed to South Africa's apartheid policy into action. Anti-apartheid demonstrations erupted throughout the country. In Queensland, the state government took the extreme step of declaring a state of emergency while the South African team visited there. This was done to prevent the tour's being disrupted or even called off.

There were other protests in 1971, particularly in the field of education. For the first time in their histories the eastern states of Australia were faced with strikes by teachers. The teachers' demands included better working conditions.

Economy

Economically, the two major problems that troubled Australia were the rise in the cost of living and the alarming fall in wool prices. The Australian Council of Trade Unions (A.C.T.U.), under the vigorous and able new President, R. J. Hawke, successfully pressed for higher wages. Meanwhile, the Federal Government partly curbed inflation by increasing certain taxes. It helped the sheepman by guaranteeing a minimum price for his wool.

The greatest threat to the Australian economy will come with the long-awaited entry of Great Britain into the European Economic Community (EEC). Australia may then be deprived of its traditional safeguards for the export of its primary products to Britain.

This unhappy economic news was partially offset by the continued mineral boom. But the frenzied excitement created by the rich discoveries of 1970 was dampened by the failure of some large companies. Mining activity and oil drilling did continue, however, but with much greater caution. This was especially so in the Northern Territory where oil, natural gas, bauxite, and uranium were discovered. In Western Australia the development of vast iron and nickel resources was stepped up. This helped make the state the fastest growing one in the Commonwealth.

Australia is a land of violent climatic contrasts. While drought still gripped many parts of northern Australia, torrential rains swept over Queensland. These rains broke a seven-year-old dry spell. They brought about great flooding of the land, but at the same time improved the prospects for the long-suffering cattle industry.

Drug Problem

Like a number of other countries throughout the world, Australia faced a growing drug problem. The increasing traffic in drugs brought great concern to the people and leaders of the major cities. The issue was discussed and debated. Clinics were established

Neville Bonner, Australia's first aboriginal senator, with fellow Senator John Carrick.

Below: Drought in northern Australia.

Port Moresby, capital of Papua New Guinea.

to treat drug addicts. Police squads were increased, and greater efforts were made to cope with this problem.

Papua New Guinea

Throughout the year the movement for home rule grew and was strengthened. A timetable for political independence with an English style of government was drawn up by Australian authorities. In June the legislature of the Territory of Papua and New Guinea passed the National Identity Bill. This bill gave the territory a new name—Papua New Guinea—as well as an official flag and emblem.

Industrial and mining activities, along with greater education, awakened and stirred native political consciousness. The most important of the mining enterprises was the Bougainville Copper Company. This company has built one of the world's largest opencut copper mines. It has also built the new mining town of Panguna on the lush island of Bougainville, which is part of the trust territory of Papua New Guinea.

Although the production of copra declined in importance, the beef industry began to expand. A vast hydroelectric project was started, to bring power to the towns of the highlands and the coast. However, the territory had a severe problem of unemployment. Many jobless natives left their villages to seek jobs in the capital city of Port Moresby and in the new mining towns.

NEW ZEALAND

The National Party Government, a well-entrenched one in New Zealand, is headed by Prime Minister Keith Holyoake. The chief concern of Prime Minister Holyoake and his Government in 1971 was to get the best terms possible for New Zealand's primary products when Britain enters the European Economic Community. On a visit to Europe, Deputy Prime Minister Jack Marshall secured what was generally regarded as a satisfactory agreement for continued export of butter to Britain. Earlier, France had called for an end to British imports of all New Zealand dairy products.

But the Government was able to do little to curb mounting inflation and the resulting industrial unrest. All labor unions demanded and won big wage increases. Of special economic importance was the failure of employers and employees to agree on the conditions under which new container cargoes should be loaded and unloaded. Special port facilities had been built for these container cargoes at great expense. The problem was therefore an urgent one.

After long negotiations, the largest shipping company in the country, the Union Steamship Company of New Zealand, which was English-owned, was sold to an Australian and New Zealand group. An extension of the limited free-trade agreement between the two countries further strengthened trading ties across the Tasman Sea.

A nationwide census gave the population of New Zealand as over 2,800,000. It also revealed that the population shift from the south continued, giving two thirds of the population to the North Island. The immigration of young Pacific islanders, especially from Tonga, Niue, and the Cook Islands, increased. Most of the newcomers went to Auckland where they soon found work. Tourism also brought a record number of visitors to New Zealand.

The problem of pollution, which is concerning the people of many industrialized countries throughout the world, has also come to plague New Zealanders. In the wake of increased urban development and manufacturing, some of the rivers and lakes of the North Island have been found to be polluted.

THE PACIFIC ISLANDS

For the peoples of Oceania, 1971 was a year of political unrest. There were some native movements toward independence and the creation of ministates. In April a meeting of Pacific Island leaders was held at Nukualofa, the capital of Tonga, to discuss common problems.

There was political discontent in the French overseas territories. The people of New Caledonia agitated for self-rule. And in the New Hebrides there was sharp criticism of the British and French control. This joint control, which has been in effect for 65 years, is called a condominium. Because of its alleged clumsiness and ineptness it is locally referred to as "Pandemonium."

In August an important South Pacific conference was held in Wellington, New Zealand. High-ranking representatives of Australia and New Zealand met with the heads of government of independent Western Samoa, Fiji, Nauru, and Tonga, and the self-governing Cook Islands. The meeting was called the South Pacific Forum, and it was announced that the forum would be a permanent organization that would meet every year.

Most island groups enjoyed prosperity in 1971. In Fiji, bauxite and manganese were discovered. Some deposits of bauxite were also found in the Solomon Islands. The production of nickel was stepped up in New Caledonia, and a search for oil was made in Tonga. A number of airstrips were built on several islands. But despite the development and prosperity, some of the islands had problems of overcrowding and unemployment. These problems were especially acute in Tonga and Samoa.

The interest of the Great Powers in the Pacific was largely strategic. Besides establishing an anti-nuclear-missile tracking station on Canton Island, the United States transferred shipments of deadly nerve gas from Okinawa to Johnston Island. In the South Pacific, France exploded nuclear devices on Mururoa, a tiny uninhabited atoll in French Polynesia.

E. J. TAPP
Former Associate Professor
The University of New England (Australia)

CANADA

NEARLY a decade ago, Lester Pearson, then Canadian prime minister, predicted that future relations between Canada and the United States would no longer be "easy and automatic." In 1971, Lester Pearson's prophecy seemed to be coming true. A time of trouble between the two nations had arrived, and the main cause was President Nixon's decision in August to impose a 10 per cent surcharge on goods imported into the United States.

The new United States trade policy came at a critical time. Canada's unemployment rate had risen to over 7 per cent, and there were fears that another 70,000 Canadians would lose their jobs as a result of the American action.

Canada is very dependent on the United States as a market for goods. About 70 per cent of all Canadian exports go to the United States. Canada, in turn, buys almost 25 per cent of all United States exports. President Nixon's surcharge was therefore a shattering blow to Canada's efforts to bring itself out of an economic slump. Thus when Nixon devalued the dollar and lifted the surcharge in December, Canadians breathed a sigh of relief.

Progressive Conservative Party leader Robert Stanfield listens to the grievances of unemployed workers in Vancouver, British Columbia. Economic problems plagued Canada during 1971.

In Washington, D.C., Canadian Prime Minister Pierre Elliott Trudeau and President Nixon discuss U.S.-Canadian relations and the President's forthcoming trip to Communist China.

Canada developed closer ties with several communist nations in 1971. Huang Hua (left) became the first Communist Chinese ambassador to Canada. President Tito of Yugoslavia (above) visited Canada. And in October, Prime Minister Trudeau and Soviet Premier Aleksei Kosygin (below) signed a cultural, scientific, and educational pact.

Despite all the political activity, Prime Minister Trudeau found time to get married, to Margaret Sinclair.

▶THE ECONOMY

Canada already had serious economic problems when the United States imposed the 10 per cent surcharge. Unemployment in Canada had reached a 10-year high, and the prediction of a further loss of 70,000 jobs because of the American policy was a staggering blow. Furthermore, Canada had been enjoying a favorable balance of trade with the United States: it was exporting a little more than it was importing from the United States. The new United States trade policy threatened to wipe out this economic advantage.

Faced with this dramatic turnabout, the Canadian Government took immediate action by beginning an $80,000,000 program to help those industries hardest hit by the surcharge. In an effort to pump more money into the sluggish economy, Finance Minister Edgar Benson cut income taxes by 3 per cent and corporation taxes by 7 per cent. In addition, Ontario, the richest of Canada's 10 provinces, reduced its provincial income and corporate taxes by the same amount.

Meanwhile, a special Canadian delegation went to Washington in an effort to persuade the United States Government to exempt Canada from the surcharge. When the mission failed, Prime Minister Pierre Trudeau commented: "I don't think they [the United States Government] know much or care much really about Canada. If they do realize what they are doing and if it becomes apparent that they just want us to be sellers of natural resources and buyers of their manu-

factured products. . . . we will have to reassess our relations with them, trading, political and otherwise."

Probably the sorest spot in United States-Canadian relations concerns recent developments in the six-year-old automobile pact. This pact has given Canada's car industry a handsome share of the North American market.

Up until 1965, Canada had a huge deficit in the auto trade. Canadian auto plants built only 4 per cent of the total North American production, while Canadians purchased 7 per cent of the output. But by 1970 the picture had dramatically changed. Canada was exporting more automotive vehicles and parts to the United States than it was importing.

In October 1971, however, U.S. Treasury Secretary John Connally made it clear that the United States would insist on the removal of several provisions in the pact that were designed to protect the Canadian auto industry. The announcement created new resentment against the United States and its economic policies.

Then, in mid-December, just two weeks after Prime Minister Trudeau had met with President Nixon in Washington, D.C., to discuss mutual problems, it was announced that the United States was removing its 10 per cent surcharge on imported goods. While this alone will not solve all the economic problems between the two nations, it was at least a step in bringing the North American neighbors closer together.

Continued high sales of lumber were one bright spot in the Canadian economic picture.

As every housewife knew, a major problem in 1971 was rising prices of food and other consumer goods.

The automobile assembly line at the General Motors plant at Ste. Thérèse, Quebec.

▶FOREIGN AFFAIRS

Many Canadians were disturbed by signs that the Trudeau Government was apparently leading the country away from its traditional friendship with the United States. At the same time, the Government seemed to be developing closer ties with the Soviet Union and other communist nations.

Since he became prime minister in 1968, Trudeau has often expressed a desire to strike out on a more independent course in foreign policy—rather than follow the policies of the United States. This became evident in 1970 when Canada established diplomatic relations with the People's Republic of China, in spite of opposition from the United States.

Prime Minister Trudeau took another step in this new direction when he and Soviet Premier Aleksei Kosygin exchanged visits in 1971. In May, Trudeau and Kosygin signed a protocol in Moscow that pledges both their countries "to enlarge and deepen consultation on important international problems of mutual interest."

At the signing ceremony, Trudeau said: "We are not only the friend, neighbor, and ally of the United States. We want to communicate even more strongly with the Soviet Union, even though she is not our ally. It will help us to as independent a point of view as possible."

Trudeau was met by enthusiastic crowds of Russians throughout his 11-day tour of the Soviet Union. This was in marked contrast to the hostile crowds that greeted Soviet Premier Kosygin when he arrived in Ottawa, in October. During the Soviet official's eight-day visit, he was the target of anti-Soviet demonstrations by members of Canada's large Jewish and Eastern European minority groups. On one occasion, Kosygin was assaulted, but not injured, by a self-styled Hungarian "freedom fighter." Prime Minister Trudeau quickly apologized for the incident.

Security was tight and Kosygin was guarded by hundreds of police as he traveled to Montreal, Toronto, and Vancouver. In each of these cities, Jewish demonstrators

On October 21, more than 1,200 demonstrators march on the Soviet Consulate in Montreal. They were protesting Soviet Premier Kosygin's visit to Canada.

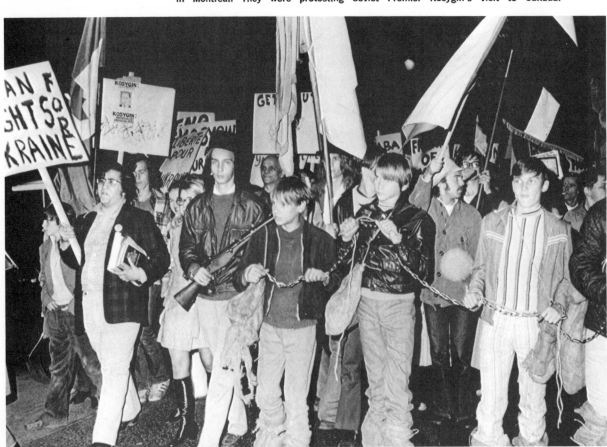

In a tense moment in Ottawa, Premier Kosygin is grabbed by Giza Matrai, a self-styled Hungarian "freedom fighter." Kosygin was not hurt. Prime Minister Trudeau is at right.

were on hand to shout their demands that Russian Jews be allowed to emigrate from the Soviet Union.

Kosygin and Trudeau signed an agreement to expand cultural, scientific, and educational relations between the two countries. Kosygin used the occasion to observe that United States protectionist trade measures forced some countries "to increase unemployment on account of the economic miscalculation of others."

This statement prompted a stern reply from Opposition Leader Robert Stanfield. He said that it was "stupid" for the Canadian Government to allow the Soviet leader to use Canada as a platform to attack the U.S.

Most observers continue to believe that the majority of Canadians favor close ties with the United States, in spite of the differences that occasionally strain relations. Trudeau felt it important to have a new appraisal of the U.S. attitude toward Canada if these problems were to be worked out. On December 6, Prime Minister Trudeau and President Nixon conferred in Washington. Trudeau returned to Canada hailing the meeting as a "fantastic" success. He said he felt that Nixon did not want Canada to be "a colony of the United States," and "wanted to respect not only our political identity, but our economic identity." This was indeed a "new statement" on U.S.-Canadian relations.

Kosygin talks with Henri Richard of the Montreal Canadiens. The Premier watched two periods of the game with the Vancouver Canucks and was given a standing ovation by the audience when he left.

In Edmonton, Alberta, Premier Kosygin wears a headdress given him by the Ermineskin Indians. The Indians named him Chief Golden Eagle.

▶ PARLIAMENT

In 1971 the Federal Parliament passed several important bills.

On January 1, 1972, an increase in unemployment benefits went into effect under a revision of the Unemployment Insurance Act. The maximum payment to a jobless worker was raised to $100 a week—nearly double the $53 allowed under the old act.

Parliament also passed a bill authorizing the formation of the Canada Development Corporation. The purpose of this $250,000,-000 public-fund corporation is to develop and maintain Canadian-controlled corporations and "give Canadians greater opportunities to invest in the economic development of Canada."

Eventually the corporation will go public and sell shares at $5.00 each. It is expected to acquire total capital of about $2,000,000,-000. Future plans include the option of purchasing 3 promising Crown corporations and the 45 per cent Government-owned share of Panarctic Oils—an association of oil-exploration companies that has already made 2 large natural-gas discoveries in the Arctic region.

A tax-reform program that became effective on January 1, 1972, freed over 1,000,-000 low-income Canadians from paying any income tax. Additional millions of working people will be paying less in taxes than before.

The new tax-reform act was a product of a nine-year study by Parliamentary committees and a Royal Commission. In announcing the passage of the bill, Finance Minister Edgar Benson said that the burden of taxation would be spread "more evenly and more fairly so that every person and every institution able to contribute will do so."

Carrying English- and French-language signs, demonstrators march past Parliament in Ottawa. In 1971 Parliament passed a bill increasing unemployment benefits.

Displaying the Canadian flag, students in Windsor, Ontario, protest the planned United States nuclear explosion at Amchitka Island in the Aleutians. The students closed the Ambassador Bridge, which connects Canada with Detroit, Michigan.

There were a number of significant changes in the rates of taxation and the types of allowable exemptions as a result of the reform bill. Among the changes were the following:

The personal-income-tax exemption was increased from $1,000 to $1,500 for a single Canadian, and from $2,000 to $2,850 for a married wage earner.

Until recently Canada was the only Western industrialized nation without a capital-gains tax. That has now changed, and the reform bill provides for the taxation of one half of profits at the same rates as personal income taxes. It is expected that this will offset the loss of revenue resulting from the increase in personal exemptions.

Smaller businesses—those earning less than $400,000 a year—will be taxed at a rate of only 25 per cent for the first $50,000 income. Thereafter the rate will increase to 50 per cent on all profits. All foreign-owned companies, regardless of size, must pay the full rate. In order to channel more investment funds into Canadian businesses, retirement savings plans and pension funds are now permitted to invest no more than 10 per cent of their funds abroad.

Expense accounts have been curtailed by limiting the items that can be deducted as business expenses. It is no longer possible to deduct such items as a yacht, or memberships in country clubs or other recreational groups.

Working mothers received new benefits under the reform plan. They may deduct up to $500 from their taxable income for day care, baby-sitters, and summer camps.

Generally speaking, the tax burden on the individual income earner has been lessened, while that on businesses and certain institutions has been increased.

▶ENVIRONMENT AND POLLUTION

According to one of the country's top scientists, Dr. Omand Solandt, Canada is rapidly reaching the saturation point in population—even though it is the world's second largest country and has fewer than 22,000,000 people. Dr. Solandt, chairman of the Science Council of Canada, stated that Canada must play a key role in stabilizing world population, controlling resource-use, and reducing pollution.

"If the human race is to have a tolerable future on planet Earth, the whole of our social organization must be drastically revised within a very few generations," he wrote in the science council's fifth annual report.

Dr. Solandt recommended strict population and immigration controls for Canada. He suggested that additional population in certain areas of the country would only spoil the natural environment. In his view, the vast Canadian Arctic, with its tiny population of 60,000 Eskimos, Indians, and whites, may already be overpopulated. Some parts of the country therefore should not be encouraged to pursue costly programs of industrialization. A pastoral life might be better for these regions.

To accomplish these goals, Dr. Solandt recommended the formation of an institute of scholars which would "define future problems and outline alternative solutions that should be taken today, tomorrow, or within a few years." He proposed a name for the institute—Futures Canada.

The city of Montreal is barely visible beneath a heavy blanket of air pollution. In early February the city went through its worst air-pollution crisis in years.

THE PRIME MINISTER

Canada's dynamic Prime Minister, Pierre Elliott Trudeau, 51, surprised nearly everyone—including members of his own Government—by marrying 22-year-old Margaret Sinclair, a daughter of a former Liberal cabinet minister, James Sinclair. Not until the wedding ceremony had been performed early in March, in a North Vancouver church, did the news finally leak out.

A vigorous and athletic man, Trudeau had long been Canada's most eligible bachelor. Before his marriage, Trudeau was seen in the company of several female celebrities. Among them were singer Barbra Streisand and actress Louise Marleau, whom he escorted to public functions.

The secrecy surrounding the unannounced wedding was typical of Trudeau. He has often maintained that his private life is not a matter of public concern, and he has tried to keep it out of the spotlight of publicity.

Trudeau is the first Canadian prime minister to marry while in office. And on Christmas Day, Mrs. Trudeau gave birth to a son, Justin Pierre. The child is the first to be born to an incumbent Canadian prime minister, since 1869.

On the government level, Prime Minister Trudeau continued to press for what he has termed a "just society." His record has been one of mixed success.

Now in his fourth year of office, Trudeau has failed to end inflation or eliminate the regional differences that still divide Canada. On the other hand, the Prime Minister has reorganized and streamlined government agencies. He has also established several new bureaus, including a department of the environment to fight pollution and conserve natural resources. During the separatist violence in Quebec, Trudeau was widely hailed for his tough stand against the French-Canadian terrorists of the Front de Libération du Québec (F.L.Q.). To ease tension between French- and English-speaking Canadians, Trudeau successfully fought to have Parliament pass an act requiring that the French language have equal status with English in Federal government offices and lawcourts.

In foreign affairs, Trudeau has had several important successes. His major triumph was the establishment of diplomatic relations with Communist China. The Trudeau Government also established closer ties with the Soviet Union. However, these improved relations with the communist countries coincide with a drift away from the United States-backed North Atlantic Treaty Organization (NATO), and this has upset some Canadians. But according to recent surveys, Trudeau continues to be a favorite with the people.

THE PROVINCES

In October, Ontario's voters went to the polls, and returned to office the Progressive Conservative Party, which has governed the province for the past 28 years. The Conservatives won 78 seats. This increased their majority by 10 in the 117-seat provincial legislature.

Led by Premier William Davis, the Conservatives beat back a determined bid for office by the socialist New Democratic Party. The election left the Liberal Party with 20 seats, and the New Democrats with 19.

In his six months in office before calling an election, Davis had pushed 103 bills through the legislature. These included a no-fault insurance law described as the best in North America, and improved benefits for senior citizens. Davis, who succeeded John Robarts as the Conservative Party leader in March, also lowered the voting age to 18. As a result, an additional 450,000 young people in Ontario were given the right to vote.

Progressive Conservatives also scored victories in Alberta, where they ended the 36-year reign of the Social Credit Party, and in Newfoundland. The Conservatives won 49 of 75 seats in Alberta's provincial legislature. Party leader Peter Lougheed thus became the first Conservative premier in Alberta's history. In Newfoundland the Progressive Conservatives won the October elections. However, as the year ended, Premier Joey Smallwood and his Liberal Party were contesting the results. The 70-year-old Smallwood, premier of the province for 22 years, had earlier said he would retire from politics.

The Liberal Party also suffered a defeat

in Saskatchewan. After seven years in office, Premier Ross Thatcher and his fellow Liberals were beaten by the socialist New Democratic Party. Canadian socialism first took root in Saskatchewan in 1944 when the province elected North America's first socialist government. In the 1971 election, the New Democratic Party won 45 of the legislature's 60 seats. Allan Blakeney became the new premier of the province.

Prairies: Farm Economy

The grain-growing farmers of the three Prairie Provinces—Manitoba, Saskatchewan, and Alberta—have witnessed a complete turnabout in their economic situation during the past two years. In 1969 they were unable to find a market for their wheat because of worldwide overproduction, and they were left with a surplus of 1,200,000,000 unsold bushels.

Peter Lougheed (right) became premier of Alberta after his Progressive Conservative Party won a majority of seats in the provincial legislature. Below: Premier William Davis of Ontario.

The trading floor of the Grain Exchange in Winnipeg, Manitoba. Canada's three Prairie Provinces produced a total of 1,500,000,000 bushels of all grains in 1971.

A sharp reduction in the acreage given over to wheat cut production in half in 1970. This was coupled with greatly improved sales abroad—a record 671,000,000 bushels in 1971. As a result, prosperity returned to the prairies in 1971.

At the urging of the government, farmers began to vary their crops. Flax, barley, rye, and rapeseed are now being grown, and in 1971 this led to a reduction in the wheat surplus. A total of 1,500,000,000 bushels of all grains were produced in 1971. The barley crop alone numbered 630,000,000 bushels, twice the 1970 output. In all, the bountiful harvest amounted to about $1,500,000,000.

Quebec

Attention shifted from problems created by French-Canadian separatists—who would like to see the province become independent of the rest of Canada—to problems created by the unfavorable economic picture.

In spite of promises by Premier Robert Bourassa that he would create 100,000 new jobs, Quebec's unemployment rate averaged over 10 per cent during 1971. Because of a decline in world markets, several key resource industries in the pulp and newsprint field had to cut back their production. A large number of workers were laid off.

One indicator of Quebec's economic woes came to light as a result of a Government report. The study pointed out that nearly half of all bankruptcies in Canada occur in Quebec. Total bankruptcies in the country numbered over 4,000. About 1,900 were in Quebec, with a total loss to creditors of $55,600,000.

To reduce unemployment, Premier Bourassa began a massive hydroelectric power

A Canadian stamp honoring Pierre Laporte was issued. Laporte had been killed by Quebec separatists in 1970. In 1971 four men were arrested and charged with his murder. They are (below, left to right, top to bottom): Jacques Rose, Paul Rose, Francis Simard, and Bernard Lortie.

project in the James Bay area of northwestern Quebec. The $6,000,000,000 project, which will harness the power of 5 rivers flowing into James Bay, is expected to provide 125,000 new jobs.

The target date for the completion of the project is 1980. When finished, it will produce 35,000,000,000 kilowatt-hours of power annually, making it the largest hydroproject in the hemisphere. Bourassa already has arranged preliminary financing of the project. Most of the power will be sold across the border to New York and the New England states, where the demand for power in recent years has exceeded the supply.

The Quebec Premier has said that the economic situation in his province can be improved only if there is a big influx of foreign investment. But this view is not held by the Federal Government. While other provinces have discouraged foreign investment, Bourassa has insisted that Quebec will decide for itself about accepting foreign capital.

The province still has not fully recovered from the wave of separatist terror that swept across Quebec in 1970. During that troubled year, Pierre Laporte, a provincial cabinet minister, and British trade commissioner James Cross were kidnaped and held for ransom by members of the radical Front de Libération du Québec. Cross was later released, but Laporte was murdered by his captors.

Four men were arrested and in 1971 were charged with the Laporte murder. Two were convicted of noncapital murder and were sentenced to life imprisonment. One is serving a prison term for kidnaping, and the fourth is awaiting trial. Out of 500 persons detained under the emergency measures imposed by Prime Minister Trudeau in 1970, about 40 are still awaiting trial. Many of them are charged with seditious conspiracy.

GUY BIRCH
News Editor, *Toronto Star*

ECONOMY

THE economic policy of the United States underwent a drastic change of course in 1971. For the first time in the nation's history, a president imposed wage and price controls on the American public in a period when there was no declared national emergency or an all-out war involving the nation.

The economy had been slowing down for several years. In 1971 industry suffered additional setbacks, and hundreds of thousands of workers were laid off around the country. Yet at the same time inflation was rampant. The prices of everything from food to clothing continued to spiral upward. Another complicating factor was that the United States was spending more abroad than it was selling. All of these problems indicated that a new economic policy was needed in the United States.

The new policy had a severe impact not only on the United States but on other nations around the world. For President Nixon announced that the United States would no longer redeem the dollar in gold at $35 an ounce and that it would impose a 10 per cent tax on most foreign goods being brought into the country.

In December came the historic decision to devalue the dollar, thus changing international monetary agreements that dated back to the end of World War II. As part of the new agreement, other Western industrialized nations would revalue their currency, and the U.S. would remove its import surcharge tax.

With inflation and the rising cost of food, poor people were especially hard hit. One way of helping the poor is the Food Stamp Program, which allows people to buy food with coupons supplied by the Federal Government.

Economic adviser Paul W. McCracken declares in July that U.S. economic performance is not living up to expectations.

Unemployment lines grew long as more and more people found themselves out of work. A ten-year high was reached in 1971 when 6.1 per cent of the labor force was unemployed.

The Office of Emergency Preparedness handled the thousands of questions that poured in after President Nixon announced the price-wage freeze.

The emblem of the new U.S. economic program, symbolizing "inflation going down."

WE FIGHT INFLATION • WE SUPPORT THE U.S. ECONOMIC PROGRAM

New units were set up to administer Phase 2. The Pay Board (above), made up of labor, management, and the public, was to keep wage hikes at 5.5 per cent. The Price Commission (below), made up of persons outside government, was to restrain price and rent increases.

The American public had expected the economy to be stronger in 1971 after turning sharply downward in 1970. The Council of Economic Advisers announced early in the year that it expected the gross national product to reach $1,065,000,000,000 in 1971. But the economy did not rebound this quickly, and many elected officials began to call upon President Nixon to do something to stimulate the economy and to slow down inflation.

President Nixon's new economic policy was designed to do just that. There were three basic reasons why the President was forced to set wage and price controls. First, inflation was rising at a rapid pace. This meant that prices for goods and services increased by more than the acceptable 2 or 3 per cent over the cost of the same item a year ago. Second, people were not buying so much as they had been buying in years past, because they did not have the money. This, in turn, caused industry, which makes and sells goods and services, to produce less. Since industry was not producing as much, fewer workers were needed, which resulted in widespread unemployment. The third reason was the balance of trade. The value of United States exports fell far short of the value of foreign imports. In other words, the nation was selling less goods abroad than it was buying.

▶ THE NEW ECONOMIC POLICY

President Nixon's new economic policy was announced on August 15, 1971. The wage and price freeze was the most startling part of it. For this meant that for a period of ninety days, starting immediately after the announcement, no one could receive a pay increase. Also, prices of goods and services were frozen and could not be raised unless the item was one of the few that did not fall under the controls. On November 14, "Phase II" of the controls program went into effect. In the second phase, price and wage increases were limited but not completely halted.

In order to give people more money to spend, President Nixon recommended to Congress that the personal-income-tax exemption be raised to $750. The President asked, too, for the repeal of the excise tax on new-automobile purchases. This meant that anyone buying a car would save up to $200. President Nixon also asked that industry, in general, be given a special tax credit so that it could buy more American-made equipment and machinery.

(In December Congress granted Nixon's requests. The personal-income-tax exemption was raised to $675 in 1971 and $750 in 1972. The 7 per cent excise tax on automobiles was repealed, and the 7 per cent investment tax credit was reinstated.)

To balance the international-trade deficit a 10 per cent surcharge tax was imposed on most goods imported into the United States from foreign countries. In this way, it was hoped that the consumer would buy American-made products because they would be cheaper than imported items. Many foreign products are produced in factories where employees are paid far less money for their work than workers in the United States. Because of this, products could be sold at a lower price in America than homemade goods. This was especially true in the field of electronics (television sets and tape recorders). With the new surcharge tax, these imported products are no longer less expensive than American-made goods.

The President also announced that the United States would no longer guarantee to redeem the dollar in gold at $35 an ounce. This did not mean very much to the consumer, because he doesn't use gold as money. But gold *is* used by all free nations of the world as the base for the value of their own currency. Therefore, President Nixon's move caused major financial concern around the globe. For more than 25 years, foreign nations have set the value of their money in relation to the dollar. These countries knew that they could always purchase gold from the United States at $35 an ounce.

President Nixon hoped that by releasing the dollar from a fixed value of $35 to an ounce of gold, he would force other countries to put a higher value on their own currency. In some cases, this did happen. However, most nations allowed their currencies to "float" rather than officially revaluing.

Economists felt that a new universal

money policy, with a fixed gold redemption base for the dollar, had to be set. In December a landmark in economic history occurred. The Group of Ten, the largest industrialized Western nations, met to realign the world's currencies. The United States agreed to devalue the dollar and fix the official price of gold at $38 an ounce. Other nations agreed to revalue their currencies upward. The effective dollar devaluation was 12 per cent. This means that American-made products will be cheaper overseas and foreign products will be more expensive in the United States.

▶ **UNEMPLOYMENT**

Early in 1971, months before the wage and price program was announced, there were signs that the nation's economy was in

"I didn't even understand the old system!"

When the Group of Ten reached a currency agreement in December, President Nixon called it "the most significant monetary agreement in the history of the world."

"Our President has frozen all allowances."

To help solve the employment situation, Congress passed a billion-dollar Public Service jobs program. Under this project, federal funds will be given to city, county, and state governments to hire 153,000 people to work in such fields as health, education, and law enforcement.

In an effort to help returning veterans, the President started a "Jobs for Veterans" program with the co-operation of government and business. Besides asking business to hire veterans, the Government provided millions of dollars for skill-training programs.

▶INDUSTRY

A major cause of the unemployment problem was that many industries were not producing at full capacity. Some were hit harder than others by the economic slowdown. Aerospace was one of these, and the airline industry was another.

The Boeing Company, one of the world's largest producers of aircraft, had to lay off

trouble. The United States was still the richest country in the world; wages were going up at record rates; and people were saving money. But the economy was not growing at the rate of increase that it had displayed in years past. Nor was it growing at the rate expected to take care of all the young people coming into the labor market and to fulfill all the needs of the people.

As a result, unemployment continued to rise. By the end of September, approximately 5,100,000 people out of a labor force of some 87,000,000 workers were unemployed. This was the highest number of jobless people in 10 years.

The unemployment problem was especially felt by the younger people, who make up a large segment of the nation's working population. Since 1965, the number of teen-age workers has jumped more than 25 per cent. Consequently, the number of teen-agers who tried and failed to get a summer job in 1971 totaled 2,400,000—280,000 more than in 1970.

But equally worrisome were the high unemployment rates in various sections of the country for adults, including highly skilled scientists and technical people. Also, hundreds of thousands of veterans of the Vietnam war were coming back into the labor market and having great difficulty finding jobs.

Of the 150 major labor areas in the country, in October the Department of Labor classified 65 as being in the "substantial" unemployment category, compared with a high of 38 in 1970.

In September about 5,100,000 people out of a labor force of 87,000,000 workers were unemployed.

In 1971 nearly 3,000,000 workers went on strike. Below left: Railroads across the country came to a standstill when signalmen left their posts. Below right: The West Coast dockworkers strike spread to the East and Gulf coasts, closing all ports in the United States. Basically, workers wanted more money. Thus, some of the strongest critics of the new economic policy were labor leaders, such as AFL-CIO President George Meany, shown at right with President Nixon discussing the wage-price freeze.

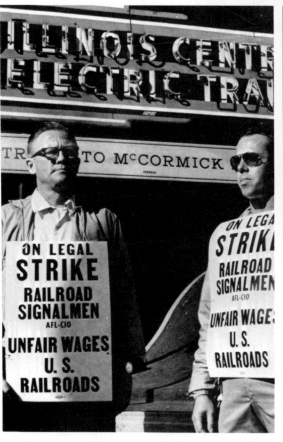

On August 16, the day after Nixon announced his new economic program, the Stock Exchange had its busiest day in history with record trading volume of 31,720,000 shares.

thousands of workers when Congress decided to stop a program developing a supersonic passenger plane. Many of the critics of this program said it would add to the noise and air pollution problems, which had already become a national concern. Supporters of the plane had strongly disagreed.

Lockheed Aircraft Company barely escaped bankruptcy in 1971. The United States Congress, after great debate, approved a $250,000,000 loan to enable Lockheed to continue developing a three-jet commercial transport plane. Without the loan, more than sixty thousand workers would have lost their jobs.

The airline industry blamed inflation—rising wages and rising costs as well as the general economy—for its troubles. Airlines in the United States pressed hard for authority from the Civil Aeronautics Board to increase fares. But many foreign airlines fought equally as hard for price decreases to encourage travel. Hundreds of thousands of young Americans did visit Europe during the summer. However, these trips were taken mostly on charter flights, or on cut-rate excursion fares offered by some airlines.

▶ LABOR

There was continued unrest in the field of labor throughout the year. During the first eight months of 1971, more than 2,500,000 workers went on strike for some length of time. According to the Labor Department in Washington, the total number of idle mandays because of strikes amounted to more than 28,000,000.

Some of the major strikes involved automobile, telephone, and railway workers. The amount of new wages negotiated by these unions, plus the steelworkers and postal unions, was more than $11,000,000,000 for a three-year period.

One of the longest and most frustrating of strikes involved dock workers on the West Coast. It began in July, and continued late into the year. To further complicate matters, dock workers struck ports on the East and Gulf coasts, as well, in the fall of 1971, closing all ports in the United States.

▶ SOME GOOD ECONOMIC SIGNS

By the end of the year the economy was not going as well as many people had thought it should. However, there were a few signs that it was still strong. The average weekly salary of a worker in non-farm industries was $129 in August, up $6.80 from a year ago. Spendable earnings (the amount left after taxes) amounted to $112.87 for the average worker with three dependents. The Federal Reserve System announced that personal savings had increased to $60,900,-000,000 by the second quarter of 1971. People who were saving money were doing so at a rate of more than 8 per cent of their income after taxes. In September the nation's commercial banks reported total deposits of $498,000,000,000.

The installment debt of the nation (what people still owed for things they had purchased) continued to be very high. At the end of July, the debt stood at $102,850,000,000.

Taxes continued to play a big part in the economic picture. The Tax Foundation estimated that by June 1972 the average household will be paying $3,165 a year in Federal taxes, including social security.

The stock market, which always serves as a good barometer, bounded back from a slow year in 1970. Trading in shares reached record levels many times throughout the year. On the day after the President announced his new economy program, sales on the New York Stock Exchange reached a new high of 31,720,000 shares, and the market's value went up a record 33 points.

There are about 32,000,000 shareholders of stocks listed on the New York Stock Exchange, and more than 2,000,000 of them are under 21 years of age. The total value of all shares listed on the exchange amounts to about $710,000,000,000.

Another good sign that the economy is making a recovery is the increase in raw-steel production. For the first half of the year, production amounted to 81,711,325 net tons as compared with 78,691,008 for the same period in 1970.

However, the state of the National Budget served to offset somewhat the positive side of the economy. President Nixon announced that for the fiscal year ending in June 1972, the deficit was expected to be about $28,000,000,000. This means that the Government will spend that much more money than it collects in taxes and other revenue and still have to borrow to pay its bills.

It is hoped that by mid-1972 the economic picture, with the help of the price and wage restraints and the President's new economic policy, will be considerably brightened.

WILBUR MARTIN
Managing Editor, *Nation's Business*

EDUCATION

EFFORTS to end segregation in United States schools made much front-page news during 1971. There was progress, although much remains to be done before integration becomes a fact everywhere. Busing, taking children out of nearby neighborhood schools and taking them by bus to other schools, came into wider use as a means of achieving racially-balanced schools. Integration was no longer thought of as exclusively a Southern problem, as cities in the North and West began to come to grips with it.

State aid to parochial schools also made headlines. The Supreme Court ruled that direct payments to private or church-run schools were unconstitutional. Lawmakers looked for other ways to give financial support to such schools to keep them from closing.

Public-school officials, too, were concerned about money. Many cities and smaller communities had to cut back on spending as voters turned down requests for increased money for education.

On college campuses, where there was less violence than in recent years, as well as in elementary and secondary schools, there was an emphasis on different ways of learning. Three new developments were schools without walls, the open university, and the open classroom.

At the Institute in Open Classroom Education, at the City College of New York, elementary-school teachers learn—through discovery—this new approach to teaching. In open classrooms, students learn to pursue their own interests; there is no set lesson plan.

A classroom at St. Cecilia Grammar School in Englewood, New Jersey. Because of a lack of funds, many parochial schools were forced to close in 1971.

Elementary-school pupils in Mecklenburg County, North Carolina. In 1971 the U.S. Supreme Court ruled that busing is an acceptable means of achieving desegregation of schools.

A storm of contention broke over the nation on the school-busing issue. In 1954 the Supreme Court had declared that desegregation of public schools should proceed with "all deliberate speed." Many people thought the "deliberate" was more obvious than the "speed" in Southern communities with separate schools for whites and blacks.

In the Charlotte-Mecklenburg decision in the spring of 1971, the Supreme Court once again took its earlier position. The court stated that desegregation must be accomplished, although the arrangements are "administratively awkward, inconvenient, and even bizarre." Busing, the court ruled, is an acceptable way to achieve desegregation.

Later in the year President Nixon spoke out against extensive forced busing. "I do not believe that busing to achieve racial balance is in the interest of better education," he said. But he made it clear that his administration would carry out the Supreme Court order.

Parents in all sections of the country began complaining when busing plans were drawn up for their areas. (One proposed plan would have required the busing of 89 per cent of local elementary pupils.) Parents said they wanted their youngsters, especially the youngest children, in neighborhood schools close to home. Most of these are attended by members of one race only, because of segregation patterns of housing.

Outside the South, action against busing took place in a number of cities. In San Francisco, Chinese parents kept children out of school. In Boston both whites and blacks protested against taking children out of the neighborhood. As a result, the city lost

School buses burned by parents opposed to the busing of their children in Pontiac, Michigan.

millions of dollars in state aid. In Pontiac, Michigan, ten new school buses were burned just before school opened.

In spite of the opposition to busing, progress toward desegregation was seen in 1971. Philadelphia, Pittsburgh, Detroit, Los Angeles, and Denver are among the cities now planning to take specific action to mix the races in their schools. Segregation in these cities results largely from concentrations of blacks, Puerto Ricans, and Mexican-Americans in the inner city and of whites on the outer edges of the city.

Often lost from sight was the purpose of integration: quality education. Studies indicate, to the satisfaction of most educators, that children learn better in racially mixed classes. The finding appears to be true for whites, as well as for blacks and other minorities.

▶ FINANCIAL PROBLEMS

Although they were concerned about racial matters, school officials in most areas looked upon dollar shortages as their most pressing problem. Voters continued to vote down bond issues for building schools and higher tax rates for running them.

Meanwhile, pay raises for school staffs and generally rising costs have increased school budgets. Some districts had to cut down on programs and staffs. Philadelphia was one of the cities hardest hit. There, six hundred teachers and eight hundred other school employees were dropped, along with some features of the school program. Plans were made to cancel all extracurricular activities, including varsity sports. But these plans were set aside when both candidates for mayor of Philadelphia pledged to find some way of paying for these activities once in office.

A California court decision indicated that school taxes may have to be collected in a different way in that state, and perhaps in other states, as well. At present, money to run the public schools comes mainly from local property taxes. Thus, in some communities where property is more valuable and taxes are higher, more money is available for schools. The court decided that the present system does not provide equal educational resources for all children. The court

Textbooks as well as schools are being "integrated." Shown here is a page from a multiethnic reader.

decision could lead to a more equal distribution of money to schools throughout a state.

In Washington there were signs that the Federal Government would eventually supply a larger share of the funds needed by public schools. But the Government was not yet prepared to do so.

▶ AID TO PAROCHIAL SCHOOLS

Parochial schools, especially Catholic schools, felt the financial pinch too. Increasing numbers of church schools are closing. Officials say more will be shut down if government aid is not greatly increased. They argue that their schools save taxpayers money by educating a portion of the population and thus deserve help. These authorities warn that an end to parochial schools would send numbers of their pupils into public schools. This would cause serious crowding.

Many state legislatures have tried to find ways to help parochial schools. One approach was the payment of money directly to the church school. But this approach was set aside by the Supreme Court during the year.

Newark schoolteachers on strike. The strike closed Newark schools for 11 weeks.

▶TEACHERS AND STUDENTS

Teacher groups were firm in their demands, striking in several large cities and in suburban communities. In Newark, New Jersey, schools were closed for 11 weeks because of a teacher walkout. When they reopened, the mayor appointed a 17-year-old black youth leader to the school board.

The number of teachers employed across the country increased again, but the rate of increase slowed. Many trained teachers looking for their first job were not hired because there were more teachers than teach-

ing jobs, and schools generally had to cut back on expenses. However, teaching positions dealing with the special problems of the poor and handicapped often went unfilled.

School enrollment was up again. A total of 60,200,000 children registered in public and private schools (kindergarten through graduate school). However, elementary enrollment dipped slightly for the second straight year. The dip reflected a declining birthrate, which in time should relieve the overcrowding in some school districts.

▶EXPERIMENTS AND NEW IDEAS

The search for new ways to make learning more interesting and meaningful to students continued.

An important trend is the open classroom, an informal approach to teaching that developed in British infant and primary schools. (The basic idea of informal education, of course, is not a new one. It was popular in the 1930's as "progressive" education.) In the open classroom, children move about freely, work alone or in small groups, and learn by following their interests. The teacher directs their work, but does not follow a set lesson plan.

The idea of the open classroom spread from Great Britain to other countries, and experimental open classrooms have been introduced in a number of schools in the United States. During the year experts warned against hoping for too much too quickly from the open-classroom approach.

Almost all activities at the Plantation Middle School take place in one room. This enormous room, which can accommodate 1,600 students, includes the library, science labs, and all classroom areas. Carpeting and high ceilings keep noise to a minimum.

Many schools began using the open-classroom approach to teaching in 1971. Below: Pupils at the Steuart Hill Elementary School in Baltimore view a filmstrip. Right: At P.S. 219 in Queens, New York, students gather in groups or study alone in their new beautifully designed open classroom.

High schools "without walls" opened in Hartford, Connecticut, and in Washington, D.C., in the fall. These were patterned after the original school without walls, Philadelphia's Parkway Project. The schools have no buildings of their own, but hold classes in business or government offices and in museums and universities. The schools use businessmen, government officials, professional people, and community workers as teachers.

Schools without walls are part of the effort to get results in education. Educators are showing greater concern for making school pay off for students. Some educators believe that one way to do this is to bring in business firms that "guarantee" pupil learning. They sign performance contracts, promising that pupils' skills or knowledge will increase more than it usually would in a school year. If the firms fail they must pay

a penalty for failing. More than 100 contracts of this kind were signed or were in effect during the year.

In terms of the number of pupils involved, the largest contract signed "guaranteed" advances in reading in Philadelphia. There 15,000 elementary pupils used reading materials supplied by the company. Regular teachers were trained by the same company. Tests given at the start and end of the 1970–71 school year showed gains by many pupils.

For each child who made 10 months' progress in the 8-month period, the school system paid the contractor $40. For some other pupils, the company received $20 a pupil. But for children in the program who attended regularly but did not show 10 months' improvement, nothing was paid. Some youngsters gained more than 3 years in reading during the period. The program will continue.

Since 1965 the Office of Education has covered the costs of many experiments in teaching methods and materials. In 1971 the new United States Commissioner of Education, Dr. Sidney P. Marland, Jr., set up a new program. The program, which would allow a whole school to introduce new ideas, is called the experimental schools program. In the fall three districts (in Minneapolis, Minnesota; Tacoma, Washington; and Berkeley, California) began operating some of their schools on this basis. Others are to be added.

Another development Dr. Marland has supported is vocational-technical training. He calls it "career education" and has named it his top priority. New approaches are being worked out in different parts of the country to go into effect in high schools and community colleges in 1972. Dr. Marland feels the program is important, since not everyone needs a college education for the work he is to do in life.

A year-round school calendar has been adopted by a school district in Romeoville, Illinois. Students have no summer vacation. All year long they go to school for periods of 45 days and then have vacations of at least 15 school days. The program is intended to ease the problem of high enrollment, since the district has no funds for building. Students go to school in 4 staggered groups, with ¼ of the students on vacation at all times.

▶CAMPUS DEVELOPMENTS

In colleges, too, new ways of learning are being tried. A report by the Carnegie Commission on Higher Education, entitled *Less Time, More Options,* served as a theme for much discussion during 1971. The report recommended that college students be given more choice about the way they learn. The report also recommended that the time spent on campus be shortened. The chancellor of the California state colleges suggested that a student's college studies could be completed in 2½ or 3 years. Several colleges are moving ahead with 3-year programs.

Off-campus studies are becoming more popular. Students have taken part in field trips and community activity for some time. But a new emphasis developed in 1970 when the university without walls came into being on 20 campuses. The approach is similar to that of the high schools without walls. The university without walls uses ways of teaching that are out of the ordinary and take students into the real world to learn.

Some educators would like to take this method one step further. Why, they ask, must a person set foot on a college campus at all in order to get an education? Why

The trend toward "schools without walls"—on the high-school as well as the college level —continued in 1971. Here, a Philadelphia jeweler teaches gemology to high-school students.

Jim Thomson, a Philadelphia architect, teaches a class in architecture to students in the Parkway Project, the original high school without walls.

can't he study at home, using correspondence courses, television, and other means to get his degree? Such a person would make college available to many young people who can't afford the usual college costs, and to older people, including those who have to work.

The plan is known as the open university, or external-degree program. There are no age limits and no time limits. Those enrolled study at their own speed and take examinations when they are ready. Their courses are college level, offered and supervised by a university.

New York opened two campusless branches of its all-new Empire State College in the fall to offer an external-degree program. California is experimenting with the idea, and Massachusetts expects to sponsor a trial program in the fall of 1972.

The number of students in colleges and universities rose from 7,900,000 to an estimated 8,400,000. Much of the increase came in state institutions and in community colleges, where charges are lower than in private colleges and universities. The enrollment of blacks and members of other minority groups increased nearly four times as fast as that of whites.

About 75 per cent of students are enrolled in publicly supported institutions of learning. The figure goes up each year. The fact explains in part the financial difficulties of independent and church-connected colleges. Many of these cut back on spending, but still face the possibility of closing down. Some state colleges and universities, too, began to feel the dollar pinch during the year.

KENNETH G. GEHRET
Education Editor
The Christian Science Monitor

ENTERTAINMENT

THE entire entertainment scene in 1971 paid homage to the growing trend of nostalgia. One of the biggest theatrical hits of the year was *No, No, Nanette*, a revival of a musical from the 1920's. Moviegoers packed movie houses that showed revivals

of such popular stars of the past as W. C. Fields, Mae West, and Humphrey Bogart. In addition, many new movies, such as *Summer of '42* and *The Last Picture Show,* were nostalgic looks at days gone by. Music moved away from hard rock to the softer ballads of the past. Even television jumped on the nostalgia bandwagon, with *It Was a Very Good Year,* hosted by Mel Torme. This popular summer series looked back at the fun and hard times of earlier years of this century.

Nostalgia fans came in droves to see "No, No, Nanette," a runaway musical hit of 1971.

THEATER

Much of the "drama" of the 1970–71 theater season took place offstage. The League of New York Theaters took the radical step of changing the Broadway evening curtain time from 8:30 to 7:30. So far, it is a change theatergoers, as well as actors and producers, seem to welcome.

In an effort to woo a new generation of young theatergoers, the League pushed through a Student Discount ticket policy for Broadway shows. However, the producers won't earn any applause until more shows support this new program.

Still another new League policy went into effect, the Limited-Gross Agreement. Under this plan a producer may voluntarily choose to limit his gross profits. The theatergoer benefits through sharply reduced ticket prices. Although it is too soon to see dramatic results, many theater people hope

this measure, too, will introduce a new, younger audience to Broadway theater.

While Broadway made these non-traditional moves to encourage a broader theatergoing audience, a crippling actors' strike took place off-Broadway. It appears that this once-freewheeling experimental wing of the theater has lost its innocence. Almost as sophisticated and complex as Broadway, off-Broadway now shares the uptown theater's problems.

▶BROADWAY

Onstage, only 45 shows were produced during the 1970–71 Broadway season, compared with 69 for the preceding season.

American playwrights did not offer a great deal in the way of original drama. Critical praise did go to Edward Albee's *All Over,* Neil Simon's *The Gingerbread Lady,* and Paul Zindel's *And Miss Reardon Drinks a Little.* However, more originality was shown by Paul Sills, whose *Story Theatre* and

"Follies," a nostalgia-filled musical, won the Drama Critics Circle Award.

Metamorphoses introduced a charming blend of dance, mime, and a storytelling narrative. *Lenny* was the season's most talked-about play thanks to Tom O'Horgan's dynamic direction. Cliff Gorman's powerful performance in the role of the controversial nightclub comedian, Lenny Bruce, also won critical praise.

A number of the season's dramatic high points were imports from London. Anthony Shaffer's *Sleuth* was a clever thriller whose ingenious plot was a real baffler. The renowned director Peter Brook brought over his brilliantly inventive version of *A Midsummer Night's Dream* for a limited run. And David Storey's *Home* was about two old men who symbolize the dying traditions of modern civilizations. Sir Ralph Richardson and Sir John Gielgud offered breathtaking performances in this subtle and moving play.

Broadway's major musical spectacle was a revival of the 1925 musical *No, No, Nanette*. Adapter/director Burt Shevelove made it one of the richest visual delights of recent years. Ruby Keeler and Patsy Kelly, stars of days gone-by, were brought back to the stage, and the nostalgia fans showed up in masses. However, Broadway staggered under several spectacular big-budget musicals that folded almost as soon as they opened. The survivors included another piece of nostalgia, *Follies*. Its weak plot was greatly helped by

TONY AWARDS

Play: *Sleuth*

Musical: *Company*

Actor-Play: Brian Bedford (*The School for Wives*)

Actor-Musical: Hal Linden (*The Rothschilds*)

Actress-Play: Maureen Stapleton (*The Gingerbread Lady*)

Actress-Musical: Helen Gallagher (*No, No, Nanette*)

Supporting Actor-Play: Paul Sand (*Story Theatre*)

Supporting Actor-Musical: Keene Curtis (*The Rothschilds*)

Supporting Actress-Play: Rae Allen (*And Miss Reardon Drinks a Little*)

Supporting Actress-Musical: Patsy Kelly (*No, No, Nanette*)

Director-Play: Peter Brook (*A Midsummer Night's Dream*)

Director-Musical: Harold Prince (*Company*)

Choreographer: Donald Saddler (*No, No, Nanette*)

Scenic Designer: Boris Aronson (*Company*)

Costume Designer: Raoul Pene duBois (*No, No, Nanette*)

DRAMA CRITICS CIRCLE AWARDS

Play: *Home*

Musical: *Follies*

American Play: *The House of Blue Leaves*

Puck (John Kane) in Peter Brook's modern version of "A Midsummer Night's Dream."

Jeff Fenholt in the title role in "Jesus Christ Superstar," 1971's controversial hit.

the direction of Harold Prince and by a hauntingly beautiful score by Stephen Sondheim. *The Rothschilds* was an interesting interpretation of the lives of the famous European Jewish banking family. *Two by Two* boasted music by Richard Rodgers which turned out to be surprisingly pallid. But its star, Danny Kaye, gave theatergoers the delight of seeing a super-popular stage star in top form.

Super-Stars

An old musical and a new musical were in the spotlight in 1971. *Fiddler on the Roof* became the longest-running musical in Broadway history. It passed the record previously set by *Hello, Dolly!* in 1970. And the phenomenal rock opera *Jesus Christ*

Superstar is on its way to becoming the most controversial hit of the 1971–72 season. Super-director Tom O'Horgan (who also staged the group rock musical *Hair*) said that *Superstar* is meant to be "a totally spiritual . . . highly mystical experience, an exaltation for the audience."

▶ OFF-BROADWAY

Off-Broadway produced 125 shows this season, which was 24 fewer than last. However, most of these were short-lived. John Guare enlivened the scene with his *The House of Blue Leaves*. This black comedy combined huge belly laughs with important comment on the undertones of violence in America. Novelist Kurt Vonnegut, Jr., made his playwrighting debut with his outlandishly plotted *Happy Birthday, Wanda June.* It was a pertinent comedy about the changing character of the American hero figure. The underground hit of the season was Andre Gregory's whimsical and offbeat version of *Alice in Wonderland.*

An ebullient rock score by Stephan Schwartz made *Godspell* off-Broadway's single fly-away musical hit. The show's vision of Christ as a Super-Clown from today's counter-culture made it a favorite with young people.

Off-Broadway, the revival trend favored drama, and the season saw the rebirth of a number of interesting plays. These ranged from modern classics like *Waiting for Godot* and *The Homecoming* to the youth-oriented *One Flew over the Cuckoo's Nest.* Claire Bloom enjoyed a personal triumph in her long-running bill of Ibsen's *Hedda Gabler* and *A Doll's House.* A stunning revival of O'Neill's *Long Day's Journey into Night* brought Geraldine Fitzgerald, Robert Ryan, and Stacy Keach together as a powerful ensemble.

▶ **REPERTORY**

Among repertory groups, the New York Shakespeare Festival Public Theater had a wonderfully rich season. Its presentations ranged from a charming revival of *Trelawny of the Wells* to a thrilling one-woman show by Siobhan McKenna. It also staged original new works by young writers such as Robert Montgomery, David Hare, and David Rabe. Rabe's play, *The Basic Training of Pavlo Hummel,* was a surrealistic antiwar story of an oddball soldier. The Shakespeare Festival's summer operations in Central Park included a disarmingly wacky version of *The Two Gentlemen of Verona,* which so captured audiences that it moved to Broadway.

The highly regarded Phoenix Theater was fortunately back in business again and produced two of the finest shows of the season. One was a sparkling revival of Molière's *The School for Wives,* with Brian Bedford performing perfectly in the high-comedy role. The other was the Rev. Daniel Berrigan's moving documentary, *The Trial of the Catonsville Nine.*

In Brooklyn, the Chelsea Theatre Center

A street-theater group in a Lincoln Center festival.

proved itself to be one of the most imaginative companies through its fine work on such unusual plays as Heathcote Williams' *AC/DC.* Two of its productions, Edward Bond's *Saved* and the rock musical *Tarot,* switched to off-Broadway.

Lincoln Center's Beaumont Theater productions were unexcitingly respectable, except for an impressive revival of Ibsen's *An Enemy of the People.* Downstairs, however, in the Forum Theater, the company did more interesting work, especially with Friedrich Dürrenmatt's clever satirical comedy, *Play Strindberg.*

▶ **STREET THEATER**

A new type of theater entertainment is springing up in more and more ghetto communities. Called "street theater," it seeks to bring theater to the people. Its productions are acted and written by people of the streets, based on or related to their experiences in their communities. Ten black community theater groups in New York formed a federation called the Black Theater Alliance. They presented a festival of their works at the home-theater of the Negro Ensemble Company. Twelve other street-theater groups staged their plays at a festival held in Lincoln Center's parks and plaza areas. The groups, which came from New York, Washington, D.C., Los Angeles, and San Francisco, represent only a small number of the community-based street ensembles active in the United States.

MARILYN STASIO
Drama Critic, *Cue* Magazine

A scene from "Summer of '42," a major box-office success of 1971.

MOTION PICTURES

The year 1971 was one of change for the motion-picture industry. During the past several years, the basis for most Hollywood films was little more than sex and violence. Sensing the public's weariness with this sort of movie fare, and in an effort to do something to boost the declining box-office receipts, motion-picture producers reverted to films with romantic and nostalgic themes.

Summer of '42, directed by Robert Mulligan, was one of the first to follow this new trend of nostalgia. It was a tender story of three adolescent boys spending the summer with their families on an island off the New England coast. The overwhelming financial success of this film set the stage for others of the same type that followed.

Joseph Losey's *The Go-Between,* starring two of Britain's most accomplished actors, Julie Christie and Alan Bates, won the Grand Prize at the 1971 Cannes Festival. The film centers on a 12-year-old boy, brilliantly played by Dominic Guard, who carries messages between two lovers, and the effect this has on him.

The Last Picture Show was director Peter Bogdanovich's second film. Adapted from a novel by Larry McMurtry, it is a story about growing up in a small town in Texas during the early 1950's. With a relatively unknown cast, the film opened to critical acclaim at the New York Film Festival in October and immediately went into successful distribution.

Love Story was reminiscent of many of the romantic, sentimental films of the 1940's. Taken from Erich Segal's best-selling novel, the film starred Ali MacGraw and Ryan O'Neal as a young married couple whose happiness is suddenly shattered by illness and death.

Ryan's Daughter, directed by David Lean, was a lyrical love story, about a sensitive schoolmaster, Robert Mitchum, who is unable to convince his bride, Sarah Miles, that love is richer than romance.

While many of this year's films dealt with sentiment and romance in a nostalgic fashion, two very important motion pictures handled these subjects in a deeper and more explicit manner. *Carnal Knowledge,* directed by Mike Nichols, featured Jack Nicholson, Candice Bergen, Arthur Garfunkel, and Ann-Margaret in a film about the lives and frustrations of two men from their college days to middle age. *Sunday, Bloody Sunday,* written by film critic and author Penelope Gilliatt and directed by John Schlesinger, was a complex love story of two men and a woman.

▶ **COMEDIES AND THRILLERS**

Multi-talented Elaine May wrote, directed and starred in *A New Leaf.* Her costar, Walter Matthau, played the part of a wealthy man who suddenly realizes that his fortune has run out. In desperation he decides to marry an heiress and then to get rid of her with all possible haste.

One of 1971's funniest films was Woody Allen's *Bananas,* a farce that almost defies description. *Bananas* has to do with, among other things, a shy American who accidentally becomes a dictator as the result of a Latin-American revolution.

Little Big Man, starring Faye Dunaway and Dustin Hoffman, was a runaway hit of the year. Dustin is first seen as a 120-year-old man who recalls his experiences with the Cheyenne Indians, Colonel Custer, and a host of other characters. Chief Dan George in a supporting role was outstanding.

Cartoonist Jules Feiffer's *Little Murders* was a satirical and provocative comedy about contemporary New York City life. Elliott Gould was especially good in the leading role.

Also appealing to general audiences were *Plaza Suite,* starring Walter Matthau in the

Above: Timothy Bottoms (left) and Ben Johnson in "The Last Picture Show." Below: Dustin Hoffman (left) and Chief Dan George in "Little Big Man."

film version of the hit Broadway show of the same name; *There's a Girl in My Soup,* teaming Peter Sellers and Goldie Hawn; and *Skin Game,* a hilarious racial comedy with James Garner and Lou Gossett.

In spite of the public outcry against blood and violence, this type of movie thriller once again proved very successful at the box office. Michael Caine appeared in *Get Carter,* a brutal gangster yarn in which the hero is involved in shootings and murder. Sean Connery, who won fame in the James Bond films, starred as an ex-convict in *The Anderson Tapes.* Based on the best-selling novel, the film had Connery leading a gang of thieves in a carefully planned heist of a luxury apartment building.

Shaft was directed by the well-known photographer, composer, and writer, Gordon Parks. This, his second film, starred Richard Roundtree as John Shaft, a New York private eye. It was the story of a hard-as-nails black detective who performs mission-impossible feats to rescue the kidnaped daughter of one of Harlem's chief hoodlums.

Jane Fonda, costarring with Donald Sutherland, gave a much-talked-about per-

formance in *Klute,* a thriller detective story. Miss Fonda played a girl who unwillingly assists and then falls in love with John Klute, a small-town cop who is out to solve the disappearance of his best friend.

Greek director Costa-Gavras followed his successful film *Z* with *The Confession.* This highly acclaimed film starred Yves Montand

A scene from "The Andromeda Strain," a science-fiction thriller about the threat of an epidemic.

in a true story of the survival of a loyal Communist who is imprisoned and tortured during the Stalinist purges.

▶ SCIENCE-FICTION AND HORROR FILMS

Mysticism, exorcism, and witchcraft underscored most of this year's horror films. Many of them were poorly made, with unknown casts. Others, of better quality, featured well-known actors.

Charlton Heston appeared in *The Omega Man,* a science-fiction horror-thriller in which one of the last survivors of a germ war finds himself pitted against zombies in a life-and-death struggle. Other films of this genre included *THX 1138,* which dealt with a computer-oriented society, and *The Andromeda Strain,* a story of four American scientists who are working against the threat of a worldwide epidemic caused by an unknown germ from outer space.

Zohra Lampert portrayed the heroine in *Let's Scare Jessica to Death.* Set in a haunted house in Connecticut, the film had a murky atmosphere and contained a variety of eerie noises.

One of Hollywood's most original horror films was brought to the screen in 1971. *Willard* starred Bruce Davison as a fumbling, neurotic young man who discovers he has a gift for communicating with rats. He forms an army of his "pets" and takes great pleasure in letting it loose on members of the community who have done harm to his family.

▶ THE DOCUMENTARY FILM

Documentary films in 1971 seemed to appeal to almost every taste. *Gimme Shelter* was an account of Mick Jagger and The Rolling Stones concert at Altamont, California. Music of a different kind was featured in *Soul to Soul,* a filmed account of an African-music festival in Ghana.

A more dramatic film was photographer Peter Gimbel's *Blue Water, White Death,* which dealt with man's quest for the largest, deadliest, most cold-blooded of sharks. One of the highlights of the film was the incredible underwater photography.

French director François Reichenbach and American disc jockey Tom Donahue

A great white shark in "Blue Water, White Death."

teamed up to follow 150 hippie youths on a cross-country trek in *Medicine Ball Caravan.*

▶ FILM FESTIVALS

The ninth New York Film Festival proved to be more successful than those held in the past. Although only 18 features were shown, capacity crowds attended every performance. A few of the films received unanimous critical acclaim and were released to the public immediately after the festival screening.

Nostalgia seemed to play a major role in festivals throughout the country. Old films were suddenly re-released, and movie stars of the past were being honored by special film festivals in theaters and on television. Stars such as Buster Keaton, Douglas Fairbanks, Mary Pickford, Greta Garbo, Jean Harlow, and Charles Chaplin were gaining a new surge of popularity, and drawing crowds to movie theaters just as they had done many years ago.

HAIG P. MANOOGIAN
Institute of Film and Television
New York University

MUSIC

Much of the year's musical excitement focused on the John F. Kennedy Center for the Performing Arts, which opened in Washington, D.C., in 1971. The Center is both a memorial to the late President and a cultural showcase for the nation's capital. Two specially commissioned works received their world premieres during the gala opening ceremonies in September. One was Leonard Bernstein's theatrical, rock *Mass,* which used orchestra, singers, and a group of performers from the Alvin Ailey Modern Dance Company. The second new work was *Beatrix Cenci,* an opera by the modernist Argentinian composer Alberto Ginastera. It is based on Shelley's tragedy about a 16th-century Roman family.

▶ THE OPERA WORLD

During the 1970–71 opera season, most of the old-line operatic establishments continued to cling to traditional styles and approaches. But a growing trend toward new stage techniques was noted among younger and more enterprising companies.

The Center Opera of Minneapolis is an experimental group based at the Tyrone Guthrie Theater. It made its first extended eastern United States tour in 1971. One opera presented by the company was *Faust Counter Faust* by H. Wesley Balk and John Gessner. The work is made up mostly of quotations from previous Faust operas and plays. Its use of slide projections, tape recordings, and other modernistic devices helped stir up controversy wherever it went.

The Opera Society of Washington, D.C., is another innovative group. It, too, made excellent use of visual projections when it revived *Koanga,* a rarely heard opera by the English composer Frederick Delius. *Koanga* is about slavery and racism. The subject matter, as well as the stage techniques, gave the opera a decidedly modern flavor.

Another production that used projections, perhaps most successfully of all, was the New York City Opera's presentation of Leos Janacek's *The Makropoulos Affair.* This strange work, by the modern Czech com-

French composer-conductor Pierre Boulez was named musical director of the New York Philharmonic.

poser, is about a woman who discovered a potion that keeps her alive for hundreds of years. With the work's semi-nude scene and other touches of eroticism, it might become the first opera eligible for an "X" rating.

There were two other notable New York City Opera presentations. *The Most Important Man,* a new work by Gian-Carlo Me-

A scene from Leonard Bernstein's two-hour "Mass," a specially commissioned work performed at the opening of the John F. Kennedy Center for the Performing Arts.

Cellist-composer Pablo Casals, 94, plays at the United Nations Day concert. Earlier he had conducted a 150-piece orchestra in the world premier of his newest work, "A Hymn to the United Nations."

notti, is about a black scientist in South Africa. The opera was impressive more as a piece of theater than as a musical achievement. Donizetti's *Roberto Devereux* gave soprano Beverly Sills an opportunity to demonstrate her rare combination of musical and acting skills in the role of Queen Elizabeth I.

At the Metropolitan Opera in New York, most of the excitement centered on the appointment of Goeran Gentele, head of the Royal Opera in Stockholm, Sweden. Gentele will become the new general manager of the Met with the departure of Sir Rudolf Bing in June 1972. Among the new productions staged during the season were Wagner's *Parsifal* and Jules Massenet's *Werther*.

▶ **ORCHESTRAL MUSIC**

At the New York Philharmonic, French composer-conductor Pierre Boulez succeeded Leonard Bernstein as musical director, beginning with the 1971–72 season. The new director is expected to place a greater emphasis on contemporary works. This might draw a new type of Philharmonic audience. An indication of this trend was seen early in 1971. A nonsubscription concert was devoted entirely to the music of, and was conducted by, the German avant-gardist Karlheinz Stockhausen. The concert was attended largely by young people, many of them blue-jeaned and long-haired.

More and more young people are gaining prominence in the music world. Twenty-six-year-old Michael Tilson Thomas was appointed music director of the Buffalo Philharmonic. And a new name, Garrick Ohlsson, was added to the roster of outstanding young pianists. Ohlsson, 22, became the first American to win the top prize at the prestigious International Chopin Piano Competition in Warsaw, Poland.

The saddest event of 1971 was the death of Igor Stravinsky. The greatest composer of the era, Stravinsky revolutionized music with such scores as *The Firebird, Petrouchka,* and *The Rite of Spring.* He remained an innovator almost to the end of his life.

HERBERT KUPFERBERG
Music Critic, *The National Observer*

POPULAR MUSIC

Ringo Starr (left) and George Harrison (center left), two of the four Beatles, were reunited onstage for the first time in more than four years; they are joined by Bob Dylan (playing harmonica) and Leon Russell at Madison Square Garden for two benefit concerts.

In 1971, rock got religion. "The day has come for God, Love, and rock and roll" ran the words of one popular song. And Linda Ronstadt sang, "We need a lot more of Jesus and a lot less of rock and roll." An early omen of the trend had been the Gold Record success of Simon and Garfunkel's disc *Bridge over Troubled Water*.

The movement from Now Rock to Rock of Ages found expression in Norman Greenbaum's *Spirit in the Sky,* Bob Dylan's *Three Angels,* Judy Collins' *Amazing Grace,* Ocean's *Put Your Hand in the Hand,* and George Harrison's *My Sweet Lord*. Then came the success of *Godspell,* an off-Broadway musical based on The Gospel according to St. Matthew.

But "Jesus rock" or "gospel rock," as it came to be known, was confirmed by *Jesus Christ Superstar. Superstar* started out as a widely acclaimed rock-opera recording by two young Englishmen, Andrew Lloyd Web-ber and Tim Rice. In October 1971 it opened on Broadway as a complete stage production. The thrust of religion in rock was even acknowledged by the Vatican radio when it played *Superstar* in its entirety.

▶ **CHANGES IN THE ROCK REVOLUTION**

The mushrooming of Jesus Freaks and Street Christians was only one symptom of the upheaval in the Rock Revolution. Another was the collapse or cancellation of one rock festival after another. The climax was the violent disruption of the time-honored Newport Jazz Festival. This was followed by the blackout of the Newport Folk Festival.

Also disturbing were the closings of San Francisco's famous rock showcase, the Fill-more auditorium, and its younger New York outlet, Fillmore East. Impresario Bill Graham, who ran both, blamed the greed of performers and their managers. He accused them of placing too little value on creativity

The Carpenters

and too much on the materialism they had once attacked. Many observers labeled the shutdowns as "the end of an era."

▶ MELODIC ROCK

In 1971, popular rock seemed to be turning away from hi-amp distortion, unmelodic thunder, and screaming vocals. Instead a softer, sweeter, and more serene sound was being heard. Acoustic guitars, literate lyrics, and solo balladry were *in*.

James Taylor was one of a new breed of singer-songwriter who attracted much attention. A hit autobiographical single, *Fire and Rain*, was followed by the Gold LP's *Sweet Baby James* and *Mud Slide Slim and the Blue Horizon*. Taylor's melodies were gentle, his vocals soft, and his style reflective.

Kris Kristofferson, a Rhodes scholar who paid his dues in Nashville, came to the fore with a flock of songs. Many of his songs, although recorded by him, were made into hits by others: Janis Joplin (*Me and Bobby McGee*), Johnny Cash (*Sunday Mornin' Comin' Down*), Sammi Smith (*Help Me Make It through the Night*), and Ray Price (*For the Good Times*).

Many regarded Rod Stewart, who is part of the Faces and records on his own, as the most productive and exciting of the new rockers. His sound is like that of country rocker Elton John and gospel rocker Leon Russell. It has the rawness, sensuality, and rhythmic punch of early rock 'n' roll.

▶ FEMALES ON THE ROCK SCENE

Many females emerged on the rock scene in 1971. Carole King, a hit-writer of the 1960's, stood out with her single *It's Too Late* and her blues-inflected album *Tapestry*.

GRAMMY AWARDS

Record of the Year: *Bridge over Troubled Water* (Simon and Garfunkel)

Album of the Year: *Bridge over Troubled Water* (Simon and Garfunkel)

Song of the Year: *Bridge over Troubled Water* (Paul Simon, songwriter)

New Artist of the Year: Carpenters

Contemporary Vocal Performance-female: *I'll Never Fall in Love Again* (Dionne Warwick)

Contemporary Vocal Performance-male: *Everything Is Beautiful* (Ray Stevens)

Rhythm and Blues Vocal Performance-female: *Don't Play That Song* (Aretha Franklin)

Rhythm and Blues Vocal Performance-male: *The Thrill Is Gone* (B. B. King)

Country Vocal Performance-female: *Rose Garden* (Lynn Anderson)

Country Vocal Performance-male: *For the Good Times* (Ray Price)

Original Score for a Motion Picture: *Let It Be* (John Lennon, Paul McCartney, George Harrison, composers)

Score from an Original-Cast Show Album: *Company* (Stephen Sondheim, composer)

Recording for Children: *Sesame Street* (Joan Cooney, producer)

Classical Album: Berlioz: *Les Troyens* (Colin Davis conducting Royal Opera House Orchestra and Chorus)

Carole King

(Her song *You've Got a Friend* was a smash for James Taylor.) Dory Previn followed her autobiographical debut album with the impressive *Mythical Kings and Iguanas*. Debut albums by Carly Simon of Manhattan, Rita Coolidge of Nashville, Kate Taylor of the James Taylor family, and Mary Travers of Peter, Paul and Mary all emphasized the balladry of love and personal relationships. The most poetic of the group was Joni Mitchell. Her probing reflections found expression in her album *Blue*.

▶ NEW VOICES

New faces and voices of 1971 included the Carpenters, a well-groomed brother-and-sister duo. They made hit singles of *Close to You, We've Only Just Begun,* and *Rainy Days and Mondays*. By summer, they were tapped as co-hosts (with Al Hirt) for NBC-TV's *Make Your Own Kind of Music* variety hour. From TV came the Partridge Family, bringing vocal stardom to young David Cassidy with their album *Up to Date*.

▶ SUPERSTARS

Although the day of the supergroup seemed past, Motown's Jackson Five continued their string of Gold Records. And the Rolling Stones returned to the recording scene with *Sticky Fingers*. Sales indicated that there was still appeal in the sneer and leer of Satan's Jesters.

The media, both Establishment and underground, made great efforts to create superstars. However, none had the charisma of the splintered Beatles, or of Janis Joplin, Jimi Hendrix, and Jim Morrison, whose deaths had a sobering impact on the rock scene. Not even the individual Beatles, each of whom had solo hit albums, had the old pizazz.

▶ PROTEST SONGS

Antiwar and protest songs were not absent from the rock scene. *Battle Hymn of Lt. Calley* was one that caused much controversy. Others included *Power to the People* by John Lennon, *Share the Land* by The Guess Who, and *Stop the War* by Edwin Starr.

ARNOLD SHAW
Author, *The Rock Revolution*

DANCE

"The Goldberg Variations," choreographed by Jerome Robbins, was set to the music of J. S. Bach.

The words "vibrant" and "alive" aptly describe the dance season in 1971. Foreign dance troupes brought creative works and exciting dancers to American audiences. U.S. dance companies thrived, and many new works were premiered.

▶FOREIGN DANCE COMPANIES

Germany's leading ballet company, the Stuttgart Ballet, under the directorship of John Cranko, performed at the Metropolitan Opera House during its stay in New York City. Their repertoire included the world premiere of Cranko's version of *Carmen.* Some critics found it disappointing. However, much praise was given to the other full-length narrative ballets: *Eugene Onegin, Romeo and Juliet,* and *The Taming of the Shrew.*

The Australian Ballet made a 14-city tour of the United States and Canada. The company was touring the United States for the first time, opening with a full-length version of *Don Quixote,* with guest star Rudolf Nureyev dancing the role of Don Basilio.

Belgium's Maurice Béjart and his modernist Ballet of the 20th Century made their U.S. debut at the Brooklyn Academy of Music early in 1971. Dazzling dancing, hip choreography, and low student rates drew young people to the Academy in droves.

Participating in an Afro-Asian festival, six nations, with over two hundred performers, brought their cultures to the United States and Canada in 1971. It began at the Brooklyn Academy, which hosted the Classical Khmer Ballet of Cambodia, the Senegalese National Dance Company, the National Dance Company of Morocco, the

Ritual Acrobats of Persia (Iran), the Dagar Brothers–Raga Singers of India, and the Sierra Leone National Dance Troupe.

Mexico's Ballet Folklorico and Poland's Mazowske Company also found appreciative audiences in U.S. dance theaters.

▶UNITED STATES DANCE COMPANIES

An outstanding event of 1971 was the presentation by the Alvin Ailey American Dance Theater of Ailey's *Cry* at the New York City Center. As dance critic Clive Barnes wrote, "the first-night audience . . . applauded and cheered it for nearly 10 minutes." Judith Jamison danced the solo

Judith Jamison in "Cry."

in this ballet about the ordeal of the black woman in America.

The Goldberg Variations, choreographed by Jerome Robbins, premiered in its final version at the New York State Theater in May. The eighty-minute ballet, a classically-elegant and powerful work, is set to the baroque music of J. S. Bach.

As far removed as possible from Bach's 18th-century classicism, was Ann Halprin's *Animal Ritual,* which was premiered at the Connecticut College American Dance Festival in August. It turned out to be a unique experience. For an hour and a half, with no intermission, the audience sat in an atmosphere of almost complete darkness, as dancers mimicked the physical and vocal characteristics of all sorts of jungle animals. In the finale the audience joined the cast onstage. This strange work aroused much comment and some controversy.

The successful and very popular Joffrey Ballet premiered several new works, one of which was the light and delightful *Reflections.* The ballet, choreographed by Gerald Arpino, is set to music by Tchaikovsky. (The Joffrey Company also boasts an active Junior Company with excellent repertoire.)

Dolly Suite, with Natalya Makarova as guest dancer, was premiered by the Boston Ballet. With music by Gabriel Fauré and John Taras' choreography, the charming ballet was well suited to the capacities of this relatively young company.

The American Ballet Theater was made the "official" company of the new John F. Kennedy Center for the Performing Arts in Washington, D.C. During opening-week ceremonies in September, the Ballet Theater's repertoire included Anthony Tudor's *Romeo and Juliet,* starring Natalya Makarova and John Prinz; Harald Lander's *Etudes,* with the exuberant dancing of Ivan Nagy; and *The River,* choreographed by Alvin Ailey, with music by Duke Ellington.

▶FINANCIAL SUPPORT

It has been estimated that the 1971 budget for U.S. dance companies was $25,000,000. Obtaining this kind of support was not easy.

Since 1965 there has been Federal assistance to the arts, and, increasingly, state arts

The Classical Khmer Ballet of Cambodia toured the United States and Canada in 1971.

councils are helping. In a March 1971 speech, President Nixon asked Federal agencies to "look around and see if there's some way you can give help to the arts." (Congress voted almost $20,000,000 to the arts in 1971.)

It was because of a $500,000 subsidy from the National Endowment for the Arts that the American Ballet Theater became the resident company of the Kennedy Arts Center. The National Endowment has also been of great help by supporting 20 modern-dance companies in a touring residency program in 1971. The Paul Taylor and Merce Cunningham troupes were among those that were particularly popular on college campuses. The Endowment also supported in 1971, for the fifth year, the Regional Ballet's summer Choreographic Workshops. Topflight artists, teaching technique, music, and dance composition, are made publicly available through these workshops.

The Ford Foundation gives major assistance to the New York City Ballet and its affiliated School of American Ballet. The Foundation also helps the Boston, Pennsyl-

vania, and San Francisco Ballets, and Utah's Ballet West.

The Rockefeller Foundation is responsible for starting and supporting both the University of Utah's Dance Repertory Theater and the professional dance company of the North Carolina School of the Arts.

Despite this encouraging trend there are a great many fine companies that continue to struggle for survival. Leading modern-dance groups, such as those of Lar Lubovitch, Paul Sanasardo, and Louis Falco, are finding it difficult to make ends meet.

Particularly tragic was the disbanding of the Eliot Feld company in 1971. This company, formed in 1969, showed great promise and had started to make a name for itself among dance audiences. It finally had to give up because of lack of funds to meet its high standards of performance.

In 1971, Dorothy Alexander, founder of the regional ballet movement, said, "the spark of dance in America has been lighted. It still needs to burst into flame."

LYDIA JOEL
Dance Consultant

TELEVISION

In 1971 television was criticized from all sides. Politicians, regulators, and ordinary viewers were dissatisfied with its performance and were determined to see change. Some were disturbed by TV news coverage, feeling that it was biased. Others attacked the bland sameness of TV entertainment and called for greater variety. Still others, mainly parents, pressured the broadcasters to upgrade children's programing and cut back the toy, cereal, and candy commercials so heavily squeezed into these shows.

▶"THE SELLING OF THE PENTAGON"

TV's news practices, already widely questioned, came under new fire after a CBS documentary, *The Selling of the Pentagon,* was aired on February 23. The controversial program dealt with the public-relations methods used by the U.S. Defense Depart-ment. The Pentagon's friends in Congress charged CBS with bias in editing film shots for the documentary and demanded to see the unused film and text. The network flatly refused. Infuriated, Rep. Harley O. Staggers, chief House of Representatives watchdog over broadcasting, advocated citing CBS and its President, Frank Stanton, for contempt of Congress. In a showdown on the House floor, the proposal was killed by a 226–181 vote. It was a close call in another battle between the Federal Government and the news media. The resentments date back to the heated debates over TV's coverage of the 1968 Democratic convention and the Chicago riots.

▶CHILDREN'S PROGRAMING

A group of Boston-area mothers calling itself Action for Children's Television (ACT) and the Federal Communications Commission (FCC) Chairman, Dean Burch, joined forces to improve children's TV fare.

The opening scene from the controversial CBS documentary "The Selling of the Pentagon."

Above: Colleen Dewhurst and George C. Scott in "The Price." Below: Tony Randall (left) and Emmy-winner Jack Klugman in "The Odd Couple."

They pressed for fewer hard-sell commercials and more educational substance in the networks' morning children's programs. ACT demanded that all advertising be taken out of shows for children. Burch urged the networks to consider jointly presenting a quality children's program each late afternoon. The networks resisted both these ideas. But they did cut down on the flood of Saturday cartoons by replacing some of them with "live action" programing with do-good overtones.

▶LOCAL STATIONS

At the local level, stations in city after city were facing challenges by citizen forces.

These were often sparked by blacks and other minority groups which felt the stations had not given proper voice to all community interests. They demanded that the FCC, before renewing a TV station's three-year license, require stronger proof that the station would present what it promised.

THE THREE-HOUR RULE

While the medium was struggling with these problems, the FCC declared that the home screen was too much under the domination of the three big commercial networks (CBS, NBC, and ABC). As a result, it acted to impose "diversity" in TV entertainment by limiting each network to three hours of programing per evening (instead of the usual 3½ hours) beginning in the fall of 1971. Local stations would have to fill a half hour of prime time each evening with new programing of their own. The FCC conceded, however, that time might be required for developing new non-network sources of programing. It allowed local stations, for a period of one year, to fill their extra time with reruns of old network series and old movies. So, the real test of how much freshness the so-called Three-Hour Rule would bring to the medium was postponed until October 1972. Needless to say, the FCC move was not overly welcomed by either the local stations or the networks. Both groups predicted that the new rule would fail to produce higher-quality shows.

A NIELSEN REPORT

For all the criticism and pressures heaped on it, television was more popular than ever. The A. C. Nielsen survey, the most quoted viewing index, found TV watching at an all-time high of "just under six hours" a day in the average U.S. household early in 1971. Nielsen also reported that men in the $15,000-plus income bracket were watching TV 20 hours a week, while their wives watched 23 hours. This should dispel the widely-held notion that TV is the poor man's diversion.

ON THE ENTERTAINMENT SCENE

The networks, ever seeking what would please the most people, seemed to find their

The cast of "All in the Family."

answer in movies. So great was the demand for movies that many broadcasters were using two-hour filmed dramas made specially for TV. "Ersatz movies," the trade paper *Variety* called them. Dozens were ordered. The public appeared to like them just as much as the pictures they had seen—or missed—at the neighborhood movie house. One network, ABC, decided to experiment with original ninety-minute movies in the daytime beginning early in 1972.

CBS, long the top-rated network, decided that its prime-time programs, popular though they were, too often had a "rural" and older-viewer appeal. In a major shake-up of its programing, the network dropped such long-standing favorites as *The Ed Sullivan Show, The Beverly Hillbillies, Green Acres, Mayberry R.F.D.,* Jim Nabors' variety hour, *Hee-Haw,* and even *Lassie* and *Family Affair.* Sullivan's show, the oldest weekly series on TV, had been around for 23 years.

Alan Rowe (left) as King William III and John Neville as John Churchill, Earl of Marlborough, in the Public Broadcasting Service's "The First Churchills."

Old-timers also got their notices at the other networks. ABC dropped Lawrence Welk, and NBC canceled Red Skelton and Andy Williams.

A midseason entry that CBS unveiled with some trepidation might develop into a new trend in TV entertainment. *All in the Family,* the first U.S. series attempting to humorously portray outrageous bigotry, was loosely based on a British TV comedy, *Till Death Us Do Part.* Because many British viewers were offended by it, CBS was prepared for the worst. But it never came. A few viewers and critics took exception to the program, but the majority enjoyed its brashness. Soon *All in the Family* was a top-rated attraction. Attempted copies of it were a certainty.

Public television claimed much attention in 1971. The Public Broadcasting Service (PBS), a network of more than two hundred noncommercial stations, delighted viewers with a run of British dramas, including *The Forsyte Saga* and *The First Churchills.* William F. Buckley Jr.'s syndicated *Firing Line* talkfests moved onto PBS. Beginning its second season in the fall of 1971, the "fourth network" promised a weekly political series leading into the 1972 election campaign. Also slated for presentation was a 26-week run of old classic movies; even public TV had the movie fever!

Television's coverage of the Apollo 14 and 15 missions provided earthlings with ever more intimate views of the moon. The second of the two 1971 lunar shows was particularly thrilling. A perfectly functioning color TV camera, mounted on the astronauts' moon buggy and remote-controlled from the Houston space center, televised David Scott and Jim Irwin ambling about in the lunar dust. The same camera got an awesome picture of the lunar module rising like a shot from the moon's surface, in the first televised launching from another world.

▶ **CABLE TELEVISION**

As cable TV (CATV) continued to reach into more homes, the FCC struggled with a complex set of proposed Federal regulations. The problems involve ending the long-standing freeze on CATV entry into urban areas while guarding against injury to broadcast television. In November the CATV and broadcast industries reached a compromise agreement: CATV will be allowed to expand into smaller cities, but its expansion into larger cities will be slowed. Also, CATV companies will have to pay film companies for movies beamed to CATV customers. This had not been done in the past.

RICHARD K. DOAN
Columnist, *TV Guide*

Young musicians on "The Electric Company," a new show produced by the Children's Television Workshop.

CHILDREN'S TV SHOWS

In 1971, children's television programing put on a new and better face. The television networks, responding to criticism, started some promising new series.

ABC began a Saturday morning hour called *Curiosity Shop,* attempting to combine learning with fun. A new Sunday morning program, *Make a Wish,* with guitar-playing singer Tom Chapin as host, tried to engage children in association of ideas. CBS contributed topical *In the News* capsules between its Saturday cartoons as well as an early Saturday afternoon children's version of the 1950's series *You Are There.* The narrator was Walter Cronkite. NBC pushed Saturday morning cartoons aside for two hours to offer a filmed undersea adventure, *Barrier Reef;* a revival of Don Herbert's

prizewinning science show, *Mr. Wizard;* and an hour-long experiment called *Take a Giant Step.* In the latter show, three teen-agers discussed their views of themselves, their families, and their friends.

On public TV, the widely acclaimed *Sesame Street* (now being shown in many countries around the world) was supplemented by *The Electric Company.* This daily half-hour show, also produced by the Children's Television Workshop, featured an adult repertory group including comedian Bill Cosby. It sought to improve the reading skills of 7 to 10 year olds. Several stations ran this program during school hours, for in-class viewing, and repeated it in the early evening.

National Educational Television began a children's entertainment series titled *Masquerade,* employing dance, mime, and dialogue to relate folklore and fairy tales.

Walter Cronkite "visits" Revolutionary America during a segment of "You Are There."

Three teen-agers talk about the sea on "Take a Giant Step," an hour-long show on NBC-TV.

Don Herbert as "Mr. Wizard." The prizewinning science show was revived for the 1971 TV season.

Youngsters perform on "Curiosity Shop," a Saturday morning fun-and-learning show.

Being developed for 1972 was a 13-week *Children to Children* series. Each program will be filmed in a different country and will show some aspect of children's life in that land.

The commercial programers also were working up additional children's fare. ABC said it would produce a weekly hour-long movie for children to be shown Saturday mornings beginning in the fall of 1972. The network also said it would televise a monthly one-hour "special" for children in the late afternoon. NBC disclosed plans to begin a Monday through Friday half hour of "balanced educational entertainment" programing for children which the network would feed over its coaxial cable to NBC outlets to air at times of their own choosing, but preferably in the late afternoon. CBS, whose *Captain Kangaroo,* a morning show, has long been the only daily moppet show on the big networks, was casting about for new and exciting ideas that would fit other times of the day.

To top all this off, the British Broadcasting Corporation's highly praised *Playschool,* for preschoolers, was introduced experimentally on a Milwaukee station and offered for showing on others.

Altogether, 1971 was a banner year for children's television.

WALT DISNEY WORLD

Walt Disney World sprawls over 27,400 acres of central Florida. At the heart of this Disney paradise is the Magic Kingdom amusement park (below and right), where fairy tales come to life.

The $400,000,000 amusement-park-resort-complex is a mixture of fun, fantasy, and nostalgia. Right: On a cruise through Adventureland, visitors see an elephant looming from the jungle. Left: Just before opening day in October, the Disney denizens gather in front of the 18-story Cinderella Castle.

ENVIRONMENT

TWO major trends marked the advance of the "environmental revolution" in 1971. One trend was a shift in public concern from talk to action. The other was the broadening of the "environmental horizon" from a national to an international scope.

Earth Week, 1971 (April 18–24), was a far different kind of event than Earth Day, 1970. Activities were more low-keyed and locally oriented. Particular problems, rather than improvement of the environment in general, were stressed. Cleanup drives were held in many communities. Seattle, Washington, organized a bike day, and Urbana, Illinois, proclaimed a walk-to-work day. In New York City, Madison Avenue was closed to traffic and turned into a pedestrian mall during the noon hours.

From such familiar matters as local air and water pollution, public concern extended to larger problems. Some of these were contamination of the oceans; the possibility, due to air pollution, of eventually changing the earth's critical "heat balance" from the sun; and the global population explosion, with the possibility that world population will double within 25 years.

For the first time in history, the world decided to examine such problems collectively. A great majority of United Nations member countries joined in preparations for an international Conference on the Human Environment, in Stockholm, Sweden, in June 1972. At this conference, joint action on environmental problems will be planned.

A display at Bronx Park Zoo in New York City, "warning that the earth is becoming unsuitable for life."

In 1971, as part of the "environmental revolution," many communities and cities sought "to return the streets to the people." As an answer to the air-polluting auto, people in hundreds of cities began bicycling to work (above). During Earth Week, New York's Madison Avenue (below) was turned into a pedestrian mall, with all traffic banned.

The "environmental revolution" in the United States dates approximately from 1969. Two events occurred in that year that attracted worldwide attention and made millions of people suddenly aware of the urgency of environmental problems. One was the Santa Barbara, California, oil-well blowout, which drenched many miles of beautiful beaches with black scum. The other event was the astronauts' sensational television pictures from the moon of the planet Earth, looking tiny and isolated. People suddenly became aware of just how dependent the earth is on the very thin layer of exhaustible resources that lies close to the globe's surface. This sudden public awareness of pollution and its effects touched off corrective efforts on many fronts.

▶ GOVERNMENT ACTION

The environmental year 1971 unfolded in a series of small crises or episodes rather than in an orderly progression.

Congress, under pressure from both conservationists and economists, ended the multibillion-dollar, Federally sponsored project to develop a supersonic transport (SST) plane. Conservationists argued that the sonic booms and gaseous emissions that the 1,800-mile-an-hour plane would generate could prove destructive.

After much debate, two large projects of the Army Corps of Engineers were halted by the Federal Government because of their possible ill effects on the environment. One was the construction of a 177-mile Cross-Florida Barge Canal between the Atlantic Ocean and the Gulf of Mexico. The other project was a $386,000,000 Tennessee-Tombigbee Waterway in Tennessee.

Similarly, the Department of the Interior withheld approval for the construction of an 800-mile oil pipeline in Alaska. The $1,000,-000,000 project, set up by a group of oil companies, would extend the pipeline from the rich petroleum fields of Prudhoe Bay in the extreme north of Alaska to the ice-free tanker-ship port of Valdez in the south. The objections of conservationists ranged from possible disruption of terrain and wildlife to the possibility of massive leaks in the pipeline.

Federal officials also reversed the position they had taken on the use of household phosphate-based detergents. Earlier in the year, the Government had warned that the discharge of these phosphates into the sewage system caused the growth of weedy plant life in waterways. Further research, however, indicated that substitutes for phosphates contained harsh chemicals of more immediate danger to people. So authorities recommended that homemakers go back to using their original detergents.

Another far-reaching Federal decision was a public warning against eating swordfish. New studies were conducted in which it was found that industrial wastes had dispersed mercury in many of the nation's waterways. Swordfish was discovered to be particularly susceptible to the absorption of mercury.

Conservationists didn't win all of their battles with the government. One conflict that became particularly intensive centered on the nuclear-test explosion a mile underground on Amchitka Island off mainland Alaska. It was the largest underground atomic explosion in the history of the United States—250 times more powerful than the World War II bomb that devastated Hiroshima, Japan.

The Department of Defense and the Atomic Energy Commission said that the explosion was necessary for the development of new weapons. Opponents of the test thought that there was too much uncertainty about the effects of such an enormous blast. They felt that there was a possibility that it might trigger an earthquake or tidal waves, and that there was great danger of radiation releases.

A year-long debate in Congress and the courts ended in a Supreme Court decision allowing the test to take place. It was conducted on November 6 with no immediately harmful results. The force of the explosion was measured at about 7 on the Richter scale of earthquake strength.

Many of these controversies stemmed from the National Environmental Policy Act of 1969. This act requires that before any project involving a Federal agency is undertaken, a study of the impact it might have on the environment must be filed with the

Two concerns of the Environmental Protection Agency: air and water pollution caused by industry.

Council on Environmental Quality, a presidential advisory agency. These declarations are then available for public discussion and public pressures on Federal policy-making.

A noteworthy administrative development was the resignation of Walter J. Hickel, controversial secretary of the interior. (The Department of the Interior has extensive environmental jurisdiction.) Hickel was replaced by Rogers C. B. Morton, a former U.S. representative from Maryland.

The Environmental Protection Agency

A new Federal organization began operation in 1971. The principal mission of the Environmental Protection Agency (EPA) is to issue and enforce standards and regulations concerning air and water pollution, solid waste, noise, radiation, and pesticides.

The year brought many developments in these fields. The Clean Air Act of 1970—which took effect early in 1971—set a schedule of limits on automobile fumes. By 1975 the emissions of major pollutants from cars should be reduced by as much as 90 per cent. Automobiles are blamed for about one half of the nation's air pollution.

During an air-pollution emergency, 23 companies in Birmingham, Alabama, shut down their plants in November, under EPA orders. It was the first emergency injunction issued under the Clean Air Act.

The EPA launched two major programs in the field of water pollution during 1971. In one project, an inventory was taken of the fluid-waste discharges of all the nation's industrial facilities. This inventory was then compared with information already available on the discharges of municipal sewage systems. These are two of the four major sources of the country's water pollution. (The others are wastes from agriculture and rainstorm runoff from urban areas. Plans for dealing with these two situations have not yet been developed.)

Industry is considered primarily responsible for controlling and treating its own wastes. The EPA's second major step in controlling water pollution was to begin enforcement of a law passed in 1899. This law requires that industrial plants obtain Federal permits for their fluid-waste discharges, to ensure that they will not be excessive. EPA Administrator William D. Ruckelshaus reported that those industries that filed for permits during 1971 were believed to account for about 90 per cent of industrial water pollution.

The EPA began tackling the growing problem of noise pollution with a series of hearings throughout the country. Airlines began modifying airplane engines to meet new restrictions on their sound levels.

EPA officials also worked to reach some agreement in the regulation of pesticides. (Pesticides are chemicals that are used to destroy insects that damage crops. Some pesticides are believed to have harmful side effects on people, animals, and plants.)

▶RECYCLING WASTE

In 1971 there were widespread demands that the nation's mounting mass of refuse ("solid waste"), totaling some 350,000,000 tons a year, be reduced by recycling. In other words, basic materials such as metals, glass, and paper would be reprocessed for reuse. Many millions of tons of waste were being recycled by private-citizen groups. But this made only a small dent in the total amount. It was obvious that large-scale re-

In 1971 airlines increased efforts to modify airplane engines to reduce noise pollution.

Collecting garbage in New York City. The U.S. produces 350,000,-000 tons of solid waste annually.

In Ann Arbor, Michigan, bottles are collected for recycling.

cycling needed a new economic pattern—one that would make recycling less expensive than the present method of taking new materials from nature's limited supply and then destroying them.

▶ **THE COST OF ENVIRONMENT CLEANUP**

Throughout the year, industry and some public officials expressed the belief that the cost of the environmental cleanup being pressed for by various levels of government might be excessive. The Council on Environmental Quality in its annual report stated that during a 5-year program the cost would amount to $21,000,000,000 a year. This equals only 2 per cent of the country's annual production of goods and services (gross national product).

President Nixon said in an environmental message to Congress ". . . the quality of our environment can be substantially improved, if only we go about that task with sufficient will and sufficient energy."

GLADWIN HILL
National Environmental Correspondent
The New York Times

THE YOUTH CAMPAIGN FOR A CLEANER ENVIRONMENT

A Toledo, Ohio, boys' club earned $3,100 toward the purchase of a bus by collecting 144 tons of old bottles. Thirty University of Maryland students received a $26,000 grant from the National Science Foundation for a summer study of water pollution in Washington, D.C.'s Rock Creek Park. In Florida, Miami-Dade Junior College students estab-

lished a chain of refuse-recycling centers that soon were yielding over a ton of paper daily.

In these ways, as well as in many others, young people in thousands of communities throughout the United States pressed the campaign for a cleaner environment in 1971.

Efforts covered a wide range of activities. One important project was undertaken by

Young people in thousands of communities all over the world joined the fight to clean up the environment in 1971. Here, youngsters collect newspapers for recycling.

the 4-H Club members of Virginia. They lobbied for stricter enforcement of pollution laws. In another area, a semester-long class project at the University of Michigan produced a public-education advertising campaign against overpopulation.

The year's most ambitious effort, however, came on June 5. Boy Scout groups across the nation organized a one-day litter cleanup drive. The project involved two million people of all ages who collected over one million tons of refuse for disposal or recycling.

"A lot of young people who joined in the original Earth Day in 1970 eventually lost their enthusiasm," commented Michael McCloskey, executive director of the Sierra Club, a leading conservation organization. "But those who stayed in the movement have twice as much determination and ingenuity, and they are attracting more support all the time."

In San Diego, California, students at the Sunnyside School (left) and at San Marcos High School (right) were paid for thousands of aluminum cans which they collected for recycling.

EUROPE

LEADERS in West and East Europe were trying to take down barriers in 1971. One especially important event occurred in August when a provisional Berlin treaty was agreed on by Great Britain, France, the Soviet Union, and the United States. The status of West Berlin had been one of the most sensitive points of conflict between East and West since World War II.

In West Europe, co-operation was achieved, after ten years of talks, when Britain and the six member countries of the European Economic Community agreed on the conditions for British membership in the trading community.

Important developments followed in East Europe in 1971 from the announcement by U.S. President Richard Nixon that he would visit Communist China. This raised the specter of a possible Washington-Peking alliance against the Soviet Union. To prevent that possibility from becoming a reality, the Soviet leaders mounted an energetic diplomatic campaign that culminated in a Soviet invitation to President Nixon to visit Moscow in 1972.

Ambassadors of France, the United Kingdom, the Soviet Union, and the U.S. sign the Berlin agreement.

Above: British newspapers report on the House of Commons decision to approve that nation's membership in the Common Market. Below: The 24th Congress of the Soviet Communist Party, at which Communist Party General Secretary Leonid Brezhnev emerged as the most powerful figure in the Soviet Union. In May 1972 Brezhnev will meet with President Richard Nixon in Moscow.

▶ EAST-WEST RELATIONS

In two important areas, East and West Europe came closer together in 1971. In addition to an agreement on the status of West Berlin, preliminary discussions began on mutual troop withdrawals and on the holding of a European security conference.

The West Berlin Agreement

The ambassadors of the "big four" nations —the United States, Great Britain, France, and the Soviet Union—had been meeting in Berlin since March 1970. They were seeking to reach an agreement that would settle some of the problems that began when Berlin, like the rest of Germany, was divided into Allied Occupation Zones in 1945, at the end of World War II. The city was divided into East and West Berlin.

West Berlin, 110 miles inside East Germany, had long been a pressure point in the cold war. In 1948–49, when the Soviets blockaded West Berlin by cutting road and rail traffic, fleets of Western planes kept it supplied for more than a year. Although the Soviets never tried to completely block it again, there was often interference with traffic into and out of West Berlin.

Western leaders saw the Berlin problem as a test of Soviet intentions. They said they would consider holding a European security conference, a favorite project of Moscow's, only after a Berlin settlement was reached.

The four ambassadors reached provisional agreement on the basic principles on August 23 and signed the draft agreement on September 3, 1971.

Under the settlement, the Soviet Union agreed to let travelers and freight enter West Berlin quickly and without complications. West German officials would be allowed to come to the city, though not to perform certain kinds of political duties. The Bonn Government would also be able to represent West Berliners abroad.

The Western Allies agreed that West Berlin was not part of West Germany. However, they wrote into the settlement their pledge that relations between West Berlin and West Germany would be kept up and developed. Also, the Soviet Union would be allowed to open a consulate in West Berlin.

The agreement was then submitted to East and West German leaders who, after difficult negotiations, worked out the final details. Next, it was returned to the four powers for signature by their foreign ministers. When this occurs, the agreement will be approved and go into effect, probably sometime in 1972.

Troop Reductions in Europe

In March 1971, Leonid Brezhnev, Soviet Communist Party general secretary, called for mutual troop reductions in sensitive areas of Europe and a European security conference. Two months later Brezhnev asked for the beginning of negotiations on the reduction of troops in Central Europe. He repeatedly spoke favorably of that idea.

At the same time, support was growing in Washington for bringing back some of the 300,000 American troops in West Europe. President Nixon made it clear, however, that there would have to be a balanced reduction of Warsaw Pact troops so as not to weaken West Europe.

In October, Brezhnev visited France for talks with President Georges Pompidou. It was the first Western country that Brezhnev had visited since he replaced Nikita Khrushchev in 1964. Brezhnev and Pompidou agreed to begin active preparation for a European security conference.

Also in October, Manlio Brosio, the former secretary-general of NATO (North Atlantic Treaty Organization), was appointed to begin exploratory talks with the Soviet Union on reducing the number of troops in Central Europe. If East and West can reach an agreement on troop reductions, a European security conference will possibly be the next step.

▶ WEST EUROPE

Reflecting the importance of normalizing East and West European relations, West German Chancellor Willy Brandt was awarded the Nobel Peace Prize on October 20, 1971. He was cited for building bridges between East and West; for his "efforts to obtain for the people of West Berlin the fundamental human rights of personal security and full freedom of movement"; and

French President Georges Pompidou (left) welcomes Soviet Communist Party General Secretary Leonid Brezhnev (right) to France. The two leaders signed a friendship treaty.

for his initiatives toward furthering the political and economic unity of West Europe.

Brandt had sought to improve relations with the communist countries of East Europe from the time he became foreign minister in 1966 and then chancellor in 1969. In 1970 he negotiated important treaties with the Soviet Union and Poland. On September 16, 1971, he flew to the Soviet Union to continue his efforts to improve relations.

Great Britain and the Common Market

In the small hours of the morning, on June 23, 1971, negotiators reached final agreement on the main conditions for British membership in the European Economic Community (also called the Common Market). It was a climax of ten years of talk and hesitation on both sides.

Britain succeeded in its third attempt, after the late President Charles de Gaulle of France had twice vetoed its applications to join, in 1963 and 1967.

The Common Market was formed in 1958 by France, West Germany, Italy, Belgium, the Netherlands, and Luxembourg. Their aim was to stimulate business and industry by letting their products circulate freely within the group.

Hard problems in the discussions on British entry came partly from the fact that Britain's trading pattern and economy were different from those of the original Common Market countries. Britain had to decide on a big readjustment in order to join. The country, which has few farmers and lives by industry and trade, has special arrangements with many countries to bring in low-priced food. It would have to give these up to join the Common Market, which keeps food prices deliberately high to support its farmers.

Even after reaching agreement, the British Government faced a big problem: the British public was still not convinced. Public-opinion polls showed a majority were against joining the Common Market. One big reason was the expected rise in food prices. The question also became a political battle when the Labor Party said it would vote against joining under the conditions the Conservative Government had agreed to. The showdown came on October 28 when, by a vote of 356 to 244, the House of Commons approved British membership. However, there are still legislative problems to be worked out. If these are overcome, Britain will become a full member on January 1, 1973. Britain's entry will help pave the way for Ireland, Norway, and Denmark. They too have applied for entry.

If these countries become members, the combined economic strength of West Europe working together in one group could be huge. The Common Market would then group 250,000,000 people of some of the most advanced nations in the world.

West German Chancellor Willy Brandt (left) with British Prime Minister Edward Heath. In 1971 Brandt won the Nobel Peace Prize. Heath reached agreement on Britain's entry into the Common Market.

The currencies of Switzerland, the Netherlands, Germany, and Austria were allowed to "float" or were revalued during the May 1971 monetary crisis.

World Monetary Crisis

In 1971 a world monetary crisis seemed to be in the making. It began in May when West Germany let its currency unit, the deutsche mark, "float" to a higher value. (The U.S. dollar's exchange rate had been fixed at a specific value in relation to other currencies. When the Germans "floated" their deutsche mark, they set it free from its fixed value to the dollar. Thus the system of supply and demand would determine the value of the deutsche mark. Because West Germany has a very strong economy, the "floated" deutsche mark was in demand. It thus rose to a higher value and was worth more in relation to the dollar.)

When the Germans let the deutsche mark "float," the Netherlands let its currency unit "float." These moves caused complications for the Common Market, where most trade arrangements depend on fixed money values.

On August 15, President Nixon set a special tax on imports (goods coming into a country) and let the dollar's value "float." The dollar's value went down in comparison with most West European currencies. This was desirable to West European countries, for they felt that the dollar had been overvalued. However, they strongly urged the United States to remove the import tax.

The world monetary system was in a process of change in 1971. Most nations felt that a fixed currency value was necessary. But the U.S. wanted West European countries and Japan to officially raise the value of their money. They in turn wanted the U.S. to officially lower the value of the dollar.

In December, in a surprise move, President Nixon agreed to a devaluation of the dollar as part of an international agreement on a realignment of currencies.

Italy Chooses a President

In December 1971 the 7-year term of Italy's President Giuseppe Saragat ended. Although the president is largely a figurehead, there is always much political drama in the elections. After numerous ballots, Italy's electoral college finally chose former premier Giovanni Leone president.

The new President has many problems to resolve. He must form a new Government, usually a long and difficult process. He will have to contend with a severe depression, one which left the country with an annual growth rate of zero in 1971. And he will have to deal with Italy's year-old divorce law which has been threatening to turn into a "religious war."

Swiss Women Win the Vote

Switzerland's men finally decided to let its women vote. In a referendum on February 7, the men voted by almost two to one for a constitutional amendment that permits women to vote in federal elections and to hold federal offices.

But the men of Switzerland's tiny neighbor, Liechtenstein, refused in a referendum on February 28 to let its women vote.

The Greek Regime

In September a military court in Greece sentenced four persons for their participation in an unsuccessful attempt to help a Greek prisoner escape. Among those convicted was Lady Amalia Fleming, the Greek-born widow of the British discoverer of penicillin. She was stripped of her Greek citizenship and deported to England.

In October, U.S. Vice-President Spiro Agnew spent a week in Greece in an official capacity and as a private visitor. During his stay he visited the town where his father had been born. Many Americans and Greeks were opposed to Agnew's visit because they felt it was a sign of U.S. support for the military-backed regime.

The Conflict in Northern Ireland

The conflict in Northern Ireland has deep roots. When Ireland gained independence in 1921, Northern Ireland remained under British control. About 1,000,000 of its people are Protestant, and about 500,000 are Catholics.

After years of protesting that they were discriminated against in jobs, housing, and voting rights, the Catholics launched a civil-rights movement in 1968. Riots and clashes with Protestants followed, partly as a result of an angry reaction from militant Protestants. The Protestant-controlled Government of Northern Ireland promised reforms, but action was slow and tempers rose.

The early demonstrations had been led by civil-rights organizers. By 1971 the conflict had reached the point of armed battles involving British troops and local police. (By the end of 1971, over 14,000 British troops were stationed in Northern Ireland.) This new and more deadly phase was spearheaded by a militant wing of the outlawed Irish Republican Army (IRA). The IRA wants Northern Ireland to be united with the mainly Catholic Republic of Ireland to the south.

In March, Prime Minister James Chichester-Clark resigned in despair and frustration over the conflict. He was succeeded by Brian Faulkner, also a Protestant.

On August 9 the new Government started a policy of preventive detention and internment, seizing suspected IRA members and holding them without trial. Hundreds of people were held in this way.

As if in answer, the bloodiest rioting in fifty years erupted. Sniper attacks or bomb explosions occurred almost every day. Bombs went off at police stations and in public areas, and troops were ambushed in roads and streets.

In the months that followed the introduction of the internment policy, over 100 soldiers, police, and civilians were killed.

Government Changes

Norway's Prime Minister Per Borten resigned in March in the midst of a political

In 1971 British troops in Northern Ireland were caught between warring Protestants and Catholics. Left: Catholic youngsters harass British troops. Far left: A girl on a Belfast street walks past anti-British, pro-IRA signs. The IRA—the Irish Republican Army—would like to see Northern Ireland united with the predominantly Catholic Republic of Ireland. Above: Pro-Protestant, anti-Catholic signs in Belfast.

scandal involving the release of a confidential report on Norway's negotiations with the Common Market. Labor Party leader Trygve Bratteli formed a new Government.

In October elections in Austria, the Socialists became the first party in the country's postwar history to win more than 50 per cent of the vote.

In Finland a dispute over agricultural policy brought down the Government of Premier Ahti Karjalainen in October. Teuvo Aura was appointed to head a caretaker Government until 1972 elections.

In the Netherlands, the coalition Government of Petrus de Jong lost its Parliamentary majority in April elections. Barend W. Biesheuvel became the new premier.

Prime Minister Hilmar Baunsgaard of Denmark resigned after September elections. His coalition Government was succeeded by a Social Democratic minority Government headed by Jens Otto Krag.

The island-nation of Iceland swung to the Left in general elections on June 13. The new left-wing coalition Government, headed by Prime Minister Olafur Johannesson, said it would close an American-manned NATO air base at Keflavik. This aroused grave concern in NATO countries. Later in the year Iceland was reconsidering, but it seemed certain there would be some revision of its defense agreement with the U.S.

Another small island-nation, Malta, produced problems for NATO after a new Government was elected in June. The Labor Party came to power with a one-seat edge and Dom Mintoff as prime minister. Mintoff immediately demanded more money from Britain and the other NATO members for their continued use of the island's military bases. In December, Mintoff declared that all 3,500 British troops must be withdrawn from Malta by January 15, 1972, unless an agreement was reached.

In August, NATO removed its Mediterranean naval headquarters from Malta at Mintoff's request and announced it would be transferred to Naples, Italy.

DAVID LAULICHT
Reuters News Service

SOVIET UNION AND EAST EUROPE

For the Soviet Union and East Europe, 1971 was a turbulent year. Poland's leader had been ousted in the closing days of 1970, and the political ruler of East Germany was dethroned in mid-1971.

By the end of 1971, the Soviet Union was engaged in its most vigorous wooing of the West in many years: Soviet Communist Party General Secretary Leonid Brezhnev visited France, and the two countries signed a ten-year trade agreement; Premier Aleksei Kosygin became the first Soviet head of government to visit Canada; the Soviet Union was one of the four major powers (with the United States, Britain, and France) to agree upon a provisional Berlin treaty; and on October 12 it was announced that U.S. President Richard Nixon would visit the Soviet Union sometime in May 1972. If this visit takes place, Nixon will become the first U.S. president to visit the Soviet Union since the end of World War II.

Soviet Internal Affairs

The 24th Congress of the Soviet Communist Party was held March 30 to April 9 in Moscow. A new five-year economic plan was approved by the Congress. For the first time, the emphasis was on more rapid development of consumer goods and agricultural production. Brezhnev proclaimed that raising the standard of living would be "the supreme aim of the party's economic policy." The Soviet leaders had finally decided to take steps to quiet the growing complaints of the Soviet consumer. However, the new economic plan did not abandon nor neglect heavy industry and military output.

Brezhnev also indicated that the Soviet Union was interested in improving relations with the West. It seemed that the Soviets were trying to ease tension on the international level so that resources could be transferred to meeting domestic needs.

As the Congress ended, it was apparent that Communist Party chief Leonid Brezhnev had emerged as the most important member, or "first among equals," of the Kremlin leadership.

In 1971, a new flexibility was evident in the way the Soviet Government responded to an unusual domestic challenge: the demand of thousands of Soviet Jews that they be permitted to emigrate to Israel. In past years the Soviet propaganda line had been that virtually no Soviet Jew had any such desire. The harshness of the Soviet attitude was seen in December 1970 when two Jewish defendants charged with planning to hijack an airplane were sentenced to death. There were worldwide protests, and the death sentences were commuted. Then, in the spring of 1971, the Soviet Government relaxed its emigration policy for Jews. By the end of the year, over ten thousand (an unprecedented number) had emigrated to Israel. Moscow had decided that it was wiser to let the loudest protesters leave the country—in the hope that, in their absence, the problem would die down. It was also part of Moscow's policy of projecting an image of moderation to the West.

Soviet Foreign Affairs

In the Middle East the Soviet position remained basically unchanged. Huge quantities of Soviet weapons, munitions, and supplies moved to that area. In particular, the Soviet Union sought to strengthen its ties with Egypt. On May 27, Egypt and the Soviet Union signed a 15-year treaty of friendship and co-operation. This occurred after an Egyptian government shake-up had purged a number of pro-Soviet ministers.

Even after Sudan put down an attempted communist take-over of its Government, the Soviets were not deterred. Moscow made it plainer than ever that it intended to remain a major factor in the Middle East indefinitely.

The Soviet Union did undertake a series of informal contacts with the Israelis. However, these contacts fell far short of restoring formal diplomatic relations between the two countries.

When President Nixon announced he was going to visit Communist China in 1972, the Soviet leaders were deeply disturbed. Their own relations with China, as Brezhnev had made plain at the 24th party Congress, were unsatisfactory and tense. There had been some minor improvements—an exchange of ambassadors and some slightly increased trade. But large numbers of Russian and Chinese troops still faced each other along the 6,000-mile Sino-Soviet border. And the Chinese made no secret of the fact that they were digging air-raid shelters everywhere in their country as defense against Soviet attack.

Of particular concern to Moscow was the evidence of increased Chinese influence in East Europe. Not only was Albania a satellite of China, but Yugoslavia had resumed full diplomatic relations with China in 1970. And Rumania's leader, Nicolae Ceausescu, had visited China for a cordial meeting with the Chinese leaders just before the Nixon announcement in July 1971. There was much speculation, in fact, that Ceausescu had played a key role behind the scenes in arranging for the visit of President Nixon's envoy, Henry Kissinger, to Peking in early July. It was during that visit, conducted in secret, that Nixon's scheduled trip to China was agreed upon. (It was also thought that Nixon's planned visit to China spurred the Soviet invitation to Nixon to visit Russia.)

The Soviets' alarm about the weakening of their position in the Balkan countries was reflected in increased tension there during the summer of 1971. Only unswerving fidelity to Moscow became the Soviet line. The implications of this became even clearer when a Hungarian newspaper, probably writing on instructions from Moscow, wrote about a "Tirana-Belgrade-Bucharest" axis that might turn into an "anti-Soviet axis." The implied threat was that if Albania, Yugoslavia, and Rumania did not cease their friendship with China, the Soviet Union might act against them "in self-defense."

To some degree, the tension was broken when Soviet party chief Brezhnev visited Belgrade in September. What emerged from the visit was a communiqué that ratified Yugoslavia's right to independence, yet at the same time pledged Yugoslavia to closer co-operation with the Soviet Union. It was noticeable that the two countries stressed different parts of the same agreement. It also did not escape world attention that when Brezhnev left Belgrade, he made short visits to Hungary and to Bulgaria, presumably to explain the results of his Yugoslavia visit. He pointedly did not visit Rumania, whose

Egyptian President Anwar el-Sadat (left) and Soviet President Nikolai Podgorny.

Soviet leader Leonid Brezhnev (right) visits with Yugoslav President Tito.

continued independence obviously disturbed the Russians.

Ceausescu's Strategy

Ceausescu's strategy in seeking to avoid a Russian invasion harked back to the lessons of Czechoslovakia in 1968. In that year the Soviet Government had justified its invasion by stating that socialism in Czechoslovakia was in danger. Hence, Ceausescu sought to demonstrate that the Communist Party was in complete control of Rumania. On his return from China in 1971, the Rumanian leader ordered an extensive campaign against Western cultural influences. This move seemed motivated by a fear that Moscow would charge such influences endangered socialism in Rumania.

The Purge in Poland

The dramatic events in Poland began in December 1970 and continued into the early weeks of 1971.

In 1968, dissatisfaction among Polish students and intellectuals erupted into riots that were easily put down. The same year, the liberal trend in Czechoslovakia posed a threat to Moscow's rule. It was such a strong threat that Czechoslovakia was invaded by Soviet and Warsaw Pact armies. Brezhnev and other communist leaders believed that

Poland's new Communist Party chief, Edward Gierek.

these moves would insure them against any more serious internal trouble in East Europe.

Perhaps it was overconfidence that can explain Wladyslaw Gomulka's historic error in raising the prices of food and other necessities only a few weeks before Christmas, 1970. Christmas is a holiday that still means much in predominantly Catholic Poland. When workers in the Baltic ports protested against the price raises, they were met by gunfire that claimed many lives. As the anger of the workers mounted, the entire future of communist rule in Poland hung in the balance. The possibility of Soviet armed intervention loomed menacingly. In this moment of crisis Gomulka was ousted, and replaced by Edward Gierek. Gierek moved swiftly to quiet popular discontent by making major concessions to the Polish workers. He repealed the price hikes, and granted wage increases for the most poorly paid workers. And he made moves to eliminate old and sorely felt complaints of the Roman Catholic church in Poland. Gomulka and his closest collaborators were made scapegoats for the unpopular policies of the past.

The events in Poland were taken as a serious warning throughout the entire Soviet bloc. New attention was focused on measures to ease popular discontent.

Ulbricht Steps Down

On May 3, 1971, Walter Ulbricht resigned and was replaced by his longtime lieutenant, Erich Honecker. Ulbricht's "resignation" was supposedly the result of ill health. But there was every reason to believe that he suffered from a more political ailment. It was well known that he looked with suspicion on a four-power agreement on Berlin. He fought bitterly against any Soviet concessions, for he feared that the Soviet Union might sacrifice East Germany's interests in order to improve Soviet relations with West Germany. For Moscow, a Berlin settlement was essential so that West Germany would ratify the West German-Soviet agreement of 1970. When Ulbricht suddenly and unexpectedly stepped down, there was speculation he had been deposed to pave the way for agreement on a four-power provisional Berlin treaty. This proved to be the case, and in August

Erich Honecker, East Germany's new Communist Party leader.

such a treaty was agreed upon. It did much to improve the atmosphere of East-West relations.

Yugoslavia's Collective Leadership

In Yugoslavia the internal situation was quite complicated. President Tito was seeking to prepare the way for Yugoslavia to continue after he, and his unifying influence, passed from the scene. For that purpose Tito took steps to establish a collective presidency. A major program of decentralization of power was carried out, one aimed at giving the various constituent republics of Yugoslavia more power. The goal was to make concessions to the rising nationalistic feelings among the major Yugoslav peoples —Croats, Serbs, Slovenes, Bosnians, Macedonians, and Montenegrins. But as 1971 neared its end there was increasing evidence that hostility among nationalities was rising and was endangering the future of Yugoslavia. This was especially true in Croatia, a relatively industrialized and rich area. There the demands for complete autonomy led to a major student strike, a purge of Communist Party leaders, and violent anti-Belgrade demonstrations.

Czechoslovakia, under Husak

In Czechoslovakia, Communist Party leader Gustav Husak kept things under control, very tight control, in 1971. The remnants of the Dubcek era had been wiped out by Husak in 1969 and 1970. In 1971 the pressure was kept up to avoid any rebirth of the liberal forces of 1968. There were no mass trials, and Dubcek himself was allowed to live as a free citizen in an obscure, ill-paid job. But virtually all government, party, and cultural institutions were purged of their liberal employees. As a result, many of Czechoslovakia's most brilliant citizens had to earn a living by working as bricklayers, messengers, and taxi drivers. The citizens of Czechoslovakia, deprived of any hope of influencing their nation's future, gave themselves up to their private concerns, hoping that someday a better and freer time might come.

HARRY SCHWARTZ
The New York Times

HOBBIES

ALTHOUGH science and industry have given us necessities and luxuries so plentifully, there is always a desire in people to make things for themselves. Thus, many old crafts are rediscovered. Macramé, candlemaking, Indian leathercraft, and ceramics were some of the popular handicrafts of 1971. Of course, stamp and coin collecting continued to be two of the world's leading hobbies. And the recent nostalgia trend found more and more hobbyists collecting such items as baseball, cigarette, and greeting cards, big little books, old posters, and other "antiques" from the late 19th and early 20th centuries.

Model trains: One hobby that can be enjoyed by the whole family.

New stamp issues of 1971 included four Historic Preservation commemoratives (above) and the second in the American Poets series, honoring Emily Dickinson (above right).

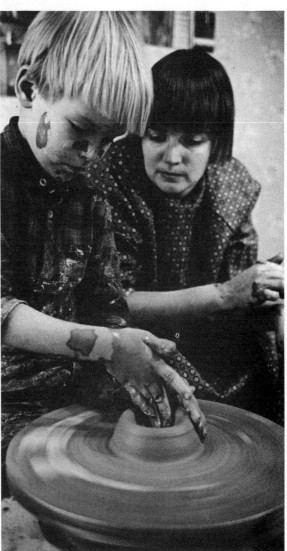

A youngster tries to master the art of "throwing" a ceramic piece on a potter's wheel.

COINS AND COIN COLLECTING

New coins issued when Great Britain changed its currency to the decimal system.

The theme for National Coin Week in 1971 was "Numismatics—the Hobby of All Ages." It was an appropriate slogan because of the exciting opportunities that coin collecting offers to veterans and beginners alike.

The story-of-the-year was the issue of the dollar coins honoring the late President Dwight D. Eisenhower. After two years of legislative battles between those who favored silver and those who favored nonsilver commemorative coins, a compromise was reached late in 1970.

A 40 per cent silver edition, created specifically for sale to collectors at premium prices, began production at the San Francisco Mint on March 31, 1971. They were the first silver dollars to be minted by the United States since 1935. A total of 150,000,000 uncirculated and proof silver dollars will be minted over the next few years.

The "sandwich" (copper-nickel clad) version of the Ike dollar is intended for general circulation. Production began at the Philadelphia and Denver Mints, and the first nonsilver commemoratives were released on November 1.

On April 20 the new "sandwich" Kennedy half-dollar coins were released. With no silver remaining in them, the half-dollar began to slowly filter back into active circulation after years of hoarding.

Several commemoratives in the U.S. Mint's official medal series were released during the year. One, a bronze miniature ($1\frac{5}{16}$ inch diameter), depicts George Washington inspecting the first U.S. coins in 1792. It is based on a 1914 oil painting by John Dunsmore.

In 1971, to commemorate the 100th anniversary of British Columbia's entry into the

President Richard Nixon presents Mrs. Dwight D. Eisenhower the first of the new silver "Ike" dollars.

Confederation, Canada issued its first silver dollars since 1967. In 1968 Canada began producing only dollars made of nickel, both for general circulation and for collectors. The 1971-dated silver dollars are intended as collector's items.

A record 10,571 people attended the American Numismatic Association's 80th-anniversary convention held in Washington, D.C., in August. Reflecting the growing interest in coin collecting among young people, young collectors had their own special day at the convention. It included a VIP tour of the White House, watching the printing of currency and souvenir sheets, and a visit to the Smithsonian's Numismatic Division.

CLIFFORD MISHLER
Coins Magazine and *Numismatic News*

STAMPS AND STAMP COLLECTING

The year 1971 was an epoch-making one for the postal system of the United States. The U.S. Post Office Department was changed into an independent government corporation. It is now called the U.S. Postal Service. Postmaster General Winton M. Blount, who had remained as head of the corporation, resigned in October. Elmer T. Klassen was named to succeed him, effective January 1, 1972. The new agency does not call for a seat in the Federal Cabinet.

For the stamp collector the difference will be slight. However, it is the hope of the new Postal Service that, with its departure from political influences, better service, efficiency, and economy will result.

An entirely new rate structure was set up by July 1, the day the U.S. Postal Service came into being. Because of the increased rates, new stamps were issued. These included an eight-cent stamp for first-class mail and a sixty-cent special-delivery stamp. Air-mail, registered, and circular rates were also increased. Parcel-post rates, increased in late 1970, were not further revised.

Topical stamps (stamps collected because they portray a certain subject) continued their intense popularity. Currently, many popular stamps are devoted to the topic of space exploration. Many countries now issue these regularly to satisfy the strong market. The stamps usually honor both American and Russian achievements in space. In 1971 the United States issued its space stamps in "twin form," two separate stamps which together form a lunar scene. Each stamp is in the eight-cent denomination. The stamps commemorate a decade of American space

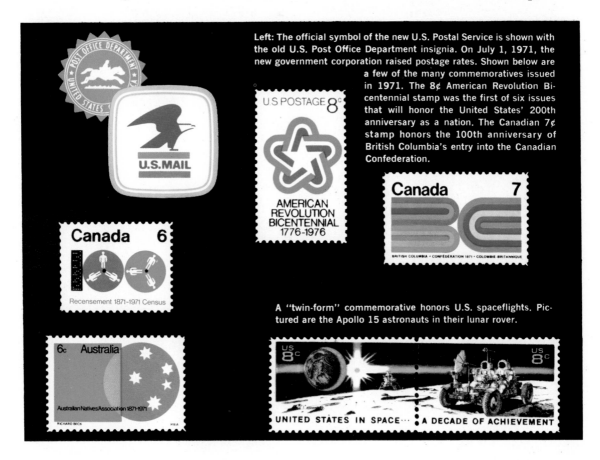

Left: The official symbol of the new U.S. Postal Service is shown with the old U.S. Post Office Department insignia. On July 1, 1971, the new government corporation raised postage rates. Shown below are a few of the many commemoratives issued in 1971. The 8¢ American Revolution Bicentennial stamp was the first of six issues that will honor the United States' 200th anniversary as a nation. The Canadian 7¢ stamp honors the 100th anniversary of British Columbia's entry into the Canadian Confederation.

A "twin-form" commemorative honors U.S. spaceflights. Pictured are the Apollo 15 astronauts in their lunar rover.

Topical stamp collecting continued to be very popular in 1971. Two topics, each with a wide variety of stamps to choose from, were youth (above) and sports.

A block of four wildlife conservation stamps was issued on June 12. They picture a trout, an alligator, a polar bear, and a California condor.

achievement. They were issued to tie in with the Apollo 15 spaceflight. The twin-form novelty was begun in 1967 with another "space twin" issue. Although it is a fairly recent issue, it now brings well over the face value when available.

Other stamps issued by the United States in 1971 covered a variety of subjects. *Wake of the Ferry,* by John Sloan, provided the design for another stamp in the American Artist series. There was a stamp to help in the prevention of drug abuse and another to commemorate the CARE program. (CARE is the organization that sends food and medical supplies to less fortunate peoples of the world.) And a commemorative postal card was issued to honor America's hospitals.

The United Nations continues to issue stamps that are both popular and beautiful. Past issues have called attention to the cause of human rights and the fight against malaria. The United Nations designated 1971 as "International Year for Action to Combat Racism and Racial Discrimination." The organization, as well as many countries, issued stamps on the subject.

To commemorate the United States' 200th anniversary of independence in 1976, the Postal Service issued, on July 4, the first in a series of annual stamps. The final one will be issued in 1976, when bicentennial celebrations will take place in many cities of the United States. The former national capital, Philadelphia, will be the center of the series of events. During that year, Philadelphia will also be host to an international stamp exhibition.

Avid collectors who follow the conventions and exhibitions had a long distance to travel in 1971. The International Exhibition was held in Tokyo, Japan, in April. The event was a success from the standpoint of interest and attendance. But the number of visitors from other countries was disappointing. The 1972 Exhibition will be held in Brussels, Belgium, in June.

With its large number of enthusiasts, stamp collecting continues to be one of the world's leading hobbies. As stamp collectors like to point out, their hobby can be pursued as inexpensively or as expensively as one wishes. And this "investment" is never lost. As a rule, with the passage of time, most stamps gain in value. Thus, a collector may have his pleasure with his hobby over a period of years, and then obtain more than the original cost of the stamps if they are sold.

HERMAN HERST, JR.
Author, *Fun and Profit in Stamp Collecting*

NOSTALGIA AND THE HOBBYIST

During 1971 a nostalgia craze swept the United States. This longing for the past, or for things of the past, touched almost every aspect of life. *No, No, Nanette,* a revival of a musical from the 1920's, was a box-office smash. Book publishers hit pay dirt with reprints of half-century-old Sears Roebuck catalogues. Young girls could be seen wearing hairstyles, makeup, and clothing dating back to the 1930's. And Buffalo Bob Smith, a star from the Howdy Doody era, when television was in its infancy, made a comeback, packing in audiences on the college-campus circuit. For the hobbyist, the nostalgia boom opened exciting new avenues for collecting. Of course, many collectable items were found to be very expensive. Some antique toys, for example, could run into the hundreds of dollars. Even Mickey Mouse watches were selling for as much as $75 in antique shops and jewelry shops.

But for the young collector with limited funds to spend on his hobby, there were many fun items that were inexpensive. Of course, the most popular of these were baseball cards. Today the major source of base-

Cards distributed by cigarette companies early in the 20th century covered a variety of topics.

ILLUSTD SWEET CAPORAL
PRIVATE 69TH REGT. N.Y.S.M.

LEIFIELD, PITTSBURG

FOREFATHERS' DAY-U.S.

PLAYER'S CIGARETTES

DAIMLER 15 SALOON

PLAYER'S CIGARETTES

AUSTIN SEVEN RUBY SALOON

ball cards is Topps Chewing Gum Inc. Each year since 1951 Topps has issued cards on every player in the major leagues. The cards can be bought—along with bubble gum—in your local candy store. Entire sets can also be purchased, from card-collector organizations. Many of these organizations advertise in such newspapers as *The Sporting News.*

For the dedicated collector, however, the most fascinating cards are those dating back to the late 19th and early 20th centuries. Cards were then issued by cigarette manufacturers. One card—that of Honus Wagner —is a rarity. Only 7 are known to exist, and if it could be purchased it would cost $1,500. Other cards are less scarce and can be bought today for 25¢ up to a dollar, de-

pending on their condition. Cigarette companies also printed cards depicting airplanes, actors and actresses, automobiles, and many other subjects.

Postcards, greeting cards, and trade cards were also popular with hobbyists. In many antique and print shops these delightfully artistic items sold for as little as 25¢, although more-elaborate cards sometimes cost $2 or $3. Big Little Books, child's fare of the 1930's and 1940's, also enticed collectors, as did back issues of *Life, Look, Colliers,* and other magazines.

Collections of nostalgia items seem sure to increase in value in the years to come. But more important, they are sure to delight this and future generations as much as they delighted generations of the past.

A.B. AEROTRANSPORT: FOKKER F. XII "VARMLAND"

DEUTSCHE LUFT HANSA   JUNKERS G 38

GREETING CARDS

Decorated notepaper was used for personal greetings before the commercial card became the tradition. Saving greeting cards has become a time-honored American custom. However, it is the 19th-century card that is the collector's item. The Valentine's Day card was the fanciest, with cupids, hearts, and flowers. Easter and Christmas cards, celebrating religious occasions, usually contained a poem or a Bible passage.

TRADE CARDS

Another item for the collector is the trade, or advertising, card. In the days before radio and television, many manufacturers issued trade cards to promote their product. Some cards came with the product, while others were handed out by commercial establishments. And, like the 19th-century greeting card, many were works of art.

BOOKS OF THE PAST

Beginning in 1968, with the publication of a facsimile edition of the 1897 Sears Roebuck catalogue, publishers have flooded the market with nostalgia books. There have been books on screen stars of the past and books on the history of American comic-book characters. While these books are certainly enjoyable to read, to hobbyists they are not the real thing. The real thing to collectors are early issues of "Life," "Colliers," and "The Saturday Evening Post," dime novels from the turn of the century, Horatio Alger books, and the delightful Big Little Books. Captain Midnight, Tarzan of the Apes, Dick Tracy, Smilin' Jack, Terry and the Pirates—these are names that bring to mind a real vision of excitement and adventure. For the collector who has the time to browse through antique shops, Big Little Books and Better Little Books featuring these comic-book heroes can be bought for as little as $3, though books in mint condition sell for as much as $10.

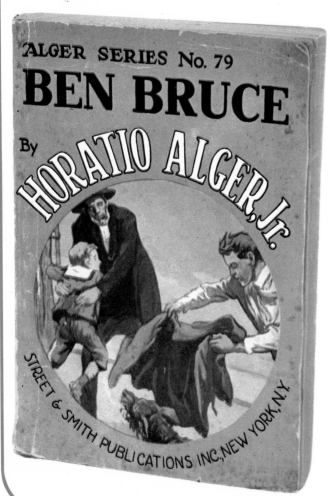

HANDICRAFTS

Before the Industrial Revolution, crafts played a very important role in everyday life. People were dependent upon the skills of their hands to produce the things they needed most. These included candles for light, hand-woven fabrics for warmth, and hand-sewn leather for clothing and shoes.

In 1971, crafts again played an important role in everyday life. People turned to crafts not because there was no other way of acquiring the things they needed, but because they appreciated the beauty of handcrafted things. They also discovered that making something is often more fun than buying it. The most popular crafts in 1971 were ones that had been practiced in earlier times.

▶ INDIAN LEATHERCRAFT

Headbands, moccasins, and beads remind us of American Indians. Because there is a great deal of interest in the American Indian, it is only natural that Indian-type crafts are popular. Several years earlier, young people discovered Indian beadcraft. In 1971, Indian leathercraft became the major interest. While the stores were selling leather jackets, moccasins, and fringed handbags, crafters found that they could make these things themselves. Some people preferred to make leather accessories from kits. These had holes for lacing already punched in the leather, and the pieces were precut. But soon more and more hobbyists decided to design and make their own creations. Often they combined leathercraft with beadwork, just as the Indians did hundreds of years ago.

Indian-style: moccasins and fringed wampum pouch.

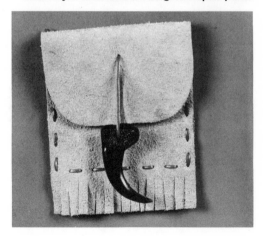

These father-and-son leather vests were made from precut parts.

►CANDLEMAKING

Even though we now have electric light at the flick of a switch, candles have a special charm. And making candles has become a very popular pastime. There are two basic ways to make candles: by dipping a wick into wax or by pouring wax into a mold. Craft manufacturers realized that pouring candles was the method preferred by hobbyists. Soon there were many kinds of molds available, so that candles could be made in all kinds of shapes. If you wanted a candle that would look like an owl, a dog, or a flower, you could find a mold to make it.

Some crafters, especially young people, enjoyed making sand-cast candles. The mold for this type of candle is simply formed in the sand. Well-dampened sand can be dug and patted with the hands into any shape. A wick is placed in the sand mold; hot wax is poured in; and the candle is formed. After the wax has cooled, the candle is removed from the sand. Some sand clings to the sides of the candle, giving it a rough texture. Every sand candle is different from every other. And it is interesting to see the variety of shapes that can be created. Sand candles can be made in a bucket filled with sand at home. But it's more fun to make them at the beach.

1. Making a sand candle: Dampened sand is dug and patted into a deep, round shape.

2. Hot wax is poured into the sand mold. The hotter the wax, the thicker the sand crust will be.

3. A wick with a metal core is coiled at one end and then lowered into the still liquid wax.

4. When the wax has completely set, the candle is dug out, and the excess sand is removed.

▶MACRAME

In the days of sailing ships, sailors who spent many months at sea whiled away the time by tying knots. Belts, bags—even curtains and hammocks—can be made simply by combining just a few kinds of knots. This knot-tying craft is called macramé. In 1971 a great many people were trying it. Macramé is easily learned because only two knots are usually used: the double half hitch and the square knot. By combining these two knots in different ways, countless designs can be made. Soon many people were wearing macramé belts, necklaces, and handbags. These macramé accessories were very much in keeping with the fashions of 1971.

SYBIL C. HARP
Editor, *Creative Crafts* Magazine

Macramé is usually done with cord or rug yarns, such as jute wrapping twine, linen, wool, and rya rug yarn. The material must be easy to use, but sturdy enough to hold the knot firmly. It is best for a beginner to start with cotton cord. Also needed are pins to hold the work in place, and a backing, such as fiberboard, on which to work. The 18-strand dog-collar choker shown in the pictures was made with one of the two basic knots, the double half hitch. The starting cord is called the knot-bearing cord. The strands that are added to it are the knotting cords. The three pictures at the right show various steps in the making of the dog collar.

The finished work: A dog-collar choker.

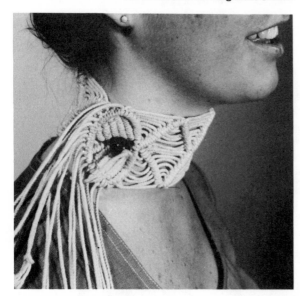

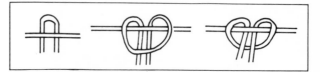

The double half hitch knot is formed in this way.

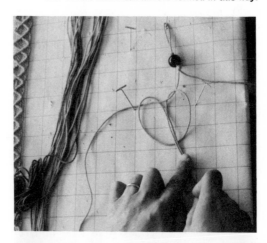

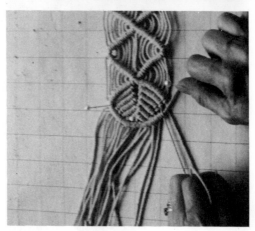

LATIN AMERICA
AND THE CARIBBEAN

EVENTS in Chile dominated the Latin-American scene in 1971. Chile's new Marxist President, Salvador Allende Gossens, followed a cautious but determined course in taking his country "along the road to socialism." Foreign (and largely U.S.-owned) copper mines were nationalized. Chile's banking industry was taken over by the state. And there was a speedup in agrarian reform. There was, however, a growing political opposition to the Marxist orientation of the Government. Chile also faced growing economic problems. Food and other consumer goods were scarce. Foreign reserves were dwindling. And earnings from copper, the nation's major export, were down. A visit by Premier Fidel Castro of Cuba in November and December precipitated anti-Government demonstrations.

Elections were held in Uruguay in late November, and many observers expected this country to follow Chile's lead and choose a socialist government. However, the Uruguayan people defeated the Leftist coalition by a margin of 4 to 1.

Elsewhere in Latin America, mounting nationalism was evident. This was often, but not always, expressed in anti-United States stands. There was also a semblance of developing Latin-American unity on issues of importance to all the countries.

The unmistakable profile of Fidel Castro, premier of Cuba.

The people of Antofagasta, Chile, give a warm reception to Castro.
Castro's visit to Chile was his first trip outside Cuba in seven years.

▶CHILE

Chilean President Salvador Allende Gossens led his nation along the road to socialism in 1971.

Foremost among his socialist programs was the nationalization of Chile's important copper industry. The copper industry had been in the hands of 3 United States corporations. It regularly accounted for 75 per cent or more of Chile's exports and is the backbone of the country's economy.

Chileans have long wanted to control the industry. In the late 1960's, under the Government of Christian Democratic President Eduardo Frei Montalva, Chile bought into the mines in a process known as "Chileanization." At that time, many observers saw the step as a move toward eventual nationalization. President Allende's nationalization effort therefore had wide support among Chile's 10,000,000 people. Even the Chilean Congress, which is dominated by the opposition parties, supported Allende on this issue. In July it passed a constitutional amendment designed to facilitate nationalization of the copper industry. This move cleared the way for President Allende's nationalization decree later in July. The decree transferred the Anaconda Company's Chuquicamata mine and the Kennecott Corporation's El Teniente mine to state hands. The Chuquicamata mine is the largest open-pit copper facility in the world. The El Teniente mine is the largest underground copper mine. Other Anaconda property as well as smaller mines belonging to the Cerro Corporation also was nationalized during the year.

In September, President Allende announced that the U.S. copper companies owed Chile more than $750,000,000 in excess profits gained over the past decade. He also announced that this amount would be deducted from any compensation due the companies. A month later Allende said that the companies would not be compensated at all.

This action was sharply criticized by the United States Government. The United States did not question Chile's right to nationalize the property. But it did argue that

An aerial view of the Chuquicamata copper mine in Chile; it was nationalized in 1971.

Cuban Premier Fidel Castro with Chilean President Salvador Allende Gossens.

some sort of compensation should be paid. In October the U.S. State Department publicly warned Chile that, if it did not compensate the copper companies, United States-Chilean relations would worsen.

In another move aimed at bringing socialism to Chile, Allende took control of the nation's banking industry. The Government purchased a majority of the stock in the 20 private banks operating in Chile. By year's end, the Chilean Government controlled 90 per cent of banking activities in the country.

A number of other industries were also nationalized. These included textile firms, machine-tool companies, transportation systems, and other medium to large organizations.

It was estimated that by the end of 1971 close to half the companies regarded by Allende as "large monopolies which ought to be in state hands" had been acquired by the Government.

In the countryside, agrarian reform was speeded up. More than 5,000,000 acres of land were brought under state control. Using agrarian-reform laws in effect when he took office, President Allende simply ordered that the large fundos, as Chilean farms are called, be broken up. This caused a great deal of disruption in rural areas. As a result, production was cut back, causing a widespread shortage of foodstuffs by the end of the year.

Moreover, Leftist extremists urged Indians and landless peasants in the agricultural south to seize and operate the fundos. At least a million acres were taken over. Production all but halted on these lands.

President Allende started 1971 with a 35 per cent across-the-board pay increase for Chilean workers. The pay boost put a great deal of purchasing power into the hands of Chileans, who promptly went on a buying spree. Allende had also put a lid on prices. But as the year went on, some prices edged up. And food and other consumer goods were in short supply. To take care of the pay raises and the cost of buying control of banks and other industries, the Government printed more money. In all, the total amount of money in circulation was increased by 80 per cent.

Because the farms were not producing food, the Government had to import $300,-000,000 worth of foodstuffs. This was an increase of nearly 100 per cent over 1970. Other imports were also stepped up. As a result, Chile's foreign reserves were nearly depleted at the end of the year. Lowered copper prices on the world market contributed to the problem.

The general view of Chile after one year of Salvador Allende and his Marxist Government was guarded. The visit by Premier Fidel Castro of Cuba in November and December pointed up the problems faced by the Allende Government. The visit sparked demonstrations by anti-Marxist groups and by thousands of Chileans protesting the shortage of food.

Juan Bordaberry, front-runner for Uruguayan presidency.

▶ URUGUAY

In November the people of Uruguay went to the polls to elect a new president. Many observers believed that Uruguay would follow the lead taken by Chile in 1970 and elect a socialist Government.

Pitted against the governing Colorado Party was a coalition of Leftist parties called the Broad Front. This coalition was made up of the Communist Party, the Socialist Party, the Christian Democratic Party, and two small left-wing splinter groups. The aim of the Broad Front was to give the people of Uruguay a choice between capitalism and a socialist form of government.

After a hard-fought campaign, however, the Broad Front was soundly defeated. But the contest was so close that a recount was under way as the year ended to determine whether Juan Maria Bordaberry or Wilson Ferreira Aldunate would be Uruguay's next president.

The Tupamaro Guerrillas

In the months before the election, Tupamaro activity had reached new highs. In January the guerrillas had kidnaped Geoffrey Jackson, the British ambassador, adding him to their list of prisoners. They were then still holding Dr. Claude Fly, a United States aid official, and Aloysio Mares Dias Gomide, the Brazilian consul. Mr. Dias was released in February after his wife and the public paid a large ransom to the Tupamaros. Dr. Fly, who was suffering from a heart condition, was released in March.

In addition to their foreign victims, the Tupamaros seized several dozen prominent Uruguayans. These included the country's attorney general, a leading newspaper editor, and a score of businessmen. All were eventually released unharmed. In some cases ransom was paid to the guerrillas.

The Tupamaros carried off several spectacular prison escapes in 1971. Over 30 women prisoners escaped from a Montevideo jail in July. Thirteen Tupamaros had slipped out of that same prison in March 1970. But the most daring escape was that of 106 Tupamaro suspects from the prison via a laboriously dug tunnel in September. Among those who escaped was Raul Sendic, the nominal leader of the Tupamaros. With his escape and that of the others, the Tupamaros released British Ambassador Jackson and announced that they would end their kidnapings until they saw the outcome of the presidential election.

▶ ARGENTINA

In March 1971, less than a year after he had engineered a change of presidents in Argentina, General Alejandro Agustin Lanusse, commander in chief of the Argentinian Army, engineered another change. This time he installed himself in the presidency, after ousting President Roberto Marcelo Levingston.

General Lanusse declared that he would return Argentina to civilian rule sometime in 1973. He appointed a Cabinet of civilian politicians, who were drawn from various political groups, including the Radicals and the Peronistas. The Peronistas are followers of former dictator Juan Peron, who was

After a week of riots in Cordoba (right), Argentinian President Levingston was ousted by the military. General Alejandro Lanusse (below) assumed the presidency. Lanusse's new Cabinet included followers of former Argentinian dictator Juan Peron (on poster, above). This marked the first time that Peronistas were allowed to take part in politics since 1955, the year Peron was ousted.

Bolivian President Hugo Banzer Suarez.

Honduran President Ramon Ernesto Cruz.

ousted in 1955 and is now in exile in Spain. The Peronistas have long been excluded from politics in Argentina. There was opposition to Lanusse's plan to include them in the 1973 election.

▶OTHER GOVERNMENT CHANGES

In August, after only ten months in office, Bolivian General Juan Jose Torres Gonzalez was ousted from the presidency by Colonel Hugo Banzer Suarez. Colonel Banzer's Government proved more effective than the preceding Government in bringing old political adversaries together and in getting Bolivia's stagnant economy moving again.

In Honduras, Ramon Ernesto Cruz, leader of the National Party, was elected president for a six-year term.

▶CHANGING ATTITUDES TOWARD CUBA

One of the most interesting developments during the year was the changing attitude toward Cuba. Marxist-oriented Chile established diplomatic relations with Cuba. Many other countries indicated that they were interested in doing the same. Both Peru and Ecuador announced that they opposed the sanctions imposed on Cuba by the Organization of American States (OAS). These sanctions, dating to the early 1960's, had been voted by OAS members after Cuba was accused of trying to export its revolution. In effect, the sanctions led to the isolation of the Cuban Government and people from the other nations of the hemisphere. Only Mexico, which refused to go along with the OAS majority, and Canada, which was not a member of the OAS, continued to maintain relations with Cuba.

Cuban Prime Minister Fidel Castro welcomed these new overtures. He affirmed, however, that he would not allow Cuba to be reseated in the OAS. He has called the organization a "lackey of the United States."

Castro's visit to Chile late in the year was seen as a further step in ending the isolation of Cuba. The visit also marked Castro's official acceptance of "other roads to socialism." Castro espouses violent revolution. Chilean President Allende does not.

At a meeting of the Organization of American States in April, U.S. Secretary of State William Rogers (left) listens to Costa Rican President Jose Figueres Ferrer attack American economic policy.

▶RELATIONS WITH THE UNITED STATES

The changing attitude toward Cuba was accompanied by changing views about the United States. The Nixon administration was sharply criticized on several occasions.

At a meeting of OAS foreign ministers in San Jose, Costa Rica, in April, the United States was accused of economic imperialism because it imposed restrictions on the use of American aid money. A similar criticism was issued in May at the Inter-American Devel-

opment Bank meeting in Lima, Peru. The Latin-American nations also drafted a statement demanding that the Nixon administration lift, for Latin America, the 10 per cent import surcharge that was part of the new U.S. economic policy.

The Latin-American nations complained that they were being penalized for problems the United States has with other parts of the world. They insisted that they have an unfavorable balance of trade with the United

The "Apollo," an American tuna boat, was seized by Ecuador for fishing in waters claimed by that country.

States, and that their economies should not be hurt further.

The Latin-American nations also reacted sharply to the U.S. Senate vote cutting off foreign aid. The United States was denounced for "failing to take the needs of the underdeveloped nations into account" and for "economic aggression against the developing nations."

In October Ecuador stepped up its seizure of United States tuna boats. Most Latin-American nations firmed up their resolve to claim 200-mile territorial sea limits and to exclude foreign fishing vessels from their waters.

Fishing rights were a major topic for discussion between President Nixon and Brazilian President Emilio G. Medici in December. The Brazilian leader had traveled to Washington to discuss various aspects of U.S.-Brazilian relations.

Panama and the United States held talks aimed at writing a new treaty on the operation of the Panama Canal. There was some evidence that the United States is prepared to give Panama sovereignty over the canal while retaining control of the canal and its operation.

▶THE CARIBBEAN

During 1971 the independent nations of the Caribbean as well as the non-self-governing islands faced increased economic problems, social unrest, and political conflict.

The economic problems were a result of overpopulation, the lack of jobs, and a very poor winter tourist season. Most of the islands depend on tourist dollars for their economic well-being. But many tourists stayed away during 1971 because of the political and social unrest in the islands, where

Jean-Claude Duvalier, Haiti's new president, holds a news conference.

black-power advocates are challenging the entrenched political parties.

Two independent Caribbean states—Guyana and Trinidad and Tobago—and five Associated States—Dominica, Grenada, St. Lucia, St. Vincent, and St. Kitts-Nevis-Anguilla—discussed the possibility of forming a Caribbean union. The islands of the Caribbean had failed in an attempt to form a federation nearly a decade earlier.

Haiti

The death of President François Duvalier raised many questions about the future of Haiti. In January, "Papa Doc," as the dictator was generally known, had named his son, Jean-Claude, as his successor. When the 64-year-old Duvalier died in April, an orderly succession took place. But behind the calm facade a power struggle took place. Luckner Cambronne, the minister of the interior,

emerged as the strong man behind young Duvalier, who, like his father, assumed the title "President for Life."

The new President received several assistance projects from the United States and opened Haiti to new foreign investment.

Trinidad and Tobago

In May elections, which were boycotted by the major opposition party, the ruling People's National Party of Prime Minister Eric Williams won all 36 seats in Parliament.

Barbados

In general elections held on September 9, Prime Minister Errol Barrow and his ruling Barbados Democratic Labor Party won 18 of the 24 seats in the House of Assembly.

JAMES NELSON GOODSELL
Latin America Editor
The Christian Science Monitor

CUBAN REFUGEES

Since Cuban Premier Fidel Castro came to power in 1959, at least one million Cubans have fled their homeland. The exact number is not known and probably never will be. But more than 600,000 are now living in the United States, with the greatest number in Florida. The remainder are scattered throughout Latin America and in the Caribbean, with a few thousand in Europe.

Many of those who went into exile soon after Castro assumed control of the island had been associated with the preceding Government, of Fulgencio Batista. But as time went on, a great number of professional people—lawyers, engineers, doctors, teachers—fled with their families because they were not in sympathy with Castro's goals and policies.

Since 1965, the United States Government, under an agreement with the Cuban Government, has operated a daily airlift for Cubans wanting to leave the island. Close to 300,000 Cubans have left in this way. But it appeared that the airlift would end in early 1972.

The mass exodus of Cubans has had important consequences for the Castro Government. Many who left were skilled and professional people. As a result, Cuban industry and agriculture suffered from the loss of managerial talent. On the other hand, the departure of thousands of unsympathetic Cubans removed a potentially dangerous element from within Cuba—one that could have posed a serious threat to Castro's leadership.

Refugees from Cuba arrive in Miami, Florida. Most of the one million Cuban refugees have settled in the United States, primarily in Florida.

The large number of Cuban refugees living in Miami has made that southern city a "little Havana." Above: A small Cuban coffee shop in the downtown area. Below left: A theater that features Spanish-language films. Below right: A fruit market owned and operated by Cuban refugees.

LITERATURE

PUBLISHERS, like everyone else, were suffering the effects of the economic slowdown in 1971. Although profits were down, however, the standards of literature were not. Few spectacular successes were produced, but the American literary scene seemed to be in very good health.

A variety of books made the best-seller list in 1971. Among them were *Honor Thy Father* by Gay Talese, *Bury My Heart at Wounded Knee* by Dee Brown, Agatha Christie's *Passenger to Frankfurt*, *QB VII* by Leon Uris, *The Day of the Jackal* by Frederick Forsythe, and Germaine Greer's *The Female Eunuch*.

Many of the books for young people stressed contemporary problems, such as drug use and ecology. The Newbery Medal for the best children's book went to *The Summer of the Swans* by Betsy Byars, and Gail E. Haley won the Caldecott Medal for her pictures in *A Story, A Story*.

THE VANTAGE POINT
PERSPECTIVES
OF THE PRESIDENCY
1963–1969
LYNDON BAINES JOHNSON

Lyndon Baines Johnson gives a personal view of his years in the presidency in "The Vantage Point."

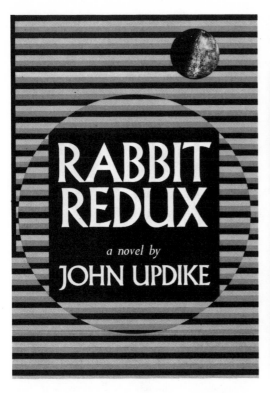

In "Rabbit Redux," John Updike brings back the hero of his earlier best-selling novel and confronts him with more-contemporary problems.

Based on treaties and speeches of Indian leaders, Dee Brown's "Bury My Heart at Wounded Knee" is a history of how the Indians lost the West.

FICTION

In *Rabbit Redux,* John Updike returns to the hero of his best-selling book *Rabbit, Run.* In his new novel, the hero, ten years older now, confronts a number of major social issues—marriage, fatherhood, drugs, and Vietnam. Walker Percy set his *Love in the Ruins* in the future, "at a time near the end of the world," while *Grendel,* by John Gardner, takes place in Anglo-Saxon England. Gardner's book is unique in that it tells the Beowulf myth from the monster's point of view.

African history is the subject of *Bound to Violence,* an epic work by Yambo Ouologuem. This first novel by a young Malian author tells of the last seven centuries of a mythical African empire and its ruling families.

John Hawkes strengthened his reputation as a writer of fables with *The Blood Oranges,* a novel dealing with love under a Mediterranean sun. Ross Macdonald's perennial detective hero, Lew Archer, pops up again in *The Underground Man,* which proves the author to be a major novelist as well as an excellent crime-fiction writer.

Two important writers proved somewhat of a disappointment. Bernard Malamud's *The Tenants* was not up to his usual standards. The story is about two writers, one black and one white, and the interaction between them and the books they are trying to write. Joyce Carol Oates' *Wonderland,* an exploration of grotesque pathology, was also disappointing.

On the other hand, Sylvia Plath's *The Bell Jar* is a moving autobiographical novel. It relates the author's twentieth year of life, during which she suffered a temporary phase of insanity.

Philip Roth came upon the literary scene with somewhat of a surprise in 1971. *Our Gang* is a short, funny, satirical novel about American political life, with President Trick E. Dixon at the helm.

The collected works of three important writers were published in 1971. *Flannery O'Connor: The Complete Stories* contains all of her published works; *The Mortgaged Heart* by Carson McCullers is a compilation of her miscellaneous writings; and *Franz Kafka: The Complete Stories* is a collection of Kafka's finest literary achievements.

AUTOBIOGRAPHIES AND BIOGRAPHIES

One of the most highly publicized books of the year was Lyndon Baines Johnson's *The Vantage Point.* This autobiography contains Johnson's views on the years of his presidency, 1963–69, as seen from his vantage point. Edmund Wilson's *Upstate* is a rather unusual book in that it is an informal history of Wilson's ancestral home and a critic's observation of his own life. *A Sort of Life,* by Graham Greene, traces the first 27 years of his life, as the troubled son of a schoolmaster to his troubled years as a novelist on the verge of success.

A recent translation of an older volume, *In the Twenties,* by Harry Kessler, gives a vivid description of life in the German Weimar Republic based on parts of his diary. It is particularly relevant because America of the 1960's and 1970's is often compared with the era of the Weimar Republic.

Werner Heisenberg, in *Physics and Beyond,* relates the excitements and frustrations of his career in atomic physics over the last fifty years. Ronald Clark, in *Einstein,* offers a well-researched account of the life and times of the great physicist.

A number of notable literary biographies made their appearance in 1971. Among the more impressive books were: *Verlaine* by Joanna Richardson; *André Breton* by Anna Balakian; *William Dean Howells: An American Life* by Kenneth S. Lynn; and Martin Lamm's classic study of *August Strindberg.* Michael Meyer's *Ibsen* and *After Great Pain,* a portrait of Emily Dickinson by psychiatrist-writer John Cody, are two very different but compelling books.

There were few outstanding biographies of major political figures in 1971. One of the more interesting was *Mohammed* by Maxime Rodinson. The book is a study of the man and the circumstances that brought about the birth and evolution of a powerful ideology.

Eleanor and Franklin is an important study of the relationship between two of the twentieth century's most renowned figures.

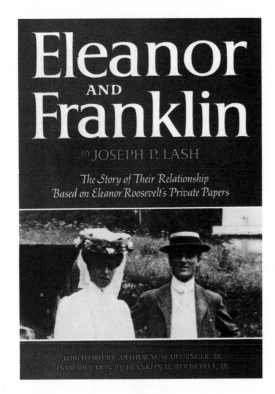

Eleanor and Franklin

BY JOSEPH P. LASH

The Story of Their Relationship Based on Eleanor Roosevelt's Private Papers

FOREWORD BY ARTHUR M. SCHLESINGER, JR.
INTRODUCTION BY FRANKLIN D. ROOSEVELT, JR.

"Eleanor and Franklin": one of the most fascinating marriages in American political history.

The book, by Joseph Lash, is based on the private papers of Eleanor Roosevelt.

Stilwell and the American Experience in China 1911–45 by Barbara Tuchman is a literary portrait of General "Vinegar Joe" Stilwell and America's disastrous China policy. The book, although not one of Miss Tuchman's best works, is nevertheless an incredible and complex story finely told.

Two very real but different personalities were the subjects of biographies in 1971. *Capone* by John Kobler covers the rise and fall of one of America's most notorious underworld figures. Mike Royko's *Boss* is the story of the very colorful and controversial Mayor of Chicago, Richard Daley.

▶ **HISTORY**

Fresh historical ground was broken by Hugh Thomas in a voluminous history of Cuba. The book, entitled *Cuba,* covers the history of that island-nation and its people from 1762 to the present. Modern-day Cuba was given spacious, if somewhat hostile, treatment by K. S. Karol in *Guerrillas in Power*. This monumental work traces the course of the Cuban Revolution under the leadership of Fidel Castro.

"Cuba," by Hugh Thomas, covers the full sweep of that island-nation's history, from 1762.

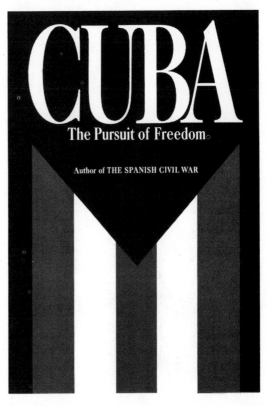

CUBA

The Pursuit of Freedom

Author of THE SPANISH CIVIL WAR

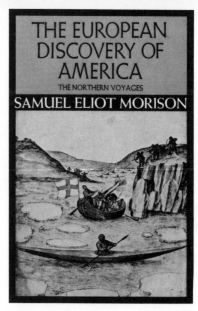

Admiral Morison's book is about the exploration of America's northeast coast.

In *The European Discovery of America,* Admiral Samuel Eliot Morison presents a survey of the transatlantic explorations of the northeastern seaboard of America up to 1600. Particular attention is paid to many 16th-century navigators, among them Cabot, Raleigh, Drake, and Verrazano.

Another subject that demanded a good historical account was the Ku-Klux Klan. Author Allen W. Trelease fulfilled that need with *White Terror,* an in-depth study of the Klan and its reign of terror during Reconstruction in the South.

In David Bergamini's book *Japan's Imperial Conspiracy,* Emperor Hirohito emerges as the prime exponent of Japan's Pacific war policies. The book has created much controversy because Mr. Bergamini, in reaching his conclusions, seems to be ignoring the documented evidence of Hirohito's nonrole in World War II, which is generally used by both Japanese and American historians.

Another major attempt at revisionist history was the surprising *India's China War* by Neville Maxwell. In Maxwell's view, China did indeed attack India in 1962, but he concludes that the hostilities were justified.

One of the most popular best sellers of 1971 was Dee Brown's *Bury My Heart at Wounded Knee.* This narrative history of how the American Indians lost the West is based in part on records of treaty councils and the words of Indian leaders.

Vietnam

The Vietnam war and its horrifying effects were the basis of many books in 1971. Several literary works were particularly well written and documented. Anthony Austin's *The President's War* is an account of the circumstances surrounding the Tonkin Gulf Resolution. *365 Days,* by Dr. Ronald Glasser, is a medic's report of his tour of duty in an Army hospital in Japan, and his encounters with casualties of the Vietnam conflict. In *Tet!,* Don Oberdorfer covers the crucial 1968 battle that received worldwide attention. The issue of war crimes in Vietnam served as the subject of several books. One notable such work is *Nuremberg and Vietnam: An American Tragedy* by General Telford Taylor. The Mylai massacre is given excellent coverage in Richard Hammer's *The Court-Martial of Lieutenant Calley.*

▶ SOCIAL AND CULTURAL CRITICISM

The first major literary comment on the 1969 moon mission came from Norman Mailer. His *Of a Fire on the Moon* not only covers the launch, the astronauts, NASA, and space technology, but also Mailer himself. In a rather prolific year, Mailer also

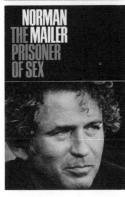

Germaine Greer, in her book "The Female Eunuch," and Norman Mailer, in his book "The Prisoner of Sex," are spokesmen for opposing views of the Women's Lib movement.

published *Prisoner of Sex,* which contains his rather controversial views on Women's Liberation and the metaphysics of sex. Another prominent Women's Liberation polemic was Germaine Greer's *The Female Eunuch.*

An extraordinary analysis of the facts and meanings of the blood-donation systems in many countries throughout the world was dramatically written in *The Gift Relationship* by Richard Titmuss. The welfare system in the United States was given radical interpretation by Frances Fox Piven and Richard Cloward in *Regulating the Poor.* In *Deschooling Society,* Ivan Illich argues against the school as an institution, while Joseph Featherstone argues for the English Free School model in *Schools Where Children Learn.*

Without Marx or Jesus, by Jean-François Revel, suggested to many surprised readers that American culture, more than any other, holds promise for the world.

Quentin Anderson suggests in *The Imperial Self* that the assumptions of some clas-sical American visionaries such as Thoreau, Emerson, and Whitman should be questioned.

Richard Poirier in *The Performing Self* and Richard Gilman in *Common and Uncommon Masks* examine new styles of books and literature. In *Fiction and the Figures of Life,* William Gass affirms the independence of art. An outstanding detailed history of rock music is offered in *The Sound of the City* by Charlie Gillett.

▶ **POETRY**

The major poetry event of the year was the publication of the facsimile reprint of T. S. Eliot's *The Waste Land.* The manuscript contains the original editorial notations and cuts by Ezra Pound.

Important collections of poems included *Archaeologist of Morning* by Charles Olson; *Collected Poems* by James Wright; and *Love and Fame* by John Berryman.

ROGER JELLINEK
Assistant Editor
The New York Times Book Review

LITERATURE FOR YOUNG PEOPLE

In 1971 many of the books for young people were about racial problems, the use of drugs, and the ecology movement.

The widening gap between whites and blacks in New York City is the subject of Louise Tanner's *Reggie and Nilma* (Farrar). Kim and Tony Bonner have been practically raised by their black housekeeper, Nilma. Nilma's son, Reggie, is their close friend until they reach their teens. The Bonner children go on to a private school, while Reggie goes to a school in Harlem that has "a drug problem." Their different environments affect their friendships and their lives. The story won *Book World*'s 1971 Children's Spring Book Festival award for teen-age books.

Younger readers will find honest fiction about blacks in John Steptoe's *Train Ride* (Harper). Harlem children, looking for something to do, sneak into the subway for a train ride to midtown Manhattan and a day of adventure. When they return home, the consequences of their mischievousness are made painfully clear.

Interesting and unusual is *Masks* (Watts) by Jay Bennett. It is about a Chinese boy and a white girl who fall in love. Peter Yeng and Jennifer Moore share joy until the prejudice of the girl's mother destroys their relationship.

Writings by young people involved in today's problems can be especially forceful. Verse and prose by black youths fill *Children*

An illustration by Ted CoConis from "The Summer of the Swans," winner of the Newbery Medal.

of *Longing* (Holt), edited by Rosa Guy. Pain, anger, hope, and pleasure burst from the lines.

Drug addicts have their say in *Heroin Was My Best Friend* (Crowell-Collier). James Berry interviewed the mother of an addict, and seven young girls and boys in a rehabilitation center. Readers will get a true picture of what using drugs can be like.

Concern for the environment appeared in numerous books. Jean Craighead George wrote *Who Really Killed Cock Robin?* (Dutton). The story is handled as a mystery investigation into the death of one bird.

There was even a science-fiction novel that was sympathetic to the ecology movement. In Adrien Stoutenburg's *Out There,* a family tries to find the almost extinct animals in the "barren" world of the 21st century. The family members find themselves struggling to survive as the early pioneers had.

Readers will get the straight facts in Margaret O. Hyde's *For Pollution Fighters Only* (McGraw-Hill). She points out how pollution occurs and gives instructions on how some types of pollution can be avoided. One interesting chapter describes what can happen to our air and water supply because of overpopulation.

▶TEEN-AGE BOOKS

Winner of the Newbery Medal for 1971, *The Summer of the Swans* (Viking) by Betsy Byars makes growing pains real for young teen-age girls. Sara Godfrey worries about her big feet and having a dull summer. When her mentally retarded brother wanders off in search of wild swans, she realizes the importance of problems other than her own.

Another girl faced with growing up dominates *A Room Made of Windows* (Little)

Above: A Children's Book Week poster. Below: A runner-up for the Caldecott Medal.

by Eleanor Cameron. As Julia Redfern observes the world from her bedroom windows, she becomes aware of different kinds of people and their problems. As she responds to them, she grows up.

"Knee-Knock Rise," a runner-up for the Newbery Medal.

Teen-agers in S. E. Hinton's *That Was Then, This Is Now* (Viking) tear themselves apart with strong emotions. Bryon and Mark have been raised together and love each other as if they were brothers. Bryon also loves Cathy. As Bryon matures, he must accept that relationships with those one loves can change with time.

Joseph P. Clancy builds a picture of King Arthur and fifth-century Britain in *Pendragon* (Praeger). The first half of the book gives a background of English tribes and related Roman history through Arthur's battles with the invading Saxons. The second half explores the sources of the King Arthur legends and how writers have since used the material.

▶FOR INTERMEDIATE AGES

The National Book Award for children's books went to *The Marvelous Misadventures of Sebastian* (Dutton) by Lloyd Alexander. A wandering Sebastian learns about life from a princess in disguise and other mysterious strangers.

Unusually good character development occurs in *The Boy, the Rat, and the Butterfly* (Atheneum) by Beatrice de Regniers, illustrated by Haig and Regina Shekerjian. During a summer walk, three friends reveal how different they really are. Each one is granted one wish. The rat's mind is mainly on himself, and the butterfly can't keep his mind on one subject long enough to make a wish. Only the boy feels a true concern for others.

Edna Barth's *I'm Nobody! Who Are You?* (Seabury) concentrates on the high points in the life of Emily Dickinson. Incidents from the poet's life are developed around stanzas of her poems. However, the charming biography does not answer the question of why the young, talented woman became a recluse.

Natalie Babbitt had a "runner-up year." Her *Knee-Knock Rise* (Farrar) was one of the near-winners for the 1971 Newbery award. And her *Goody Hall* (Farrar) was a runner-up in the Children's Spring Book Festival. This second book is a fascinating kind of Gothic mystery about life in an English country house.

Thought-provoking poems fill *The Geranium on the Window Sill Just Died, But Teacher You Went Right On* (Quist) by Albert Cullum. The book takes a harsh look at the adult world from the eyes of the young. And they are often disappointed in what they see.

▶PICTURE BOOKS

Gail E. Haley received the Caldecott Medal for her pictures in *A Story, A Story* (Atheneum). This lovely book illustrates an African legend about Ananse the Spider Man. Miss Haley's woodcuts triumphed over the artwork of runners-up Blair Lent, Arnold Lobel, and Maurice Sendak.

Sendak's *In the Night Kitchen* (Harper) created an uproar because it showed pictures of a naked boy. But many adults said, "Nudity, prudity! Who cares? The main trouble, is, it's a dull story." Undaunted, in 1971 the publisher brought out *In the Night Kitchen Coloring Book*. This brought complaints from those who feared that letting children color the pictures would make them even more aware of nudity.

Because of its lively and imaginative pictures, *Hello, Small Sparrow* (Lothrop) could be a future prizewinner. It is illustrated by Tony Chen and contains short poems by Hannah Johnson. Similar to Japanese haiku, the verses give sparkling glimpses of nature.

Admirers of Tasha Tudor were delighted

One of Tony Chen's beautiful illustrations in "Hello, Small Sparrow."

when she won the 1971 Regina Medal for "continued distinguished contribution to the field of children's literature." Her newest book, *Corgiville Fair* (Crowell), is illustrated in full color. It describes a festival at which a goat and a nasty cat play important roles.

Some artists told stories without words. Pat Hutchins did in *Changes, Changes* (Macmillan), achieving drama and humor. Two figures made of building blocks keep changing their environment, also made of blocks, until they are content with their world.

No words are needed to express love, the theme of *The Blue Balloon* (McGraw-Hill) by Frank Asch. When his green balloon bursts, a young boy lovingly puts it back together. When something sad happens in the boy's life, the balloon expresses sorrow in a surprising way.

With lovely pictures by Don Bolognese, Jean Craighead George's *All Upon a Stone* (Crowell) won the Children's Spring Book Festival award for a picture book. This informative story is about the life of a mole

An illustration from "Changes, Changes," a book without words by Pat Hutchins.

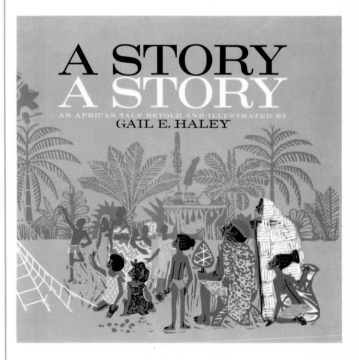

"A Story, A Story" by Gail Haley was awarded the 1971 Caldecott Medal for its beautiful woodcuts.

cricket. For the cricket, a large stone is a complete world. On it he finds adventure and, in time, happiness.

With catchy verse and humorous pictures, Byrd Baylor's *Plink Plink Plink* (Houghton) tells what night sounds might seem to be—pirates, giraffes—and what they really are. Less poetic, but even funnier, are the verses of Patricia Thomas in *Stand Back, Said the Elephant, I'm Going to Sneeze!* (Lothrop). Wallace Tripp's pictures echo the humor as a jungle full of animals faces a disaster.

Two unusual picture books will captivate young readers. Humor combines with a puzzle element in *The Adventures of the Three Colors* (World). Using three colors and transparent pages, Annette Tison and Talus Taylor play tricks that have educational value. And *Do You Want to Be My Friend?* (Crowell) by Eric Carle provides a guessing game, a story told in eight words, and a satisfying ending.

CHARLES PAUL MAY
Author, *Stranger in the Storm;*
Bats; Veterinarians and Their Patients

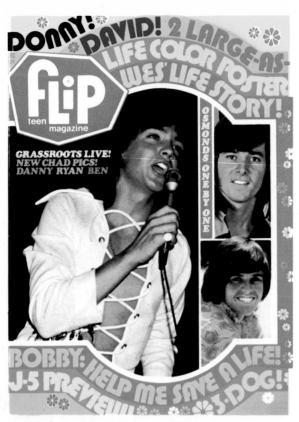

YOUTH MAGAZINES

Several popular, mass-circulation magazines have folded in recent years. *The Saturday Evening Post* and *Look* are but two examples. On the other hand, magazines aimed at specific audiences have flourished. Among the fastest-growing groups of specialized magazines is the one geared to young people. Many of these youth-oriented magazines are aimed at teen-agers, and much of their content deals with rock music. *Flip* and *Circus,* shown at left, are two examples of this type of magazine.

In late 1970, however, a new and very unusual magazine for young people was published. Called *Kids* (below), it is written "by kids for kids." The editorial staff and all the contributors of *Kids* are between the ages of 5 and 13. Their accomplishments are amazing. The magazine is professional in quality and contains stories, poetry, paintings, photographs, cartoons, and many other creative features.

DoDo Bird

Illustrations of a dodo bird (above) and a whale (below) from an article in "Kids" on vanishing species of animals. Drawings are by 6th-graders at the Parkwood Elementary School, Kensington, Maryland.

"Typewriter Man," by Paul Bruggeman, a pupil at St. Agnes School, Cincinnati, appeared in "Kids."

Rain
Falling Down
From the Clouds
Hear it fall on your umbrella
From the Clouds
Falling Down
Rain

Poetry is a popular feature of "Kids." Jane Leong, 11, did the illustrated poem above. Mary Mattos, 12, and Maryann Micchelli, 12, the coauthors of "Our 2¢ School" (below), live in Kearny, New Jersey.

Our 2ᶜ School

by Mary Mattos and Maryann Micchelli

We're sitting on 2¢ chairs
 And doing cheap Arithmetic problems
  And having a Social Studies test that
   Isn't Worth half a penny
    We're using 25¢ Science books
     And 50¢ spelling books
      The $30 thermometer says 90°
       But we're sweating on our 2¢ chairs
        Doing worthless Science words
         The 25¢ school bell rings
          And whether you have 1¢ or
           $100 dollars
            You are $100,000,000 happy

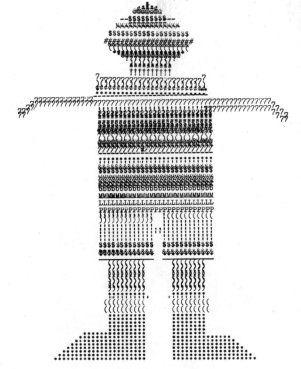

MEDICINE AND HEALTH

THE year 1971 was marked by a number of important advances in various fields of medicine and health sciences. Progress was made in many areas, including cancer research. Smallpox has become such a rarity in the Western world that beginning in 1971 routine smallpox vaccinations were no longer required for school-children or travelers to other countries.

Another notable event of 1971 was the celebration of the 50th anniversary of the discovery of insulin. This substance has saved the lives of millions of sufferers from diabetes. In 1921 two young Toronto scientists, Dr. Frederick Grant Banting and Charles Herbert Best, succeeded in producing insulin, an essential hormone that controls blood-sugar levels in the body.

On a less pleasant note, 1971 will be remembered as a year when a devastating cholera epidemic swept across parts of Asia, Africa, and Europe. In the United States, a death resulting from botulism, an acute food poisoning, was a source of concern.

At the National Cancer Institute, Dr. Alfred Hollman uses a special device to handle a virus culture. Most medical researchers now believe that at least some human cancers are caused by viruses.

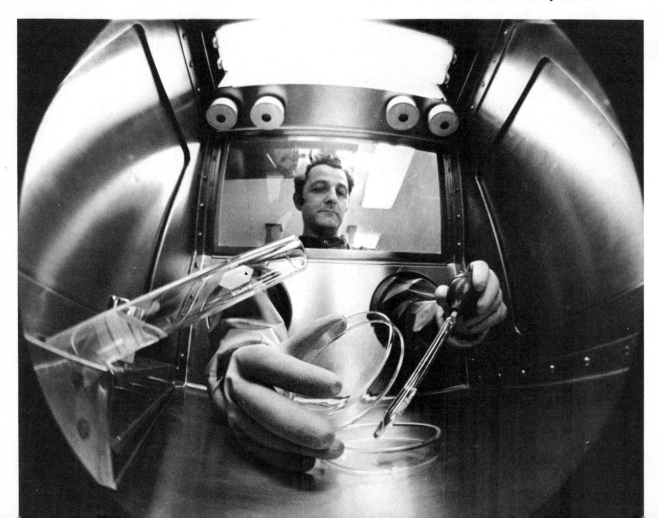

In 1971 Dr. Choh Hao Li, director of the hormone-research laboratory at the University of California Medical Center, synthesized a molecule of human growth hormone. His accomplishment holds out hope that children born as pituitary dwarfs will someday be cured.

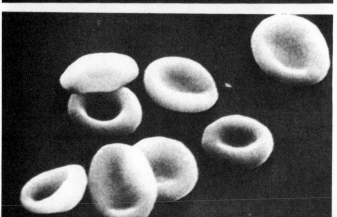

Work continued during 1971 on ways to diagnose and treat sickle-cell anemia. In the United States, this disease affects black people almost exclusively. At left are red blood cells that are sickled (top) and red blood cells from the same patient after he was treated (bottom). The sickle-shaped cells block some arteries, often causing death.

CANCER RESEARCH

With but one exception—heart diseases—cancer kills more people in the United States than any other disease. Yet many of these deaths can be prevented if cancer can be detected in its early stages—before it becomes too advanced to be cured.

In January 1971, President Richard Nixon announced that "the time has come in America when the same kind of concerted effort that split the atom and took man to the moon should be turned toward conquering this dread disease." In answer to the President's plea, the Congress approved a bill allocating $1,600,000,000 for cancer research over the next three years.

Meanwhile, medical investigators all over the world continued their efforts to find new ways of detecting and treating the disease. Medical researchers in Israel reported that they had possibly developed a blood test that would enable the detection of cancer in its early stages. And Phil Gold, a Canadian doctor, devised a test to detect one form of cancer—cancer of the colon. These results are very encouraging, but they need a great deal more testing and refining.

Recent research into the causes of cancer has concentrated upon the science of virology, the identification and control of viruses. Many researchers believe that some types of cancer are caused by specific viruses. Hodgkin's disease, or cancer of the lymph glands, is believed to be caused by a virus, but tests are not yet conclusive. It is encouraging to note that Hodgkin's disease, considered incurable ten years ago, is now successfully treated in 75 per cent of the cases at some large medical centers.

A type of virus associated with Hodgkin's disease is thought to cause Burkitt's lymphoma, another kind of lymph-gland cancer. This disease is relatively common among children in one region of equatorial Africa. In July a group of researchers at the M. D. Anderson Hospital and Tumor Institute in Houston, Texas, reported success in growing a specific virus taken from a young boy suffering from this type of cancer. However, much work needs to be done before it can definitely be established that the virus that was isolated actually causes the cancer.

Dr. Leon Dmochowski and Dr. Elizabeth Priori of the M. D. Anderson Hospital and Tumor Institute. In July they succeeded in isolating a cancer virus.

PRESS DOWN FIRMLY ON HARD SURFACE WITH BALL POINT PEN OR BLUNT PENCIL. LETTERS OR NUMBERS WILL RAISE AS FINGER RUBS OVER THEM. A FEW PRACTICE TRIALS WILL PERFECT TECHNIQUE.

NU-VU NO. 310
PATENT PENDING

In 1971 Bosch & Lomb, an optical company, developed a soft contact lens. It is easier to put in place and more comfortable than the hard contact lenses.

Mrs. Ruth Barr (below) works with a special paper that allows blind people to "read" without learning Braille. The process is described above.

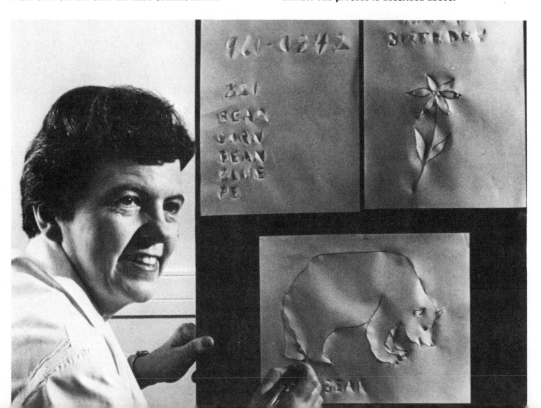

HUMAN GROWTH

Each year, in the United States alone, some 7 million children are born with a condition known as pituitary dwarfism. This results from a malfunctioning or underdeveloped pituitary gland. The pituitary gland secretes a chemical known as human growth hormone. If enough of this hormone is not secreted, the child will not grow. Pituitary dwarfs are normal in every way—except that they remain very small.

Thus far the only treatment available to pituitary dwarfs is injections of human growth hormone. However, this hormone can be obtained only from human pituitary glands. Efforts to have people bequeath their pituitary glands have met with only moderate success. There has not been enough human growth hormone available to treat even a small percentage of those youngsters born as pituitary dwarfs.

In 1971 an enormous stride forward was made in this area. A research team at the University of California Medical Center, headed by Dr. Choh Hao Li, synthesized a molecule of the growth hormone. Many scientists believe that in the near future drug companies will be able to manufacture growth hormone on a large scale, and most pituitary dwarfs who have not passed their teen years will be treated and cured.

HEART DISEASES

Heart diseases continued to be the leading cause of death among Americans in 1971. And cigarette smoking continued to be blamed, in part, for the high incidence of heart disease. The U.S. Surgeon General's report to Congress in January 1971 stated that "Cigarette smoking is a significant factor in the development of heart disease."

One hopeful sign is that during the past five years the number of people who smoke cigarettes has dropped from 52 per cent to 42 per cent. Dr. Dan Horn of the National Clearing House for Smoking and Health feels that by 1975 this figure should drop to 25 per cent.

In 1971 a new instrument in the fight against heart disease was developed—the cardiac sensor. This instrument can produce an electrocardiogram (a record of the heart action) in less than three seconds. This makes it possible to determine quickly the type of heart irregularity from which a patient is suffering. Lifesaving treatment can thus be started at once.

SICKLE-CELL ANEMIA

Sickle-cell anemia is a hereditary blood disorder that in the United States affects black people almost exclusively. About 10 per cent of all black Americans carry 1 gene for sickle-cell anemia, and 1 in 500 black Americans have inherited 2 genes—1 from each parent—and therefore have the disease.

In sickle-cell anemia, the red blood cells become sickle-shaped, and block some arteries. As a result, not enough oxygen is carried throughout the body. Children born with sickle-cell anemia have only a 50 per cent chance of surviving the first year of life.

In 1971, five new tests were developed to diagnose the disease. One of the tests can be done rapidly and inexpensively, making possible worldwide testing of the black population. Other groups of investigators reported limited success in treating children with blood transfusions and chemotherapy.

HEPATITIS

Serum hepatitis, a liver disease which kills about three thousand Americans each year, is often caused by a transfusion of blood that contains the hepatitis virus.

A method of testing blood in human transfusions for the hepatitis virus has been devised. This should prove of help in controlling the spread of the disease.

In March, Dr. Saul Krugman of the New York University Medical Center announced that he and a team of researchers had developed a method of immunizing people against serum hepatitis. The researchers immunized a small group of children with heat-treated blood serum that contained the serum-hepatitis virus. The blood serum stimulated the production of antibodies (substances in the blood that fight disease-causing germs), protecting the children from hepatitis when they were later exposed to it.

Dr. Krugman said he hoped his work would eventually lead to a vaccine that would prevent serum hepatitis.

▶ PROSTAGLANDINS—NEW MIRACLE DRUG?

Since the early 1930's, medical researchers have been working on a family of hormonelike substances called prostaglandins. These substances are of great interest because they give promise of having many medical uses, including treatment of ulcers, asthma, high blood pressure, and problems involved in pregnancy. The body produces very little of these highly potent substances, but researchers have now begun synthesizing prostaglandins. This means there will be enough of the substance for research.

▶ BOTULISM

Botulism is acute food poisoning caused by a bacterium that creates what many scientists believe to be the deadliest poison known to man. In July 1971 the American public was shocked by the report of a death from botulism. The victim had eaten a cold canned soup made by Bon Vivant, a small canning company in New Jersey. All products of this canning company were recalled, and no further deaths were reported.

Canned foods can be made safe if they are boiled for 15 minutes. The death from botulism raised questions about the quality of safety precautions and sterilization procedures used by the vast food-processing industry.

▶ CHOLERA EPIDEMIC

Cholera is spread by water or food that is contaminated by certain bacteria. With proper medical care—antibiotics and replacement of body fluids—recovery from cholera is generally swift and certain. Deaths from cholera occur only in areas without medical facilities.

In the spring of 1971 a widespread cholera epidemic killed thousands of East Pakistani refugees in India. As happens in this day of jet travel, the disease spread rapidly, reaching even into Lapland. The African nations were unusually hard hit, but the World Health Organization believed that the epidemic had been brought under control by late fall.

LEONARD I. GORDON
Internist, New York City

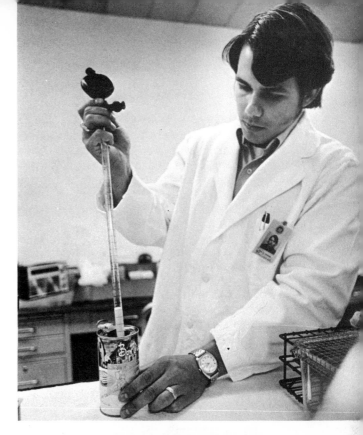

Above: A can of soup is checked for botulism, an acute food poisoning that killed one person in New York. **Below:** Cans of the soup are stacked up at the Bon Vivant plant in New Jersey after they were ordered recalled by the Food and Drug Administration.

CHINESE ACUPUNCTURE

Doctors in China today are schooled in both modern, or "Western" style, medicine and the Chinese traditional medical practice of acupuncture. Acupuncture is sometimes called "needling," because it is the art of healing by puncturing the skin at certain points, using long needles.

In China this ancient practice has been used in some form since 1000 B.C. to help kill pain and cure such ailments as stomach cramps, headaches, stiff limbs, and arthritis. Although the basic principles remain the same, acupuncture has been modernized, and Chinese doctors are continually finding new uses for it. In 1968 two new discoveries were made which are now widely used throughout China. These are the use of acupuncture needles as the only anesthetic in major surgery; and the application of acupuncture to cure deafness caused by a childhood disease.

In order to understand acupuncture from the Chinese point of view, it is necessary to look at its origin and the complex philosophy behind it. The Chinese were among the first people to break away from the old medicine men who, because of ignorance and superstitious fears, conjured up the supernatural powers to cure the sick. Instead in China they developed acupuncture and the use of herbal medicines. Even in the oldest of all Chinese medical books, *The Yellow Emperor's Classic of Internal Medicine* written in 1000 B.C., reference was made to acupuncture.

The basic philosophy of Chinese traditional medicine is that health is dependent upon the balance of harmony within the body. To obtain this there must be a free and unimpeded circulation of energy flowing through the body's organs. This life-force runs along a complex network of twelve invisible channels, called meridians. These meridians are divided into two elemental forces known as yin and yang.

Yin is feminine, the shady side of the hill, dark, cold, moist. Yang is masculine, the sunny side of the hill, bright, warm, dry. The interaction of these two forces must be kept

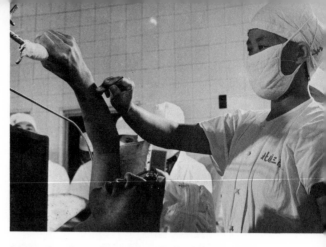

Acupuncture is used as an anesthetic during surgery.

in perfect balance, or disease will occur. The Chinese concept of the yin and yang energies, strange as it may seem, may to some extent be compared with our theories of the functioning of the sympathetic and parasympathetic nervous systems.

The technique of acupuncture is based on the theory that all illnesses stem from an imbalance of the flow of energy or life-force. The aim is to break down the blockage and restore the free flow of energy through the meridians, and thus improve the functioning of the organ and restore the patient to health. This is done by inserting long needles into specific acupuncture, or nerve, points in the skin related to the affected organ. New nerve points are continually being discovered. The old books say 365 points, but the new ones now claim up to 800.

The insertion of the needle is painless, but as the needle is twisted a nerve point is reached. Then a prick is felt, and often the sensation of a small electric charge zings through the body. The needle is inserted up to 1½ inches into the body. In some cases, results are felt immediately; in others the treatment is given regularly for longer periods of time.

Obviously there is no scientific logic in the Chinese philosophical explanation of acupuncture. Modern Chinese doctors do not even express this rather fanciful theory. They prefer to base their healing techniques on the results of hundreds of years of painstaking research and recorded clinical observations of the results. They say there is no scientific explanation, but it works—like aspirin.

Chinese doctors trained in Western medi-

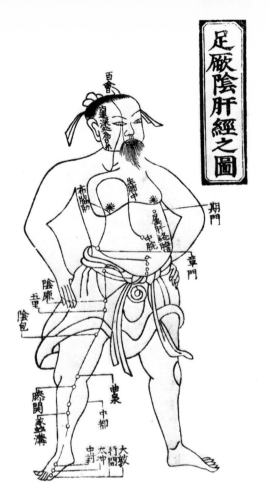
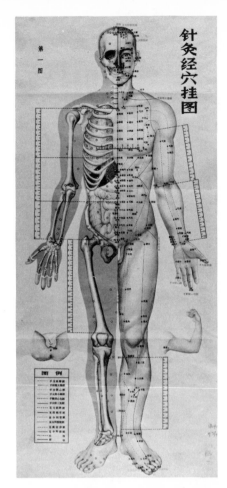

Above left: A diagram from an ancient Chinese medical book, showing the points in the body where acupuncture needles should be inserted. Above right: A modern diagram.

cine no longer scoff at acupuncture. They use it side by side with modern methods. It is now used in all the modern hospitals in China, as well as in the clinics, state farms, factory complexes, housing developments, and sanitariums.

Many Western medical men are highly skeptical of any form of acupuncture. Some put it in the same category as witchcraft. It is "just rubbish," wrote Nobelist Sir John Eccles in *Medical World News*. In the same article Case Western Reserve neurosurgeon Robert J. White expressed his doubts and suggested that acupuncture used as an anesthetic during major surgery "must be due to hypnotic suggestion." Western observers, however, who have witnessed the operations report that there was no evidence of hypnotism.

Two American biologists, Dr. Arthur W. Galston of Yale University, and Dr. Ethan Signer of the Massachusetts Institute of Technology, witnessed four major operations where the only anesthetic used was acupuncture needles. The patients remained fully conscious during the procedure. Dr. Galston said he thought that "Western pharmacology had much to learn from traditional Chinese medicine." "Like everyone else in the West," said Dr. Signer, "I was skeptical about the whole thing. That was until we saw the operations using only acupuncture as anesthetic. As far as I could tell there was no other means of anesthetic. The patients were conscious throughout and they were happy."

The Chinese doctors pay little heed to this controversy in the West and continue to practice the art of acupuncture as they have for many centuries.

AUDREY R. TOPPING

MIDDLE EAST

THERE was little actual fighting in the Middle East during 1971. But the region's pressing political disputes remained unresolved. The Arab-Israeli dispute smoldered, ready at any time to explode again into bitter warfare. Little progress was made in the Cyprus controversy. Rivalry increased among the various Arab states. And the consequences of the announced British withdrawal from the Persian Gulf added to the tensions in the area. In short, the Middle East in 1971 remained one of the crucial trouble spots in the world.

Internally, most of the states of the region continued to experience political instability. There was an unsuccessful coup in Morocco. In Sudan, a military coup succeeded for a few days, and then, in a countercoup, General Nimeiry regained power. In Turkey, the military forced a change in the civilian government. There were attempted assassinations and political acts of violence in many of the states of the Middle East. There were also major cabinet shake-ups in the governments of Egypt, Iraq, and Yemen (Sana).

U.S. Secretary of State William Rogers meets with Jordan's King Hussein in May.

Above left to right: Israel Foreign Minister Abba Eban, U.S. Secretary of State Rogers, Israeli Prime Minister Golda Meir, and Deputy Prime Minister Yigal Allon. The "Rogers Mission" to the Middle East in May met with little success, but the U.S. continued to press for indirect talks between Israel and Egypt. Israel warned that it would not participate unless the U.S. resumed its sales of F-4 Phantom warplanes (left). In December the U.S. decided to sell Israel the jets.

"... and this little old gray-haired lady asks me, 'Are they Phantom jets, young man?' and I says, 'Yes, ma'am, they are.' And then she slugged me!"

►ARAB-ISRAELI CONFLICT

The most significant development in the Middle East during 1971 was the maintenance of the Arab-Israeli cease-fire. This cease-fire went into effect in August 1970. Since then it has been twice extended and then allowed to lapse, although it continued to be observed. In September 1971 it appeared that fighting would flare up again along the Suez Canal following the shooting down of an Egyptian and an Israeli aircraft. But neither side was keen to resume the conflict.

The Jarring Talks

The year opened with the resumption of indirect contacts through Gunnar V. Jarring, special representative of United Nations Secretary-General U Thant. Both the Egyptians and the Israelis sent memoranda to Jarring. They outlined their positions for the implementation of UN Security Council Resolution 242 for an overall Arab-Israeli peace settlement. This resolution calls for Israel to withdraw from Arab territories occupied during the six-day war in June 1967. It also calls for the Arab states to acknowledge Israel's independence and Israel's right to be secure within its boundaries.

Both the Egyptians and the Israelis restated their old positions. Israel said it would not withdraw. The Egyptians said they would not settle for anything less than a complete Israeli withdrawal.

Early in February, Jarring tried to break the impasse. He asked Israel to commit itself to the complete withdrawal from Egyptian territory, minus the Gaza Strip. Egypt was asked to commit itself to a peace settlement and also to agree to recognize Israel. Further, the borders between the two states would then be demilitarized. Security would be provided for Israel in the Sharm al-Sheik region. And Israel would be allowed freedom of navigation in the Suez Canal. With the above agreement, Israel and Egypt would then proceed, along with Jordan, on a reciprocal basis to implement Security Council Resolution 242.

Egypt indicated its willingness to proceed along the lines outlined by Jarring. Israel, however, refused. The Israeli Government ruled out a total withdrawal from Egyptian territory. The stalemate which has been troubling the world continued. In March, Jarring suspended his mission and returned to his post as Swedish ambassador to the Soviet Union. The cease-fire officially lapsed on March 7. However, both sides agreed not to break it so long as there was a possibility of fruitful negotiations.

The Rogers Mission

With the suspension of the Jarring mission, the United States tried to prevent renewed hostilities. Washington thought that a step-by-step approach to the Arab-Israeli problem would get better results than an attempt to achieve an immediate overall settlement.

An Israeli patrol boat and a fire-fighting tug pass through the Strait of Tiran. Egypt's closing of the Strait in 1967 had been one of the causes of the six-day war.

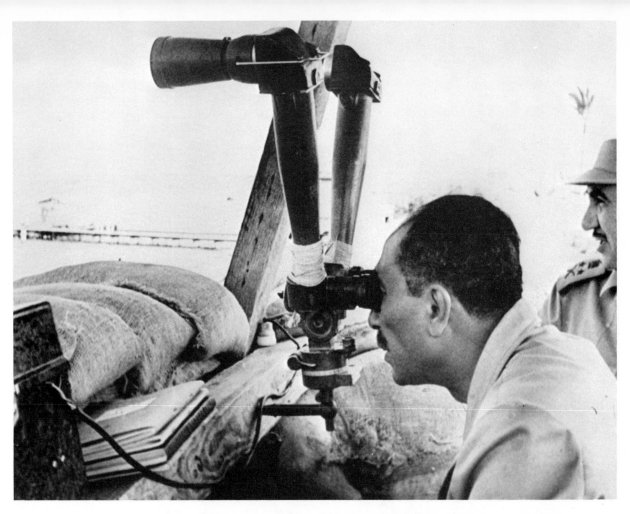

Egyptian President Anwar el-Sadat scans the Israeli-occupied east bank of the Suez Canal. Both Israel and Egypt would like to see the canal reopened, but cannot agree on conditions.

In April, Egyptian President Anwar el-Sadat again offered to extend the cease-fire and to open the Suez Canal if Israel would agree to a partial withdrawal of its troops in the Sinai. This idea was pressed for by United States Secretary of State William Rogers on his visit to the Middle East in May.

While both sides agreed that the Suez Canal should be reopened, they could not agree on the conditions for opening it. When the United States was not successful in reconciling these major differences, the matter was referred to the fall meeting of the United Nations General Assembly.

At the United Nations, on October 4, Secretary Rogers submitted a new plan. The six-point proposal called for: 1) a partial Israeli withdrawal; 2) the reopening of the Suez Canal; 3) an expanded UN peace-keeping force; 4) an extension of the cease-fire; 5) an Egyptian presence in the Sinai; and 6) the free use of the international waterway by all states, including Israel. Rogers also emphasized that the Suez accord would be a step toward the full implementation, within a reasonable period, of Security Council Resolution 242.

Israel continued to insist that the cease-fire should be for an unlimited period and that no Egyptian armed forces should enter the areas vacated by the Israeli forces. Israel also stated that the Suez accord should stand on its own merits and not be tied to other commitments. Israeli Prime Minister Golda Meir warned that no talks would take place until the United States lifted its embargo on the delivery of jet aircraft to Israel. In November it was announced that the Soviet

Union had sent to Egypt several bombers capable of carrying air-to-ground missiles. This further heightened Israeli fears that the delicate arms balance in the Middle East was being tipped in the Arabs' favor.

On December 13 the General Assembly adopted a resolution calling on Israel to withdraw from all occupied territory. The United States was one of the 36 nations that abstained. Israel announced that it would not abide by the Assembly demand.

Unless further progress for a peaceful settlement in the Arab-Israeli dispute is made, fighting may break out again. On the other hand, an Israeli withdrawal from the Suez Canal is, in itself, no guarantee that peace will be kept. The Israelis seem convinced that it is safer to stay put than to move to a less defendable position. The Israelis are also beginning to question the ability or willingness of the United States to help them in the event of another Arab-Israeli

war. They therefore resent pressure from Washington to give up their current military and strategic advantages.

The Arabs, however, fear that Israel will use every excuse not to budge from the Sinai and other occupied territories. They see in an unlimited cease-fire a permanent Israeli occupation of their territory.

▶ **JORDAN AND THE PALESTINIANS**

In 1970 the Palestinian liberation movement was a formidable force in the Middle East, particularly in Jordan. In 1971, however, the movement lost much of its influence and prestige in the Arab world.

In September 1970 the guerrilla forces of the Palestinian liberation movement suffered near-defeat at the hands of the Jordanian Army. However, agreements were made allowing the Palestinians to operate against Israel from Jordanian territory. The agreements were soon violated. King Hus-

In Amman, Jordanian soldiers conduct a house-to-house search for Palestinian guerrillas and weapons.

An underground Palestinian group was responsible for the assassination of Jordan's Premier Wasfi Tal.

Three Mideast leaders (left to right), Anwar el-Sadat of Egypt, Muammar al-Qaddafi of Libya, and Hafez al-Assad of Syria, formed the Federation of Arab Republics. Sadat was named president.

sein was determined to regain full sovereignty over Jordan. The more radical elements of the liberation movement were more interested in overthrowing Hussein's government than in fighting the Israelis. Hussein moved against the guerrilla forces, and by the end of July 1971 they were completely defeated.

The defeat of the Palestinian liberation forces in Jordan was due also to a deepening rift within the liberation movement, to the lack of money, and, most important, to the unwillingness of the Arab governments to come to their defense. Without exception, these governments waited until it was too late before lodging complaints with the Jordanian Government.

As 1971 ended, the Palestinian liberation movement was largely an underground operation. It was one underground group that claimed responsibility for the assassination of Jordan's Premier Wasfi Tal on November 28. Tal had aroused bitter antagonism because of his stern measures against the Palestinian guerrillas. Thus, while the Palestinians are not strong enough to sabotage an Arab settlement with Israel, they cannot be ignored in the final settlement of the "Palestine" question.

▶ **THE FEDERATION OF ARAB REPUBLICS**

In November 1970, Egypt, Syria, Libya, and Sudan announced a projected four-state federation. This plan was partially realized in 1971. In April, Presidents Sadat of Egypt, Assad of Syria, and Qaddafi of Libya declared that agreement on the details of the projected federation had been reached. A referendum was held in September in each of the three states, and the Federation of Arab Republics was officially established. Sudan was expected to join at a later date, following the settlement of some of its internal problems.

The federation has a loose structure and fairly flexible rules. It calls for one flag, one anthem, and one capital. There is to be close co-operation, but no abdication of authority. It is essentially a co-ordinating body. The Presidential Council will be made up of the rulers of the three states. All important issues must be approved unanimously. No important decision can be imposed on any of the three states.

Although the federation calls for joint defense and foreign policies, the armed forces remain under national commands. Each state can enter into separate treaties and agreements with other states. Egypt, for example, could enter into an agreement with Israel, even if Libya or Syria objected.

There is a provision that any two states can intervene militarily in the third to restore matters to normal. This can be done even if the government is not in a position to ask for assistance. The anticoup provision was apparently prompted by the experience in Sudan earlier in the year. A Leftist coup was attempted in that country in July, and for a few days General Nimeiry was out of office. Libya and Egypt helped him crush the coup and regain power.

The formation of the Federation of Arab Republics is not likely to change the military balance in the Middle East. But it may help strengthen the position of the rulers of the member states. A move against Sadat, Assad, or Qaddafi could be viewed as undermining the struggle for Arab unity. Also, any opponent of any one of the three regimes would have to consider the possibility of intervention by the other federation members.

▶TURKEY'S POLITICAL CRISIS

Turkey started out the year on the brink of anarchy. Student violence and urban-guerrilla terrorism were rampant throughout the nation. In March, the military threatened to take over the country if Premier Suleyman Demirel did not resign. They demanded a strong government that would carry out far-ranging economic and social reforms, and bring about an end to the civil disorder.

A coalition Cabinet was installed on March 26 headed by Nihat Erim, a law professor. Although Premier Erim tried to bring about reform measures, there were many clashes between radical and conservative members of parliament. Twice during the year Erim resigned, but each time was persuaded to withdraw his resignation. In December a more moderate Cabinet was installed as a concession to the conservatives. Erim then announced that the political crisis "is finished."

Nihat Erim became the new premier of Turkey after Suleyman Demirel was forced to resign.

Right: The Shah of Iran, Empress Farah, and their family. In October the Shah hosted more than 500 guests from 70 nations at a spectacular celebration—the 2,500th anniversary of the founding of the Persian Empire by Cyrus the Great. Below: In Persepolis, the ancient capital, one of the many parades celebrates the event.

In December six Trucial States on the Persian Gulf declared their independence as the Union of Arab Emirates. Spread over 32,000 square miles and with a population of 200,000, the Union also became a member of the United Nations. Dubai is one of the richest emirates because of its extensive oil wealth. It boasts a modern medical center (below), excellent schools, and a jetport. Right: An enormous underwater oil storage tank in Dubai is the first of its kind and is considered to be one of the most ingenious engineering feats in history.

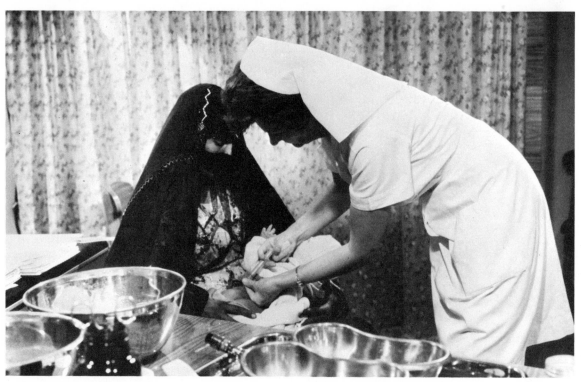

UNEASY TRUCE IN CYPRUS

In Cyprus no progress was made on the crucial issue of local government. The Greek Cypriots insisted that the Turks accept individual equality and a protected minority status in a unitary state. The Turkish Cypriots continued to insist on nothing less than communal equality. This equality would be expressed in separate political, economic, and social structures. This could result in a complete partition of the two communities.

In 1971 there were some new developments in the Cyprus problem. The Greek and Turkish governments showed a growing impatience with the talks. And the secret return of General George Grivas from Greece caused much concern. These developments could provide the impetus to a greater involvement of the United Nations, Britain, and the United States in the process of conciliation. But they could also mean a new eruption of violence in 1972. Turkey and Greece may again try to impose a solution in Cyprus, as was done in 1959. General Grivas, who wants a union of Cyprus with Greece, may again bring the island to the brink of civil war.

As the year ended, the UN peace-keeping force was still stationed on Cyprus.

IRAQ AND THE KURDS

In Iraq, the major achievement of the Arab Baathist Government was the maintenance of the March 1970 cease-fire. This cease-fire brought to an end almost ten years of war between the Kurds and the Arabs. On the other hand, Iraq did not make much progress in reaching a lasting accommodation with its two million Kurds. The agreements of March 1970 were not fully implemented, and the Kurds still demanded a greater share of political and governmental power.

However, there does not seem to be much chance of another outbreak of war. The Kurds need time to consolidate their gains and to recover from the years of war. The Baathist Government needs friends. It has alienated much of Iraqi society. Because of its foreign policies, it has become isolated from the rest of the Arab world.

THE PERSIAN GULF

Britain's plans to pull out of the Persian Gulf area after the end of 1971 compelled the rulers of the nine Arab Emirates to move into action. During 1971, two of the Emirates—Qatar and Bahrain—chose independence. Six of the seven Trucial States became independent as the Union of Arab Emirates. The six states are Abu Dhabi, Dubai, Sharjah, Umm al-Qaiwain, Ajman, and Fujairah. The seventh Trucial State, Ras al-Khaimah, held out for better terms.

The events leading up to the formation of the Union of Arab Emirates caused much protest in the Arab world. On November 30, Iran occupied three strategically located islands in the Persian Gulf: Abu Musa, Greater Tumb, and Lesser Tumb. Having given up its claim to Bahrain in 1970, Iran insisted that its claim to these islands must be satisfied before it would recognize the proposed Union. The landing on Abu Musa was by agreement with the ruler of Sharjah. However, Ras al-Khaimah, which claimed sovereignty over the two Tumbs, lodged a strong protest with Britain, which was responsible for the Trucial States' defense.

The following day Britain ended its treaty obligations with the seven Trucial States. And on December 2 the Trucial States, except Ras al-Khaimah, proclaimed the Union of Arab Emirates and signed a friendship treaty with Britain.

Arab anger exploded. Many suspected that Britain had purposely allowed Iran to occupy the islands so the new Union could be formed. Iraq, with the Persian Gulf as its only access to the sea, accused Iran of threatening the security of the region, and broke relations with Iran and Britain.

Many have doubts whether the Union will succeed. There are still traditional rivalries, territorial disputes, and a disparity of wealth among its members. And there are external pressures. Revolutionary elements in and around the Gulf region have long waited for the final withdrawal of the British forces. Saudi Arabia can at any time press its longstanding claim to a large slice of Abu Dhabi.

HARRY J. PSOMIADES
Queens College of the University
of the City of New York

BAHRAIN AND QATAR BECOME INDEPENDENT

On August 14, 1971, Bahrain declared itself an independent state. In the following month, on September 1, Qatar also chose complete independence. Both Persian Gulf States were granted membership in the United Nations. Bahrain had been a British "Protected State" since 1820, and Qatar since 1916. Both states had treaties granting Britain exclusive control of their foreign relations in return for a promise of British protection.

▶ BAHRAIN

The Bahrain archipelago is a group of several islands located in the Persian Gulf between the Qatar peninsula and the mainland of Saudi Arabia. It has a population of about 200,000, and the total land area, most of which is flat, sandy desert, is 231 square miles. The principal island, Bahrain, from which the country takes its name, is 30 miles long and 10 miles wide. Among the other islands, the most important is Muharraq, which is connected to Bahrain by a causeway and motor road. The majority of the population lives on these two islands.

The capital and chief commercial center of the archipelago is Manama. It has a population of over 80,000.

Most of the people of Bahrain are Muslim Arabs, but there are sizable communities of Indians, Pakistanis, Persians, and Europeans. Although there is some fruitgrowing, fishing, pearling, and light industry, the country's main source of revenue is derived from its vast oil operations. Bahrain earns more than $20,000,000 a year in the production and refining of crude oil. This small island group also serves as a center of air and sea communications in the Gulf area.

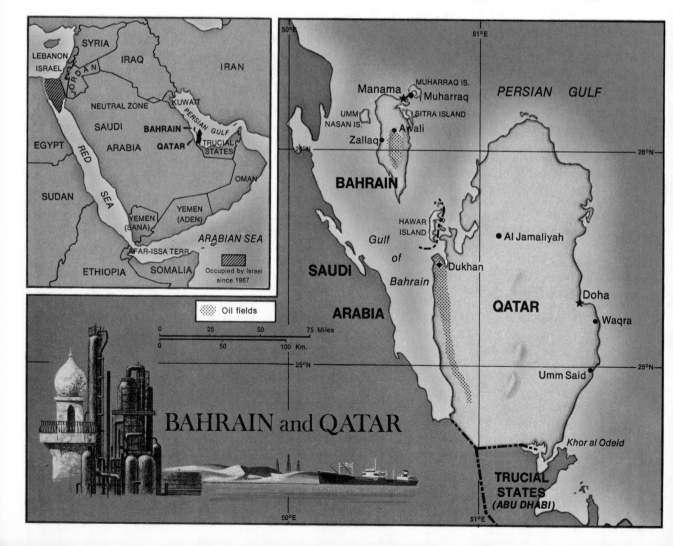

BAHRAIN and QATAR

The ruler of the archipelago, Sheik Isa bin Sulman al-Khalifa, represents an Arab dynasty that has been in power since 1782. The government is an absolute monarchy, with most of the important state positions held by members of the ruling dynasty. However, the constitution is in the process of being changed to allow the citizens of Bahrain a greater voice in their country's government.

QATAR

Qatar is a barren and desolate peninsula lying midway along the west coast of the Persian Gulf. It has a land frontier with Saudi Arabia and Abu Dhabi (one of the Trucial States), the limits of which have never been clearly defined. The total land area is 4,000 square miles, and the country has a population of about 110,000. This includes a large number of merchants, technicians, and workers from neighboring states as well as from distant regions of the Arab world. Because of the expansion of Qatar's oil industry, the population has quadrupled in the past decade.

Doha, the capital, contains more than half the population of the country. Other important towns are Umm Said, the major port and oil terminal, and Dukhan, the center of oil production.

The majority of the people are Muslim Arabs, although the large working force is made up mostly of non-Arabs. Qatar's rapidly expanding social services are free. Oil is Qatar's only significant commodity, and until oil production began in 1949, the people eked out their living from the traditional pursuits of fishing, pearling, and nomadic herding.

Oil revenues are well over $120,000,000 annually. The output from new offshore fields and expected increases in oil prices will greatly increase Qatar's oil revenues.

Qatar is an absolute monarchy. The present ruler, Sheik Ahmad bin Ali al-Thani, appears determined to use wisely the tremendous wealth brought by the oil reserves for the benefit of all the people.

Like that of Bahrain, the security of Qatar is threatened by revolutionary movements from abroad, and internally by the new social

A street scene in Doha, capital of Qatar: a castle built during the Middle Ages and modern soda machines.

forces created by the rapid increase in prosperity. Qatar also shares with the other small but wealthy oil-producing states of the Gulf the problem of how to live with the more powerful states of the region, and not to become politically and socially dominated by them.

MODERN LIVING

THERE were many exciting trends in contemporary living in 1971. Fashion came back to life again when even antifashion young people, both male and female, donned hot pants, the most popular clothing fad to sweep the nation. However, blue jeans were far from out and continued to be the "uniform" of today's youth. Furnishings were "fanciful," and many a child's room was designed with fun in mind: Raggedy Ann seats, steering-wheel lamps, and gym-shoe chairs. And the popularity of recreational vehicles grew. Bicycles, snowmobiles, and dune buggies were practical means of transportation and fun to use.

1900   1913   1919   1928

1929   1929   1940   1947

The fashion picture of the 20th century: Hemlines rose and dipped and rose again as women fell in with the fashions of the day. By 1971 the dictates of the fashion Establishment were no longer accepted. The girls said "everything goes," and maxi, midi, and mini lengths were equally popular. Hemlines reached new heights when hot pants (right) became the latest fad.

1958

1967

1970

1971

FASHION

In 1971, fashion came back to life again after the industry had been seriously shaken by the youth-generated, antifashion, pro-blue-jean movement.

The first fad to sweep the scene in the spring of 1971 was hot pants, so named by the editors of *Women's Wear Daily*. They were worn instantaneously in Paris, London, New York, and Rome. Hot pants took the dowdyism out of the long maxicoats and gave girls a chance to show off their legs again. The popularity of hot pants continued even into winter, when they were worn with colorful tights and boots.

A fad of the summer—perhaps the logical follow-up to bullet belts—was the uniform. St. Tropez, the French resort where European fashion surfaces, seemed like an armed camp, with both men and women in the U.S. Army look. *The New York Times* reported that T-shirts in olive green, decorated with shoulder patches and insignia, had replaced 1970's tie-dyed T-shirt as the everyday uniform among the young. Multi-zippered pilots' jackets and fatigues-green shorts and pants, were everywhere.

But blue jeans were far from dead. Although blue jeans had been popular for at least three years, 1971 was the year Levi Strauss was recognized for its worldwide (though unintentional) fashion contribution. Blue jeans were definitely the basic wearing apparel of most young people. Hot-pant blue jeans, cut off as short as the wearer dared, were the newest variation of the original Levis.

Clothes that hugged the body were the best, and the body stocking became a way of life. The older looking and more personally decorated these clothes were, the better. Faded bodyshirts, faded and body-shaped jeans, personal jewelry, and belts were "in." Even Geraldine Stutz, the president of New York's fashionable Henri Bendel, proclaimed it very out to look "in" in somebody else's designed clothes.

As fall approached, the American "classics"—simple, comfortable, and uncluttered clothes—seemed the new trend. The big controversy over skirt lengths was over. Whatever felt most comfortable was worn. But the new fad was ankle-length, worn by youthful students as well as older women.

The one old-fashioned look that really boomed was in shoes. Wedgies and platforms in shocking heights and color combinations surfaced first. Then came ankle-strap shoes in even-higher heels.

Jean Guilder, fashion director of *Glamour* magazine, explained the fall picture for young girls: "Long, shining hair, curled at the ends. Lips very red. Eyes sparkly. Fluffy hair. Fuzzy hair. Bright red nails. Vampy eyes. Campy shoes. Clogs and ankle straps. Wedgies. Wedgie boots. Ballet slippers. Paratroop boots, combat boots, work shoes. Plastic vinyl, Bakelite bracelets. Beaded bracelets. Ubiquitous little pins. Rhinestone pins. People, places and things decorating the body in amusing ways. Marvelous legs, opaque textured. Colorful. Barrettes on hair. Sou'westers. Pulled-down hats. Berets. Little leather gloves. Got the picture?"

▶ MALE FASHION TRENDS

Boys' and men's fashions continued to be as personal and exhibitionist as the girls'. Young men plunged into "hot pants" for summer, and knickers tucked into high boots in the fall. This was basically a street look that worked best when most casual. The jeans jacket was universally favored in not only denim, but dressier fabrics.

The influx of layered looks in the fall was popular with both sexes—tight-fitting shrink sweaters worn over shirts with deep pointed collars in as varied color combinations as one could manage. Pants and trousers continued to have a Fred Astaire look to them—wide pants legs with cuffs.

Reaction to all this color set in at some levels, especially on Wall Street. White shirts reappeared as a fashion and couldn't be found in stock in most department stores. *The Wall Street Journal* announced, "Right now, even finding a white shirt to buy can be a headache. . . ." A spokesman for Wallachs stores explained, "The overall atmosphere in terms of business conditions is a rather sober one now. . . . More conservative clothing is in order."

In answer to the mini-midi controversy, hot pants became the fashion rage of 1971.

Men's shoes tended to the work-shoe category—anything with a clunky look; many male trend-setters were wearing shoes and boots with three-inch heels.

▶ THE FASHION DESIGNER

As established *couturier* designers were settling back into their elegant but not extreme mode of dressing their private customers, young designers were making an impact in Establishment circles. Stephen Burrows, a noteworthy young black designer, was nominated for the prestigious Coty Fashion Critics' Award in his second

year as a special designer at Henri Bendel in New York.

Betsey Johnson, who designs for a firm called Alley Cat, was also nominated and won a Coty "Winnie." Betsey is one of the youngest winners in Coty history. She is only seven years out of school. Her public is the late-teen-ager or young married who wants something more picturesque and personal than most big-name designers provide. Her designs are basically for the do-it-yourselfer who needs help in putting together the right fashion ingredients.

France's most successful trend-setters were ready-to-wear designers who had the body-hugging formula for clothes down pat. Sonia Rykiel's fashions are narrow and body hugging at the top and flaring at the bottom, built the way most girls and young women are.

Yves Saint Laurent, easily the most influential *couturier* in France, announced that he would no longer do any *couture* collections, and devoted himself to ready-to-wear. This was a logical step for Saint Laurent, who had been doing all the designing for both collections himself. His ready-to-wear collections are as influential as his *couture* designs, and are much less expensive. They are now sold in Saint Laurent Rive Gauche boutiques in Paris, New York, and Chicago.

Karl Lagerfeld, a youngish German designer who designs for Chloe in Paris, started a return-to-the-forties look that was picked up and parodied by Yves Saint Laurent and by designers in the United States.

Probably the most prophetic collections of 1971 were the Oriental ones. Young Japanese designers emerged strongly with their own brand of hip style. Missy Miyake of Tokyo had a successful showing in New York, and Enzo in Paris designed curiously updated Oriental gear for a shop called "Jap" in Paris.

The complete switch away from big-name fashion designers, especially among the young, was possibly accomplished in 1971. Giorgio di Sant'Angelo explained to fashion

In the fall, the layered look became "the look," with colorful, body-hugging little vests worn over blouses with deep-pointed collars.

Fashion accessories: 1930's-style pulled-down hats, clunky shoes, skinny crochet vests, and little plastic pins in a variety of colors.

columnist Eugenia Sheppard that "If something good is backed up by a name, so much the better, but the only thing women really care about now is the final product."

CHANEL AND MAINBOCHER

Coco Chanel died in Paris at the age of 87, and Mainbocher retired in New York at the age of 81. Both represented a fashion era that dressed wealthy "society" women and set the style for status-seeking followers. Both represented elegance and understatement, qualities that seem part of the past. Mainbocher was famous for "little nothing" dresses. He invented the decorated cashmere sweater, the basic black crepe, the short evening dress, the sleeveless daytime dress, and black mink.

Chanel was best known for her box-jacket suits, her little jersey dresses, and for making costume jewelry popular.

FASHION AND ECOLOGY

Concern with ecology was taking over even in the fashion world. As student protests were shifting from antiwar to proenvironment, furs became taboo. Personality types like Candice Bergen signed "the pledge" never to wear furs. As a result, furriers made a big issue of "safe furs," such as hides that are raised to be worn and chemical furlike fabrics. Fur designer Jacques Kaplan showed a collection of safe furs with designs by Paloma Picasso, the daughter of Pablo Picasso.

HOMEMADE FASHIONS

The passion for making things at home continued to grow. Knitting, crocheting, needlepoint, sewing, and macrame instruction books and kits were best sellers. Well-known designers also helped the home sewer by designing precut patterns which could easily be stitched up at home. To some this looked like killing the goose that lays the golden egg. But as designer Don Simonelli explained, "The craft thing will be to the '70's what gourmet cooking was to the '60's. It's a means of personal identification—but it doesn't mean you won't go to a restaurant again."

JO AHERN SEGAL
Former Fashion Editor
Look Magazine

FANCIFUL FURNITURE

Beds, chairs, and other furnishings are usually considered utilitarian: most are designed to be useful rather than fanciful. In 1971, however, several designers decided to put a little fun into their furniture. Darrell Howe, for example, thought that a Raggedy Ann seat would be a perfect resting-place for a young girl. For young boys, he designed an entire room with but a single theme: cars. The table was made from a replica of an automobile engine, and the lamp from a steering wheel and other automobile parts. The racing-car bed alone costs $270—and it has no motor.

The giant gym-shoe seat was designed by a whimsical Englishman, Tony Wright. Inside the shoes is a comfortably padded seat. Other giant chairs designed by Wright and by Jon Weallean include a king-size telephone and a wide-open mouth—teeth included—with a plush cushion that looks strangely like a tongue.

Gym-shoe seat (left), Raggedy Ann chair (right), and a boy's room designed around a race-car bed (below).

RECREATIONAL VEHICLES

A dune buggy speeds across the desert. There are 100,000 dune-buggy fanciers in the United States.

A motorcycle racer.

Today people have more leisure time than ever before in which to pursue their favorite activities. In 1971 it seemed that almost everyone's favorite activity was to jump in or on some kind of recreational vehicle—and get away from it all.

The topography of North America is suited to the variety of recreational vehicles being produced. In the north there is snow for snowmobiling. In the Southwest—to the delight of dune buggyists—there are vast stretches of desert. And there are beautiful open spaces for the casual cyclist. Many recreational vehicles can be dangerous: scores of people have been killed or injured —especially on snowmobiles and minibikes. Yet the boom continues: In 1971 nearly 2,000,000 snowmobiles were sold in the United States and Canada; sales of bicycles in the U.S. were over 8,000,000.

During 1971 the minibike (left) and the snowmobile (above) were among the most popular of the motorized recreational vehicles. But because of the number of accidents in which these vehicles were involved, many states and communities took steps to regulate their use. Below: A group of bicyclists enjoy a summer outing.

PERSONALITIES

Canada's Newlyweds: On March 4 Canada's most eligible bachelor, Prime Minister Pierre Elliott Trudeau, 51, married Margaret Sinclair, 22. On Christmas Day, Mrs. Trudeau gave birth to a son, Justin Pierre.

White House Wedding (left): On June 12, Tricia Nixon, daughter of the President, was married to Edward Finch Cox, a Harvard law student.

Chess on His Mind: When Bobby Fischer (above) beat Soviet chess master Tigran Petrosian in 1971, he became eligible to play another Russian, world champion Boris Spassky. If Bobby wins, and he expects to, he will become the first U.S. world chess champion.

Frank Sinatra: America's teen-age idol, 1940's. . . .

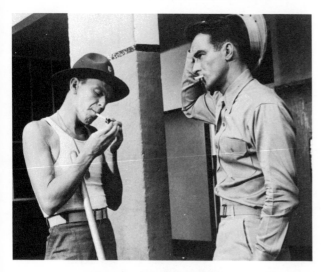

. . . .Academy Award winner for best supporting actor in "From Here to Eternity," 1953. . . .

. . . .with The Clan (Dean Martin, Peter Lawford, Joey Bishop, and Sammy Davis, Jr.), 1960. . . .

Bowing Out: Frank Sinatra, 55, gives his farewell performance, ending a career that spanned three decades and included 58 motion pictures, 100 albums, and nearly 2,000 individual recordings, June 14, 1971.

First at Sea: In 1971 Samuel L. Gravely, Jr., commander of a guided-missile frigate, became the Navy's first black admiral.

First in the Air: In 1971 Jeanne M. Holm, director of Women in the Air Force (WAF), became the United States Air Force's first woman general.

Baby Lenore: Mr. and Mrs. Nick DeMartino fled to Florida to avoid a New York court ruling ordering them to surrender their adopted baby to her natural mother. For the DeMartinos, the story ended happily when a Florida court awarded them custody of Lenore.

DEATHS

Hugo L. Black, 85 (above left), the Supreme Court associate justice whose liberal philosophy had a strong influence on the Court for 34 years, died on September 25. John M. Harlan, 72 (above right), the Supreme Court associate justice appointed in 1955 and described as the Court's "conservative conscience," died on December 29. Both Black and Harlan had resigned in September.

Nikita S. Khrushchev, 77, the Soviet Communist Party leader who had held power for 11 years, died on September 11. His denunciation of Stalin, the Soviet dictator who died in 1953, was a turning point in Soviet history. Khrushchev, with his fiery temper, infectious smile, and earthy wit, lived in obscurity after he was deposed in 1964.

Dr. Ralph J. Bunche, 67, one of the United Nations' most influential diplomats since its founding in 1945, died on December 9. Bunche won the 1950 Nobel Peace Prize for his efforts in negotiating the armistice between the Arab states and the new nation of Israel.

Whitney M. Young, Jr., 49, the civil-rights leader, died on March 11. Executive Director of the National Urban League since 1961, Young strove to help the black American poor gain self-sufficiency.

URBAN LEAGUE CITIES

Igor Stravinsky, 88, the Russian-born composer, whose works, such as *The Firebird* and *Petrouchka*, revolutionized music, died on April 6. Left: Picasso's 1920 sketch of Stravinsky.

Louis Armstrong (Satchmo), 71, the virtuoso jazz trumpeter with the sandpapery voice, died on July 6. The master showman delighted millions on his worldwide tours.

Gabrielle (Coco) Chanel, 87, the French couturière, whose elegant and simple designs long dominated the fashion world, died on January 10. Famous Chanelisms: jersey and tweed, Chanel suit, Chanel No. 5.

ACHESON, DEAN, 78, U.S. statesman. Secretary of State (1949–53) under President Harry S. Truman, he strongly influenced American foreign policy. October 12.

ALLEN, JAMES E., JR., 60, U.S. Commissioner of Education (1969–70). October 16.

ANDREWS, GEORGE, 65, Democratic representative from Alabama since 1944. December 25.

ANGELI, PIER, 39, Italian-born motion-picture actress. September 10.

BERLE, ADOLF A., JR., 76, American lawyer, professor, diplomat, and presidential adviser. February 17.

BOURKE-WHITE, MARGARET, 67, American photo-journalist. August 27.

BYINGTON, SPRING, 77, American motion-picture, theater, and TV character actress. Starred in TV series *December Bride.* September 7.

CERF, BENNETT, 73, American book publisher, writer, and TV personality. Cofounder of Random House publishing company. August 27.

CORBETT, ROBERT J., 65, U.S. politician. Republican representative from Pennsylvania (1939–41, and from 1945 until his death). April 25.

DEWEY, THOMAS E., 68, U.S. politician. Governor of New York (1943–55), and Republican presidential nominee in 1944 and 1948. March 16.

DODD, THOMAS J., 64, U.S. politician. Democratic senator from Connecticut (1959–Jan. 1971). In 1967 he became the 6th senator in U.S. history to be censured by his Senate colleagues (for diverting campaign funds for personal use). May 24.

DUPRÉ, MARCEL, 85, French master organist, famous for his original improvisations. May 30.

DUVALIER, FRANÇOIS ("Papa Doc"), 64, President-dictator of Haiti, the world's oldest black republic, since 1957. April 21.

FERNANDEL, 67, French motion-picture comedian. February 26.

FLIPPEN, JAY C., 70, American motion-picture and television character actor. February 3.

FULTON, JAMES G., 68, U.S. politician. Republican representative from Pennsylvania since 1945. October 6.

GILBERT, BILLY, 77, American stage and motion-picture comedian. September 23.

GOSLIN, LEON (GOOSE), 70, American League baseball batting star. Elected to baseball's Hall of Fame in 1968. May 15.

GUGGENHEIM, HARRY F., 80, American financier, philanthropist, horseman, and publisher. January 22.

GUTHRIE, SIR TYRONE, 70, British theatrical director and producer. Established regional repertory group in Minneapolis, Minnesota, in 1963. May 15.

HAYWARD, LELAND, 68, American theatrical producer. March 18.

HEFLIN, VAN, 60, American motion-picture and stage actor. Winner of 1942 Academy Award for best supporting actor for his role in *Johnny Eager.* July 23.

HICKENLOOPER, BOURKE B., 75, U.S. politician. Republican senator from Iowa (1945–69). September 4.

JOHNSON, ALVIN, 96, American educator. Founder of the New School for Social Research in New York City. June 7.

JONES, BOBBY, 69, American golf master. He was the only player ever to have won golf's grand slam (in 1930). December 18.

KARRER, PAUL, 82, Swiss chemist. Shared 1937 Nobel Prize in Chemistry. June 18.

KENT, ROCKWELL, 88, American landscape and graphics artist and book illustrator. March 13.

LEE, MANFRED B., 65, American author who, with his cousin, created the "Ellery Queen" mystery series. April 2.

LEMASS, SEAN, 71, prime minister of Ireland (1959–66). May 11.

LISTON, CHARLES (SONNY), 38, world heavyweight boxing champion (Sept. 1962–Feb. 1964). Found dead on January 5.

LLOYD, HAROLD, 77, American motion-picture comedian. His portrayals of a fumbling, bespectacled youth made him one of the great silent-film stars. March 8.

LUKACS, GYÖRGY, 86, Hungarian Marxist philosopher, writer, and literary critic. June 4.

LUKAS, PAUL, 76, American motion-picture and stage actor. Winner of 1943 Academy Award for best actor for his role in *Watch on the Rhine.* August 15.

MURPHY, AUDIE, 46, most-decorated American soldier of World War II, and motion-picture actor. May 28.

NASH, OGDEN, 68, American poet and humorist. Master of droll and witty verse with unconventional rhymes. May 19.

NEVINS, ALLAN, 80, American historian and biographer. Winner of 1933 and 1937 Pulitzer Prizes in biography. March 5.

NIEBUHR, REINHOLD, 78, American Protestant theologian, political philosopher, and author. June 1.

ORR, LORD BOYD, 90, Scottish nutritionist. First director of the UN Food and Agricultural Organization (FAO). Winner of 1949 Nobel Peace Prize. June 25.

PENNEY, J. C., 95, American businessman. Founder of the department-store chain bearing his name. February 12.

PROUTY, WINSTON L., 65, U.S. politician. Republican senator from Vermont since 1959. September 10.

RENNIE, MICHAEL, 62, British-born motion-picture and TV actor. June 10.

ROPER, ELMO B., JR., 70, American public-opinion analyst. Among the first to develop modern political polls. April 30.

RUGGLES, CARL, 95, American composer of atonal and dissonant music. October 24.

RUSSELL, RICHARD B., 73, U.S. politician. Democratic senator from Georgia since 1933, and chairman of the Senate's Armed Services Committee (1951–69). January 21.

SARNOFF, DAVID, 80, American broadcasting pioneer and chairman of the board of the RCA Corporation. December 12.

SEFERIS, GEORGE, 71, Greek diplomat and poet. Winner of 1963 Nobel Prize for Literature. September 20.

SKOURAS, SPYROS P., 78, Greek-born motion-picture magnate. Builder of the 20th Century-Fox empire. August 16.

SOONG, T. V., 77, Chinese financier and statesman. Served as finance minister, foreign minister, and premier in Chiang Kai-shek's Nationalist Government before the Communist Chinese takeover in 1949. April 25.

STANLEY, WENDELL M., 66, American biochemist. Shared 1946 Nobel Prize in Chemistry. June 15.

STERN, BILL, 64, American sportscaster. November 19.

SVEDBERG, THEODOR H. E., 86, Swedish nuclear scientist. Winner of 1926 Nobel Prize in Chemistry. February 26.

TAMM, IGOR Y., 75, Russian physicist. Shared 1958 Nobel Prize in Physics. April 12.

THATCHER, W. ROSS, 54, premier of Canadian province of Saskatchewan (1964–June 1971). July 23.

TIGER, DICK, 42, Nigerian boxing champion. Holder of world middleweight title (1962–63; 1965–66) and world light-heavyweight title (1966–68). December 13.

TISELIUS, ARNE, 69, Swedish biochemist. Winner of 1948 Nobel Prize in Chemistry. October 29.

TUBMAN, WILLIAM V. S., 75, president of Liberia, Africa's oldest independent republic, since 1944. July 23.

WATTS, JOHN C., 69, U.S. politician. Democratic representative from Kentucky since 1951. September 24.

WYLIE, PHILIP, 69, American author. Novels and essays included *The Disappearance* and *A Generation of Vipers,* in which he coined the word "momism." October 25.

RELIGION

MANY of the religious denominations were shaken by conflicts in 1971. Controversy arose within several Protestant churches between those who would like a return to the religious traditions of the past and those who desire more social involvement. At the five-week Roman Catholic Synod of Bishops held in the Vatican, there was debate on the subject of celibacy of priests, and the question of women's role in the church. For the Jewish population, a matter of concern was the status of Jerusalem—whether it should be an internationalized city or under the control of Israel.

Pope Paul convokes the Roman Catholic Synod of Bishops, held September 30–November 6.

In a campaign of harassment protesting Soviet treatment of Jews, the Jewish Defense League demonstrates outside the Russian Mission in New York City.

A new religious movement called "The Jesus People" spontaneously sprang up on many college campuses in 1971. Above: Followers of the movement emerge from the baptismal waters.

PROTESTANTISM

In 1971, many Protestant denominations were shaken by conflicts between the conservatives and the moderates and liberals. Conservatives would like a return to "old-time" religion because they want to keep the traditions of the past. They believe in Bible study, personal salvation, and the preaching of the gospel. Moderates and liberals feel it is necessary to adapt to the ways of the present. They want the church to be more concerned with social action, and they believe in Christian unity, or ecumenism.

▶ **CONTROVERSY WITHIN THE CHURCH**

In July, the 2,800,000-member Lutheran Church–Missouri Synod held its biennial convention. The delegates were greeted by a large sign with a dove on it and the words "Sent to Reconcile." This sentiment pointed up the many bitter disagreements between conservatives and moderates during the past two years. Many compromise measures were adopted at the convention. However, the conservatives, led by President J. A. O. Preus, lost several important battles.

The 1,000,000-member Presbyterian Church in the U.S. (Southern) also had major clashes between conservatives and liberals. In August, conservative Southern Presbyterians announced plans to form a new denomination, "loyal to the Scriptures and to the Reformed Faith." One of the reasons for conservative dissatisfaction was the proposed reunion with the United Presbyterian Church in the U.S.A. (Northern).

The United Presbyterian Church was having problems of its own. In May, the Committee on Church and Race made a $10,000 grant to the Angela Davis Defense Fund. More than 7,000 letters of protest were received, even though a group of black clergy repaid the money. (Miss Davis, an avowed Communist, has been in a California prison, charged with being an accomplice in the murder of a judge in 1970.) Presbyterian officials made the grant to help ensure that she would receive the same justice a white, well-to-do non-Communist might be expected to receive.

The Rev. Ralph D. Abernathy (above) and Dr. J. H. Jackson (below) were chosen by "Ebony" magazine as two of the most influential black leaders in the U.S.

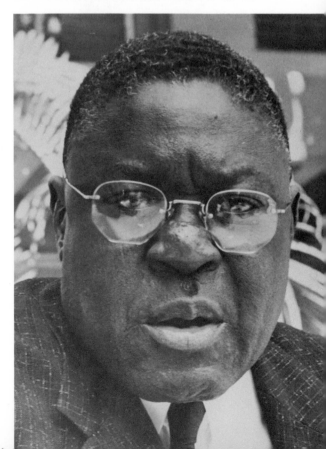

Rev. Dr. Wilmina Rowland of the United Presbyterian Church: the first woman to give the opening prayer in the U.S. Senate.

Lois Stair, first woman to become spiritual leader of the United Presbyterian Church.

Protestants, as well as the rest of the country, continued to be divided over the war in Southeast Asia. Episcopal Bishop Robert L. DeWitt of Philadelphia and William P. Thompson, top staff official of the United Presbyterian Church, joined a Holy Week vigil and fast for peace at the White House. The Methodist Board of Missions became one of the first national church agencies to urge that the war end by December 31, 1971.

President Nixon's plan to visit Communist China was praised by many of the leaders of the National Council of Churches, the United Methodist Church, and other church groups. Many Protestant groups had long advocated U.S. recognition of mainland China and its membership in the United Nations. The United Church of Christ had done so as early as 1961. Conservative denominations tended to oppose recognition of Communist China. They supported Nationalist China, based on Taiwan. Taiwan President Chiang Kai-shek and his wife are Christian.

YOUTH AND RELIGION

Most Protestant churches were surprised by a new religious movement called "The Jesus People" or "Jesus Freaks." This unorganized movement, spontaneously springing up around the country, focuses on personal witnessing and Bible study. The young followers combine "hip" language ("Get high on Jesus") and 19th-century revivalism ("Are you saved?"). The churches were not sure whether this was a desirable spiritual revival or a new addiction, for many former drug addicts were members.

The opera *Jesus Christ Superstar,* which could be described as a hard-rock Passion play, was another manifestation of youth interest in religion. Opening on Broadway in late 1971, the work had several early performances in Protestant churches.

BIBLICAL PROPHECY

As astrology and interest in the occult flourished in the United States, a Conference on Biblical Prophecy was held in Jerusalem. Sponsored by American Protestant conservatives, it was attended by 1,400 people. The conference concerned itself with the Second Coming, or the return of Jesus to earth.

BLACK RELIGIOUS LEADERS

Six Protestant ministers were among 100 persons selected by *Ebony* magazine as the most influential blacks in America. They included the Rev. Ralph D. Abernathy, president of the Southern Christian Leadership Conference; Dr. J. H. Jackson, president of the 5,500,000-member National Baptist Convention, U.S.A. Inc., the largest black denomination in the nation; and Rev. Leon Sullivan, pastor of Philadelphia's Zion Baptist Church and the first black member of the General Motors board of directors.

REINHOLD NIEBUHR

Reinhold Niebuhr, one of the world's most influential Protestant theologians and political philosophers, died on June 1. He had been the chief architect of an intellectual, political movement called "Christian realism."

KENNETH L. WILSON
Editor, *Christian Herald* Magazine

ROMAN CATHOLICISM

▶THE SYNOD OF BISHOPS

The major event of interest to Roman Catholics in 1971 was a meeting of Catholic bishops, called a "synod," held in Vatican City during October and November. About two hundred bishops from many countries gathered to discuss what was happening in the world and to advise the Pope on church policies. The two main subjects discussed at the synod were social justice and the problems of Catholic priests. Once more the bishops supported the Pope in his decision not to change the rule of celibacy, which forbids priests to marry. A majority of priests today believe they should be allowed to marry if they wish. But the Pope and the bishops think that by being celibate a priest can serve God and the people more fully.

In their discussion of world justice the bishops at the synod strongly criticized the governments of the world for spending too much money on weapons and too little on helping the poor. Some of the speakers also criticized the church itself for similar reasons. They said that bishops and priests should live more simply and not use so much money for church buildings.

The synod also gave more attention than ever before to the question of the place of women in the church. This is not really a new question. But suddenly many Catholics, including at least a few bishops, are coming to believe that it is unfair to keep women from entering the priesthood. The synod made no real decisions on this subject, but those who favor a new policy felt that some progress was made.

One practical reason why churchmen are discussing the possibility of married priests and even of women priests was that in 1971, as in several previous years, there were a large number of resignations from the priesthood. The rule of celibacy was not the only reason for the resignations. Some priests (especially in the United States) no longer felt that serving in the church was the best and most useful way they could spend their lives. Surveys showed that among lay people, and especially young people, there was less interest in the church and less respect for its authority. Another growing problem was the financial one; nearly 500 of the nation's 11,000 Catholic grade and high schools went out of operation in September 1971 because of lack of money.

▶POLITICAL ACTIVISM

But not all Catholics were discouraged by these developments. In fact many Catholics, including priests, were becoming more politically active than they had been for years. Two American Catholic priests, the brothers Philip and Daniel Berrigan, were serving prison sentences for destroying Selective Service records. They had done this to show their resistance to the Vietnam war.

In 1971 Philip Berrigan and seven others were indicted on charges of conspiracy to kidnap Dr. Henry Kissinger, President Nixon's national security adviser. It was also alleged they planned to set off explosives in the heating system serving U.S. government buildings in Washington. Their purpose, the Government said, was to try to stop the war in Vietnam. Known as the "Harrisburg Eight," the defendants said they would never have planned a kidnaping or a bombing, since they did not believe in violence. By the end of 1971 the Harrisburg Eight had not been brought to trial, so the case remained a puzzle. Quite apart from any particular case, many American Catholics were proud of those priests who opposed the Vietnam war; they felt that their opposition showed the continuing power of religious conscience in world affairs. Progressive leadership also appeared in some Latin-American countries, where church leaders sided more and more with the poor and oppressed.

After the synod the U.S. Catholic bishops agreed at a meeting in Washington that the Indochina war should be ended because its bad effects outweigh whatever good results it might have. This was the strongest criticism the Catholic Church had ever made of American policy in Vietnam. The bishops also asked an end to the arms race and urged forgiveness for young Americans who left the country because they did not want to fight in Vietnam.

Jozsef Cardinal Mindszenty (left) with Pope Paul VI at the opening of the Synod of Bishops. Released by the Hungarian Government just two days earlier, Mindszenty had spent fifteen years in self-imposed confinement in the U.S. Embassy in Budapest.

► JOZSEF CARDINAL MINDSZENTY

In September an event that brought back memories of religious-political activism of another kind took place. The Holy See arranged with the Hungarian Government for the release of Jozsef Cardinal Mindszenty, Roman Catholic Primate of Hungary, from his self-imposed confinement in the American Embassy in Budapest. Cardinal Mindszenty finally agreed to voluntary exile and in September left forever his beloved Hungary.

In 1949 the Cardinal had been sentenced to life in prison on a charge of high treason against the communist Government. He was released from prison in 1955 because of poor health. When Soviet troops crushed the Hungarian uprising in 1956, the Cardinal, a firm opponent of the communist regime, took refuge in the U.S. Embassy. Despite pleas from the Vatican and the Hungarian Government, he had refused to go into voluntary exile.

ROBERT G. HOYT

JEWS AND JUDAISM

Three important concerns marked Jewish life in 1971. They were: the plight of the Soviet Jew; the continued tension in the Middle East; and the growing number of mixed marriages in the United States.

▶ JEWS IN THE SOVIET UNION

Despite official statements by the Soviet Government that there is no anti-Semitism in Russia, Jews do suffer hardships. There are no Jewish schools, and the teaching of Hebrew and Yiddish is not permitted. Jewish books and newspapers are not allowed to be published. Therefore it is impossible for Russian Jews to study the culture and history of the Jewish people.

In 1971 the Soviet Union relaxed its restrictions on Jewish emigration. Thousands of Jews were allowed to leave for Israel. However, there are still thousands more who would like to go to Israel but continue to be denied exit visas.

In September, more than nine hundred Soviet Jews signed an open letter addressed to Soviet leaders and to the United Nations General Assembly, appealing for help in emigrating to Israel.

In London, British Jews protest alleged Soviet mistreatment of Russian Jews.

New buildings in the old city of Jerusalem. Arabs and others have protested the Israeli building program; Israel insists that Jerusalem is one undivided city and an integral part of Israel and that it can therefore build housing projects for Jews in the Old City.

Originally from Chicago, this family of "Black Israelites" emigrated to Liberia, staying there for two years before moving to Israel in 1969. Settling in the Negev town of Dimona, they were soon joined by some 400 other Black Israelites. In 1971, however, the Israeli Government sought to put an end to the wave of black immigrants and refused entry to a large group arriving from the United States. The Israeli Government said that the blacks "are not Jews and thus are not entitled to immigrant rights." The blacks insisted that they are "Israelites claiming our land . . ."

▶ISRAEL

In 1971 the uneasy Middle East cease-fire was generally maintained by Israel and its Arab neighbors. Anwar el-Sadat, Egypt's new president, continued the late Gamal Abdel Nasser's anti-Israel policies.

Israel continued to insist that only when Israeli and Arab leaders meet face to face, without preconditions, can the issues dividing them be resolved. The Arab world continued to reject this proposal, refusing to recognize Israel as a sovereign state.

The issue of the status of Jerusalem remained a problem. Israel declares that Jerusalem is an undivided city, and an integral part of Israel. Israel guarantees that Christian, Muslim, and Jewish holy shrines in Jerusalem will be safeguarded and all worshipers shall have free access to them.

Others insist Jerusalem should become an internationalized city. They feel Israel alone should not have control of Jerusalem, and especially of the religious shrines in the Old City (The Old City is that part of Jerusalem that had been under Arab control before the six-day war.)

In the fall, the Synagogue Council of America invited spiritual leaders of all faiths in the United States to hold a special meeting to discuss the status of Jerusalem.

▶AMERICAN JEWISH LIFE

In America, the increasing number of mixed marriages has become an important problem. Many Jewish men and women are marrying non-Jews who have not converted to the Jewish faith.

Orthodox and Conservative rabbis will not officiate at a marriage if either party is not of the Jewish faith.

Although Reform Judaism is officially opposed to mixed marriages, there are a number of Reform rabbis who will officiate at them. However, there is sharp disagreement on the most valid way of handling it. Some Reform rabbis require a promise to bring up the children in the Jewish faith. Some require that the couple become affiliated with a Jewish congregation, or read certain Jewish texts. Still others require that the couple maintain a Jewish home.

It is likely that the 1972 convention of the Central Conference of American Rabbis (the national Reform wing) will consider the matter, and will determine Reform Judaism's responsible role in dealing with mixed marriages.

JACOB PHILIP RUDIN
Past President, Central Conference
of American Rabbis and Synagogue
Council of America

SCIENCE

IN 1971 scientists applied themselves to a great variety of studies. Their work ranged from research on the basic parts of matter, less than a billionth of an inch across, to studies of quasars, billions of light-years away.

Physicists studied evidence pointing to the existence of quarks and partons, which may be the fundamental particles of matter. Other scientists announced that they had created a new element. And the dream of almost unlimited electrical power for the world came closer with the building and operation of a number of tokamaks, machines whose purpose is to help find a way to carry on continuous nuclear fusion.

Attention was given in 1971 to the location of two newly discovered galaxies, and to new evidence that quasars are the most distant objects in the universe. New evidence was also found that strengthened the theory that some dying stars disappear into a strange state called a "black hole."

Earth scientists uncovered new evidence to explain the cause of many earthquakes, and continued experiments aimed at controlling the distribution and fall of rain, snow, and hail.

Two newly discovered galaxies, Maffei 1 and Maffei 2, were photographed in 1971 on infrared film. Other objects in this photo are ordinary stars in the Milky Way.

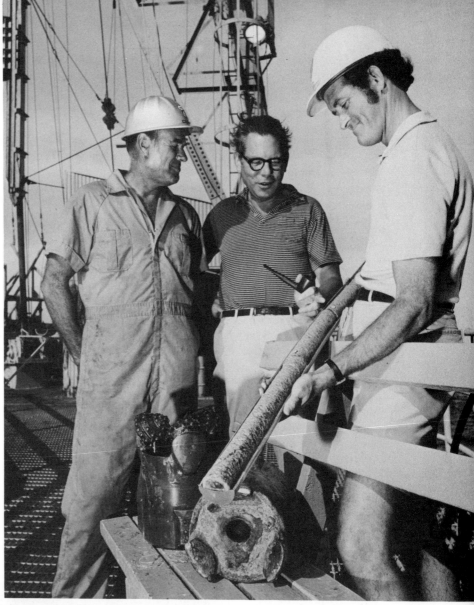

Scientists aboard the "Glomar Challenger," a specially designed and equipped ship, study a core of rock and sediment brought up from the ocean floor. Some of the findings of this Deep-Sea Drilling Project indicate that the floor of the Pacific Ocean has moved northward nearly 1,800 miles in 100,000,000 years.

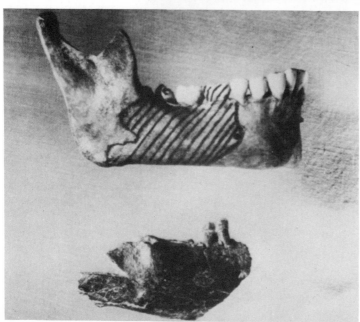

In 1967 archeologists discovered part of the lower jaw of an early ancestor of man called Australopithecus in Kenya, Africa. In 1971 scientists determined that the specimen (bottom) was about 5,500,000 years old. The ancient jawbone fragment is compared here with a jawbone fragment from a modern man (top). Shading on the modern jawbone indicates area comparable to prehistoric fragment.

Quarks and Partons

Everything in the world is made of matter. Nearly 2,500 years ago, Democritus, a Greek philosopher, wrote about his ideas on matter. Matter can be divided again and again into smaller pieces, he said, but a point will be reached when the pieces can no longer be divided. Democritus believed that these tiny solid pieces were the basic particles which make up matter. He called the particles "atoms," meaning "something that cannot be cut." As scientists studied matter, the idea of solid indivisible atoms had to be given up. Experiments done in the early 1900's showed that atoms are made up of various smaller particles. Protons and neutrons form the nucleus of the atom, and electrons surround the nucleus. In time, with the aid of powerful atom-smashing machines, many more parts, or subatomic particles, were discovered. Are the subatomic particles the basic particles that make up matter?

One modern theory states that subatomic particles are, in turn, made up of still smaller particles. These particles were given the name of quarks. According to this theory a proton, for example, is made up of three quarks. No one has shown for certain that quarks actually exist.

In 1971 experimenters at the Stanford Linear Accelerator Center and Brookhaven National Laboratory fired electrons and other particles into protons obtained from hydrogen. Their results indicated that protons are made up of smaller parts, to which they gave the name of partons. Now scientists are trying to learn whether quarks and partons are the same thing, or whether they are related in some way, and whether science has finally found the true basic particles of matter—the "something that cannot be cut."

Making New Elements

In the 1860's about sixty chemical elements were known. Their characteristics or properties varied tremendously. There were liquids, gases, and solids. Some elements were light, and others were very heavy.

Chemists tried to arrange the elements in some way that would give them a better understanding of the reasons for the great variety of properties. Dmitri Ivanovich Mendeleev, a Russian chemist, worked out an arrangement in chart form, known as the Periodic Table of the Elements. It is still in use. The properties of an element can be accurately predicted from its place in the table. Mendeleev had to leave some empty spaces to make all the known elements fit into the table. He predicted that elements not yet discovered would fit into those spaces and told what their properties would be. Later, as each element was discovered, its properties were found to be exactly those that Mendeleev had predicted.

Today 105 elements, 13 of them manmade, are known. Two more man-made elements, numbers 106 and 107, may have been created in 1971. Scientists continue to predict the properties of new man-made elements before they are made. Most of these elements are unstable, breaking down only a few millionths of a second after their creation. But one element, which will fit into the 114th space in the periodic table, is expected to be stable. In 1971 a group of British, American, and Israeli scientists attempted to make element 114. They succeeded in producing an element that may be number 112.

Tokamaks—A Step toward Nuclear Fusion

An atomic bomb does its damage by releasing enormous amounts of energy. The energy comes from the splitting, or fission, of the atomic nuclei of heavy radioactive substances such as uranium. All the nuclei split at nearly the same time, in one millionth of a second or less. A hydrogen bomb causes far more damage, as the atomic nuclei of a hydrogen isotope join together in the process of nuclear fusion.

Nuclear fission is used in more than one hundred power stations throughout the world to generate electricity. This and other peaceful uses of fission are possible because the rate of splitting of the nuclei can be accurately controlled. In place of the sudden explosive release of energy in the bomb, a slow release of energy, in the form of heat, takes place. The heat is used to make steam which is used to drive electrical generators.

Scientists in many countries are seeking a way to use fusion reactions for generating much-needed electricity. The fuel for fusion can be heavy hydrogen, which can be prepared from seawater. Vast amounts of energy are obtainable from a small amount of fuel. Another advantage of fusion is that its waste products, unlike those of fission, are not dangerously radioactive.

Fusion takes place only at temperatures of many millions of degrees. A fusion bomb has a fission bomb built into it. The explosion of the fission bomb provides the high temperatures needed to trigger the fusion reaction. So far, no one has found a successful method for releasing energy gradually by fusion. The fuel must be heated to a temperature of many millions of degrees, and kept at that temperature if fusion is to continue.

To date, the most promising device is a Russian-developed machine called the tokamak. It has heated plasmas to near-fusion temperatures, but only for about one hundredth of a second. (A plasma is the only form in which matter exists at extremely high temperatures. It is a gas whose atoms have had one or more electrons torn away by the great heat. Powerful magnetic fields keep the plasma confined within the tokamak, away from the walls of the machine.)

In 1971, scientists and engineers at Oak Ridge National Laboratory, Princeton University, and other places built and operated tokamaks of various designs in the hope of achieving a breakthrough toward controlled, sustained fusion. If they succeed, nuclear fusion may become the world's greatest source of electric power.

▶ASTRONOMY

How Stars Die

A star may give off enormous amounts of heat and light for billions of years. But it dies when it runs out of nuclear fuel. Its death may come about in one of several ways. A small star, about the size of our sun, cools down slowly until no heat is left in it, and it shrinks to about the size of the earth. The cold, shrunken star is called a white

The Ormak—an American-designed tokamak—at Oak Ridge National Laboratory.

dwarf. A large star may collapse suddenly, then blow apart to form a glowing cloud of gas, called a supernova. Some of the matter in the star's center is packed together tightly, forming a pulsar or neutron star. Such a star is extremely dense. A bit of its matter no bigger than a cube of sugar would weigh hundreds of millions of tons.

Scientists believe that there is still another way in which a very large star may die. As the star collapses, the densely packed atoms increase its gravitation enormously. The gravitation prevents the escape of any material from the collapsed star. Even light cannot escape, so the object cannot be seen. The existence of these invisible objects, called "black holes," was predicted in 1939 by J. Robert Oppenheimer and Hartland Snyder.

In 1971 a satellite detected X rays coming from a source within the constellation Cyg-

An artist's conception of how a very large star can collapse into a "black hole." As the star collapses, its gravity becomes so great that even light cannot escape; the light rays are pulled into the hole.

nus (the Swan). Neither light nor radio waves can be detected from the source. Scientists are giving close attention to this development, for these observations are exactly what could be expected if the source of the X rays were a black hole.

Two New Galaxies

The sun and billions of other stars make up our galaxy—the Milky Way. Huge as the Milky Way seems to us, it is only one of millions of galaxies in the universe. Galaxies are not spread evenly through the universe; they are gathered in groups. The Milky Way is part of a group of about twenty galaxies, called the local group. In 1968 an Italian astrophysicist, Paolo Maffei, reported finding two faint cloudlike patches in the sky. He believed that they were two galaxies of the local group, not previously observed. During 1971 scientists at several observatories in California and in France were studying the patches, named Maffei 1 and 2, trying to learn whether they really are our neighbors in the local group.

The Mysterious Quasars

The most mysterious objects in astronomy are starlike objects called quasars. One puzzle concerns the tremendously powerful light and radio waves given off by quasars. Although it is about the size of a star, a quasar emits more light and radio energy than a whole galaxy, which may be made up of billions of stars. One explanation offered is that a quasar is a collapsing star. During the collapse, large amounts of matter are changed to energy, and this is the energy that is given off.

A second mystery about quasars concerns

their distance. They appear to be the most distant objects in the universe, as well as the oldest. Some scientists disagree with these findings, pointing out that extremely strong gravitational fields can affect the measurements. Such powerful gravitation may exist around quasars.

In 1971, however, Dr. James E. Gunn of the California Institute of Technology, using pictures made through the 200-inch telescope of the Palomar Observatory, presented strong evidence that quasars are really the most distant objects in the universe.

▶ EARTH SCIENCE

Earthquakes

A new theory has made the last few years exciting ones for earth scientists. It is the plate-tectonics theory, and it appears to have answers to some old geological mysteries, such as the cause of continental drift, and of many earthquakes. According to the theory, the earth's crust is made up of six great plates and several smaller ones. The plates move slowly. Places where two plates move past one another are especially liable to have earthquakes and other disturbances. The San Andreas Fault in California, where two large plates meet, is such a place. Instead of slipping past smoothly at the usual rate of one or two inches per year, the plates may block one another. Tremendous pressure builds up, until there is a sudden release, and the plates jump suddenly, causing the movement that is an earthquake.

On February 9, 1971, a severe earthquake shook the Los Angeles area. Understandably, new interest was aroused in finding ways to prevent earthquakes and to lessen damage. Knowing when and where an earthquake will occur would be a big step in lessening the quake's toll.

Geologists and geophysicists are moving toward a science of earthquake prediction. They can accurately measure factors connected with earthquakes, such as built-up strains along faults, changes in the tilt of the ground, and changes in the earth's magnetic field. Studies are made of the frequency of quakes in given areas. Attention is also being given to the possibility of stopping big, disastrous jumps in the earth's crust by causing small quakes to occur. It may be possible to do this by setting off underground explosions, or by flooding underground areas with water.

The Deep-Sea Drilling Project

Much evidence to support the plate-tectonics theory has come from the Deep-Sea Drilling Project, which is sponsored by a group of universities and oceanographic laboratories in the United States. Since 1968 their specially designed and equipped ship, *Glomar Challenger,* has been drilling holes in the floors of the Atlantic and Pacific Oceans and the Mediterranean Sea. Cores of rock and sediment are brought up for study by scientists. In 1971, during the 17th trip of the *Glomar Challenger,* cores were taken in the mid-Pacific region. The sedi-

Left to right: Dr. Hyron Spinrad, Dr. Ivan King, and Dr. Nan Dieter, astronomers at the University of California. In 1971 they studied Maffei 1 and Maffei 2, two newly discovered galaxies.

The "Glomar Challenger," the drilling vessel of the Deep-Sea Drilling Project. The derrick that houses the huge drill stands 194 feet above the ship's waterline.

Skeletons (magnified 100 times) of radiolarians—marine protozoans—found on the Pacific Ocean floor by the Deep-Sea Drilling Project. By studying these skeletons, oceanographers hope to learn about the history of the ocean.

An important archeological find was a 200,000-year-old human skull. It is matched here with a jawbone found in the same area of France in 1970.

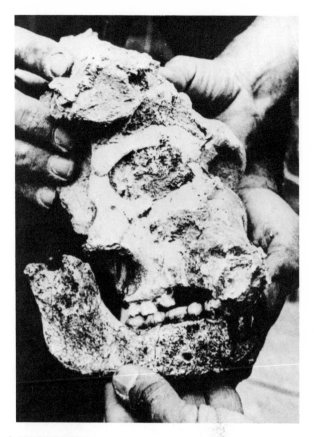

ments in the cores contain the remains of microscopic plants and animals. Cores taken at a considerable distance north of the equator contained fossils of a type that grew at the equator. This evidence indicates a northward movement of the ocean floor. The finding agrees with previous studies of the earth's magnetic field in this area, which show that the ocean floor has moved northward nearly 1,800 miles in 100,000,000 years. However, later trips indicated that this movement of the ocean floor had not been steady and continuous, but had undergone temporary reversals in direction.

Controlling the Weather

Man has always suffered from disasters caused by the weather. Today there is hope that some kinds of extreme weather conditions can be controlled.

In the 1940's scientists began to "seed" clouds by dropping pellets of Dry Ice into them from airplanes. Later, crystals of silver iodide were also used. The pellets and crystals provide centers, or nuclei, around which raindrops can form. In this way, rain can sometimes be made to fall in an area where it is needed.

Late in 1971, the National Oceanic and Atmospheric Administration began an experiment that may lessen the huge snowfalls around Buffalo, New York. The plan is to drop large amounts of silver-iodide crystals to provide great numbers of nuclei on which snowflakes can form. The larger the number of snowflakes, the smaller will be their size and weight. It is hoped that some of the smaller, lighter snowflakes will be carried off by winds, instead of falling on the city.

Each year, in the United States alone, crop damage from hailstorms amounts to hundreds of millions of dollars. In 1971, the National Center for Atmospheric Research, in Boulder, Colorado, began a five-year experiment to find ways of preventing hailstorms. One method to be tested will be cloud seeding with silver-iodide crystals.

▶ARCHEOLOGY

Man's Ancestors

Africa is the source of the oldest remains of hominids, or manlike creatures. Remains discovered in 1924 in South Africa were given the name of *Australopithecus*. Similar remains found later on were estimated to be nearly 2,000,000 years old. In 1967 an expedition sponsored by Harvard University found part of the lower jaw of an *Australopithecus* creature near Lake Rudolf in Kenya. In 1971 scientists studying the specimen determined it was about 5,500,000 years old. This means that man's ancestors go farther back in time than was previously thought. One of the leading scientists in the hunt for man's ancestors is Dr. Louis S. B. Leakey. He is preparing to explore a site which he believes may yield hominid remains going back as far as 7,000,000 years.

J. W. GEORGE IVANY
Columbia University

ONTARIO SCIENCE CENTRE

There are no "please do not touch" signs at the Ontario Science Centre in the heart of Toronto. Here people are encouraged to handle the exhibits and participate in the scientific demonstrations. And so it is no surprise that more than 2,000,000 visitors have flocked to this educational Disneyland since it opened on September 27, 1969.

Each week some 20,000 adults and schoolchildren stroll past the reception hall's 100 fountains and into the large rooms that house the Centre's nearly 500 exhibits. These exhibits include a giant laser that punches holes in solid brick, and a replica of a lunar-landing module complete with control panels and closed-circuit television. There is also a ticktacktoe-playing computer that visitors can compete against.

The Science Centre is unlike any other museum. In the psychedelic Science Arcade, you may pedal a bicycle which activates a generator that puts your image on a television screen and at the same time sets off a record player that blasts out rock music. A walk through an innocent-looking door brings you into a crazily-tilted house that causes you to stumble about like a drunken man.

It's all a lot of fun, but it's also educational. And that's the main point. While pedaling the bike, you learn something about how generators work. While trying to walk through the tilted house, you are getting a lesson in how the body's senses can become distorted and confused.

As one student wrote after his visit, "Today I have seen and learned what high-school teachers have been trying to show us in words for years."

Young visitors to the Ontario Science Centre learn how paper is made.

A demonstration of a laser beam that is powerful enough to cut through an asbestos brick.

While testing his strength, a youngster learns how pulleys work.

Youngsters play ticktacktoe with a computer in the Science Centre's Hall of Communications.

Two young boys watch a fish through a magnifying lens in the Science Centre's Hall of Life.

STAR TRACING

A star tracer in the Science Arcade shows visitors how hand and eye co-ordination can be thrown off when they try to do a simple but unfamiliar task while looking in a mirror.

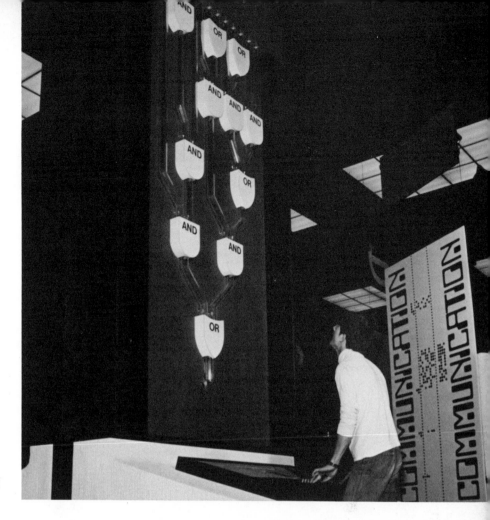

A logic game in the Hall of Communications.

A youngster discovers he has inherited the ability to roll his tongue—something not everyone can do.

Which two colors are the same? A youth tests his ability to perceive different colors.

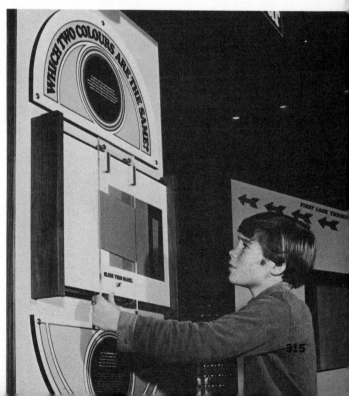

315

SPACE EXPLORATION

AFTER the near disaster of Apollo 13 in 1970, many people were concerned about the safety and practicality of future space-flights. However, in 1971 the United States manned-spaceflight program produced some impressive results. In January, Apollo 14 successfully landed two astronauts on the moon. And during the Apollo 15 flight in July, David Scott and James Irwin became the first men to travel upon the lunar surface in a battery-powered vehicle.

The Soviet Union, in an effort to boost its lagging space program, assembled a 25-ton space station and placed it in earth orbit in June. The station, named Salyut, and Soyuz 11, which had docked with it, set a new record for duration of manned orbital flight. However, the project ended in disaster when the Soviet crew died in their spacecraft while returning to earth.

Because of this tragedy, and the possibility of others like it, the United States and the Soviet Union have taken steps to ensure future co-operation in space. In 1971, officials of both countries held several top-level meetings to discuss the co-ordination of space-exploration programs.

Soviet cosmonauts Georgi Dobrovolsky (front left), Viktor Patsayev (rear), and Vladislav Volkov. Their flight aboard Soyuz II ended in disaster: all three died while returning to earth.

Tracks made in the lunar dust by the Modularized Equipment Transporter (MET) lead away from the Apollo 14 lunar module. The MET, a two-wheeled cart, was used to carry instruments and lunar rock samples.

The Apollo 14 crew: Air Force Major Stuart A. Roosa (left), the command-module pilot; Navy Captain Alan B. Shepard, Jr. (center), the spaceship commander; and Navy Commander Edgar Dean Mitchell, the lunar-module pilot. In 1961, Shepard had been the first American to make a spaceflight.

Apollo 15 is considered the most successful manned spaceflight. For three days astronauts David R. Scott and James B. Irwin explored the lunar surface, using the electrically powered lunar rover (above). Below: Irwin salutes the U.S. flag, planted near the lunar lander.

Splashdown was a tense moment for the Apollo 15 astronauts: one of the parachutes did not open properly. As a result, the command module hit the water with greater impact than expected (above left). But astronauts Alfred M. Worden, Irwin, and Scott (above right, left to right) were not hurt. Below: Navy frogmen prepare the command module for lifting onto the deck of the USS "Okinawa."

THE APOLLO PROGRAM

Many people wondered whether the Saturn-Apollo space program could do anything more than land men on the moon for brief periods of time. The flights of Apollo 14 and 15 in 1971 put all suspicions to rest. The public was able to witness, by color television, lunar missions that lasted for several days and covered many miles of the moon's surface.

Apollo 14, launched on January 31, landed astronauts Alan Shepard and Edgar Mitchell in the rugged Fra Mauro highlands on February 5. On that day, and the next, the men pulled a cart full of tools and instruments during their working excursions. Climbing up Cone Crater, they made their way among boulders, many of which measured 10-12 feet in height. The astronauts took numerous photographs of the moon and the heavens. They also placed several instruments in the lunar soil, dug a 20-inch core sample from the surface, and gathered many rocks.

Apollo 15 was launched toward the moon on July 26. Four days later David Scott and James Irwin landed near Hadley Rille, at the base of the towering Apennine Mountains. Besides the astronauts, the lunar module carried a battery-powered "car," the lunar rover. The men drove this vehicle many miles around the landing site, thus becoming the first "motorists" on the moon. Scott and Irwin set up several instruments, completed numerous experiments, and gathered rocks. One of these fragments, called the "Genesis rock," later proved to be anorthosite, a material associated with the early history of earth. Initial dating of this rock puts its age at about 4,150,000,000 years, the oldest rock fragment yet found on the moon. This date suggests that the earth and moon have similar early histories.

While the two astronauts remained on the lunar surface for nearly three days, Alfred Worden stayed in the command module, circling the moon. He operated new Apollo instruments for photographing and identifying surface materials on the moon and released a small scientific satellite into lunar orbit.

When Scott and Irwin blasted off from the moon's surface to rejoin the orbiting command ship on August 2, the whole world was able to watch the event. For the first time, a television system left behind on the lunar rover transmitted to earth a launch from another world.

Some of the results of the Apollo flights are yet to be known. However, one surprising discovery has been revealed. Scientists from Rice University think that gases detected by Apollo 12 and 14 instruments left on the moon might be geysers of water vapor emerging from deep inside the moon through cracks caused by moonquakes. Apollo 17 will carry instruments to explore this possibility.

THE PROBLEM OF WEIGHTLESSNESS

Charles Berry, director of space medicine for NASA, revealed that Stuart Roosa, Apollo 14 crew member, suffered ill effects on his return to earth. Roosa, who remained with the command module in lunar orbit, was in a noticeably weaker state than were his fellow crew members, who landed on the moon. It also took Roosa longer to reacclimatize to earth gravity. And all the Apollo 15 astronauts recovered unusually slowly from the effects of weightlessness.

Doctors are not exactly sure what this means. Almost all of the American astronauts have had different physical reactions after spending time in a weightless environment. Because of the effect weightlessness has on the heart, circulatory system, and skeleton, future astronauts will probably need "artificial gravity" (rotation of the spaceship) on long flights.

MARINER 9

In May, Mariner 9, an unmanned American spacecraft, blasted off for Mars. It reached its destination on November 13, and became the first spacecraft ever to orbit another planet. Initial photographing of the planet was hampered by a violent sandstorm that was raging over much of Mars. Nearly all surface details were obscured. However, as the storm began to subside, photographs became clearer. The pictures sent back by Mariner 9 during its three-month mission will help scientists map the mysterious planet

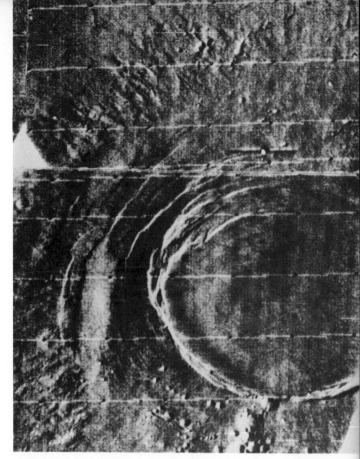

A photograph of the planet Mars taken by Mariner 9 from a distance of 445,000 miles.

A close-up of a Martian crater seventy miles in diameter, photographed by Mariner 9.

and determine whether or not some form of life exists on Mars.

▶ SOVIET SPACE PROGRAMS

In April, the Russians launched the Salyut space station. The 3-man Soyuz 10 spacecraft was launched 4 days later and successfully docked with the space station for 5½ hours before returning to earth. On June 6, the Russians sent off Soyuz 11, another 3-man spacecraft, which also docked with the space station to form an orbiting manned spaceship. On June 23, the Salyut crew broke the record for duration of a manned spaceflight held by the Soyuz 9 cosmonauts. The Salyut crew separated the Soyuz 11 from the station on June 29 for their return to earth. The landing of the spacecraft appeared normal, but when the rescue crew opened the ship's hatch, they found all 3 cosmonauts dead. Russian officials later announced that the 3 men had died from a rapid change in the air pressure in their capsule. This could have been due to a failure in securing the hatch of their spacecraft when they left the space station, or to a leak in the spacecraft.

Russia's remotely controlled lunar rover, Lunokhod 1, launched in November 1970, continued to operate off and on until October 1971.

The Russians launched two unmanned spacecraft to Mars in May 1971. Both were successfully injected into interplanetary orbit. On November 27, the Mars 2 spacecraft reached the vicinity of the planet and went into orbit. A capsule was ejected from the spacecraft, placing an emblem displaying the Soviet hammer and sickle on the surface of Mars. This is the first man-made object to be landed on that distant planet. In early December, Mars 3 joined her sister ship in orbit. This craft released a capsule that made a soft landing on Mars. Signals were transmitted to earth for 20 seconds and then ceased suddenly.

The Soviet Union has had much success with its development of orbital superbombs and satellite-interceptor spacecraft. (Cosmos 400, launched on March 19, was intercepted by Cosmos 404 on April 3.) However, their success with these destructive weapons has won the Russians few friends and little, if any, military advantage.

▶ SPACE CO-OPERATION

In January, George Low, then acting NASA Administrator, visited Moscow to discuss greater international co-operation in space. Low held his talks with Mstislav V. Kildysh, president of the U.S.S.R. Academy of Sciences and head of the Russian space program. An agreement was announced on exchanging samples of lunar material, procedures for co-ordinating work in meteorology, earth resources, and space biology and medicine, and joint docking designs. The two countries also agreed to exchange data acquired from the American and Russian Mars spacecraft.

In the midst of the ill-fated Soyuz 11 flight in June, a team of Russian engineers was visiting the NASA Manned Spacecraft Center in Houston, Texas. This meeting was one of a series held throughout the year. They were there to discuss with the American space officials common docking arrangements and space rescue. An agreement on these subjects had been reached in 1970. Co-operation between the two nations might mean that further unfortunate incidents, such as the Soyuz 11 tragedy, could be avoided.

NASA officials announced in April the selection of 108 scientists from seven countries (Canada, the United Kingdom, Denmark, West Germany, France, Sweden, and the United States) to help plan Grand Tour missions. This technically demanding project will result in exploratory unmanned space missions to the outer planets of Jupiter, Saturn, Neptune, and Uranus.

World co-operation in satellite meteorology has been steadily increasing. The United States has been preparing all nations in the use of earth-resource surveys. The first group working on the Earth Resources Technology Satellite, scheduled for launch in 1972, includes scientists from 22 countries. Representatives from India, Greece, Australia, Norway, Venezuela, Chile, as well as from many other nations, are involved in this ambitious project.

▶ COMMUNICATIONS SATELLITES

A new era of co-operative use of space was opened in Washington, D.C., on August 20. Representatives of 54 nations, including the United States, signed a permanent charter for the international communications "consortium" called INTELSAT. The new arrangement will lessen U.S. control of the world's satellite communications.

The first satellite of the Intelsat 4 series was launched by NASA in January. This satellite is able to carry as many as 9,000 telephone calls or up to 12 television programs between Europe and the United States.

Germany, France, and Japan announced plans in 1971 to build domestic communications satellites. In April, NASA and the Canadian Department of Communications signed an agreement to place an advanced domestic communications satellite in orbit by 1974.

▶ REUSABLE SPACE TRANSPORTATION SYSTEM

Not every satellite launched in 1971 proved to be a success. NASA launch-rockets failed to put a solar observatory into planned orbit in September, and failed to orbit a weather satellite in October.

If these satellites had been flown into space by a rocket-powered airplane, had been inspected and released there, and the airplane had been returned to earth for reuse, the successful deployment of the satellites would have been much more certain. Such a launch would be less expensive, perhaps only a half as much. With this idea in mind, NASA engineers worked on the development of a rocket-powered space plane, or reusable space shuttle. NASA has also tried to interest European nations in contributing to the development of a reusable space transportation system.

JOHN NEWBAUER
Editor in Chief, *Astronautics & Aeronautics*

AFTER APOLLO

IN December 1972, after the flights of Apollo 16 and Apollo 17, the Apollo program will come to an end.

▶ SKYLAB

The next step in the manned exploration of space is the Skylab program. Skylab will reach the flight stage early in 1973, when three manned missions are planned.

Skylab is a space workshop—a kind of space station made by taking the third stage of the Apollo moon rocket and turning it into living and working quarters for three astronauts. The workshop will be launched, unmanned, from Cape Kennedy and placed into earth orbit. The first crew would then be sent up in an Apollo spacecraft a day or so later to rendezvous and dock with the workshop. They would remain in space for 28 days. The second and third crews would remain for 56 days.

The most important experiments to be accomplished in the Skylab compose the study of the effect of spaceflight on man himself: on the blood vessels, heart, and on the ear and eye systems that affect balance. Surveys of earth's resources and studies of the sun are also planned. An Astronaut Maneuvering Unit will be tested, as well. This unit is designed to provide men in outer space the freedom of movement they need for assembling large structures in space and performing other strenuous tasks.

▶ SPACE SHUTTLE

During the latter part of the 1970's a new type of vehicle, the Space Shuttle, will be developed and tested. This amazing new vehicle will combine features of the rocket, the spacecraft, and the airplane. Unlike space vehicles of the past, it will be reusable.

The Space Shuttle will consist of two stages: the booster and the orbiter. The orbiter will be launched by the booster in a vertical takeoff to a speed of about 5,000 feet per second. The orbiter engines will then ignite, thrusting the vehicle into orbit. The rocket fuel and oxygen are carried by the orbiter in tanks that are dropped off after it reaches orbit. When the orbiter completes its mission in space, it will fire its retrorockets and re-enter the atmosphere, using atmospheric drag to slow it down to airplane speeds. It will then use its wings to fly back to its base on earth. The booster will be recovered at sea.

Indeed, the Space Shuttle could change space operations completely. It will greatly reduce the cost of space operations because it is reusable. It will carry men into space to visit space stations or to do scientific experiments in orbit in the Shuttle itself. It will place weather, communications, earth-resource, and other kinds of satellites in orbit. If necessary, it could bring the satellites back to earth for repair. Its quick-turnaround features will make it ideal for emergency situations, such as space rescue.

▶ PROJECT VIKING

During the next few years various unmanned space missions will be flown. One of the most interesting is called Viking. The goal of this project is to land an unmanned spacecraft on Mars in 1976. After the spaceship lands, it will send back information to the earth on the makeup of Mars' soil.

▶ THE GRAND TOUR

Another project under consideration is called the Grand Tour. In this an unmanned spacecraft would go far out into space and send back information on the characteristics of the outer planets.

▶ LUNAR STATION

It seems certain that man will return to the moon. A permanent lunar base and international colony is likely to be the next goal. From Apollo, space scientists have learned that such a base could supply its own needs. It could produce its own power from the sun, and supplies of water and air from the chemicals that exist on the moon. Men and women could live and work there in comfort, and perhaps, in time, in luxury. Such a base would be a great scientific workshop. And it would encourage the best kind of international co-operation.

ROBERT R. GILRUTH
Director, NASA Manned Spacecraft Center

SPORTS

THE 1971 sports scene will not only be remembered for spectacular victories, but also for the defeats of teams and individuals regarded as unconquerable. In the National Hockey League the Boston Bruins set dozens of records in regular-season play, and then were eliminated in postseason competition as the Montreal Canadiens captured the Stanley Cup.

In the National Basketball Association, the great New York Knicks were supplanted by the Milwaukee Bucks, who surpassed most of the Knicks' achievements.

The Baltimore Orioles, "the greatest baseball club in history," according to their own manager, were defeated by the Pittsburgh Pirates in a seven-game World Series.

Muhammad Ali, who had been insisting "I am the greatest," failed to match his own vocal appraisal in the ring, as Joe Frazier became the undisputed heavyweight champion.

On the golf course Lee Trevino, in a one-month "impossible" streak, won the U.S., Canadian, and British Opens.

Tennis unveiled a 19-year-old Australian youngster, Evonne Goolagong. The surprise winner of the Wimbledon tournament, she defeated pros like Margaret Court and Billie Jean King.

Ack Ack, being ridden here by Willie Shoemaker, was named 1971's Horse of the Year.

Evonne Goolagong, a 19-year-old Australian, astounded the tennis world by capturing the Wimbledon women's singles title.

Lee Trevino, winner of the U.S., Canadian, and British Opens, leans over Jack Nicklaus as they ponder a shot in the World Cup Golf Championship. In this international team match, the two Americans defeated South Africa's top team of Harold Henning and Gary Player.

AUTO RACING

Jackie Stewart of Scotland became 1971's world driving champion. He captured 6 of the 11 Grand Prix Formula One races.

Two of the world's leading Grand Prix circuit drivers were killed in crashes during the year: Mexico's Pedro Rodriguez, 31, died on July 11; and Jo Siffert, 35, of Switzerland, died on October 24.

Peter Revson of California became the first American racing driver to win the Canadian-American Challenge Cup. The English-built McLaren cars, which have always dominated Can-Am racing, won 8 of the 10 races.

The U.S. Auto Club offered a record prize total of $2,640,000 for its 11-race championship series in 1971. While Joe Leonard finished at the top of the point standings, the greatest share of the bulging purse went to Al Unser. Unser captured 5 events, including the rich Indianapolis 500.

WORLD DRIVING FORMULA 1 CHAMPIONSHIPS

Grand Prix	Driver
South African	Mario Andretti, U.S.
Spanish	Jackie Stewart, Scotland
Monaco	Jackie Stewart
Dutch	Jacky Ickx, Belgium
French	Jackie Stewart
British	Jackie Stewart
German	Jackie Stewart
Austrian	Jo Siffert, Switzerland
Italian	Peter Gethin, Britain
Canadian	Jackie Stewart
U.S.	François Cevert, France

World Driving Champion: Jackie Stewart

OTHER CHAMPIONSHIPS

NASCAR Grand National Champion: Richard Petty, U.S.
SCCA Canadian-American Challenge Cup: Peter Revson, U.S.
USAC Champion: Joe Leonard, U.S.
Indianapolis 500: Al Unser, U.S.

Jackie Stewart races across the finish line at the British Grand Prix.

BASEBALL

Earl Weaver, manager of the Baltimore Orioles, has called his team "the greatest baseball club in history." But in 1971 the Orioles were beaten by the Pittsburgh Pirates in a dramatic, 7-game World Series.

Spurred by Frank and Brooks Robinson and a fabulous pitching staff, the Orioles have won 318 games and three American League pennants in three years. But they have lost two of the three World Series. They were defeated by the Mets in 1969 and by the Pirates in 1971, after sandwiching in a success against Cincinnati.

During each of those three seasons, Baltimore coasted to the American League's Eastern Division title. The team then went on to sweep the play-off competitions from the Western Division champions. In 1971 the Orioles defeated the West's Oakland Athletics, who had been spurred on to victory by Vida Blue, a 22-year-old left-hander with 24 victories.

Blue and his teammates were unable to check the Orioles, who had four 20-game winners of their own: Dave McNally (21-5), Jim Palmer (20-9), Mike Cuellar (20-9), and Pat Dobson (20-8).

In the National League the Pirates had a fairly easy time, finishing with a 7-game margin in the Eastern Division. In the Western Division, the San Francisco Giants struggled through the stretch to hold off the surging Los Angeles Dodgers by a single game. In the play-off for the pennant, the Giants managed to win the opening game, but lost the next three to the Pirates.

In the Series, the Orioles appeared to justify their manager's appraisal as they won the first two games in their home park, 5–3 and 11–3. A sharp, unbelievable turnabout occurred when the Series moved to Pittsburgh. Steve Blass turned back the Orioles

The Pirates' Roberto Clemente, named outstanding player of the World Series, connects for a triple.

FINAL MAJOR-LEAGUE STANDINGS

AMERICAN LEAGUE

Eastern Division

	W	L	Pct.	GB
*Baltimore	101	57	.639	
Detroit	91	71	.562	12
Boston	85	77	.525	18
New York	82	80	.506	21
Washington	63	96	.396	38½
Cleveland	60	102	.370	43

Western Division

	W	L	Pct.	GB
Oakland	101	60	.627	
Kansas City	85	76	.528	16
Chicago	79	83	.488	22½
California	76	86	.469	25½
Minnesota	74	86	.463	26½
Milwaukee	69	92	.429	32

NATIONAL LEAGUE

Eastern Division

	W	L	Pct.	GB
*Pittsburgh	97	65	.599	
St. Louis	90	72	.556	7
New York	83	79	.512	14
Chicago	83	79	.512	14
Montreal	71	90	.441	25½
Philadelphia	67	95	.414	30

Western Division

	W	L	Pct.	GB
San Francisco	90	72	.556	
Los Angeles	89	73	.549	1
Atlanta	82	80	.506	8
Cincinnati	79	83	.488	11
Houston	79	83	.488	11
San Diego	61	100	.379	28½

* pennant winners

MAJOR-LEAGUE LEADERS

BATTING
(425 or more at bats)

American League

	G	AB	H	Pct.
Oliva, Minnesota	126	487	164	.337
Murcer, New York	146	529	175	.331
Rettenmund, Baltimore	141	491	156	.318
Tovar, Minnesota	157	657	204	.311
Carew, Minnesota	146	577	177	.307
Otis, Kansas City	147	555	167	.301
May, Chicago	139	496	145	.292
White, New York	147	524	153	.292
Buford, Baltimore	122	449	130	.290
Horton, Detroit	119	450	130	.289

National League

	G	AB	H	Pct.
Torre, St. Louis	161	634	230	.363
Garr, Atlanta	154	641	219	.342
Beckert, Chicago	131	530	181	.342
Clemente, Pittsburgh	132	522	178	.341
H. Aaron, Atlanta	139	495	162	.327
Sanguillen, Pittsburgh	138	533	170	.319
Jones, New York	136	505	161	.319
Alou, St. Louis	149	608	192	.316
Brock, St. Louis	157	640	200	.313
Staub, Montreal	162	599	186	.311

PITCHING

	W	L	ERA
Seaver, New York, NL	20	10	1.76
Blue, Oakland, AL	24	8	1.82
Wood, Chicago, AL	22	13	1.91
Downing, Los Angeles, NL	20	9	2.68
Palmer, Baltimore, AL	20	9	2.68
Jenkins, Chicago, NL	24	13	2.77
McNally, Baltimore, AL	21	5	2.89
P. Dobson, Baltimore, AL	20	8	2.90
Lolich, Detroit, AL	25	14	2.92

HOME RUNS

	HR
Stargell, Pittsburgh, NL	48
H. Aaron, Atlanta, NL	47
L. May, Cincinnati, NL	39
Johnson, Philadelphia, NL	34
Williams, Atlanta, NL	33
Bonds, San Francisco, NL	33
Melton, Chicago, AL	33
Cash, Detroit, AL	32
Jackson, Oakland, AL	32

1971 WORLD-SERIES RESULTS				
	R	H	E	Winning/Losing Pitcher
1. Pittsburgh	3	3	0	Ellis
Baltimore	5	10	3	McNally
2. Pittsburgh	3	8	1	Johnson
Baltimore	11	14	1	Palmer
3. Baltimore	1	3	3	Cuellar
Pittsburgh	5	7	0	Blass
4. Baltimore	3	4	1	Watt
Pittsburgh	4	14	0	Kison
5. Baltimore	0	2	1	McNally
Pittsburgh	4	9	0	Briles
6. Pittsburgh	2	9	1	Miller
Baltimore	3	8	0	McNally
7. Pittsburgh	2	6	1	Blass
Baltimore	1	4	0	Cuellar

Vida Blue, top pitcher of the American League, finished the season with a 24–8 record.

with a 3-hitter, 5–1; Bruce Kison, a 21-year-old reliever, limited the Birds to one hit in six innings for a 4–3 decision; and Nelson Briles shut them out 4–0.

Back in Baltimore, the Birds evened the Series with a 3–2 verdict in 10 innings. But in the seventh game, Blass hurled the Bucs to their first Series success in 11 years with a 4-hitter for a 2–1 victory. The batting hero of the Series was the Pirates' 37-year-old outfielder, Roberto Clemente. He batted .414 in the 7 games and hit two home runs, one in the vital seventh game. The Puerto Rican veteran also sparkled defensively, with spectacular catches and great throws.

Individual honors during the major-league season were fairly well scattered. Joe Torre of the St. Louis Cardinals won the National League batting title with a .363 average and was the leader in runs batted in with 137. Willie Stargell of the Pirates paced the home-run hitters with 48. Tony Oliva of the Minnesota Twins captured the batting crown in the American League with .337; Bill Melton of the Chicago White Sox led in homers with 33; and Harmon Killebrew of the Twins led in runs batted in with 119. Ferguson Jenkins of the Chicago Cubs topped National League pitchers in victories with 24. Mickey Lolich of the Detroit Tigers enjoyed that distinction in the American League with 25.

BASKETBALL

The nation's horde of basketball aficionados thought it had seen the peak of team artistry when the New York Knickerbockers rolled to the National Basketball Association title during the 1969–70 season. Then, in 1970–71, along came Milwaukee. Lew Alcindor was joined by Oscar Robertson through a trade from Cincinnati. With this strength the Bucks made a shambles of the competition during the regular season. Their 66–16 record surpassed the Knicks' 1969–70 total wins by 6 games.

Milwaukee was just as overpowering in the play-offs, as it swept through San Francisco, Los Angeles, and Baltimore. Battered physically, the Knicks were eliminated by Baltimore in the semifinal series. The Bullets in turn were demolished by the Bucks in four straight engagements. A member of the league for only three years, Milwaukee became the second team in NBA history to capture the championship series with a four-game sweep. The Boston Celtics had done the same to the Minneapolis Lakers in 1959.

Alcindor was the high scorer as the Bucks romped toward the crown, and was voted most valuable player in the league. Veteran Robertson, who had waited 11 years to play with a championship outfit, was the spearhead in the 118–106 victory game that closed out the final series. The "Big O" led his club with 30 points and directed a spectacular defense.

In the American Basketball Association, the Los Angeles franchise was transferred to the salt flats. As the Utah Stars, they finished second to the defending champion Indiana Pacers in regular-season play. They then eliminated the Pacers in the semifinal play-off series. The Stars went on to defeat Kentucky for the title. Equally surprising was the subsequent departure of the Utah coach, Bill Sharman. He signed with the Los Angeles Lakers of the NBA.

In the college ranks, the unstoppable UCLA team gained its fifth consecutive NCAA title. Villanova's Howard Porter, named best player in the NCAA tournament, made an outstanding effort to hold off UCLA. Despite this, the Uclans of coach Johnny Wooden defeated the Wildcats in the final, 68–62.

Lew Alcindor of the Milwaukee Bucks scores against the Baltimore Bullets in the NBA championship series. The Bucks beat the Bullets in four straight games.

FINAL NBA STANDINGS

EASTERN CONFERENCE

Atlantic Division

	W	L	Pct.
New York	52	30	.634
Philadelphia	47	35	.573
Boston	44	38	.537
Buffalo	22	60	.268

Central Division

	W	L	Pct.
Baltimore	42	40	.512
Atlanta	36	46	.439
Cincinnati	33	49	.402
Cleveland	15	67	.183

WESTERN CONFERENCE

Midwest Division

	W	L	Pct.
Milwaukee	66	16	.805
Chicago	51	31	.622
Phoenix	48	34	.585
Detroit	45	37	.549

Pacific Division

	W	L	Pct.
Los Angeles	48	34	.580
San Francisco	41	41	.500
San Diego	40	42	.488
Seattle	38	44	.463
Portland	29	53	.354

NBA Championship: Milwaukee

FINAL ABA STANDINGS

East Division

	W	L	Pct.
Virginia	55	29	.655
Kentucky	44	40	.524
New York	40	44	.476
Floridians	37	47	.440
Pittsburgh	36	48	.429
Carolina	34	50	.405

West Division

	W	L	Pct.
Indiana	58	26	.690
Utah	57	27	.679
Memphis	41	43	.488
Texas	31	54	.365
Denver	30	55	.353

ABA Championship: Utah

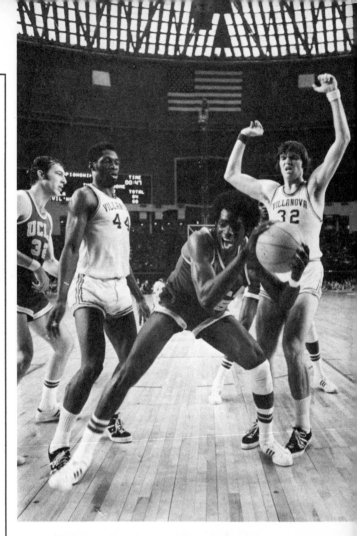

Sidney Wicks outmaneuvers two Villanova players in NCAA title match. UCLA won its fifth consecutive title.

COLLEGE BASKETBALL

Conference Champions

Atlantic Coast: South Carolina
Big Eight: Kansas
Big Ten: Ohio State
Ivy League: Pennsylvania
Mid-American: Miami (Ohio)
Missouri Valley: Drake
Pacific Eight: UCLA
Southeastern: Kentucky
Southern: Furman
Southwest: TCU
West Coast Athletic: Pacific
Western Athletic: Brigham Young
Yankee: Massachusetts

NCAA: UCLA
National Invitation Tournament: North Carolina

BOXING

Muhammad Ali continued to be the focal point of interest in world boxing in 1971. But he's no longer world champion.

After 3½ years in "exile" because of legal difficulties involving the military draft, Ali had resumed fighting in 1970. In March 1971 he fought Joe Frazier, who had been recognized by most people as heavyweight king during Ali's absence. Frazier became the undisputed champion with a 15-round decision at Madison Square Garden. It was a bruising battle that sent both fighters to the hospital for repairs. Each participant received a guarantee of $2,500,000. Receipts for closed-circuit television in theaters and arenas across the United States were estimated at $20,000,000.

While Frazier relaxed, Ali fought in many exhibitions and bouts. He will probably try to recapture the title in 1972.

U.S. fighters once dominated pugilism. But at the end of the year, Frazier and light-heavyweight champion Bob Foster were the only U.S. boxers listed on the World Boxing Association's and World Boxing Council's rosters of champions.

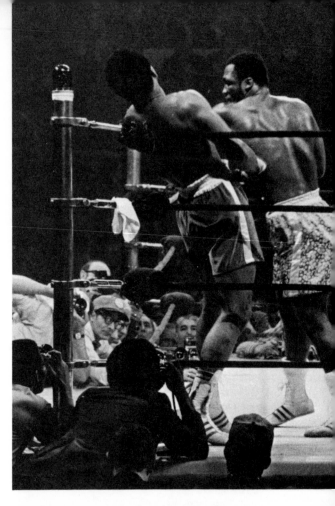

Joe Frazier staggers Muhammad Ali. . . .   . . . .Ali heads for the canvas in the 15th round. . . .

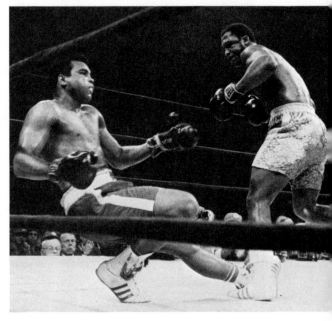

. . . .Ali hits the canvas for an 8-count.

WORLD BOXING CHAMPIONS

Division	Champion
Heavyweight	Joe Frazier, U.S.
Light Heavyweight	Bob Foster, U.S.
(disputed)	Vicente Rondon, Venezuela
Middleweight	Carlos Monzon, Argentina
Jr. Middleweight	Carmelo Bossi, Italy
Welterweight	Jose Napoles, Mexico
Jr. Welterweight	Bruno Arcari, Italy
(disputed)	Nicolino Locche, Argentina
Lightweight	Ken Buchanan, Scotland
Jr. Lightweight	Ricardo Arrendondo, Mexico
(disputed)	Alfredo Marcano, Venezuela
Featherweight	Kuniaki Shibata, Japan
(disputed)	Antonio Gomez, Venezuela
Bantamweight	Ruben Olivares, Mexico
Flyweight	Erbito Salavarria, Philippines
(disputed)	Masao Ohba, Japan

BOWLING

AMERICAN BOWLING CONGRESS CHAMPIONS

Classic Division

Singles: Vic Iwlew
Doubles: Bill Zuben-Barry Warshafsky
Team: Chester Iio Investments (Houston, Texas)
All-Events: Gary Dickinson

Regular Division

Singles: Al Cohn
Doubles: Tony Maresca-Bill Haley
Team: Carter Tool & Die Corp. (Rochester, N.Y.)
All-Events: Al Cohn

WOMEN'S INTERNATIONAL BOWLING CHAMPIONS

Open Division

Singles: Ginny Younginer
Doubles: Dorothy Fothergill-Mildred Martorella
Team: Koenig & Strey Real Estate (Wilmette, Ill.)
All-Events: Lorrie Koch

DOG SHOWS

Above: Trixie, Dog Hero of the Year, helped save her two-year-old master from drowning. Below: Ch. Chinoe's Adamant James, Best in Show at the Westminster and International dog shows. Below right: Alaskan malamutes: Best Brace at Westminster.

WESTMINSTER KENNEL CLUB

Best in Show: Ch. Chinoe's Adamant James

Hound: Ch. Vin-Melca's Vagabond, Norwegian Elkhound

Nonsporting: Ch. Tally Ho Tiffany, miniature poodle

Sporting: Ch. Chinoe's Adamant James, English springer spaniel

Terrier: Ch. O'Connell of Kerry Oaks, Kerry Blue

Toy: Ch. Duke's Lil Red Baron of O'Kala, Pomeranian

Working: Ch. Pavo de la Steingasse, standard schnauzer

INTERNATIONAL KENNEL CLUB

Best in Show: Ch. Chinoe's Adamant James

Hound: Ch. The Rectory's Rabbi, bloodhound

Nonsporting: Ch. Haus Brau Executive of Acadia, standard poodle

Sporting: Ch. Chinoe's Adamant James, English springer spaniel

Terrier: Ch. De Go Hubert, West Highland white

Toy: Ch. Continuation of Gleno, Yorkshire terrier

Working: Ch. Dolph von Tannenwald, Doberman pinscher

FOOTBALL

Standings in the National Football League had a familiar look as the regular season ended, except for one surprise. In the National Conference, Dallas led the Eastern Division for the sixth straight year; Minnesota topped the Central group for the fourth consecutive campaign; and San Francisco was a repeater in the West.

The American Conference likewise followed form closely. The Baltimore Colts, Super Bowl champions a year ago, Kansas City, Cleveland, and Miami survived the 14-game schedule and were in positions to bid for the Super Bowl bonanza.

The surprise entry in the postseason competition was Washington, which hadn't enjoyed anything approaching championship stature since 1945. George Allen, released by the Los Angeles Rams, was installed as head coach and led the Redskins into the play-offs by trading for a collection of veterans. Called the "over-the-hill gang," the Redskins qualified for the play-offs with the best second-place record in the NFC.

Beaten in the 1971 Super Bowl by Baltimore, the Cowboys handed the key role of quarterback to Roger Staubach midway through the 1971 campaign. Staubach completed 133 passes before he was intercepted in the season's finale. En route to their 11–3 record, Dallas won 7 straight games with Staubach quarterbacking. Staubach then led Dallas to a 24–3 victory over the Miami Dolphins in the 1972 Super Bowl.

In college football, Nebraska and Alabama concluded their regular seasons with perfect records and were ranked Nos. 1 and 2 in the various polls. In climactic Thanksgiving weekend battles of unbeaten teams, Nebraska defeated Oklahoma, 35–31, and Alabama romped over Auburn, 31–7. That set up the Nebraska-Alabama clash in the Orange Bowl as the decisive contest. By defeating Alabama 38–6, Nebraska was rated the nation's number one college team.

Despite the presence of outstanding ball carriers such as Johnny Musso of Alabama, Greg Pruitt of Oklahoma, and Ed Marinaro of Cornell, the Heisman Trophy was captured by Auburn passer Pat Sullivan.

Miami's Larry Csonka crashes through the Kansas City line for a touchdown.

FINAL NFL STANDINGS

NATIONAL CONFERENCE

Eastern Division

	W	L	T	Pct.	PF	PA
Dallas	11	3	0	.786	406	222
Washington	9	4	1	.692	276	190
Philadelphia	6	7	1	.462	221	302
St. Louis	4	9	1	.308	231	279
N.Y. Giants	4	10	0	.286	228	362

Central Division

	W	L	T	Pct.	PF	PA
Minnesota	11	3	0	.786	245	139
Detroit	7	6	1	.538	341	286
Chicago	6	8	0	.429	185	276
Green Bay	4	8	2	.333	274	298

Western Division

	W	L	T	Pct.	PF	PA
San Francisco	9	5	0	.643	300	216
Los Angeles	8	5	1	.615	313	260
Atlanta	7	6	1	.538	274	277
New Orleans	4	8	2	.333	266	347

Conference Champion: Dallas

AMERICAN CONFERENCE

Eastern Division

	W	L	T	Pct.	PF	PA
Miami	10	3	1	.769	315	174
Baltimore	10	4	0	.714	313	140
N.Y. Jets	6	8	0	.429	212	299
New England	6	8	0	.429	238	325
Buffalo	1	13	0	.071	184	394

Central Division

	W	L	T	Pct.	PF	PA
Cleveland	9	5	0	.643	285	273
Pittsburgh	6	8	0	.429	246	292
Houston	4	9	1	.308	251	330
Cincinnati	4	10	0	.286	284	265

Western Division

	W	L	T	Pct.	PF	PA
Kansas City	10	3	1	.769	302	208
Oakland	8	4	2	.667	344	278
San Diego	6	8	0	.429	311	341
Denver	4	9	1	.308	203	275

Conference Champion: Miami

1972 Super Bowl Winner: Dallas

COLLEGE FOOTBALL

Conference Champions

Atlantic Coast: North Carolina
Big Eight: Nebraska
Big Ten: Michigan
Ivy League: Dartmouth; Cornell (tied)
Mid-American: Toledo
Pacific Eight: Stanford
Southeastern: Alabama
Southern: Richmond
Southwest: Texas
Western Athletic: Arizona State
Yankee: Connecticut; Massachusetts (tied)

Heisman Trophy: Pat Sullivan, Auburn
Lambert Trophy: Penn State

In the Orange Bowl, Nebraska's Jerry Tagge laterals to teammate Jeff Kinney. Nebraska beat Alabama 38–6.

Dallas Cowboy quarterback Roger Staubach scrambles for a first down in the National Football Conference championship game with the San Francisco 49ers. Dallas won 14–3 and then went on to beat the Miami Dolphins 24–3 in the Super Bowl.

GOLF

With the help of an incredible one-month streak, Lee Trevino of El Paso, Texas, became the dominant figure in golf in 1971. From mid-June to mid-July, the merry Mexican-American swept to victory in the United States, Canadian, and British Open tournaments, three of the world's major golfing events. Remarkably poised under pressure, Trevino acquired two of his major crowns in play-offs. He was tied with Jack Nicklaus after the regulation 72 holes in the U.S. Open, and with Art Wall in the Canadian Open.

Trevino was slowed during the summer by an emergency appendectomy, and failed to muster a challenge in the four-man World Series of Golf. This tournament was won by Masters champion Charles Coody.

During the 1971 season Trevino earned $231,202. However, it was Jack Nicklaus who reached a record high in single-season earnings with a total of $244,490.

PROFESSIONAL

Individual
U.S. Open: Lee Trevino, U.S.
Masters: Charles Coody, U.S.
British Open: Lee Trevino
Canadian Open: Lee Trevino
PGA: Jack Nicklaus, U.S.
World Series of Golf: Charles Coody
Ladies PGA: Kathy Whitworth, U.S.
U.S. Women's Open: JoAnne G. Carner, U.S.

Team
World Cup: United States
Ryder Cup: United States

AMATEUR

Individual
U.S. Amateur: Gary Cowan, Canada
U.S. Women's Amateur: Laura Baugh, U.S.
British Amateur: Steve Melnyk, U.S.

Team
Curtis Cup: United States
Walker Cup: Great Britain

Charles Coody blasts out of a sand trap during second-round play in the 1971 Masters.

HOCKEY

The Boston Bruins carried off almost everything the National Hockey League has to offer in the way of trophies and records. But they were somewhat numbed spectators as the Montreal Canadiens captured the most prized possession of all, the Stanley Cup.

During the regular 78-game season, the Bruins, defending cup champions, had adding machines clicking overtime as they shattered 32 team and individual records. A notable team record was their total of 57 victories, compared with the previous high of 46. Phil Esposito erased 9 individual marks, including the scoring record with his 76 goals, a major contribution to the club's total of 399. Two years earlier, the Bruins had set the previous standard of 303 goals.

"This is the greatest hockey team ever assembled," chortled rabid New England fans —until the Bruins were toppled by the Canadiens in the opening play-off series for the Stanley Cup. Rookie goalie Ken Dryden and Pete Mahovlich, likewise lacking prior play-off experience, were outstanding performers in the upset of the Bruins, 4 games to 3.

The Canadiens went on to eliminate Minnesota in the second round in 6 games. Led by old pro Henri Richard, they then snatched the championship in a bitterly fought 7-game series with the Chicago Black Hawks. Richard accounted for the tying and winning goals in the 3–2 triumph in the seventh and decisive contest. The victory gave Montreal

its 16th Stanley Cup. It was a remarkable comeback for the team that a year earlier had suffered through its worst season and had failed to qualify for the play-offs.

FINAL NHL STANDINGS

East Division

	W	L	T	Pts.
Boston	57	14	7	121
New York	49	18	11	109
Montreal	42	23	13	97
Toronto	37	33	8	82
Buffalo	24	39	15	63
Vancouver	24	46	8	56
Detroit	22	45	11	55

West Division

	W	L	T	Pts.
Chicago	49	20	9	107
St. Louis	34	25	19	87
Philadelphia	28	33	17	73
Minnesota	28	34	16	72
Los Angeles	25	40	13	63
Pittsburgh	21	37	20	62
California	20	53	5	45

Stanley Cup: Montreal

Art Ross Trophy (scoring): Phil Esposito, Boston
Calder Trophy (rookie): Gil Perreault, Buffalo
Georges Vezina Trophy (goalie): Ed Giacomin and Gilles Villemure, New York
Hart Trophy (most valuable player): Bobby Orr, Boston
Lady Byng Trophy (sportsmanship): Johnny Bucyk, Boston
Norris Trophy (defense): Bobby Orr

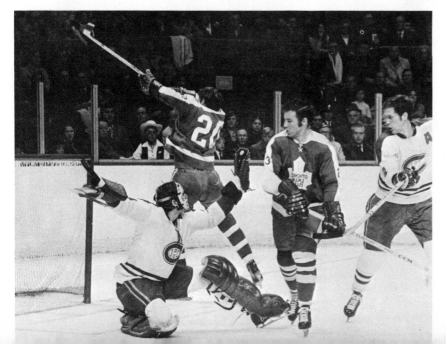

Canadien goalie Ken Dryden makes a one-handed save during regular-season play against the Toronto Maple Leafs. Dryden's outstanding performance in the Stanley Cup play-offs helped Montreal defeat Boston, Minnesota, and Chicago.

HORSE RACING

HARNESS STAKES WINNERS

Race	Horse
Cane Futurity	Albatross
Dexter Cup Trot	Quick Pride
Hambletonian	Speedy Crown
International Trot	Une de Mai
Kentucky Futurity	Savoir
Little Brown Jug	Nansemond
Messenger Stakes	Albatross
Realization Pace	Windy Way
Realization Trot	Timothy T.
Yonkers Futurity	Quick Pride

THOROUGHBRED STAKES WINNERS

Race	Horse
Belmont Futurity	Riva Ridge
Belmont Stakes	Pass Catcher
Flamingo Stakes	Executioner
Jockey Club Gold Cup	Shuvee
Kentucky Derby	Canonero II
Preakness	Canonero II
Suburban Handicap	Twice Worthy
Travers	Bold Reason
United Nations Handicap	Run the Gantlet
Wood Memorial	Good Behaving

ICE SKATING

FIGURE SKATING

North American Championships

Men: John M. Petkevich, U.S.

Women: Karen Magnussen, Canada

Pairs: Jo-Jo Starbuck-Ken Shelley, U.S.

Dance: Judy Schwomeyer-James Sladky, U.S.

World Championships

Men: Ondrej Nepela, Czechoslovakia

Women: Beatrix Schuba, Austria

Pairs: Irina Rodnina-Aleksei Ulanov, U.S.S.R.

Dance: Ludmila Pakhomova-Aleksandr Gorshkov, U.S.S.R.

SPEED SKATING

World Championships

Men: Ard Schenk, Netherlands

Women: Nina Statkevich, U.S.S.R.

Canonero II, winner of the Kentucky Derby, crosses the finish line to win the Preakness.

Canada's Karen Magnussen: women's North American figure-skating champion.

Barbara Cochran, winner of the women's slalom in the 1971 U.S. Alpine Senior Championships.

SKIING

WORLD CUP CHAMPIONSHIPS

Men: Gustavo Thoeni, Italy
Women: Annemarie Proell, Austria

U.S. ALPINE SENIOR CHAMPIONSHIPS

Men
Downhill: Bob Cochran, U.S.
Giant Slalom: Bob Cochran
Slalom: Otto Tschudi, Norway
Combined: Bob Cochran

Women
Downhill: Cheryl Bechdolt, U.S.
Giant Slalom: Laurie Kreiner, Canada
Slalom: Barbara Cochran, U.S.
Combined: Judy Crawford, Canada

NCAA CHAMPIONSHIPS

Downhill: Otto Tschudi, University of Denver
Slalom: Otto Tschudi
Cross-Country: Ole Hansen, University of Denver
Jumping: Vidar Nilsgard, University of Colorado
Nordic Combined: Bruce Cunningham, University of New Hampshire
Alpine Combined: Otto Tschudi
Team: University of Denver

SWIMMING

Shane Gould

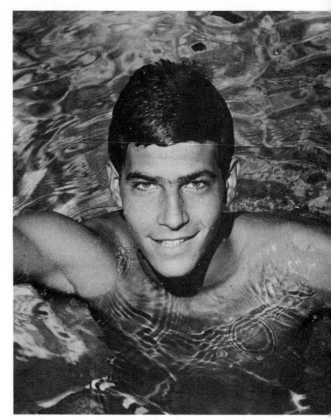

Mark Spitz

WORLD SWIMMING RECORDS SET IN 1971

Event	Holder	Time
	Men	
100-meter backstroke	Roland Matthes, E. Germany	0:56.7
200-meter backstroke	Roland Matthes	2:05.6
100-meter butterfly	Mark Spitz, U.S.	0:55.1
200-meter butterfly	Hans Fassnacht, W. Germany	2:03.3
200-meter freestyle	Mark Spitz	1:53.5
400-meter freestyle	Tom McBreen, U.S.	4:02.1
800-meter freestyle	Graham Windeatt, Australia	8:28.6
	Women	
200-meter butterfly	Ellie Daniel, U.S.	2:18.4
200-meter freestyle	Shane Gould, Australia	2:05.8
400-meter freestyle	Shane Gould	4:21.2
800-meter freestyle	Shane Gould	8:58.1
1,500-meter freestyle	Shane Gould	17:00.6

TENNIS

A bright, new, sparkling figure appeared on the world tennis scene. Evonne Goolagong, a 19-year-old youngster from a remote area of Australia, swept to the women's title on the historic Wimbledon courts. In the process, she upset Billie Jean King in the semifinal and Margaret Smith Court in the final. Each had been a three-time winner at Wimbledon, and Mrs. Court had been the winner in 77 major tournaments. Earlier, Miss Goolagong had captured the French championship.

Another Cinderella was unveiled in the U.S. Open at Forest Hills. Sixteen-year-old Chris Evert advanced to the semifinals before she was eliminated by Mrs. King, who went on to win the title. In men's singles, John Newcombe of Australia was the Wimbledon victor. U.S. honors went to Stan Smith, in the absence of many topflight professionals.

Players who were under contract to World Championship Tennis, Inc., were barred from Forest Hills. But they competed in a series of tournaments for prize money that reached substantial proportions. By the end of the year, the spectacular Australian "Rocket" Rod Laver had become tennis' greatest money-winner with a nine-year career total of over $1,000,000.

Sixteen-year-old Chris Evert at Forest Hills.

TOURNAMENT TENNIS

	U.S. Open	Wimbledon	Australian Open	French Open
Men's Singles	Stan Smith, U.S.	John Newcombe, Australia	Ken Rosewall, Australia	Jan Kodes, Czechoslovakia
Women's Singles	Billie Jean King, U.S.	Evonne Goolagong Australia	Margaret Court, U.S.	Evonne Goolagong, Australia
Men's Doubles	John Newcombe, Australia-Roger Taylor, Britain	Roy Emerson-Rod Laver, Australia	John Newcombe-Tony Roche, Australia	Arthur Ashe-Marty Riessen, U.S.
Women's Doubles	Rosemary Casals, U.S.-Judy Dalton, Australia	Billie Jean King-Rosemary Casals, U.S.	Margaret Court, U.S.-Evonne Goolagong, Australia	Françoise Durr-Gail Chanfreau, France

Davis Cup Winner: United States

WORLD TRACK AND FIELD RECORDS SET IN 1971

Event	Holder	Time or Distance
Men		
440-yard dash	John Smith, U.S.	44.5
2-mile run	Emile Puttemans, Belgium	8:17.8
1,000-meter run	Tom Von Ruden, U.S.	2:20.4
120-yard hurdles	Rod Milburn, U.S.	13.0
high jump	Pat Matzdorf, U.S.	7' 6¼"
hammer throw	Walter Schmidt, W. Germany	250' 8"
triple jump	Pedro Perez, Cuba	57' 1"
Women		
800-meter run	Hildegard Falck	1:58.3
1,500-meter run	Karin Burneleit, E. Germany	4:09.6
high jump	Ilona Gusenbauer, Austria	6' 3½"
discus throw	Faina Melnik, U.S.S.R.	212' 10½"

At Berkeley, California, during a U.S.-Soviet track-and-field meet, Pat Matzdorf of Wisconsin clears the bar at 7' 6¼" to set a new world record in the high jump.

In what has been called the "Dream Mile," Marty Liquori of Villanova and Jim Ryun, holder of the world record for the mile, race toward the finish line. Liquori won—by less than a yard.

The opening ceremonies at the Pan-American Games, held in Cali, Colombia.

THE PAN-AMERICAN GAMES

Amateur athletes from the United States reaped the customary harvest of medals at the sixth Pan-American Games in Cali, Colombia. Still, they returned home in a slight daze after being defeated in basketball and baseball, two basically North American sports. Brazil was the victor in basketball, Cuba in baseball.

Individually the U.S. performers were overpowering. They won 105 gold medals, 73 silver, and 40 bronze out of a total of 595 medals that were available to the 4,150 athletes from 30 competing nations. Cuban athletes made a surprisingly strong showing, winning 30 gold medals, 50 silver, and 25 bronze.

In men's track and field, the U.S. squad captured 20 of 24 gold medals, and in men's swimming and diving, the United States accounted for 16 victories in 17 events.

Individually, John Crosby, a gymnast from Southern Connecticut State College, collected the most medals: 2 gold, 5 silver, and 1 bronze in 8 events. Frank Heckl, a 6'5" swimmer from the University of Southern California, won 6 gold medals (3 in individual races and 3 in relays) and 1 silver.

Roxanne Pierce, a 16-year-old high-school senior from Kensington, Md., dazzled spectators at the gymnastic competition by winning 6 medals. These included the coveted gold medal in the all-around competition.

Queen of the swimmers was a Canadian, Leslie Cliff. She captured gold medals in the 200- and 400-meter individual medley and a silver medal in the 100-meter butterfly. She also was a member of the winning 400-meter medley-relay team.

Left: American gymnast John Crosby, winner of eight medals. Below: Debbie Van Kiekebelt of Canada, winner of the women's pentathlon. Below left: the Cuban and Brazilian basketball teams in a crucial playoff game; Brazil won the gold medal.

The United States team bats against Cuba in the baseball competition. In a stunning upset, the Cubans defeated the United States, and went on to win the gold medal in baseball.

Duane Bobick of the United States: heavyweight boxing champion of the Pan-American Games.

MEDAL WINNERS				
COUNTRY	GOLD	SILVER	BRONZE	TOTAL
United States	105	73	40	218
Cuba	30	50	25	105
Canada	19	20	41	80
Brazil	9	7	14	30
Mexico	7	11	23	41
Argentina	6	4	12	22
Colombia	5	9	14	28
Jamaica	4	3	4	11
Puerto Rico	2	4	7	13
Venezuela	2	3	4	9
Netherlands Antilles	1	2	1	4
Trinidad-Tobago	1	1	5	7
Panama	1	1	4	6
Ecuador	1	0	2	3
Guatemala	1	0	0	1
Chile	0	3	4	7
Peru	0	1	4	5
Barbados	0	1	0	1
Uruguay	0	0	3	3
Guyana	0	0	1	1
TOTAL	**194**	**193**	**208**	**595**

These countries did not win medals in the Pan-Am Games: Bahamas, Bermuda, Costa Rica, Dominican Republic, El Salvador, Haiti, Nicaragua, Paraguay, Surinam, and Virgin Islands.
These countries did not participate in the Pan-Am Games: Bolivia, British Honduras, Honduras.

Canada's Nancy Robertson in the diving competition. She won a gold medal in the 10-meter platform event.

Track-and-field events always command the most attention in international competition. The classic event, the 1,500-meter run, resulted in an easy triumph for Martin Liquori. The 21-year-old Villanova alumnus set a Pan-Am record of 3:42.1, the equivalent of a 3:59 mile.

A crowd of 60,000 watched the opening ceremonies at Pascual Guerrero Stadium, and Frank Shorter of Boulder, Colo., began the competition by winning the 10,000-meter run. He closed the track program with a spectacular triumph in the marathon. The only other double winner in the men's track and field was Don Quarrie of Jamaica in the 100- and 200-meter dashes. His time for the longer sprint, 19.81 seconds, equaled the world record.

Two world records were broken during the Games. The U.S. men swimmers completed the 800-meter freestyle relay in a time of 7:45.82. And in the triple jump, Pedro Perez, a Cuban, soared 57 feet 1 inch.

There were riotous scenes at the Pan-Am Games when a U.S. Marine boxer, Reginald Jones, was awarded a decision over a Colombian, Bonifacio Avila. And there were political overtones in the defection of a Cuban fencer, Jose Diaz Hernandez, who reputedly slipped away to Miami. But for the Cubans, that minor item was overshadowed by their baseball team's 4–3 triumph over the United States. The Cubans won all of their eight games in the round-robin tournament en route to the gold medal. The United States was second with a 6–2 record.

In basketball the United States was eliminated in the preliminaries on a point system. Brazil finally captured the gold medal with a 5–0 record in the final competition.

TRANSPORTATION

THE biggest story in transportation in 1971 was the airline rate war. It gave students and others under the age of 26 the lowest transatlantic fares ever offered by scheduled airlines.

Perhaps of greater long-range importance was the United States Congress vote to end research and development on the American supersonic transport (SST) program. During 1971 the Anglo-French supersonic transport, the Concorde, and the Soviet TU-144 made a number of supersonic test flights.

On the ground, the future of United States railroads remained a matter of deep concern. The Penn Central, the country's biggest railroad, continued to be in serious financial trouble. The government-created National Railroad Passenger Corporation (known as Amtrak), a system of long-distance passenger routes, began operation on May 1. But late in the year it went back to Congress to ask for more money.

Outside the United States, the emphasis was on developing faster train service and on introducing improved equipment.

Deepwater shipping companies generally found 1971 a difficult year. However, a new design of ship, known as LASH, promised great advantages for cargo carrying.

In the United States the automobile industry set a one-month record for sales. More than one million new cars were sold in the month of October.

During the airline rate war of 1971, young people were offered overseas fares at bargain prices.

1972 AUTOMOBILES

Thunderbird

Dodge Colt

Chevrolet Nova

Dodge Dart Swinger

AMC Hornet Sportabout

Ford Gran Torino

Pontiac Sprint

Plymouth Fury

The great youth air fare war of midsummer 1971 started simply enough. The Belgian Government had approved the purchase of 747 jumbo jets for Sabena, the Belgian airline. The Government soon found that its new $25,000,000 airplanes were flying with cabins practically empty.

To cover costs on the jumbos, late in May the Belgian Government set a new policy. It directed that Sabena put into effect a $220 round-trip fare for students traveling between Brussels and New York during the summer-vacation period. At other times, the student fare would be $200.

Sabena, like most other scheduled international airlines, is a member of the International Air Transport Association (IATA). This is an organization set up by the airlines to establish and supervise international ticket prices. Ordinarily, all IATA members must charge the rate for a given route that has been agreed on at IATA meetings. However, member airlines are permitted to set their own fares when ordered to do so by their own governments. The Belgian Government had given Sabena such an order. In such cases all member airlines are free to change their fares to meet the competition.

Other airlines followed Sabena's example. Air France took the rate cuts one step further. Trans World Airlines acted to match both the Air France and Sabena fares. Eventually, Alitalia announced a youth-fare round trip between New York and Rome for $199. The only condition was that passengers had to be between 12 and 26.

The youth fares raised a storm of criticism from older passengers and from airlines that met the low rates to stay in the competition, but disapproved of the whole idea.

The United States National Air Carrier Association, which represents supplemental, or charter, airlines, filed a complaint with the United States Civil Aeronautics Board. The association charged that student and youth fares were unlawful. Other charter airlines, including West Germany's Atlantis Airways, promised to fight back with still lower charter and group rates.

Late in the year the IATA members met. A new fare schedule for transatlantic trips was agreed upon, with rates falling somewhere between the old fares and the low

Drawings of the planned Boeing supersonic transport. In 1971 Congress voted to end the project.

The Concorde, a supersonic transport built jointly by France and Great Britain.

The TU-144, the Russian-built supersonic transport, was displayed at the Paris Air Show.

Boeing employees hear a company spokesman announce that the SST program would be halted.

rates announced during the summer air fare war. Youth fares were actually slightly raised, but the new accord had lower fares for just about everyone else.

In the United States 1971 also marked the end of an eight-year program to develop an 1,800-mile-an-hour supersonic jet transport. Almost $1,000,000,000 had already been spent to develop the SST when Congress ended the program.

Early in the year, Rolls-Royce, Ltd., makers of fine British cars, declared bankruptcy. The company was developing the jet engine for Lockheed's wide-body airliner, the TriStar airbus. Rolls-Royce blamed its financial troubles on constantly rising costs in developing the jet engine. Lockheed laid off 6,500 workers at its Burbank and Palmdale, California, plants and warned that it faced bankruptcy without a government loan. The British company was nationalized as Rolls-Royce (1971) Ltd. Lockheed was given Federal loan guarantees, and work on the TriStar continued.

▶ **RAILROADS**

Amtrak, the first nationwide passenger rail system in the United States, began operation on May 1. Amtrak was created by the National Railroad Passenger Corporation, a government corporation. It took over the job of managing passenger service to more than 300 cities. Previously more than 20 different passenger railroads had served these cities. Amtrak was something less than a smash hit in its first 6 months. Late in the year it went back to Congress to ask for more money.

Amtrak noted at the Congressional hearings that fewer than half of its trains ran on time. Passengers who had been putting up with late trains for years seemed generally pleased that the trains were running at all, and Amtrak seemed likely to get the extra government help it needed.

An 18-day strike by men in certain jobs on 10 United States railroads ended in August with an agreement between management and the United Transportation Workers. The agreement provided for a 42 per cent wage increase over a period of 42 months. The agreement also provided for changes in some costly work rules.

Auto Train Corporation, a private company, announced the start of a new service for travelers and automobiles between Lorton, Virginia, near Washington, and Sanford, Florida, near the new Disney World. A kind of overland ferry, the Auto-Train will load cars of Florida- or Virginia-bound passengers on a train and carry the passengers in coach lounges or, for extra fare, in double bedrooms. Thirteen hours later the passengers will arrive at either the Florida or Virginia terminal. The trip by car takes more than 20 hours. Rates were announced as $190 one way for a car with driver and up to 3 passengers.

In countries outside the United States, high-speed rail service remained a major goal. Great Britain continued to cut the time of the 400-mile trip between Glasgow, Scotland, and London by extending electrified lines. West Germany tested an electromagnetic train capable of speeds up to 350 miles an hour. In Italy the 389-mile trip between Rome and Milan was cut to 5½ hours. Japan announced that work to extend its famous Tokyo-Osaka line would be completed in 1972. Trains will run at a top speed of 155 miles an hour.

▶ **MASS TRANSIT**

In 1971, Federal funds set aside for ground transit rose to about $600,000,000

INTERCITY PASSENGER ROUTES
NATIONAL RAILROAD PASSENGER CORPORATION
MAY 1, 1971

Amtrak board member David W. Kendall explains how the new national rail network will tie together 85 per cent of the major U.S. metropolitan areas.

In Virginia, a Florida-bound motorist drives his car aboard Auto-Train. He can then travel in comfort in the train's coach-lounge or bedroom.

The 155-mile-per-hour Super Limited Express speeds from Tokyo to Osaka, Japan.

from 1970's total of $435,000,000. And the Nixon administration has promised increased funds for future years. These figures are attractive to many depressed companies. They are looking at the possibility of breaking into the mass-transit market, a very rough business, even for established suppliers. The aerospace industry, especially, is making a determined effort to take a big share of the transit business away from the established carbuilding companies. In favor of this is New York's Metropolitan Transportation Authority (MTA). MTA is the largest purchaser of transit equipment in the world. MTA has been plagued by technical difficulties in its new designs from established builders of U.S. rail passenger cars.

However, the San Francisco Bay Area Rapid Transit District (BART) ordered its fleet of 250 new cars from Rohr Corporation, an aerospace manufacturer. Problems with the first 10 model cars caused BART to postpone the start of service from the fall of 1971 until the spring of 1972. And Rohr appeared to be finding its venture into transit an expensive one.

▶SHIPPING

Those concerned with the environment won a victory in January. President Nixon ordered that construction of the cross-Florida barge canal be permanently stopped. Already $50,000,000 had been spent on the project. The canal was being dug through

Volkswagens await delivery in the United States, where foreign-made compact cars continued to sell very well.

north central Florida near the wild Okla-waha River. Conservationists feared that the canal would ruin the area for the turkey, deer, and bear that now live in it.

Deepwater shipping companies generally found 1971 a difficult year. Long strikes, first on the West Coast, then on the East and Gulf coasts, tied up the ports and cut into profits. On the North Atlantic there was an oversupply of containerships which led to price-cutting and rate wars.

At the same time, containership operators faced competition from a new design of ship: LASH (for Lighter Aboard Ship). Container freighters must tie up and load and unload, using cranes based on shore. LASH ships carry their cargoes in lighters (another name for barges). These are lowered straight into the water by the ship's own cranes, thus cutting down on the time spent in a port.

▶ **AUTOMOBILES**

American automobile companies got a boost at midyear from President Nixon's attempt to control inflation. The President froze prices on goods produced in the United States, placed a surcharge on imports, and asked Congress to repeal the 7 per cent excise tax on automobiles.

These economic moves gave the American auto industry a price advantage that it had not had earlier in the year. There was a buying splurge that pushed auto sales in the last 4 months of the year to record highs. Profits for the industry were 589 per cent higher than those for the same 4 months of 1970. General Motors alone earned $217,000,000 in the third quarter of the year. In 1970 the company had lost $77,-000,000 in the same 3-month period.

But customers also snapped up the foreign autos shipped before the surcharge took effect. This resulted in a record year for auto sales in the United States. Combined sales of imported and domestic cars exceeded 10,000,000 for the first time, topping the 1968 record.

There was still another troublesome sign for highway interests. In the November election voters in New York State turned down a $2,500,000,000 bond issue. Half would have gone for highways, and half for mass-transit uses. The proposal was strongly supported by almost all elected leaders of both parties. Yet it was defeated by a big margin.

Part of the opposition to the bond issue came from a widespread feeling that the state already had too many highways and not sufficient mass transit. Four years earlier a similar bond issue had been approved. At that time, studies showed that the transit projects had been approved because they went along with highway projects. The change in the attitude of voters seemed to be an advance warning: opposition by conservation and other groups to huge public spending for highways could no longer be overlooked.

RODERICK CRAIB
Contributing Editor, *Business Week*

UNITED NATIONS

THE year 1971, the 26th year of the existence of the United Nations, marked an important change in the world organization. For the first time in more than 20 years, the 773,000,000 people of mainland China were represented in the UN.

The seating of the delegates of the People's Republic of China has given the UN an entirely new orientation. Ever since the signing of the UN Charter in San Francisco in 1945, the smaller member countries have tended to take their lead in international problems from one of the two "superpowers," the United States and the Soviet Union. The seating of Communist China means the establishment of a third center of influence in world affairs.

The United Nations witnessed another important event in 1971, the departure of Secretary-General U Thant. The Burmese statesman had headed the world organization for ten years. Kurt Waldheim, Austria's representative to the United Nations, was chosen U Thant's successor.

Chiao Kuan-hua, chairman of Communist China's UN delegation, addresses the General Assembly.

Kurt Waldheim of Austria was chosen the new secretary-general of the United Nations.

U Thant (left), the outgoing UN secretary-general, sits with Indonesian Foreign Minister Adam Malik. Mr. Malik was elected president of the General Assembly.

COMMUNIST CHINA AND THE UN

In 1949 the Nationalist armies of President Chiang Kai-shek of the Republic of China were defeated by the communist armies of Mao Tse-tung. President Chiang and some two million of his followers made their way to the island of Formosa, now better known as Taiwan, off the Chinese coast.

In the intervening years, both the Nationalist Government on Taiwan and the Communist Government in Peking had claimed to represent all China. For all these years the Nationalists had continued to represent China in the UN General Assembly, the Security Council, and all other UN bodies.

Nations friendly to Communist China sought to persuade the United Nations to reject the Nationalist Chinese representatives and admit instead a delegation from the mainland. The efforts consistently failed.

In 1971, President Richard Nixon announced that he would visit mainland China. To many countries friendly to the United States, this announcement signaled a drastic change in American policy. These countries foresaw a switch from a period of more than twenty years of enmity toward Communist China (dating from the Korean war in 1950) to a policy of peaceful collaboration and possibly even friendship with the regime that controls almost one quarter of the world's population. These countries also believed that the United States had come to the view that the Nationalist Chinese Government could no longer be regarded as the true representative of China.

Under these circumstances, a number of governments announced that they would no longer vote to have the Nationalist Government remain as China's sole representative in the United Nations.

The United States agreed that the People's Republic of China should take the permanent China seat in the UN Security Council. The United States also agreed that a Peking delegation should join the General Assembly and other UN bodies. But the United States hoped that a place in the Assembly could be retained for the Nationalist Chinese.

However, the Chinese Communist Govern-

Above: Tanzanian and Albanian UN delegates applaud defeat of a U.S. resolution calling for a two-thirds majority vote to expel Nationalist China. Later, the Nationalists were expelled and Communist China admitted. Left: Chinese-American opponents (above) and supporters (below) of Communist China.

ment said it would refuse to send a delegation to the UN so long as the Taiwan Government retained its UN representation, and the issue was placed before the member countries. When the final vote came on October 25, the General Assembly voted overwhelmingly (76 for, 35 against, 17 abstentions) to remove Nationalist China and admit Communist China. About three weeks later the delegation of the People's Republic of China, led by Deputy-Minister of Foreign Affairs Chiao Kuan-hua, arrived in New York.

▶WHAT THE PRESENCE OF MAINLAND CHINA MEANS

The presence of mainland China's representatives is certain to make the United Nations more realistic and more able to deal with problems of international peace and security. Mainland China will be a third major power in the United Nations, seeking to attract support from the communist countries which in the past took their lead from the Soviet Union. The Chinese will also look for support from among the Asian countries friendly to the United States and from the uncommitted Asian and African countries sometimes referred to as the "Third World."

▶ RETIREMENT OF U THANT

Early in 1971, Secretary-General U Thant stated that he would resign when he completed his second five-year term on December 31. U Thant became secretary-general in 1961 after Dag Hammarskjöld was killed in an airplane crash while on a peace mission to the Congo.

Twice during 1971 U Thant was ill enough to require hospital treatment. In spite of pressure from many governments urging him to serve another term, it soon became apparent that he meant to stand by his decision to retire.

Election of a new secretary-general is done by the General Assembly on recommendation of the Security Council. This means that each of the five permanent members of the Council, now including Communist China, can veto any candidate.

Several well-known diplomats emerged as possible successors to U Thant. After three days of balloting, the Security Council nominated Kurt Waldheim, Austria's UN representative. His nomination was ratified by the General Assembly. Waldheim had been a foreign minister of his country and a candidate for the presidency of Austria.

▶ UN ACTIVITIES IN THE MIDDLE EAST

During 1971, efforts to resolve the problems of relations between Israel and its Arab neighbors continued.

Following the so-called "Six Day War" in 1967, U Thant had appointed Gunnar Jarring, Swedish ambassador to Moscow, as his personal representative to try to bring about a peace agreement. Early in 1971 Ambassador Jarring resumed his contacts with the countries concerned. In February he took the initiative by asking both Egypt and Israel to give him commitments which he believed necessary for progress. From Israel, Mr. Jarring requested a commitment to withdraw from occupied Egyptian territory. From Egypt he sought a commitment to enter into a peace agreement with Israel. Egypt agreed to the commitment, but Israel

UN Middle East peace envoy Gunnar Jarring.

George Bush, the United States' new UN ambassador.

Pakistani UN Ambassador Agha Shahi at an emergency session of the UN Security Council. In the foreground, at left, is India's UN Ambassador, Samar Sen. Shahi called on the Council to make India "desist from its war of aggression."

in effect rejected Ambassador Jarring's peace proposal.

In December the General Assembly overwhelmingly voted for an Egyptian-sponsored resolution calling on Israel to withdraw from all occupied Egyptian territory. Israel announced it could not accept the resolution.

▶PAKISTAN AND INDIA

At first, the civil war in Pakistan and the resulting tension between Pakistan and India did not come directly before the United Nations. Pakistan claimed that its suppression of the East Pakistan autonomy movement was an internal situation. And under its Charter, the United Nations is unable to exercise jurisdiction in a country's internal affairs.

Eventually, the tension snapped into open warfare between India and Pakistan. Cease-fire and troop-withdrawal resolutions were introduced in the Security Council, but they were vetoed by the Soviet Union. Because it was unable to act in the crisis, the Security Council transferred the debate to the General Assembly. The Assembly voted 104 to 11 for a resolution calling for a cease-fire and troop withdrawal. However, Assembly decisions are only recommendations and cannot be enforced.

India, which was winning the brief war, disregarded the appeal and continued fighting until Pakistan accepted an armistice.

The UN was able to channel aid to the Pakistan refugees in India and to the homeless people in East Pakistan.

The UN continued to help underdeveloped countries in 1971. Shown here are Zambians in a UN-assisted program designed to encourage youngsters to stay on the land. They are taught farming and nutrition.

The official symbol for the UN Conference on Human Environment.

▶WORLD DISARMAMENT

Late in 1969 the United States and the Soviet Union had joined in Strategic Arms Limitation Talks (SALT). These talks continued during 1971, though no agreements were reached. In September, however, the Geneva Disarmament Conference drafted a treaty to ban weapons of biological warfare. The United States and the Soviet Union supported the draft treaty, and it was sent to the United Nations General Assembly. The treaty will go into effect when it is signed and ratified by 22 governments. Governments that sign the treaty will be required to destroy their stocks of bacteriological weapons.

▶OTHER UN ACTIONS

The United Nations continued to condemn aspects of colonialism such as apartheid, or separation of the races, in South Africa; the rule of the small white minority in Rhodesia; and South African control of South-West Africa (Namibia). But little action could be taken to eliminate the remaining few areas of colonialism, for the countries involved ignored UN recommendations.

▶ECONOMIC AND SOCIAL PROGRESS

The brightest horizons of the United Nations in 1971 were in economic and social fields.

The UN Development Program carried on more than 3,500 projects to raise living standards in over one hundred countries. Many activities were included, from improving health to finding new sources of food. UN experts undertook projects to provide better food, better health, and a better future for millions of people around the world.

▶THE CONFERENCE ON HUMAN ENVIRONMENT

During 1971, plans advanced for the UN-sponsored Conference on Human Environment. The conference will be held in Stockholm, Sweden, in June 1972. This will be the first time that the peoples of the world will get together to consider solutions to the worldwide problems of air and water pollution and how these affect man's health and welfare.

JOHN MACVANE
United Nations Correspondent
American Broadcasting Company

UNITED STATES

PRESIDENT Richard M. Nixon was personally responsible for four of the most important events of 1971. On July 15 he announced that he would visit Communist China before May 1972. This announcement followed a trip to China by an American Ping-Pong team—at the request of the Chinese. These events heralded a dramatic change in the twenty-year history of United States relations with Communist China.

In August, President Nixon made another startling announcement. Determined to halt inflation and to reduce unemployment, he ordered a ninety-day freeze on wages and prices.

President Nixon's third surprise announcement, on October 12, was that he would travel to Moscow in May 1972 for meetings with leaders of the Soviet Union.

In December, President Nixon made the first move to break the impasse in the international money crisis by declaring that he would devalue the United States dollar.

PING-PONG DIPLOMACY: An American Ping-Pong team competes in Communist China. Three months later, on July 15, President Nixon announced that he would visit Communist China early in 1972.

These four actions by the President of the United States seemed likely to influence the course of American and world history during the next few years.

In preparation for his visits to China and the Soviet Union, President Nixon met with leaders of several friendly nations. These included Canadian Prime Minister Pierre Elliott Trudeau, British Prime Minister Edward Heath, French President Georges Pompidou, Brazilian President Emilio Medici, West German Chancellor Willy Brandt, and Japanese Prime Minister Eisaku Sato. Earlier, in a gesture of friendship toward Japan, President Nixon had met with Emperor Hirohito in Alaska. This was the first time an American president and a Japanese emperor had ever met.

Also on the international scene, the United States reduced its military role in Indochina; tried, but failed, to bring about a peaceful solution to the Middle East crisis; and suffered setbacks in its relations with the nations of Latin America.

On the domestic scene, 1971 was a year of political preparation for the 1972 presidential election. The nation's economic problems, bloodshed in prisons, and an increase in crime rates contributed to a mood of anxiety.

GOODWILL VISIT: In an effort to improve Japanese-American relations, President and Mrs. Richard Nixon meet with Japanese Emperor Hirohito and his wife in Anchorage, Alaska.

Vice-President Spiro T. Agnew.

Presidential adviser Henry Kissinger.

Secretary of State William Rogers.

THE U.S. AND CHILE: United States relations with Latin America, in general, and with Marxist-governed Chile, in particular, took a turn for the worse during 1971. The Chilean Government of Salvador Allende Gossens took over American-owned copper mines and declared that it would not compensate the owners. Above: Young socialist supporters of Allende.

TRAVELING AMERICANS: While President Nixon prepared for his 1972 trips to Communist China and the Soviet Union, other high-ranking U.S. officials traveled to many parts of the world. Vice-President Agnew visited Greece, his ancestral homeland, and other countries in Europe and the Middle East. Presidential adviser Henry Kissinger twice visited Communist China to make preparations for President Nixon's visit. Secretary of State William Rogers went to the Middle East in an effort to find a solution to the crisis there.

INDOCHINA WAR: Even though more and more U.S. troops were leaving Vietnam, the Indochina war continued to divide the American people. In late April and early May, opponents of the war, including Vietnam veterans, staged demonstrations in Washington, D.C. Daniel Ellsberg, a former Defense Department aide, was indicted by a Federal grand jury for turning over to various newspapers a secret Pentagon study of the U.S. role in Vietnam.

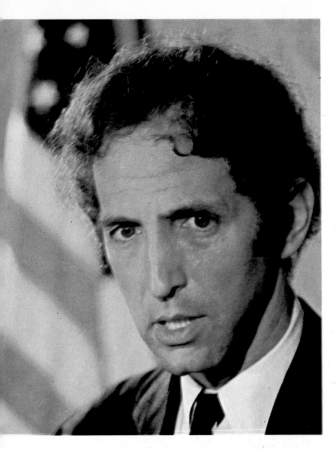

Anti-Vietnam-war activist Daniel Ellsberg.

U.S. troops prepare to leave Vietnam.

In the nation's capital, veterans opposed to the Vietnam war stage a massive demonstration.

DOLLAR CRISIS: Young Americans wait to exchange U.S. dollars at an American Express office in Athens, Greece. The international money crisis of May made U.S. dollars less than welcome in Europe. The crisis was finally ended in December, when the United States, Japan, and other industrialized Western nations agreed to revalue their currencies.

WAGE-PRICE FREEZE: Inflation and growing unemployment caused great concern during 1971. As a result, President Nixon put a three-month freeze on wage and price increases. The freeze was ended in mid-November. In its place, the Government began a system that would limit wage increases to an average of 5.5 per cent and price increases to an average of 2.5 per cent.

YOUTH VOTE: In 1971 the 26th Amendment to the United States Constitution was ratified. This amendment gave millions of 18 to 21-year-olds the right to vote in all elections for the first time. The full impact of this development on the American political scene will be felt for the first time in 1972, during the November presidential election.

ATTICA: On September 9, at Attica Correctional Facility in upstate New York, more than 1,000 prisoners revolted and seized 32 hostages. Four days later, 1,500 state troopers, prison guards, and sheriff's deputies attacked the area held by the prisoners. More than 40 people were killed.

The Economy

In 1933, President Franklin D. Roosevelt initiated the New Deal. The purpose of this broad economic policy was to end the depression and start the nation along the path of economic recovery. Not since the days of the New Deal has an American president embarked on an economic course so daringly activist as the one outlined by President Nixon on August 15, 1971.

The President took several steps. First, he froze all salaries and prices. This was the first time such a freeze had been imposed since the Korean war was being fought twenty years earlier. Second, the President ended the traditional convertibility of U.S. dollars into gold. This step allowed the dollar to float freely in the world currency markets. Third, he promised to reduce the number of people working for the Government and to reduce Federal spending by nearly $5,000,-000,000. The President also put a 10 per cent surcharge on goods imported into the United States and asked Congress to end excise taxes on American-made automobiles. (This action encouraged Americans to buy more than 1,000,000 autos in October—a one-month record for the auto industry.)

The President also provided tax incentives for industry and permitted the $650 Federal personal exemption for individual taxpayers to rise to $675 in 1971 and to $750 in 1972.

The new policies were a startling departure from the "economic game plan" followed by the Nixon administration during its first two years in power. Mr. Nixon had

In July, White House press secretary Ron Ziegler briefs newsmen about the nation's economic situation. He reported that unemployment was continuing to rise.

"Look, George! I think it's begun."

served as a minor official in the Office of Price Administration early in World War II. From this experience, he came to believe that wage and price controls cannot work effectively. He stated several times that he would not use such controls. Similarly, the administration had been opposed to tax cuts. It felt that tax cuts are inflationary.

However, Mr. Nixon did impose wage and price controls and did reduce taxes. Why? As one observer noted, President Nixon has always shown a willingness to abandon his traditional approach on any question and try a new approach. "Nixon clings to what is familiar until the last moment. Then, when everything overwhelms him or something happens in his gut, he decides to act, and nothing stands very long in his way."

Reactions to the President's new policy were varied. Almost all business leaders hailed his actions. Wall Street thundered its approval as the New York Stock Exchange registered the largest one-day price jump in its history.

The leaders of organized labor, on the other hand, questioned the fairness of the freeze. George Meaney, president of the AFL-CIO and titular spokesman for 14,-000,000 workers, called the program discriminatory against workers.

As the freeze began, however, public-opinion polls indicated that a majority of union members thought the freeze a good idea. But by October many housewives and consumer groups charged that prices had risen despite the freeze. Government statistics seemed to confirm these complaints. The consumer price index for September, after the first full month of the freeze, rose 0.2 per cent. In New York, Philadelphia, and other cities, the increase was even greater. Moreover, the Internal Revenue Service was criticized for the way it followed up complaints of violations.

On November 14, Phase 2 of the economic plan went into effect. Under this phase, the wage and price freeze was ended. However, the Government called for voluntary restraints and issued guidelines on how much wages and prices could be increased. It was suggested that an average of 5.5 per cent be the limit for increases in wages. Price increases were limited to an average of 2.5 per cent.

In a late development, in December, President Nixon announced that he would devalue the United States dollar. At the same time, he removed the 10 per cent surcharge on foreign goods imported into the United States.

George Jackson, one of three black prisoners known as the Soledad Brothers. In 1971 he was killed while trying to escape from San Quentin Prison in California.

Prisons

During 1971 the United States saw little of the racial riots and student unrest that it had seen in previous years. However, it did see violence in a new and, to many, an unexpected area: the nation's prisons.

San Quentin Prison in California is one of the nation's most famous maximum-security prisons. Attica Correctional Facility in upstate New York is not well known at all. In 1971 both were the sites of violent death and heated controversy.

George Jackson was one of three black convicts known as the Soledad Brothers. The three had been charged with murdering a guard at Soledad Prison in California. On August 21, Jackson was shot while he apparently was trying to escape from San Quentin. Also killed during the escape attempt were two other prisoners and three prison guards. Prison authorities believed that a visitor had smuggled a gun to Jackson. California authorities began a search for Stephen M. Bingham, a lawyer believed to have been the last person to visit Jackson. Friends of Jackson charged that he had been "set up" by prison authorities who planned his murder.

On September 9, over 1,000 convicts at Attica seized 32 hostages, most of them prison guards. They then presented a list of demands to prison authorities and to the New York State Commissioner of Correction, Russell G. Oswald. The demands included an end to prison censorship of reading material, the removal of the Attica

At Attica Correctional Facility, the flag flies at half-staff after 43 persons were killed as a result of a prisoner revolt. Investigations of the tragedy were begun.

Warden, and modernization of the inmate education system.

State authorities dealt with the prisoners through a committee of negotiators named by the prisoners. The negotiators included William Kunstler, a prominent attorney associated with radical political causes, and New York Congressman Herman Badillo. The authorities agreed to most of the prisoners' demands. But they were unwilling and unable to grant amnesty for criminal acts that might have been committed during the uprising. (One guard had been injured during the prisoner uprising, and later died in a hospital.)

On September 13, Commissioner Oswald ordered nearly 1,500 state troopers, sheriff's deputies, and prison guards to enter the prison and put down the revolt. The entire operation lasted about one hour. In all, 43 persons—32 prisoners and 11 hostages—were either killed immediately or later died from their wounds. Autopsies indicated that all had died from gunshot wounds inflicted by the assault force.

In the wake of the tragedy, the actions of Commissioner Oswald and New York Governor Nelson Rockefeller became the focal point of angry debate. Many praised them for the firm action they had taken. But critics wondered if the state's response had not been too hasty. They declared that the Governor should have gone to Attica and talked to the prisoners, as they had demanded. Congressional and state inquiries were authorized to investigate the incident.

Later in the year there were other, smaller, incidents or revolts in other prisons, including one in New Jersey. Here, bloodshed was avoided when New Jersey Governor William Cahill agreed to consider the inmates' demands.

Politics

The Democrats will not nominate a candidate to run against President Nixon until July 1972. Yet the race for the Democratic nomination began in January 1971. During that month Senator George McGovern of South Dakota officially entered the race. McGovern is widely regarded as a one-issue candidate because of his stand against the Vietnam war.

McGovern was not the early front-runner for the Democratic nomination. This distinction belonged to Senator Edmund Muskie of Maine, although he had not officially declared his candidacy. Muskie had been the Democratic vice-presidential candidate in 1968. During the first half of 1971 he enjoyed broad support in nearly every section of the country. And during the year, he led President Nixon in several presidential preference polls. Muskie started a minor controversy in September when he stated that he would not favor a black running mate in 1972. His reasoning was that a black-white ticket was "not electable" and therefore would not serve the purposes of the Democratic Party or the cause of civil rights.

Two other figures from the 1968 campaign were ready to challenge Muskie. Eugene McCarthy of Minnesota still enjoyed a following from his 1968 effort. In October he threw his hat into the ring for 1972. Another Minnesotan, Senator Hubert H. Humphrey, the Democratic standard-bearer in 1968, did not try to conceal his ambition to try again.

Several other probable entries came to the fore during the year, including Senator Henry Jackson of Washington, Senator Fred Harris of Oklahoma, and Congressman Wilbur Mills of Arkansas. Jackson is a conservative with a record of supporting the Vietnam war. Harris sought to weld together a coalition of lower- and middle-class black and white farmers and small businessmen. Mills is chairman of the powerful Ways and Means Committee of the House of Representatives and a popular figure in the South and border states.

An unexpected name entered into consideration when New York City Mayor John V. Lindsay quit the Republican Party

New York Mayor John Lindsay entered the 1972 presidential race after switching to the Democrats.

Rep. Paul McCloskey will challenge President Nixon for the 1972 Republican presidential nomination.

"Right on, Pop! I'm home to vote."

and registered as a Democrat. Many Democratic leaders believed that Lindsay's switch had come too late to permit him to be considered as a serious contender for the nomination. But others felt that Lindsay should be considered because of his strong appeal to blacks and young people and because of his "television charisma." It is expected that young people will play an increased role in American politics with the ratification of the 26th Amendment in 1971. This amendment lowered the voting age to 18.

Perhaps the strongest potential candidate was a man who repeatedly stated that he would not run in 1972: Senator Edward Kennedy of Massachusetts. Kennedy's name may automatically appear on the ballots in several primaries. Many observers believe he could win some of these primaries without campaigning. In the case of a deadlocked convention in July 1972, Kennedy might be the man the delegates turn to.

In the off-year elections of November 1971, political analysts watched for possible barometers for 1972. The racial polarization of some American cities was shown by the victory of conservative "law and order" candidates Frank L. Rizzo in Philadelphia and Ralph Perk in Cleveland. Their victories could be interpreted as a continuation of a trend set in 1969. In Boston, however, liberal

mayor Kevin White defeated Louise Day Hicks, well known for her aggressive law-and-order stance, by a wide margin.

In a race that drew national attention, Charles Evers, the black mayor of Fayette, Mississippi, lost to William Waller, a moderate on racial issues, in the contest for the governorship of Mississippi.

The 1971 elections also provided the first chance to evaluate the significance of the 26th Amendment to the Constitution. This amendment made millions of 18 to 21-year-olds eligible to vote for the first time.

The new voters had a marked impact on those elections taking place in towns and cities that contained large universities in states that permitted on-campus voting. Thus, in Boulder, Colorado, a graduate of the University of Colorado won election to the City Council. In East Lansing, Michigan, two students from Michigan State University captured seats on the municipal governing board. And in Bloomington, Indiana, a recent graduate of Indiana University Law School became mayor with the help of student votes. In Newcomerstown, Ohio, 19-year-old Ron Hooker became one of the nation's youngest mayors.

Despite these results, leaders of both parties were uncertain about the nationwide influence of the new voters.

Congress

The record of the first session of the 92d Congress was not impressive. The draft was extended. The Senate passed an amendment calling for the withdrawal of U.S. troops from Vietnam in six months, providing the North Vietnamese release all American prisoners of war. And Congress passed a child-development program, including daycare centers. But this bill was vetoed by the President. No action was taken in Congress on the President's welfare-reform and revenue-sharing programs.

On October 29 the Senate defeated the administration's $3,200,000,000 foreign-aid bill. Many observers believed that this totally unexpected defeat was due to the ouster of Nationalist China by the United Nations. Certainly part of the coalition that defeated the bill by a vote of 41–27 consisted of senators anxious to strike at the UN: $143,-000,000 of the funds was earmarked for the world organization. But the concept of foreign aid also has fallen into disfavor with such liberal Democratic senators as Frank Church of Idaho and Majority Leader Mike Mansfield. Some foreign aid seems destined to continue. But the program of bilateral aid that had begun with the Marshall Plan in 1948 at a cost of $143,000,000,000 has apparently been ended.

Twice during the year the White House and the Congress became involved in disputes centering on the American aircraft industry. In March the House and Senate voted to cut off funds for the proposed supersonic transport plane (SST). The House later reversed itself. But in May the Senate again voted against further development of the aircraft. Opponents of the SST objected to rising costs and to possible danger to the environment.

The administration proved more successful in persuading Congress to pass legislation permitting a $250,000,000 Federally backed loan to the Lockheed Aircraft Corporation. Supporters of the Lockheed bill said that without the loan Lockheed would go bankrupt. This would have thrown tens of thousands of workers out of jobs. The legislation passed the House by three votes and the Senate by one vote in early August.

MAJOR LEGISLATION

Cancer Program
Cancer Act of 1971 (December 23)* authorizes $1,600,000,000, over a three-year period, for an expanded cancer-research program.

Draft
Military Selective Service Act Amendment (September 28) extends the draft until June 30, 1973, and calls on President Nixon to set a "date certain" for withdrawal of U.S. troops from Indochina, subject to the release of all American prisoners of war.

Emergency Employment
Emergency Employment Act of 1971 (July 12) authorizes $2,250,000,000 to provide state and local public-service jobs for unemployed persons for a period of two years.

Lockheed
Emergency Loan Guarantee Act (August 9) provides for a $250,000,000 loan guarantee for the Lockheed Aircraft Corporation, because its failure would seriously affect the national economy.

Social Security
Social Security Act Amendment (March 17) provides for a 10 per cent increase in social-security benefits, retroactive to January 1, 1971.

Taxes
Revenue Act of 1971 (December 10) increases the personal exemption from $650 to $675 in 1971 and to $750 in 1972; repeals the 7 per cent excise tax on automobiles; and reinstates the 7 per cent business tax credit for investment in new equipment. Added to the bill is a provision enabling a taxpayer to specify that $1.00 of his tax money could go into a fund for financing presidential elections, beginning with 1976.

Voting Age
26th Constitutional Amendment lowers the voting age in all elections to 18. The proposed amendment was ratified on June 30 when the 38th state approved it.

Wage-Price Controls
Economic Stabilization Act Amendment of 1971 (Dec. 22) extends until April 30, 1973, the president's authority to control prices and wages.

* the date on which President Nixon signed the bill into law.

William H. Rehnquist, 47, an assistant U.S. attorney general, was named to the Supreme Court in 1971.

Supreme Court

It is not unusual for a president to serve a full four-year term without making a single appointment to the United States Supreme Court. But in 1971, President Nixon had the opportunity to name two men to the court. Two other Nixon nominees had been confirmed in 1969 and 1970.

Justice Hugo Black, a member of the court since 1937, resigned in 1971; he died later in the year. Justice John Harlan resigned for reasons of health. These two resignations gave President Nixon an opportunity to place on the bench two judges who share his philosophy of judicial conservatism.

At first it appeared that Nixon would appoint a woman: Judge Mildred L. Lillie of California. But this was not the case. The President sent the names of Lewis F. Powell, Jr., of Virginia and William H. Rehnquist to the Senate. They were both approved in December.

Lewis F. Powell, Jr., 64, the second Nixon appointee to the Supreme Court in 1971, is a lawyer from Virginia and a former president of the American Bar Association.

MAJOR DECISIONS OF THE SUPREME COURT

Abortion

United States v. Vuitch (April 21) upheld 5–2 the constitutionality of the District of Columbia's abortion law, allowing abortions only to protect the mother's life and health. The law is a typical abortion law of many states.

Amchitka

The Committee for Nuclear Responsibility, Inc. et al. v. Schlesinger et al. (November 6) ruled 4–3 to allow the underground hydrogen-bomb test at Amchitka Island.

Church and State

Earley v. Dicenso; Robinson v. Dicenso (June 28) ruled 8–1 that it is unconstitutional for states to reimburse parochial and other church-related schools for instruction in nonreligious subjects.

Civil Rights

Grigg v. Duke Power Co. (March 8) ruled 8–0 that employers cannot use job tests that in effect screen out Negroes if the tests do not measure ability to do the work.

Palmer v. Thompson (June 14) ruled 5–4 that a community may close its publicly owned recreational facilities rather than obey court orders to desegregate them.

Reed v. Reed, Administrator (November 22) struck down unanimously an Idaho statute that gave men preference over women in administering deceased persons' estates. It was the first time the court invalidated a state law because of sex discrimination.

Criminal Law

Mayberry v. Pennsylvania (January 20) ruled unanimously that in a disrupted courtroom a judge may immediately impose a contempt-of-court sentence. However, if he waits until the end of the trial, he should let another judge pass sentence.

McGautha v. California; Crampton v. Ohio (May 3) upheld 6–3 the capital-punishment procedures by which juries in many courts throughout the United States are empowered to impose the death penalty.

United States v. Freed (April 5) upheld unanimously a Federal law that makes it a crime to possess unregistered weapons.

Housing

James v. Valtierra; Shaffer v. Valtierra (April 26) upheld 5–3 the constitutionality of state referendum laws that allow a majority of voters in a community to block the construction of low-rent housing for the poor.

Juveniles

McKeiver et al. v. Pennsylvania (June 21) ruled 6–3 that a jury trial is not required for juveniles, thus preserving informal protective proceedings sought under the juvenile-court system.

Pentagon Papers

The New York Times Company v. United States; United States v. The Washington Post Company et al. (June 30) ruled 6–3 that any attempt by the Government to block news articles before publication bears "a heavy burden of presumption" against its constitutionality. The ruling freed *The New York Times* and *The Washington Post* to resume publication of articles based on the secret Pentagon Papers on the origins of the Vietnam war.

School Desegregation

Swann v. Charlotte-Mecklenburg Board of Education (April 20) upheld unanimously the constitutionality of busing children as a means of "dismantling the dual systems" of the South. The decision did not affect Northern-style desegregation based on neighborhood patterns.

Selective Service

Gillette v. United States; Negre v. Larsen (March 8) ruled 8–1 that for men to qualify for draft exemption as conscientious objectors, they must be opposed to all wars and not just the Vietnam war.

Clay v. United States (June 28) ruled 8–0 that the conviction of Muhammad Ali (Cassius Clay) for refusing to be inducted was invalid because his request for exemption as a conscientious objector had been improperly handled.

Welfare

Wyman v. James (January 12) ruled 6–3 that homes of welfare recipients can be inspected by welfare officials, and funds cut off if recipients refuse entry.

A New China Policy

On July 15, 1971, President Nixon announced to the nation that he would visit Communist China sometime before May 1972. (The dates for the visit by the President and Mrs. Nixon were later set at February 1–8.) Thus, in a few minutes President Nixon altered twenty years of American policy regarding the People's Republic of China.

The United States does not formally recognize Communist China. Since 1949 it has supported the claims of the Nationalist Chinese Government on the island of Taiwan as the legal government of all of China. Mr. Nixon's move seemed to have the immediate effect of lessening criticism of his handling of the Vietnam war. However, the State Department declared that the trip had no direct relation to that war. Further, the President warned the American people not to expect a quick settlement of current problems involving the United States and China. What was hoped for was the beginning of discussions leading to long-range plans for peaceful relations.

Preparations for the President's trip had been made by Henry Kissinger, his assistant for national security affairs.

Reaction to the President's planned visit was varied. The Nationalist Chinese were angered and dismayed. The South Vietnamese were apprehensive. The Russians were suspicious. In the United States, a majority of the nation supported the President. But several conservative politicians, including Senators Barry Goldwater of Arizona and James Buckley of New York, strongly disapproved.

Following the President's decision to travel to China, the State Department revealed that it would favor a two-China policy with regard to the United Nations. That is, it would like to see Communist China seated in the world organization, but without the expulsion of Nationalist China.

As events developed, the United States was unable to gain acceptance of this plan. In October, by a vote of 76 to 35 with 17 abstentions, the UN General Assembly ap-

Presidential adviser Henry Kissinger (left) talks with Communist Chinese Premier Chou En-lai in Peking.

proved an Albanian resolution admitting Communist China and ousting Nationalist China. This action caused a great deal of indignation in the United States. In fact, President Nixon declared that the "shocking spectacle" of anti-American floor demonstrations following the deciding vote in the General Assembly could result in serious loss of U.S. support for the UN and foreign aid in general. Some observers believed that the President's display of anger had been calculated to blunt some of the outrage in Congress. To many observers, the vote in the UN was predictable, given the fact that the United States itself had made a radical departure in its China policy.

One further consideration of the Nixon overtures toward China involved the reaction of the Soviet Union. Relations between the United States and the U.S.S.R. have been steadily improving over the past decade. The administration thus sought to assure the Russians that its new stance toward Peking did not imply any change in policy toward the Soviet Union. Therefore, on October 12, the White House announced that the President would journey to Moscow in May 1972. The new relationship with Communist China, it was made clear, would not be made at the cost of ending negotiations and accommodation with the Soviets.

In 1971, 1st Lt. William Calley was convicted of murdering civilians at Mylai, South Vietnam, in 1968.

The Indochina War

In mid-1971, for the first time since January 1966, the number of U.S. troops serving in Vietnam dropped below the 200,000 level. In November, President Nixon announced that by February 1972 there would be only 139,000 U.S. troops left in that war-torn country. American casualties also declined. But most interest in the Vietnam questions centered on events taking place in the United States.

The court-martial of 1st Lt. William Calley attracted a great deal of public attention. Calley's trial started on November 12, 1970. He was convicted by a military jury on March 29, 1971. The jury found Calley guilty of the premeditated murder in 1968 of no less than twenty South Vietnamese civilians at Mylai.

Calley's lawyers had not denied that he took part in the killings. But they insisted that he regarded the civilians as the enemy and that he had acted on the "order of the day" issued by Captain Ernest Medina. (In September a military jury acquitted Captain Medina of all charges brought against him in connection with the Mylai killings.)

Calley received a sentence of life imprisonment at hard labor. The verdict aroused an angry response from supporters of the war. Many of them declared that the morale of the men remaining in Vietnam would be shattered if the sentence was allowed to stand. Many opponents of the war also attacked the verdict. They felt that one man had, in effect, been charged with the entire responsibility for the tragic mistakes caused by American involvement in Vietnam.

Public opinion, as judged from polls as well as from telegrams and letters sent to the White House, favored clemency for Calley. President Nixon said that he would review the case, and Calley was released from the stockade at Fort Benning, Georgia, pending the completion of the review process. In August, Calley's life sentence was reduced to twenty years.

During 1971, the number and extent of antiwar protests declined. However, the People's Coalition for Peace and Justice attracted over 320,000 people to Washington, D.C., for 2 weeks of demonstrations

The Pentagon Papers disclosed how the United States became involved in the Vietnam War.

© Herblock in The Washington Post

'The government says publication of those documents on the war can be injurious'

beginning on April 24. At one point the demonstrators tried to create massive traffic jams in the capital. As a result, Washington police and Federal troops arrested more than 7,000 demonstrators. Several antiwar congressmen criticized the mass arrests. They termed them a violation of the constitutional rights of the demonstrators. However, Attorney General John Mitchell defended the tactics as necessary to keep the capital "open for business." Most of those arrested were eventually released, and the charges against them were dropped.

The Pentagon Papers

On June 13 *The New York Times* began publishing a series of articles that purported to show how and why the United States became involved in Vietnam. The articles—the so-called Pentagon Papers—were based on top secret Government documents.

The Pentagon Papers seemed to indicate that the administration of President Lyndon Johnson had made a covert commitment to send combat troops into Vietnam several months before the famous Tonkin Gulf in-

cident of 1964. The Tonkin Gulf incident, in which North Vietnamese boats attacked ships of the U.S. Navy, has long been regarded as the reason for U.S. intervention. Indeed, as the *Times* and other newspapers continued the series, there appeared to be some doubt that the Tonkin Gulf incident had occurred at all—or at least that it had occurred in the manner in which it had been presented to the United States and the public.

The Government attempted to halt publication of the Pentagon Papers. But the Supreme Court ruled that the Justice Department could not restrain the newspapers from publishing the documents.

It was discovered that the Pentagon Papers had been given to the *Times* and other newspapers by Daniel Ellsberg. Formerly a supporter of the war, Ellsberg came to believe that American involvement was immoral. Ellsberg had been a Defense Department aide and had helped prepare the study of American involvement.

JOHN B. DUFF
Professor of History
Seton Hall University

YOUTH

IN 1971, the various youth organizations throughout the United States continued their work on projects of immediate concern to their communities. They also assumed new and varied responsibilities. The Boy Scouts of America, Boys' Clubs of America, Camp Fire Girls, 4-H Clubs, Future Farmers of America, and Girl Scouts of the U.S.A. looked at the problems facing the world today, and vowed to do something about them.

One of the most important issues of the decade is pollution. All of the youth organizations planned new, ambitious programs to help combat this worldwide problem. Anti-litter drives were held in major cities throughout the country; many rivers and streams were cleared of unsightly refuse; and at the urging of the youth organizations, recycling centers, for such items as paper, glass, and tin, were established in many communities.

Another problem of equal importance is the lack of communication that exists among different members of our society. In an effort to bring these people together, many of the organizations have thrown open their doors. Membership drives were undertaken to recruit children of minority groups living in city ghettos and rural areas. In a surprising move, the National Council of Camp Fire Girls announced in November that they would be opening some areas of their organization to boys.

One of the major goals of youth organizations during the year was to help fight against all kinds of environmental pollution. Above: FFA boys participate in a cleanup drive.

In 1971 the 26th Amendment to the U.S. Constitution was passed, giving 18–20-year-olds the right to vote in all elections. Right: Students at the University of Michigan register to vote.

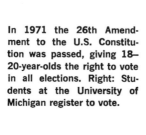

REGISTER TO VOTE

Participating in Project SOAR, Scouts plant trees to help restore a Los Angeles park.

BOY SCOUTS OF AMERICA

1971 was the third year of the Boy Scouts of America's BOYPOWER '76 plan. The aim of this program is to bring Scouting to at least one third of all American boys from 8 to 17 years of age, by 1976. To achieve this goal, the Scouts sought new means of reaching boys in rural poverty areas as well as urban ghettos. Storefront Scout "centers" were set up in many cities throughout the United States. Motor vans also provided meeting places for Scout units located in areas far from the larger cities.

During 1971, the Scouts began new programs and expanded old ones. The high-adventure program was stepped up with the opening of a 4,000,000-acre Maine-Matagamon Wilderness Base in northwest Maine.

The highlight of Project SOAR (*Save Our American Resources*) was "Keep America Beautiful Day" on June 5, 1971. About 2,000,000 Scouts and leaders, joined by representatives of other organizations, participated in this nationwide antilitter drive. A million tons of rubbish was collected. Importance was placed on the recycling of wastepaper, aluminum and steel cans, glass containers, and other material. Discussions were held to determine the success of the project and to prepare plans for another "Keep America Beautiful Day" in 1972.

An educational program geared to the drug problem was also launched in 1971, and will be expanded in 1972.

Exploring, the program for young men and women 15 through 20 years of age, attracted thousands of participants to its national activities throughout 1971. Explorer events included a Grand National Safe-Driving Road Rally in Detroit, Michigan, and an

Boy Scouts from urban ghetto areas find that pitching a tent and camping in a vacant lot (above) can be almost as much fun as camping-out in the country (below).

Explorer Space Seminar at the John F. Kennedy Space Center in Florida. A dinner was given by the Explorers Club of New York City to honor 12 outstanding teen-age scientists. Later, the young scientists were placed on an expedition or research project related to their career interests. Sea Explorers took part in regattas in Florida and Washington, and a sailing championship in Chicago.

The Boy Scouts held its 61st annual meeting in Atlanta, Georgia, in 1971. Norton Clapp, chairman of Weyerhaeuser Co., Seattle, Washington, was elected president. At the meeting, six young men and women were presented with Young American Awards in recognition of their personal achievements and high ideals.

Membership in the Boy Scouts of America reached 6,287,284 boys and leaders in 157,116 packs, troops, and posts.

ALDEN G. BARBER
Chief Scout Executive, Boy Scouts of America

BOYS' CLUBS OF AMERICA

Since the Boys' Clubs of America was established as a national organization in 1906, its purpose has been to "offer boys a place to go and a way to grow, a chance and a choice." The Clubs' role has been that of a guardian. It receives a community's "natural resources" and returns to that community healthy, respectable men, ready to assume responsible positions in society.

Like many other organizations the Boys' Clubs reacted strongly in 1971 to the winds of change that swept the country. A wide review of the role the Clubs played in some 600 communities throughout the United States was undertaken. The directors of the Boys' Clubs examined, too, the programs that provided daily activities and guidance to a membership that numbered over 950,000 boys from 7 to 17 years of age.

Many of the time-honored traditions of the Boys' Clubs were analyzed. Club services were questioned and substitute services were suggested and considered by the executive board. The possibility that the Boys' Clubs should extend its concerns to the community itself, as well as to the individual boy, was also considered. The question was raised that if changes were made, could they be carried out without damage to the Clubs' youth-serving functions?

There was general agreement that provision should be made for the needs of unserved boys, without sacrificing the quality of the services. The decision was also made to provide more meaningful programs for all age levels, with the possible concentration on the older boys.

If 1971 was a year of change, it was also a year of growth for the Boys' Clubs of America. There was an addition of 46 new Clubs during the year, bringing the total number of Clubs to 935. Growth was also the key word at the 65th annual Boys' Clubs Convention held in Atlanta, Georgia, in mid-May. A record attendance of more than 1,200 Boys' Club leaders from 46 states, including Hawaii and Alaska, and from Canada, Puerto Rico, and England was recorded.

In a White House ceremony, President Nixon "installs" Pelton Stewart as the Boys' Clubs "Boy of the Year."

By year's end, the Boys' Clubs movement was rapidly approaching its immediate goal set forth by the late President Herbert Hoover, who served as Boys' Club board chairman for 28 years. He once declared that the objective of the Clubs should be "1,000 Boys' Clubs for One Million Deserving Boys."

E. J. STAPLETON
Boys' Clubs of America

Taking part in the AWARE '71 Conference, Camp Fire Girls gather in Washington, D.C., to consider the problems facing young people in today's world.

CAMP FIRE GIRLS

The Camp Fire Girls' AWARE '71 Conference was held in Washington, D.C., Denton, Texas, and Davis, California, during June and July 1971. The meeting was attended by 1,200 teen-agers from many parts of the United States. They participated in active discussions of many of the current issues and challenges facing young people today. The delegates concerned themselves with such problems as changing morals, drugs, prejudice, school, family relationships, and dissent. Awareness films on each subject, made by young people for young people, were presented to individual groups.

Step one of a campaign to recruit new members was undertaken at the National Council Meeting in Des Moines, Iowa. Using the slogan "Take a Stand," the national volunteers and professional staff of the Camp Fire Girls outlined the goals and designs of a five-year Membership Growth Campaign. They also planned new programs that would be of particular interest to teen-age members. The workshops held at this meeting were so successful that further discussion groups are being planned for another conference in the spring of 1972. Step two of the Growth Campaign is a major item for discussion at that meeting.

In April 1971, Pittsburgh, Pennsylvania, was the scene of a well-attended plant-in. Five hundred Camp Fire Girls, their leaders, and their families took part in planting five thousand white-pine seedlings. In years to come, this evergreen grove, known as Camp Fire Forest, will bring pleasure to visitors and members of the Pittsburgh community.

One of the most exciting new projects undertaken by the Camp Fire Girls in 1971 was the introduction of a new magazine, *Today's Girl*. It is intended for the young lady who has just entered, or will soon be entering, her teen years. The magazine contains works of fiction and includes articles about fashion, ecology projects, and the making of handicrafts.

A series of program booklets for Camp Fire members from 6 through 18 years of age was published in October 1971. The first set deals primarily with Horizon Club members (girls of high-school age). These pamphlets are for members, officers of the Club, and for program committees. Each kit also includes a newspaper to guide leaders in planning new programs, and a Medallion Chart for Camp Fire Girls who wish to undertake special programs.

In 1971 Camp Fire Girls went co-ed and approved admission of boys to its high-school-age Horizon Clubs. And leadership of Camp Fire groups was opened to men.

LESLIE VERTER
Camp Fire Girls, Inc.

GIRL SCOUTS OF THE U.S.A.

In 1971 the objectives of the Girl Scouts of the U.S.A. were emphasized through two major programs: ECO-ACTION, a nationwide effort to improve the environment, and ACTION 70, a program designed to help eliminate prejudice and foster greater human understanding.

Across the country, local Girl Scout groups carried out the national goals of ACTION 70 in a variety of people-to-people service projects. These included working with youngsters from ghetto and rural areas, children of migrant workers, physically or mentally handicapped persons, and the elderly. Several of the projects received national attention when Girl Scout troops placed first and third in the 1970–71 *Parents' Magazine* Youth Group Achievement Awards. Another 29 troops received Certificates of Honor.

As part of their ECO-ACTION campaign, the Girl Scouts joined with government and community leaders in seeking out and trying to eliminate sources of water pollution. In other projects to help the environment, the Girl Scouts created mini-parks and playgrounds. Campsites and mountain and forest trails were improved. Girl Scouts planted window-box gardens, sorted glass for recycling, organized smoke-pollution alerts, started soil-erosion projects, and held ECO-ACTION teach-ins. The Girl Scouts also worked with the Interior Department's National Fish and Wildlife Service to establish new projects that will enable girls to explore careers in refuge or hatchery operation.

In 1971 the Girl Scouts continued to seek new and better ways to maintain and extend Girl Scouting in low-income city and rural areas. To help accomplish this goal, 21 selected Girl Scout councils received matching-fund grants from the Julie Nixon Eisenhower Fund. The $81,000 gift from President Nixon's daughter represented her share of profits from the sale of a crewel kit she designed.

Several regional and national conferences were held during the year to discuss the needs and interests of girls and women who belong to minority groups. One, called "Girl Scouting, Mexican-American Style," was held in August at Prescott, Arizona. It dealt with the problems and desires of the Spanish-speaking community.

In Wyoming, Girl Scouts on Project "Dig Mankind" search for Indian artifacts. Working with students and teachers from the University of Wyoming, the girls learned to sift for fossils and to catalog their finds.

After a day on the archeological dig, the girls gather to discuss their finds and to share discoveries with friends.

A seminar on urban living was held in July at the Edith Macy Girl Scout Center near Pleasantville, New York. This conference brought together more than 160 Girl Scouts who were placed into interracial teams to study the problems of "The City: Now! Tomorrow!" New York City was used as a sample urban center.

During the summer, approximately 4,000 girls took part in international, national, and council-operated Girl Scout events in the United States and abroad. Nearly 150 American girls and adults went on exploration trips, camping events, attended conferences and visited abroad. These projects were financed in part by the Juliette Low World Friendship Fund. About 130 Girl Guides and Scouts from member countries of the World Association of Girl Guides and Girl Scouts attended national and council-operated events in the United States.

In June 1971, more than 2,000 girls from 35 states and Puerto Rico took part in a "Wyoming Trek" to Girl Scout National Center West, a large wilderness reserve in Wyoming's Big Horn Basin. The girls spent two weeks participating in such activities as primitive camping, archeological digs, hiking, backpacking, and horseback riding.

They also studied the history and legends of the Indians and early Wyoming settlers.

During 1971, thousands of Girl Scout "camperships" were given to boys and girls from minority groups and from families of limited means. Among these was a special DeWitt Wallace Reader's Digest Foundation Scholarship Fund. This "campership" enabled 95 girls from various low-income areas to go to Girl Scout National Center West.

The Reader's Digest Foundation also gave financial backing to 23 Senior Girl Scout service projects. Because of these grants, a wide variety of action-oriented projects were undertaken: the development of a community drug-education center; the establishment of day camps for children of migrant workers, city and rural children, and handicapped youngsters; and setting up classes in sewing skills for Spanish-speaking adults.

The world of fashion had a most unexpected but welcome effect on the Girl Scouts in 1971. New, up-to-date Senior and Adult Girl Scout uniforms, with optional pantsuits, were introduced. This was the first uniform change for the 14-through-17-year-old Senior girls in many years.

RICHARD G. KNOX
Girl Scouts of the U.S.A.

FUTURE FARMERS OF AMERICA

In 1971, thousands of FFA members participated in activities aimed at improving their communities through the FFA "Building Our American Communities" program. This project, begun in 1970, is an effort by the FFA to involve its members in meaningful activities that will improve job opportunities and living conditions for the people of rural America. At the annual FFA Convention held in October, a National Citation was presented to the Berrien FFA Chapter of Nashville, Georgia, in recognition of its excellent work to improve the community.

Six National FFA officers, who had been elected by delegates at the 1970 Convention, traveled a total of more than 250,000 miles in 1971. During their travels, the officers were guest speakers at many adult and youth conventions and meetings. They appeared on radio and television programs and met with many of the organization's 430,000 members in the 7,845 FFA chapters across the United States.

Throughout 1971, the FFA continued its efforts to expand opportunities for nonfarm youths interested in agribusiness careers. In recent years, there has been an increasing demand for people with training in off-the-farm occupations related to agriculture: horticulture, agricultural sales and services, food processing, natural-resources development, and conservation.

The 44th National FFA Convention was held in Kansas City, Missouri, in October 1971. Approximately 13,400 members and their guests attended the conference. Elections were held for national officers for the 1971–72 term. Tim J. Burk, 20, of New Hampton, Iowa, was elected president of the Future Farmers of America.

One of the highlights of the convention was the awards program. Lonney Eastvold, 22, of Hartland, Minnesota, was named Star Farmer of America. Wayne Robert Morris, 19, from Fullerton, California, was honored with the Star Agribusiness award.

During the year, the FFA International Program helped to place 47 students from other countries on farms in the United States. In addition, through the FFA Work Experience Abroad Program, 22 FFA members from the United States spent three summer months living and working on farms in Europe and Latin America.

A. D. Reuwee
Future Farmers of America

On a field trip, FFA members learn about high-yield hybrid corn.

4-H CLUBS

The theme for the 4-H Clubs during 1971 was "4-H Bridges the Gap." During the year, more than 4,000,000 young people took part in the *H*ead-*H*eart-*H*ands-*H*ealth programs. This record enrollment comprised 9 to 19-year-old youths from all social, racial, and economic backgrounds. 4-H'ers came from towns, cities, and suburbs, as well as from farms, to "create roads of unity."

To "bridge gaps," the young people worked hand in hand with adults in a national campaign against air and water pollution. They became involved in programs to promote health and safety, combat drug abuse, and to aid the mentally retarded and physically handicapped. Parents and 4-H'ers alike worked together to build better communities and promote understanding the peoples of other lands.

The National 4-H Conference was held in Washington, D.C., in April 1971. The meeting was attended by about 225 delegates from the 50 states, the District of Columbia, and Puerto Rico. The conference highlight was a reception held at the White House. President Richard M. Nixon welcomed the delegates to Washington, and Mrs. Nixon was honored as a new "Partner-in-4-H." The delegates spent much of their week in discussion groups. The topics of concern included education, environment, changing life-styles, and respect for others.

National 4-H Week was observed throughout the United States from October 3 to October 9, 1971. The members discussed different ways to increase membership in local communities and the role parents could play in 4-H activities.

In late November, about 1,600 senior 4-H members attended the National 4-H Congress in Chicago. All the participants were state, regional, or national winners of awards and college scholarships. 1971 marked the Golden Anniversary of both the National 4-H Congress and the National 4-H Service Committee, a nonprofit educational corporation that co-ordinates private donor support.

In his 1971 message to 4-H'ers, President Nixon wrote: "A grateful Nation is intensely proud of the young men and women who participate in the 4-H educational program. . . . 4-H members are proving how effectively youth can meet the challenges of the Seventies, and are setting an example throughout this Nation and the world."

E. DEAN VAUGHAN
Director, 4-H Programs

4-H'ers study soil and forestry as part of their effort to improve the environment.

THE YOUTH VOTE

Both major political parties, and hopeful candidates for federal, state, and local political offices are out to win favor with the nation's largest and potentially most important new voting bloc—youth.

Twenty-five million young people will be eligible to vote for the first time in 1972. And in view of President Nixon's narrow margin of victory in 1968, the "youth vote" could play an important part in the forthcoming presidential election.

Roughly 11,000,000 of these new voters are 18, 19, and 20-year-olds who were granted the right to vote by the 26th Amendment to the U.S. Constitution, ratified in 1971. The rest of the 25,000,000 youthful voters consists of those who have reached the age of 21 since the 1968 presidential election. They would have been eligible to vote, in any event, by the old minimum voting age of 21.

The change in the voting law has raised many serious questions in the minds of politicians throughout the country. First and foremost is the question of whether or not young people will vote as a bloc. If they do, will they favor candidates who are liberal, moderate, or conservative? Will they vote mainly for Democrats or Republicans?

The two major parties aren't going to trust to luck. Republicans and Democrats alike have already mapped out expensive campaigns aimed at attracting young people to their respective parties.

The stakes are very high. In the presidential election 1968, just under 120,000,-000 Americans were eligible to vote. About 60 per cent—some 73,000,000—actually did so. An estimated 140,000,000 people will be eligible to take part in the 1972 election. If the percentage who vote remains at 60 per cent, it would mean a turnout of 84,000,000 at the polls.

Assuming voters in the 18–20-year-old age bracket cast ballots in the same proportion, there would be a "youth vote" of more than 6,500,000. And if this vote is cast mainly for the candidates of one particular party, it could have a tremendous impact on the 1972 election. The 1960 and 1968 elections are good illustrations of how a few hundred thousand votes can spell victory or defeat in a tight presidential race. In 1960, President John Kennedy was elected by a slim plurality of 118,500 votes; President Richard Nixon won by only 500,000 votes in a close contest eight years later.

However, many political analysts believe that young people will not vote as a group. These analysts predict that the youth vote will generally run along the same lines as the voting patterns of older people. In other words, young people will be influenced less by their age and more by other considerations, such as social and economic factors, regional attitudes and prejudices, and ethnic background.

But if a "youth vote" should materialize, it could sharply alter the American political scene. One instance of youth voting power occurred in Berkeley, California, site of the University of California's main campus. In 1971, students waged a determined campaign to capture local political offices. As a result, students and their supporters won half the seats on the Berkeley city council.

Such political activism by young people has run into strong opposition in many college towns where students often outnumber the local people. Residents of these towns fear that if students are permitted to vote where they go to school rather than where they live, they will take over many college communities. The question of where college students should vote will probably have to be settled in the courts.

But college students are still a minority among the 11,000,000 voters in the 18–20-year age group. According to the U.S. Census Bureau, a little over 5,000,000 are full-time workers or housewives. About 4,000,000 attend college, and an additional 900,000 are high-school students. The remaining several hundred thousand are serving in the armed forces.

Whatever the background or occupations of these young people, politicians will be trying to gain their support. For many political candidates are convinced that the "youth vote" may be the deciding factor in the 1972 presidential election.

Above: President Nixon signs the Constitution's 26th Amendment, granting 18-year-olds the right to vote. Below left: A new voter, Carol Fulton, 18, of Columbus, Ohio, learns how to use a voting machine. Not content just to vote, some young people ran for office. Ronald Hooker, 19 (below right), was elected mayor of Newcomerstown, Ohio.

PAGE SCHOOL

At 6 A.M. every school-day morning, classes start for a very special group of high-school students. Six in the morning may seem a bit early, but there haven't been any complaints from the students. For they hold highly coveted jobs as pages in the United States Senate, the House of Representatives, and the U.S. Supreme Court. As pages, they have an opportunity to watch history in the making—and perhaps eventually to make it themselves. Several members of the present Congress began their political careers as pages.

Although the pages have full-time jobs, they must also go to school. And so from 6 A.M. to 9:30 A.M. on school days, they attend the page school, which holds classes in rooms on the third floor of the Library of Congress. The working day for pages runs from 9:30 A.M. to 5:30 P.M. As a result, they have time only for four 45-minute classes each day. The principal of the page school is John C. Hoffman, who was formerly with the District of Columbia school system. There is a faculty of six.

Congress began the page system in 1827. Youngsters were needed to run errands and to do various chores, such as filling the inkwells and snuffboxes that were standard items on the desks. Today's pages no longer have to worry about snuffboxes, but there is plenty for them to do as messengers and clerical workers.

Congress appoints the pages on the basis of nominations made by individual congressmen. Some pages are nominated for short terms, such as the summer-vacation period. But most serve from two to four years. The salaries of the pages vary. Senate pages are paid $7,380 a year, while those in the House receive $6,767. Supreme Court pages get $6,938 annually. There are 84 full-time pages. The House has 50 to serve its 435 members; the Senate has 30 for its 100 members; and the Supreme Court has 4 for its 9 justices.

Pages range in age from 14 to 17. At work, boys have to wear dark suits, white shirts, and ties. Until recently, only boys

The first girl pages (left to right): Julie Price, Paulette Desell, and Ellen McConnell. Standing are Senators Jacob Javits (left) and Charles Percy.

could be pages. But in 1971 the rules were changed and three girl pages were appointed. All but a few of the pages go on to college. But since pages serve an average of two years, not all graduate from the four-year page school. The last graduating class of the page school had 22 members.

Pages must maintain a C average or better in their classwork. When they are not attending class or working, pages participate in sports and other activities. Basketball is the major sport, and the school's team competes against the District of Columbia high schools. Some pages also work on the school yearbook and serve on the student council. Before 1947, a part-time school was operated under the District of Columbia Board of Education. Since then, Congress has had its own accredited school for pages.

What sort of youngsters are the pages? According to Principal Hoffman, "They're very normal kids."

Most of the pages live in rooming houses during their stay in the nation's capital. There are plans to construct a building to house the school, and there have been proposals to build a page dormitory. The new school building will be named in honor of John W. McCormack of Massachusetts, a former Speaker of the House.

STATISTICAL SUPPLEMENT

(as of January 1, 1972)

Nations of the World

The United Nations

The Congress of the United States

United States Cabinet

United States Supreme Court

Executive Office of the President

Governors of the United States

Nobel Prizes

Pulitzer Prizes

NATIONS OF THE WORLD

NATION	CAPITAL	AREA (in sq. mi.)	POPULATION (in millions)	GOVERNMENT
Afghanistan	Kabul	250,000	17.4	Mohammad Zahir Shah—king Abdul Zahir—prime minister
Albania	Tirana	11,100	2.2	Enver Hoxha—communist party secretary Mehmet Shehu—premier
Algeria	Algiers	919,593	14.5	Houari Boumedienne—president
Arab Emirates, Union of	Abu Dhabi	32,000	.2	Zayd ben Sultan—president
Argentina	Buenos Aires	1,072,158	24.7	Alejandro Agustin Lanusse—president
Australia	Canberra	2,967,909	12.8	William McMahon—prime minister
Austria	Vienna	32,374	7.5	Franz Jonas—president Bruno Kreisky—chancellor
Bahrain	Manama	231	.2	Isa bin Sulman al-Khalifa—head of state
Barbados	Bridgetown	166	.3	Errol W. Barrow—prime minister
Belgium	Brussels	11,781	9.7	Baudouin I—king Gaston Eyskens—premier
Bhutan	Thimphu	18,000	1.0	Jigme Dorji Wangchuk—king
Bolivia	La Paz	424,163	4.8	Hugo Banzer Suarez—president
Botswana	Gaborone	231,804	.6	Sir Seretse Khama—president
Brazil	Brasilia	3,286,478	95.7	Emilio Garrastazu Medici—president
Bulgaria	Sofia	42,823	8.6	Todor Zhivkov—communist party secretary Stanko Todorov—premier
Burma	Rangoon	261,789	28.4	Ne Win—prime minister
Burundi	Usumbura	10,747	3.7	Michel Micombero—president
Cambodia	Pnompenh	69,898	7.3	Lon Nol—premier (titular) Sisowath Sirik Matak—premier-delegate
Cameroon	Yaoundé	183,569	5.9	Ahmadou Ahidjo—president
Canada	Ottawa	3,851,809	21.7	Pierre Elliott Trudeau—prime minister
Cen. African Rep.	Bangui	240,535	1.6	Jean Bedel Bokassa—president
Ceylon	Colombo	25,332	12.9	Sirimavo Bandaranaike—prime minister
Chad	Fort-Lamy	495,754	3.8	François Tombalbaye—president
Chile	Santiago	292,259	10.0	Salvador Allende Gossens—president
China (Communist)	Peking	3,691,512	772.9	Mao Tse-tung—chairman Chou En-lai—premier

NATION	CAPITAL	AREA (in sq. mi.)	POPULATION (in millions)	GOVERNMENT
China (Nationalist)	Taipei	13,885	14.3	Chiang Kai-shek—president C. K. Yen—premier
Colombia	Bogota	439,736	22.1	Misael Pastrana Borrero—president
Congo	Brazzaville	132,047	1.0	Marien Ngouabi—president
Costa Rica	San Jose	19,575	1.9	Jose Figueres Ferrer—president
Cuba	Havana	44,218	8.6	Fidel Castro—premier Osvaldo Dorticos Torrado—president
Cyprus	Nicosia	3,572	.6	Archbishop Makarios III—president
Czechoslovakia	Prague	49,370	14.8	Gustav Husak—communist party secretary Ludvik Svoboda—president Lubomir Strougal—premier
Dahomey	Porto-Novo	43,483	2.8	Hubert Maga—president
Denmark	Copenhagen	16,629	5.0	Frederik IX—king Jens Otto Krag—premier
Dominican Rep.	Santo Domingo	18,816	4.4	Joaquin Balaguer—president
Ecuador	Quito	109,483	6.3	Jose Maria Velasco Ibarra—president
Egypt	Cairo	386,660	34.9	Anwar el-Sadat—president Mahmoud Fawzi—premier
El Salvador	San Salvador	8,260	3.6	Fidel Sanchez Hernandez—president
Equatorial Guinea	Santa Isabel	10,830	.3	Francisco Macias Nguema—president
Ethiopia	Addis Ababa	471,777	25.6	Haile Selassie I—emperor
Fiji	Suva	7,055	.533	Ratu Kamisese Mara—prime minister
Finland	Helsinki	130,120	4.7	Urho K. Kekkonen—president Teuvo Aura—premier
France	Paris	211,207	51.5	Georges Pompidou—president Jacques Chaban-Delmas—premier
Gabon	Libreville	103,346	.5	Albert B. Bongo—president
Gambia	Bathurst	4,361	.4	Sir Dauda K. Jawara—president
Germany (East)	East Berlin	41,610	16.2	Erich Honecker—communist party secretary Willi Stoph—premier
Germany (West)	Bonn	95,743	58.9	Willy Brandt—chancellor Gustav Heinemann—president
Ghana	Accra	92,099	9.3	Kofi A. Busia—prime minister Edward Akufo Addo—president
Greece	Athens	50,944	9.0	George Papadopoulos—premier Constantine II—king (in exile)

NATION	CAPITAL	AREA (in sq. mi.)	POPULATION (in millions)	GOVERNMENT
Guatemala	Guatemala City	42,042	5.3	Carlos Arana Osorio—president
Guinea	Conakry	94,926	4.0	Sékou Touré—president
Guyana	Georgetown	83,000	.8	Forbes Burnham—prime minister Arthur Chung—president
Haiti	Port-au-Prince	10,714	5.4	Jean-Claude Duvalier—president
Honduras	Tegucigalpa	43,277	2.8	Ramon Ernesto Cruz—president
Hungary	Budapest	35,919	10.3	Janos Kadar—communist party secretary Jenö Fock—premier
Iceland	Reykjavik	39,768	.2	Kristjan Eldjarn—president Olafur Johannesson—prime minister
India	New Delhi	1,261,813	547.0	Indira Gandhi—prime minister V. V. Giri—president
Indonesia	Jakarta	575,894	124.9	Suharto—president
Iran	Tehran	636,294	29.2	Mohammad Reza Pahlavi—shah Amir Abbas Hoveida—premier
Iraq	Baghdad	167,925	10.0	Ahmad Hassan al-Bakr—president
Ireland	Dublin	27,136	3.0	Eamon de Valera—president John M. Lynch—prime minister
Israel	Jerusalem	7,992	3.0	Golda Meir—prime minister Schneor Zalman Shazar—president
Italy	Rome	116,303	54.1	Emilio Colombo—premier Giovanni Leone—president
Ivory Coast	Abidjan	124,503	4.4	Félix Houphouët-Boigny— president
Jamaica	Kingston	4,232	2.0	Hugh Shearer—prime minister
Japan	Tokyo	142,811	104.7	Hirohito—emperor Eisaku Sato—prime minister
Jordan	Amman	37,738	2.4	Hussein I—king Ahmad al-Lawzi—premier
Kenya	Nairobi	224,959	11.2	Jomo Kenyatta—president
Korea (North)	Pyongyang	46,540	14.3	Kim Il Sung—premier
Korea (South)	Seoul	38,922	32.9	Chung Hee Park—president Kim Chong Pil—premier
Kuwait	Kuwait	6,178	.8	Sabah al-Salim al-Sabah—head of state Jabir al-Ahmad al-Jabir—prime minister
Laos	Vientiane	91,429	3.1	Savang Vatthana—king Souvanna Phouma—premier

NATION	CAPITAL	AREA (in sq. mi.)	POPULATION (in millions)	GOVERNMENT
Lebanon	Beirut	4,015	2.9	Suleiman Franjieh—president Saeb Salam—premier
Lesotho	Maseru	11,720	1.1	Leabua Jonathan—prime minister
Liberia	Monrovia	43,000	1.2	William R. Tolbert—president
Libya	Tripoli	679,360	1.9	Muammar al-Qaddafii—premier
Liechtenstein	Vaduz	61	.023	Francis Joseph II—prince
Luxembourg	Luxembourg	999	.4	Jean—grand duke Pierre Werner—premier
Malagasy Rep.	Tananarive	226,657	7.1	Philibert Tsiranana—president
Malawi	Zomba	45,747	4.6	Hastings K. Banda—president
Malaysia	Kuala Lumpur	128,430	11.1	Abdul Halim Muazzam—king Tun Abdul Razak—prime minister
Maldive Islands	Male	115	.111	Ibrahim Nasir—president
Mali	Bamako	478,765	5.2	Moussa Traoré—president
Malta	Valletta	122	.3	Dom Mintoff—prime minister
Mauritania	Nouakchott	397,954	1.2	Moktar O. Daddah—president
Mauritius	Port Louis	720	.9	Sir Seewoosagur Ramgoolam—prime minister
Mexico	Mexico City	761,602	52.5	Luis Echeverria Alvarez—president
Monaco	Monaco	0.4	.024	Rainier III—prince
Mongolia	Ulan Bator	604,248	1.3	Yumzhagiyn Tsedenbal—communist party secretary
Morocco	Rabat	172,997	16.3	Hassan II—king Mohammad Karim Lamrani—premier
Nauru		8	.007	Hammer DeRoburt—president
Nepal	Katmandu	54,362	11.5	Mahendra Bir Bikram Shah Deva—king Kirti Nidhi Bista—prime minister
Netherlands	Amsterdam	15,766	13.1	Juliana—queen Barend W. Biesheuvel—premier
New Zealand	Wellington	103,736	2.86	Keith J. Holyoake—prime minister
Nicaragua	Managua	50,193	2.1	Anastasio Somoza Debayle, Jr.—president
Niger	Niamey	489,190	4.0	Hamani Diori—president
Nigeria	Lagos	356,668	56.5	Yakubu Gowon—head of state
Norway	Oslo	125,181	3.9	Olav V—king Trygve M. Bratteli—prime minister

NATION	CAPITAL	AREA (in sq. mi.)	POPULATION (in millions)	GOVERNMENT
Oman	Muscat	82,030	.6	Qabus ibn Said—sultan
Pakistan	Islamabad	365,528	141.6	Zulfikar Ali Bhutto—president
Panama	Panama	29,205	1.5	Omar Torrijos Herrera—head of state
Paraguay	Asuncion	157,047	2.5	Alfredo Stroessner—president
Peru	Lima	496,223	14.0	Juan Velasco Alvarado—president
Philippines	Quezon City	115,830	39.4	Ferdinand E. Marcos—president
Poland	Warsaw	120,724	33.3	Edward Gierek—communist party secretary Jozef Cyrankiewicz—president Piotr Jaroszewicz—premier
Portugal	Lisbon	35,553	8.7	Marcelo Caetano—premier Americo Thomaz—president
Qatar	Doha	4,000	.1	Ahmad bin Ali al-Thani—head of state
Rhodesia	Salisbury	150,333	5.2	Ian D. Smith—prime minister Clifford Dupont—president
Rumania	Bucharest	91,699	20.6	Nicolae Ceausescu—communist party secretary Ion Gheorghe Mauer—premier
Rwanda	Kigali	10,169	3.7	Gregoire Kayibanda—president
Saudi Arabia	Riyadh	829,997	8.0	Faisal ibn Abdul Aziz—king
Senegal	Dakar	75,750	4.0	Léopold Senghor—president Abdou Diouf—prime minister
Sierre Leone	Freetown	27,699	2.7	Siaka P. Stevens—president Sorie I. Koroma—prime minister
Singapore	Singapore	224	2.2	Lee Kuan Yew—prime minister Benjamin H. Sheares—president
Somalia	Mogadishu	246,200	2.9	Mohammad Siad Barre—head of state
South Africa	Pretoria Cape Town	471,444	20.6	Balthazar J. Vorster—prime minister J. J. Fouche—president
Spain	Madrid	194,884	33.6	Francisco Franco—head of state
Sudan	Khartoum	967,497	16.3	Gaafar al-Nimeiry—president
Swaziland	Mbabane	6,704	.4	Sobhuza II—king Makhosini Dlamini—prime minister
Sweden	Stockholm	173,649	8.1	Gustaf VI Adolf—king Olof Palme—prime minister
Switzerland	Bern	15,941	6.5	Nello Celio—president
Syria	Damascus	71,498	6.4	Hafez al-Assad—president

NATION	CAPITAL	AREA (in sq. mi.)	POPULATION (in millions)	GOVERNMENT
Tanzania	Dar es Salaam	362,820	13.6	Julius K. Nyerere—president
Thailand	Bangkok	198,456	37.4	Bhumibol Adulyadej—king Thanom Kittikachorn—head of state
Togo	Lomé	21,622	1.9	Etienne Eyadema—president
Tonga	Nuku'alofa	270	.086	Taufa'ahau Tupou IV—king Prince Tu'ipelehake—prime minister
Trinidad & Tobago	Port of Spain	1,980	1.1	Eric Williams—prime minister
Tunisia	Tunis	63,378	5.3	Habib Bourguiba—president Hedi Nouira—prime minister
Turkey	Ankara	301,381	36.5	Cevdet Sunay—president Nihat Erim—premier
Uganda	Kampala	91,134	8.8	Idi Amin—president
U.S.S.R.	Moscow	8,649,512	245.0	Leonid I. Brezhnev—communist party secretary Aleksei N. Kosygin—premier Nikolai V. Podgorny—president of presidium
United Kingdom	London	94,212	56.3	Elizabeth II—queen Edward Heath—prime minister
United States	Washington, D.C.	3,615,123	208.5	Richard M. Nixon—president Spiro T. Agnew—vice-president
Upper Volta	Ouagadougou	105,869	5.5	Sangoulé Lamizana—president
Uruguay	Montevideo	68,536	2.9	Jorge Pacheco Areco—president
Venezuela	Caracas	352,143	11.1	Rafael Caldera Rodriguez—president
Vietnam (North)	Hanoi	61,294	21.6	Le Duan—communist party secretary Ton Duc Thang—president Pham Van Dong—premier
Vietnam (South)	Saigon	67,108	18.3	Nguyen Van Thieu—president Tran Van Huong—vice-president Tran Thien Khiem—premier
Western Samoa	Apia	1,097	.146	Malietoa Tanumafili II—head of state Tupua Tamasese Lealofi IV—prime minister
Yemen (Aden)	Medina al-Shaab	112,000	1.3	Salem Ali Rubaya—head of state Ali Masir Mohammad—prime minister
Yemen (Sana)	Sana	75,290	5.9	Abdul Rahman al-Iryani—head of state
Yugoslavia	Belgrade	98,766	20.8	Josip Broz Tito—president Dzemal Bijedic—premier
Zaire (former Congo)	Kinshasa	905,565	17.8	Joseph D. Mobutu—president
Zambia	Lusaka	290,585	4.4	Kenneth D. Kaunda—president

THE UNITED NATIONS

THE SECRETARIAT
Secretary-General: Kurt Waldheim

THE GENERAL ASSEMBLY
President: Adam Malik (Indonesia)

Afghanistan	Denmark	Kenya	Portugal
Albania	Dominican Republic	Kuwait	*Qatar
Algeria	Ecuador	Laos	Rumania
*Arab Emirates, Union of	Egypt	Lebanon	Rwanda
Argentina	El Salvador	Lesotho	Saudi Arabia
Australia	Equatorial Guinea	Liberia	Senegal
Austria	Ethiopia	Libya	Sierra Leone
*Bahrain	Fiji	Luxembourg	Singapore
Barbados	Finland	Malagasy Rep.	Somalia
Belgium	France	Malawi	South Africa
*Bhutan	Gabon	Malaysia	Soviet Union
Bolivia	Gambia	Maldive Is.	Spain
Botswana	Ghana	Mali	Sudan
Brazil	Great Britain	Malta	Swaziland
Bulgaria	Greece	Mauritania	Sweden
Burma	Guatemala	Mauritius	Syria
Burundi	Guinea	Mexico	Tanzania
Byelorussia	Guyana	Mongolia	Thailand
Cambodia	Haiti	Morocco	Togo
Cameroon	Honduras	Nepal	Trinidad & Tobago
Canada	Hungary	Netherlands	Tunisia
Central African Rep.	Iceland	New Zealand	Turkey
Ceylon	India	Nicaragua	Uganda
Chad	Indonesia	Niger	Ukraine
Chile	Iran	Nigeria	United States
China	Iraq	Norway	Upper Volta
Colombia	Ireland	*Oman	Uruguay
Congo	Israel	Pakistan	Venezuela
Costa Rica	Italy	Panama	Yemen (Aden)
Cuba	Ivory Coast	Paraguay	Yemen (Sana)
Cyprus	Jamaica	Peru	Yugoslavia
Czechoslovakia	Japan	Philippines	Zaire
Dahomey	Jordan	Poland	Zambia

* admitted in 1971

THE SECURITY COUNCIL

Argentina (until 1972)	Guinea (until 1973)	Somalia (until 1972)
Belgium (until 1972)	India (until 1973)	Soviet Union (permanent)
Britain (permanent)	Italy (until 1972)	Sudan (until 1973)
China (permanent)	Japan (until 1972)	United States (permanent)
France (permanent)	Panama (until 1973)	Yugoslavia (until 1973)

THE CONGRESS OF THE UNITED STATES

UNITED STATES SENATE

Alabama
John J. Sparkman (D)
James B. Allen (D)

Alaska
Ted F. Stevens (R)
Mike Gravel (D)

Arizona
Paul J. Fannin (R)
Barry Goldwater (R)

Arkansas
John L. McClellan (D)
J. William Fulbright (D)

California
Alan Cranston (D)
John V. Tunney (D)

Colorado
Gordon Allott (R)
Peter H. Dominick (R)

Connecticut
Abraham A. Ribicoff (D)
Lowell P. Weicker, Jr. (R)

Delaware
J. Caleb Boggs (R)
William V. Roth, Jr. (R)

Florida
Edward J. Gurney (R)
Lawton Chiles (D)

Georgia
David H. Gambrell (D)*
Herman E. Talmadge (D)

Hawaii
Hiram L. Fong (R)
Daniel K. Inouye (D)

Idaho
Frank Church (D)
Len B. Jordan (R)

Illinois
Charles H. Percy (R)
Adlai E. Stevenson 3d (D)

Indiana
Vance Hartke (D)
Birch Bayh (D)

Iowa
Jack Miller (R)
Harold E. Hughes (D)

Kansas
James B. Pearson (R)
Robert J. Dole (R)

Kentucky
John S. Cooper (R)
Marlow W. Cook (R)

Louisiana
Allen J. Ellender (D)
Russell B. Long (D)

Maine
Margaret Chase Smith (R)
Edmund S. Muskie (D)

Maryland
Charles McC. Mathias, Jr. (R)
J. Glenn Beall, Jr. (R)

Massachusetts
Edward M. Kennedy (D)
Edward W. Brooke (R)

Michigan
Philip A. Hart (D)
Robert P. Griffin (R)

Minnesota
Walter F. Mondale (D)
Hubert H. Humphrey (D)

Mississippi
James O. Eastland (D)
John C. Stennis (D)

Missouri
Stuart Symington (D)
Thomas F. Eagleton (D)

Montana
Mike Mansfield (D)
Lee Metcalf (D)

Nebraska
Roman L. Hruska (R)
Carl T. Curtis (R)

Nevada
Alan Bible (D)
Howard W. Cannon (D)

New Hampshire
Norris Cotton (R)
Thomas J. McIntyre (D)

New Jersey
Clifford P. Case (R)
Harrison A. Williams, Jr. (D)

New Mexico
Clinton P. Anderson (D)
Joseph M. Montoya (D)

New York
Jacob K. Javits (R)
James L. Buckley (C)

North Carolina
Sam J. Ervin, Jr. (D)
B. Everett Jordan (D)

North Dakota
Milton R. Young (R)
Quentin N. Burdick (D)

Ohio
William B. Saxbe (R)
Robert Taft, Jr. (R)

Oklahoma
Fred R. Harris (D)
Henry L. Bellmon (R)

Oregon
Mark O. Hatfield (R)
Robert W. Packwood (R)

Pennsylvania
Hugh Scott (R)
Richard S. Schweiker (R)

Rhode Island
John O. Pastore (D)
Claiborne Pell (D)

South Carolina
Strom Thurmond (R)
Ernest F. Hollings (D)

South Dakota
Karl E. Mundt (R)
George S. McGovern (D)

Tennessee
Howard H. Baker, Jr. (R)
William E. Brock 3d (R)

Texas
John G. Tower (R)
Lloyd M. Bentsen, Jr. (D)

Utah
Wallace F. Bennett (R)
Frank E. Moss (D)

Vermont
George D. Aiken (R)
Robert T. Stafford (R)*

Virginia
Harry F. Byrd, Jr. (I)
William B. Spong, Jr. (D)

Washington
Warren G. Magnuson (D)
Henry M. Jackson (D)

West Virginia
Jennings Randolph (D)
Robert C. Byrd (D)

Wisconsin
William Proxmire (D)
Gaylord Nelson (D)

Wyoming
Gale W. McGee (D)
Clifford P. Hansen (R)

* Appointed in 1971

(R) Republican
(D) Democrat
(C) Conservative
(I) Independent

UNITED STATES HOUSE OF REPRESENTATIVES

Alabama
1. J. Edwards (R)
2. W. L. Dickinson (R)
3. vacant
4. W. Nichols (D)
5. W. Flowers (D)
6. J. H. Buchanan, Jr. (R)
7. T. Bevill (D)
8. R. E. Jones (D)

Alaska
N. J. Begich (D)

Arizona
1. J. J. Rhodes (R)
2. M. K. Udall (D)
3. S. Steiger (R)

Arkansas
1. W. V. Alexander, Jr. (D)
2. W. D. Mills (D)
3. J. P. Hammerschmidt (R)
4. D. Pryor (D)

California
1. D. H. Clausen (R)
2. H. T. Johnson (D)
3. J. E. Moss (D)
4. R. L. Leggett (D)
5. P. Burton (D)
6. W. S. Mailliard (R)
7. R. V. Dellums (D)
8. G. P. Miller (D)
9. D. Edwards (D)
10. C. S. Gubser (R)
11. P. N. McCloskey, Jr. (R)
12. B. L. Talcott (R)
13. C. M. Teague (R)
14. J. R. Waldie (D)
15. J. J. McFall (D)
16. B. F. Sisk (D)
17. G. M. Anderson (D)
18. R. B. Mathias (R)
19. C. Holifield (D)
20. H. A. Smith (R)
21. A. F. Hawkins (D)
22. J. C. Corman (D)
23. D. Clawson (R)
24. J. H. Rousselot (R)
25. C. E. Wiggins (R)
26. T. M. Rees (D)
27. B. Goldwater, Jr. (R)
28. A. Bell (R)
29. G. E. Danielson (D)
30. E. R. Roybal (D)
31. C. H. Wilson (D)
32. C. Hosmer (R)
33. J. L. Pettis (R)
34. R. T. Hanna (D)
35. J. G. Schmitz (R)
36. B. Wilson (R)
37. L. Van Deerlin (D)
38. V. V. Veysey (R)

Colorado
1. J. D. McKevitt (R)

2. D. G. Brotzman (R)
3. F. E. Evans (D)
4. W. N. Aspinall (D)

Connecticut
1. W. R. Cotter (D)
2. R. H. Steele (R)
3. R. N. Giaimo (D)
4. S. B. McKinney (R)
5. J. S. Monagan (D)
6. Ella T. Grasso (D)

Delaware
P. S. duPont 4th (R)

Florida
1. R. L. F. Sikes (D)
2. D. Fuqua (D)
3. C. E. Bennett (D)
4. W. V. Chappell, Jr. (D)
5. L. Frey, Jr. (R)
6. S. M. Gibbons (D)
7. J. A. Haley (D)
8. C. W. Young (R)
9. P. G. Rogers (D)
10. J. H. Burke (R)
11. C. D. Pepper (D)
12. D. B. Fascell (D)

Georgia
1. G. E. Hagan (D)
2. D. Mathis (D)
3. J. T. Brinkley (D)
4. B. B. Blackburn (R)
5. F. Thompson (R)
6. J. J. Flynt, Jr. (D)
7. J. W. Davis (D)
8. W. S. Stuckey, Jr. (D)
9. P. M. Landrum (D)
10. R. G. Stephens, Jr. (D)

Hawaii
1. S. M. Matsunaga (D)
2. Patsy T. Mink (D)

Idaho
1. J. A. McClure (R)
2. O. Hansen (R)

Illinois
1. R. Metcalfe (D)
2. A. J. Mikva (D)
3. M. F. Murphy (D)
4. E. J. Derwinski (R)
5. J. C. Kluczynski (D)
6. G. W. Collins (D)
7. F. Annunzio (D)
8. D. D. Rostenkowski (D)
9. S. R. Yates (D)
10. H. R. Collier (R)
11. R. C. Pucinski (D)
12. R. McClory (R)
13. P. M. Crane (R)
14. J. N. Erlenborn (R)
15. vacant
16. J. B. Anderson (R)

17. L. C. Arends (R)
18. R. H. Michel (R)
19. T. F. Railsback (R)
20. P. Findley (R)
21. K. J. Gray (D)
22. W. L. Springer (R)
23. G. E. Shipley (D)
24. C. M. Price (D)

Indiana
1. R. J. Madden (D)
2. E. F. Landgrebe (R)
3. J. Brademas (D)
4. J. E. Roush (D)
5. E. H. Hillis (R)
6. W. G. Bray (R)
7. J. T. Myers (R)
8. R. H. Zion (R)
9. L. H. Hamilton (D)
10. D. W. Dennis (R)
11. A. Jacobs, Jr. (D)

Iowa
1. F. Schwengel (R)
2. J. C. Culver (D)
3. H. R. Gross (R)
4. J. H. Kyl (R)
5. N. Smith (D)
6. W. Mayne (R)
7. W. J. Scherle (R)

Kansas
1. K. G. Sebelius (R)
2. W. R. Roy (D)
3. L. Winn, Jr. (R)
4. G. E. Shriver (R)
5. J. Skubitz (R)

Kentucky
1. F. A. Stubblefield (D)
2. W. H. Natcher (D)
3. R. L. Mazzoli (D)
4. M. G. Snyder (R)
5. T. L. Carter (R)
6. W. P. Curlin, Jr. (D)*
7. C. D. Perkins (D)

Louisiana
1. F. E. Hébert (D)
2. H. Boggs (D)
3. P. T. Caffery (D)
4. J. D. Waggonner, Jr. (D)
5. O. E. Passman (D)
6. J. R. Rarick (D)
7. E. W. Edwards (D)
8. S. O. Long (D)

Maine
1. P. N. Kyros (D)
2. W. D. Hathaway (D)

Maryland
1. W. O. Mills (R)*
2. C. D. Long (D)
3. E. A. Garmatz (D)
4. P. S. Sarbanes (D)

5. L. J. Hogan (R)
6. G. E. Byron (D)
7. P. J. Mitchell (D)
8. G. Gude (R)

Massachusetts
1. S. O. Conte (R)
2. E. P. Boland (D)
3. R. F. Drinan (D)
4. H. D. Donohue (D)
5. F. B. Morse (R)
6. M. J. Harrington (D)
7. T. H. Macdonald (D)
8. T. P. O'Neill, Jr. (D)
9. Louise Day Hicks (D)
10. Margaret M. Heckler (R)
11. J. A. Burke (D)
12. H. Keith (R)

Michigan
1. J. Conyers, Jr. (D)
2. M. L. Esch (R)
3. G. Brown (D)
4. E. Hutchinson (R)
5. G. R. Ford (R)
6. C. E. Chamberlain (R)
7. D. W. Riegle, Jr. (R)
8. J. Harvey (R)
9. G. A. Vander Jagt (R)
10. E. A. Cederberg (R)
11. P. E. Ruppe (R)
12. J. G. O'Hara (D)
13. C. C. Diggs, Jr. (D)
14. L. N. Nedzi (D)
15. W. D. Ford (D)
16. J. D. Dingell (D)
17. Martha W. Griffiths (D)
18. W. S. Broomfield (R)
19. J. H. McDonald (R)

Minnesota
1. A. H. Quie (R)
2. A. Nelsen (R)
3. W. Frenzel (R)
4. J. E. Karth (D)
5. D. M. Fraser (D)
6. J. M. Zwach (R)
7. B. Bergland (D)
8. J. A. Blatnik (D)

Mississippi
1. T. G. Abernethy (D)
2. J. L. Whitten (D)
3. C. H. Griffin (D)
4. G. V. Montgomery (D)
5. W. M. Colmer (D)

Missouri
1. W. L. Clay (D)
2. J. W. Symington (D)
3. Leonor K. Sullivan (D)
4. W. J. Randall (D)
5. R. Bolling (D)
6. W. R. Hull, Jr. (D)
7. D. G. Hall (R)
8. R. H. Ichord (D)

9. W. L. Hungate (D)
10. B. D. Burlison (D)

Montana
1. R. G. Shoup (R)
2. J. Melcher (D)

Nebraska
1. C. Thone (R)
2. J. Y. McCollister (R)
3. D. T. Martin (R)

Nevada
W. S. Baring (D)

New Hampshire
1. L. C. Wyman (R)
2. J. C. Cleveland (R)

New Jersey
1. J. E. Hunt (R)
2. C. W. Sandman, Jr. (R)
3. J. J. Howard (D)
4. F. Thompson, Jr. (D)
5. P. H. B. Frelinghuysen (R)
6. E. B. Forsythe (R)
7. W. B. Widnall (R)
8. R. A. Roe (D)
9. H. Helstoski (D)
10. P. W. Rodino, Jr. (D)
11. J. G. Minish (D)
12. Florence P. Dwyer (R)
13. C. E. Gallagher (D)
14. D. V. Daniels (D)
15. E. J. Patten (D)

New Mexico
1. M. Lujan, Jr. (R)
2. H. L. Runnels (D)

New York
1. O. G. Pike (D)
2. J. R. Grover, Jr. (R)
3. L. L. Wolff (D)
4. J. W. Wydler (R)
5. N. F. Lent (R)
6. S. Halpern (R)
7. J. P. Addabbo (D)
8. B. S. Rosenthal (D)
9. J. J. Delaney (D)
10. E. Celler (D)
11. F. J. Brasco (D)
12. Shirley A. Chisholm (D)
13. B. L. Podell (D)
14. J. J. Rooney (D)
15. H. L. Carey (D)
16. J. M. Murphy (D)
17. E. I. Koch (D)
18. C. B. Rangel (D)
19. Bella S. Abzug (D)
20. W. F. Ryan (D)
21. H. Badillo (D)
22. J. H. Scheuer (D)
23. J. B. Bingham (D)
24. M. Biaggi (D)
25. P. A. Peyser (R)
26. O. R. Reid (R)
27. J. G. Dow (D)
28. H. Fish, Jr. (R)
29. S. S. Stratton (D)
30. C. J. King (R)
31. R. C. McEwen (R)
32. A. Pirnie (R)
33. H. W. Robison (R)
34. J. H. Terry (R)
35. J. M. Hanley (D)
36. F. Horton (R)
37. B. B. Conable, Jr. (R)
38. J. F. Hastings (R)
39. J. E. Kemp (R)
40. H. P. Smith III (R)
41. T. J. Dulski (D)

North Carolina
1. W. B. Jones (D)
2. L. H. Fountain (D)
3. D. N. Henderson (D)
4. N. Galifianakis (D)
5. W. D. Mizell (R)
6. L. R. Preyer (D)
7. A. A. Lennon (D)
8. E. B. Ruth (R)
9. C. R. Jonas (R)
10. J. T. Broyhill (R)
11. R. A. Taylor (D)

North Dakota
1. M. Andrews (R)
2. A. A. Link (D)

Ohio
1. W. J. Keating (R)
2. D. D. Clancy (R)
3. C. W. Whalen, Jr. (R)
4. W. M. McCulloch (R)
5. D. L. Latta (R)
6. W. H. Harsha (R)
7. C. J. Brown (R)
8. J. E. Betts (R)
9. T. L. Ashley (D)
10. C. E. Miller (R)
11. J. W. Stanton (R)
12. S. L. Devine (R)
13. C. A. Mosher (R)
14. J. F. Seiberling, Jr. (D)
15. C. P. Wylie (R)
16. F. T. Bow (R)
17. J. M. Ashbrook (R)
18. W. L. Hays (D)
19. C. J. Carney (D)
20. J. V. Stanton (D)
21. L. Stokes (D)
22. C. A. Vanik (D)
23. W. E. Minshall (R)
24. W. E. Powell (R)

Oklahoma
1. P. Belcher (R)
2. E. Edmondson (D)
3. C. B. Albert (D)
4. T. Steed (D)
5. J. Jarman (D)
6. J. N. Camp (R)

Oregon
1. W. Wyatt (R)
2. A. Ullman (D)
3. Edith Green (D)
4. J. Dellenback (R)

Pennsylvania
1. W. A. Barrett (D)
2. R. N. C. Nix (D)
3. J. A. Byrne (D)
4. J. Eilberg (D)
5. W. J. Green (D)
6. G. Yatron (D)
7. L. G. Williams (R)
8. E. G. Biester, Jr. (R)
9. J. H. Ware 3d (R)
10. J. M. McDade (R)
11. D. J. Flood (D)
12. J. I. Whalley (R)
13. L. Coughlin (R)
14. W. S. Moorhead (D)
15. F. B. Rooney (D)
16. E. D. Eshleman (R)
17. H. T. Schneebeli (R)
18. H. J. Heinz 3d (R)*
19. G. A. Goodling (R)
20. J. M. Gaydos (D)
21. J. H. Dent (D)
22. J. P. Saylor (R)
23. A. W. Johnson (R)
24. J. P. Vigorito (D)
25. F. M. Clark (D)
26. T. E. Morgan (D)
27. vacant

Puerto Rico
J. L. Cordova**

Rhode Island
1. F. J. St. Germain (D)
2. R. O. Tiernan (D)

South Carolina
1. M. J. Davis (D)*
2. F. D. Spence (R)
3. W. J. B. Dorn (D)
4. J. R. Mann (D)
5. T. S. Gettys (D)
6. J. L. McMillan (D)

South Dakota
1. F. E. Denholm (D)
2. J. Abourezk (D)

Tennessee
1. J. H. Quillen (R)
2. J. J. Duncan (R)
3. L. Baker (R)
4. J. L. Evins (D)
5. R. H. Fulton (D)
6. W. R. Anderson (D)
7. L. R. Blanton (D)
8. E. Jones (D)
9. D. H. Kuykendall (R)

Texas
1. W. Patman (D)
2. J. Dowdy (D)
3. J. M. Collins (R)
4. R. Roberts (D)
5. E. Cabell (D)
6. O. E. Teague (D)
7. W. R. Archer (R)
8. B. Eckhardt (D)
9. J. Brooks (D)
10. J. J. Pickle (D)
11. W. R. Poage (D)
12. J. C. Wright, Jr. (D)
13. G. Purcell (D)
14. J. Young (D)
15. E. de la Garza (D)
16. R. C. White (D)
17. O. Burleson (D)
18. R. D. Price (R)
19. G. H. Mahon (D)
20. H. B. Gonzalez (D)
21. O. C. Fisher (D)
22. R. R. Casey (D)
23. A. Kazen, Jr. (D)

Utah
1. K. G. McKay (D)
2. S. P. Lloyd (R)

Vermont
vacant

Virginia
1. T. N. Downing (D)
2. G. W. Whitehurst (R)
3. D. E. Satterfield III (D)
4. W. M. Abbitt (D)
5. W. C. Daniel (D)
6. R. H. Poff (R)
7. J. K. Robinson (R)
8. W. L. Scott (R)
9. W. C. Wampler (R)
10. J. T. Broyhill (R)

Washington
1. T. M. Pelly (R)
2. L. Meeds (D)
3. Julia B. Hansen (D)
4. M. McCormack (D)
5. T. S. Foley (D)
6. F. V. Hicks (D)
7. B. Adams (D)

Washington, D.C.
Walter Fauntroy (D)**

West Virginia
1. R. H. Mollohan (D)
2. H. O. Staggers (D)
3. J. Slack (D)
4. K. Hechler (D)
5. J. Kee (D)

Wisconsin
1. L. Aspin (D)
2. R. W. Kastenmeier (D)
3. V. M. Thomson (R)
4. C. J. Zablocki (D)
5. H. S. Reuss (D)
6. W. A. Steiger (R)
7. D. R. Obey (D)
8. J. W. Byrnes (R)
9. G. R. Davis (R)
10. A. E. O'Konski (R)

Wyoming
T. Roncalio (D)

* elected to office in 1971
** nonvoting delegate

UNITED STATES CABINET

Secretary of State: William P. Rogers
Secretary of the Treasury: John B. Connally, Jr.
Secretary of Defense: Melvin R. Laird
Attorney General: John N. Mitchell
Secretary of the Interior: Rogers C. B. Morton
Secretary of Agriculture: Earl L. Butz
Secretary of Commerce: Maurice H. Stans
Secretary of Labor: James D. Hodgson
Secretary of Health, Education, and Welfare: Elliot L. Richardson
Secretary of Housing and Urban Development: George Romney
Secretary of Transportation: John A. Volpe

UNITED STATES SUPREME COURT

Chief Justice: Warren E. Burger (1969)

Associate Justices:
William O. Douglas (1939)
William J. Brennan, Jr. (1956)
Potter Stewart (1958)
Byron R. White (1962)
Thurgood Marshall (1967)
Harry A. Blackmun (1970)
Lewis F. Powell, Jr. (1972)
William H. Rehnquist (1972)

EXECUTIVE OFFICE OF THE PRESIDENT

Counsellors: Robert H. Finch, Donald Rumsfeld
Assistants: Peter M. Flanigan, H. R. Haldeman
Assistant for Domestic Affairs: John D. Ehrlichman
Assistant for National Security Affairs: Henry A. Kissinger
Assistant for International Economic Affairs: Peter G. Peterson
Counsel for Congressional Relations: Clark MacGregor
Science Adviser: Edward E. David, Jr.
Director of Communications: Herbert G. Klein
Press Secretary: Ronald L. Ziegler
Office of Management and Budget: George P. Shultz, director
Council of Economic Advisers: Herbert Stein, chairman
Central Intelligence Agency: Richard Helms, director
National Aeronautics and Space Council: William A. Anders, executive secretary
Office of Economic Opportunity: Phillip V. Sanchez, director
Office of Emergency Preparedness: George A. Lincoln, director
Council on Environmental Quality: Russell E. Train, chairman
Office of Consumer Affairs: Virginia H. Knauer, director

GOVERNORS OF THE UNITED STATES

State	Governor	State	Governor
Alabama	George C. Wallace (D)	Montana	Forrest H. Anderson (D)
Alaska	William A. Egan (D)	Nebraska	J. James Exon (D)
Arizona	Jack Williams (R)	Nevada	Mike O'Callaghan (D)
Arkansas	Dale Bumpers (D)	New Hampshire	Walter R. Peterson, Jr. (R)
California	Ronald Reagan (R)	New Jersey	William T. Cahill (R)
Colorado	John A. Love (R)	New Mexico	Bruce King (D)
Connecticut	Thomas J. Meskill (R)	New York	Nelson A. Rockefeller (R)
Delaware	Russell W. Peterson (R)	North Carolina	Robert W. Scott (D)
Florida	Reubin Askew (D)	North Dakota	William L. Guy (D)
Georgia	Jimmy Carter (D)	Ohio	John J. Gilligan (D)
Hawaii	John A. Burns (D)	Oklahoma	David Hall (D)
Idaho	Cecil D. Andrus (D)	Oregon	Tom McCall (R)
Illinois	Richard B. Ogilvie (R)	Pennsylvania	Milton J. Shapp (D)
Indiana	Edgar D. Whitcomb (R)	Rhode Island	Frank Licht (D)
Iowa	Robert D. Ray (R)	South Carolina	John C. West (D)
Kansas	Robert Docking (D)	South Dakota	Richard F. Kneip (D)
Kentucky	Wendell H. Ford (D)*	Tennessee	Winfield Dunn (R)
Louisiana	John J. McKeithen (D)	Texas	Preston Smith (D)
Maine	Kenneth M. Curtis (D)	Utah	Calvin L. Rampton (D)
Maryland	Marvin Mandel (D)	Vermont	Deane C. Davis (R)
Massachusetts	Francis W. Sargent (R)	Virginia	Linwood Holton (R)
Michigan	William G. Milliken (R)	Washington	Daniel J. Evans (R)
Minnesota	Wendell R. Anderson (D)	West Virginia	Arch A. Moore, Jr. (R)
Mississippi	William L. Waller (D)*	Wisconsin	Patrick J. Lucey (D)
Missouri	Warren E. Hearnes (D)	Wyoming	Stanley K. Hathaway (R)

* elected to office in 1971

NOBEL PRIZES

Chemistry: Gerhard Herzberg, Canada, of the National Research Council of Canada in Ottawa, for his research on the structure of the molecule, and especially free radicals (highly active fragments of molecules that combine easily with other molecules).

Literature: Pablo Neruda, Chile, poet, diplomat, and communist leader, for "poetry that, with the action of an elemental force, brings alive a continent's destiny and dreams." His works include *Canto General* (General Song), which has become accepted as the epic of Latin-American man. Neruda is the author of about 20 books of poetry, and his work is clear and lyrical. It is imbued with tender love as well as with social and political commentary.

Peace: Willy Brandt, West Germany, chancellor of West Germany since 1969, for his efforts to bring about a reconciliation between West Germany and East Europe. As a result of these efforts, which began when he became foreign minister in 1966, West Germany signed friendship treaties with the Soviet Union and Poland. Brandt was also cited for helping to build *détente* between East and West Europe, and for trying to obtain for all West Berliners personal security and a complete freedom of movement.

Physics: Dennis Gabor, Great Britain, professor emeritus at the Imperial College of Science and Technology in London, and staff scientist for the Columbia Broadcasting System Laboratories in Stamford, Connecticut, for inventing and developing holography. Holography is a method of three-dimensional photography without the use of a lens. Using special beams of light, holography provides a way of recording a whole image—and not just the flat surface reproduced in an ordinary photograph.

Physiology or Medicine: Earl W. Sutherland, Jr., United States, professor of physiology at Vanderbilt University, for his research in explaining the action of hormones (chemical substances that are secreted by glands and carried by the bloodstream to other parts of the body, where they influence the activities of various cells).

Memorial Prize in Economics: Simon Kuznets, United States, professor emeritus at Harvard University, for his "empirically founded interpretation of economic growth which has led to new and deepened insight into the economic and social structure of development." He developed the concept of using the GNP (gross national product—the sum of a nation's goods and services) as a measure of a nation's growth.

PULITZER PRIZES

JOURNALISM

Cartoons: Paul Conrad, editorial cartoonist, *Los Angeles Times*

Commentary: William A. Caldwell, associate editor, *The Record* (Hackensack, N.J.), for column on Bergen County local affairs

Criticism: Harold C. Schonberg, senior music critic, *The New York Times*

Editorial Writing: Horance G. Davis, Jr., editorialist, *Gainesville Sun* (Florida), for editorials supporting peaceful desegregation of Florida's schools

Feature Photography: Jack Dykinga, staff photographer, *Chicago Sun-Times,* for pictures illustrating deplorable conditions at two schools for the retarded

Spot-News Photography: John Paul Filo, Kent State University (Ohio) photography student, for widely-used photo of grief-stricken girl kneeling by the body of a student killed at Kent State in 1970

International Reporting: Jimmie Lee Hoagland, Africa correspondent, *The Washington Post,* for reports on the effects of South Africa's apartheid policy

Local Reporting, general: The Staff of the Akron Beacon Journal (Ohio), for deadline-pressure coverage of the Kent State tragedy

Local Reporting, special: William Hugh Jones, reporter, *Chicago Tribune,* for investigation and exposé of Chicago police being bribed to steer sick people in poor areas to private ambulance companies

National Reporting: Lucinda Franks and Thomas Powers, reporters, United Press International, for their documentary study of Diana Oughton, the young radical who died in a Greenwich Village "bomb factory" in 1970

Public-Service Gold Medal: Journal-Sentinel newspapers (Winston-Salem, N.C.), for coverage of environmental problems

LETTERS AND MUSIC

Biography: Lawrance R. Thompson, for *Robert Frost: The Years of Triumph, 1915–1938*

Drama: Paul Zindel, for *The Effect of Gamma Rays on Man-in-the-Moon Marigolds*

Fiction: No award given

History: James MacGregor Burns, for [Franklin D.] *Roosevelt: The Soldier of Freedom*

Music: Mario Davidovsky, for *Synchronisms No. 6 for Piano and Electronic Sound*

Nonfiction: John Toland, for *The Rising Sun*

Poetry: William S. Merwin, for his seventh volume of poems, *The Carrier of Ladders*

DICTIONARY INDEX

A

Airbus. A very large commercial jet transport airplane. The term is applied especially to the new Lockheed L–1011 TriStar, a 250-seat American airplane that can carry 400 passengers. It is powered by British Rolls-Royce RB–211 engines. This plane was much in the news in 1971. Money problems threatened to end production of the plane and the life of both companies involved in its making (Lockheed Aircraft Corporation and Rolls-Royce Ltd.). The British Government had to take over the financing of the engine manufacture for the project, and the U.S. Congress passed a bill providing a $250,000,000 U.S. Government loan guarantee to Lockheed to ensure completion of the project.

Amtrak. The National Railroad Passenger Corporation, which began operation on May 1, 1971. This company operates U.S. passenger trains in a single coast-to-coast network linking major cities. It is a semi-public corporation. It receives funds from the U.S. Government but uses equipment and resources of the railroad industry. Thus the U.S. Government and privately owned railroads are, in effect, partners in the operation. The system was set up to aid the railroads, which had found passenger service unprofitable. It has cut the number of train routes sharply but seeks to make the remaining service more modern, more efficient, and in time profitable. *See also* 354

B

Bahrain 271–73
Ballet 182–84
Ballet of the 20th Century 182
Baltimore Orioles, baseball team 327, 329
Banda, Hastings, president of Malawi 77
Bangladesh 66, 112, 122–23, pictures 112, 114–15
Banzer Suarez, Hugo, Bolivian president 58, 234
Barbados 237
Baseball 327–29
  Pan-American Games 349, picture 348
Basketball 330
  Pan-American Games 349, picture 347
Belfast, Northern Ireland, picture 59
Belluschi, Pietro, Italian-American architect 107
Berlin, Germany
  West Berlin agreement 204, 212–13, picture 202
Berrigan, Daniel and Philip, U.S. Catholic priests 300
Bhutto, Zulfikar Ali, Pakistani president 66, 122–23
Bicycle riding 282, picture 80, 283
Biesheuvel, Barend W., Netherlands premier 209
Biography 242–43
Biology see Medicine and health
Birkert, Gunnar, architect 108
Bishop, Joey, U.S. performer, picture 287
Black, Hugo L., U.S. Supreme Court justice 60, picture 290
Black hole, dead star 307–08
Blacks
  books about 246
  Israelites, picture 303
  Protestantism 299, pictures 298
  sculpture and sculptors 101
Blindness and sight problems, aids for, pictures 257
Blue, Vida, U.S. baseball player 327, picture 329
Blue Water, White Death, movie 175
Bobick, Duane, U.S. athlete, picture 348
Body clothes 276, pictures 277, 278
Boeing Company 151–52
Bolivia 58, 234
Bonner, Neville, Australian senator, 126, picture 127
Books see Literature
Bordaberry, Juan, Uruguayan leader 232
Borlaug, Norman E., U.S. agronomist, picture 83
Boston Museum of Art 92
Bottoms, Timothy, U.S. actor, picture 173
Botulism, food poisoning 259
Boulez, Pierre, French composer-conductor 178, picture 176
Bourassa, Robert, Quebec premier 144–45
Bowling 333
Boxing 332–33
BOY POWER '76 386
Boys' and men's fashions 276, 278
Boys' Clubs of America 388
Boy Scouts of America 386–87
Brandt, Willy, West German chancellor 204–05
  awarded Nobel Peace prize 204, 206
Bratteli, Trygve M., Norwegian prime minister 48, 209
Brazil 44, 236
Brezhnev, Leonid, Soviet Communist Party chief 204, 210, pictures 205, 211
Bronx Park Zoo, New York City, pollution display, picture 194
Brown, Dee, U.S. historian 244, picture 241
Bucher, Giovanni Enrico, Swiss diplomat 44
Bucks, Milwaukee basketball team 330
Budget, United States 155
Bunche, Ralph J., U.S. diplomat to UN 62, picture 291
Burgess, Lowry, U.S. artist 95

Bush, George, U.S. ambassador to United Nations, picture 362
Business
  Canada 140, picture 134, 135
  Nixon's economic policies 372–73
  youthful consumers 37–41
Busing, of school children 158–59
Butz, Earl L., U.S. secretary of agriculture 64, picture **83**

C

Cabinet of the United States 408
Cable television (CATV) 188
Caldecott Medal 240, 248, picture 251
Calley, William L. Jr., U.S. Army officer 48, 50, 382
Cambodia
  Sirik Matak, Sisowath, premier-delegate 46
  war in 119
Cameroon, picture 80
Camp Fire Girls 389
Canada 130–45
  Ontario Science Centre 312, pictures 312–15
  protest against Amchitka nuclear test, picture 64
Canada Development Corporation 139
Cancer research 256, pictures 254, 256
Candlemaking 226
Canonero II, race horse, picture 340
Capitals of the world 398–403
Caribbean 236–37
  See also individual countries
Carpenters, American singers 181, picture 180
Carson, Rachel, U.S. author 34, picture 33
Cartoons
  Chinese ping-pong player, picture 113
  Middle East, picture 263
  monetary crisis, picture 151
  Pentagon Papers, picture 383
  pollution, picture 194
  South Vietnam elections, picture 120
  United States economy, picture 373
  wage-price freeze, picture 152
  youth vote, U.S. picture 377
Casals, Pablo, Spanish cellist-composer, picture 178
Castro, Fidel, Cuban premier 64, 231, 234, pictures **228**, 231
Catholicism 300–01, picture 296
Cattle, cross-breeding 86
Ceausescu, Nicolae, Rumanian leader 211, 212

Celestial mechanics. The branch of learning that deals with the motion of celestial bodies (planets and stars) as they are influenced by the principles of dynamics and Newton's law of gravitation. In effect, the study of how forces from without, especially gravity, affect the motion and equilibrium of bodies in the heavens. This branch of learning, combining physics and astronomy, has taken on new importance as man has begun to explore outer space.

Celibacy, for Catholic priests 300
Center Opera of Minneapolis 176
Central America see Latin America
Ceramics, picture 215
Ceylon, rebellion in 123
Cézanne, Paul, French artist 94
Chad 74–75, picture 70
Chanel, Gabrielle (Coco), French couturière, picture 293
Charlotte-Mecklenburg decision, of Supreme Court
  school desegregation 158, picture 157
Chemistry 306
  Nobel prize winner 409

E

Earth art. Art that uses the earth in one of its natural forms as a means of creating or expressing something. In most branches of art, an artist works with materials such as paint, canvas, plaster, or bronze, and the thing he creates is displayed in a gallery or museum. The earth artist instead uses nature directly, and usually his work must be seen outdoors where it is created. Examples of earth art are a field of grain in which the path of the harvesting machine forms a design; a patch of snow-covered land marked by sled runners; an area of desert in which a pattern of holes or other excavations has been made; and a stretch of shoreline draped with plastic. See also 95

Ecocide. The deliberate destruction of the environment by man, as a long-range process. Acts that contribute to the process include the polluting of the air and streams and the spraying of forests and other vegetation with chemicals that are harmful to animal life. Anything that upsets the balance of nature upon which human and animal life depends for survival and healthy growth is an act of ecocide.

Econometrics. In economics, the use of mathematics and statistics as tools. They are used by economists in finding the answers to problems and in working out laws and theories of economics. For example, if the price of a certain product rises a given amount, econometrics can determine in advance what the effect should be on the demand for this product by the people who use it.

Eutrophication. A process in which the supply of dissolved oxygen in a body of water is gradually reduced.
At the same time, the mineral and organic material increases and in turn causes a further reduction of oxygen.
Gradually the environment that results favors plant life
over animal life. In present-day studies of the environment, eutrophication is a term used to describe how
such a cycle of change causes lakes to become marsh-
land, then to solidify gradually, and in time to disappear.
The pollution of lakes and streams by modern industrial
wastes has been called an important factor in this un-
desirable process.

F

G

H

K

L

M

Machismo. In Latin America, an informal term for the qualities that make up manliness. The cult of machismo, which has developed in Latin America over centuries, reflects a belligerent pride in virility, strength, courage, and aggressiveness, and the idea that men are superior to women.

Male chauvinism. Beliefs and attitudes held by men that claim for men a natural superiority over women. "Chauvinism" is, literally, boastful devotion to one's country. The phrase "male chauvinism," as used by those in the movement for women's liberation, is devotion of men to ideas and customs that keep for them a favored position in government, in employment, in the home and family, and in all situations where the sexes might be considered to have competing roles.

N

No-fault insurance. Automobile insurance that provides payment to injured persons who hold such policies, regardless of who is at fault in an accident. Usually there is a limit on the amount paid by the insuring company under this system. (The maximum is $2,000 in Massachusetts, where the first no-fault insurance law was passed in August 1970.) The purpose of such insurance is to speed settlements of claims. No-fault insurance makes it unnecessary to investigate most accidents to fix blame according to law. It is designed especially for cases involving small insurance claims, which slow up the work of the courts when one of the parties in an accident sues the other. The no-fault system does not rule out court suits, however, if damages to one or both parties exceed a certain fixed amount.

O

OTB. An abbreviation for off-track betting. This refers to
legal betting away from the track on horse races under
terms of a law that provides part of the profit for a city
or state, as in New York City, which has an Off-track Betting Corporation. (In earlier usage, off-track betting was
used for all betting away from the track, including that
handled illegally by bookmakers.)

P

Picturephone. A special telephone that permits the user
to see the person with whom he is talking. Each of the
persons in the conversation is equipped with a Touch-
Tone telephone connected to a small control box and
to what looks like a small television receiving set. The
pictures of the speakers appear on the receiving screens
(each 5 by 5½ inches in size), and they can be switched
off at the will of the persons involved. Printed material
or photographs also can be viewed at one end of such
calls, when sent from the other. A camera is mounted in
the receiving set directly above the screen. The control
unit permits adjustment of picture brightness, field of
view, and sound volume. Experimentation with this equipment began in 1927. Bell Telephone Laboratories showed
its first Picturephone at the New York World's Fair in
1964. The Bell Telephone System set up its first regular
commercial service, with a new model, in Pittsburgh in
June 1970. The service is limited to subscribers. Plans
have been announced for local service in other large
U.S. cities and later for long-distance service.

Pompidou, Georges, president of France 72, 204, picture 205
Pontiac Sprint, automobile, picture 351
Popular music 179–81
Population
    control in Canada 141
    nations of the world 398–403
    New Zealand 129
Porter, William J., U.S. diplomat 56
Port Moresby, Papua New Guinea, picture 128
Post Office, U.S. *see* United States Postal Service
Powell, Lewis F., U.S. Supreme Court justice 66, 379
Presbyterian Church 298–99
Presidential candidates, United States 376–77
Price, Julie, page in U.S. Congress, picture 396
Prisons
    Attica Correctional Facility, revolt in 60, 374–75, pic-
        tures 60–61, 371, 375
    New Jersey State Prison revolt, picture 65
    violence in 374–75
Prizes and awards
    Academy awards 174
    Drama Critics Circle awards 169
    Emmy awards 186
    Grammy awards 181
    literature for adults 240
    literature for children 247, 248
    Nobel prizes 409
    Pulitzer prizes 409
    Tony awards 169
Programing, television 185–86
Project SOAR, Boy Scouts 386
Prostaglandins, new drug 259
Protestantism 298–99, picture 297
Protest movements
    Australia 126, picture 125
    See also Demonstrations
Protest songs 181
Public Broadcasting Service (PBS) 188
Public opinion polls, TV programs 187
Pulitzer prizes 409

Q

Qaddafi, Muammar al-, Libyan premier 267
Qatar 272, 273
Quarks, particles of matter 306
Quasars, distant objects in the universe 308–09
Quebec, Canada 144–45

R

Racing
    auto racing 326
    horse racing 340
Rahman, Sheik Mujibur, of Bangladesh 49, 66, 121, 122–
    23, picture 67

Railpax. The name first given to the undertaking that became the National Railroad Passenger Corporation. The
name was formed from the words "railroad" and "passengers." *See* Amtrak.

Railroads 354, pictures 355, 356
    strikes 155, picture 153
Randall, Tony, U.S. actor, picture 186
Raphael, Italian artist, painting by 92, picture 93
Recordings 180–81
    Grammy awards 181

Recreational vehicles 282–83

Recycle. To use again, after treatment; also, to make
something usable again, after processing, for the same
or another purpose. The term is now used especially for
the processing of waste material that is thrown away.
Recycling of collected metal cans and containers involves
making the metal available for use again. Experiments
have been made in recycling industrial waste matter so
as to change it chemically into soil. A much earlier example is the treatment of water, by purification or filter-
ing, after it has been used one or more times. *See also*
198–99, pictures 198–201

Refugees
    Bengali, picture 49
    Cuban, in U.S. 238, pictures 238–39
Regency Hyatt House, Chicago, Illinois 110
Rehnquist, William H., U.S. Supreme Court justice 66, 379
Religion 296–301, pictures 78–79
Repertory theater 171
Reston, James, U.S. newspaper columnist 12

Revenue sharing. The granting by the Federal Government
of a portion of its revenue to state or city governments
for use by them. (The Federal Government's revenue is
its income, chiefly in the form of money paid in taxes
by the people to cover public expenses.) In the United
States, there are two proposed forms of revenue sharing.
General revenue sharing is the granting of such money
to be used for any lawful public purpose chosen by the
states or cities. Special revenue sharing is the granting
of money for public uses that are stated in advance by
the Federal Government.

Rhodesia 77
    compromise agreement with Britain 64
    United Nations activities in 365
Richard, Henry, Canadian athlete, picture 138
Rivers, Larry, U.S. painter and sculptor, picture 91
Rizzo, Frank L., U.S. mayor 377
Robertson, Nancy, Canadian athlete, picture 349
Rockefeller Foundation 184
Rockefeller, Nelson A., U.S. governor, 375, picture 60
Rock music 179
Rogers, William, U.S. secretary of state 265, pictures 235,
    262, 263, 368
Rolls-Royce, Ltd., declared bankrupt 354
Roman Catholicism 300–01, picture 296
Roosa, Stuart A., U.S. astronaut 46, 320, picture 317
Rose, Jacques, Canadian separatist, picture 145
Rose, Paul, Canadian separatist, picture 145
Rothko Chapel, Houston, Texas 92
Rowe, Alan, British actor, picture 188
Rowland, Rev. Dr. Wilmina, U.S. minister, picture 299
Rudolph, Paul, U.S. architect 108
Rugby, in Australia, picture 125
Rumania 211–12
Russell, Leon, U.S. singer 180, picture 179
Ryun, Jim, U.S. athlete, picture 345

S

Sabena, Belgian airline 352
Sadat, Anwar el-, Egyptian president 265, 267, picture 211
Saint Laurent, Yves, French fashion designer 278
Saint Mary's Cathedral, San Francisco 107, pictures 106,
    107
Salary and wages, United States 155
    See also Wage-price freeze
SALT (Strategic Arms Limitation Talks) 365

Sick-in. An organized protest by workers against an em-
ployer as a means of gaining higher pay or better working conditions. It is a form of work slowdown in which
some or many of the workers in a company or branch of
government service do not report for duty and instead
call in to say that they are sick. Also called a **sick-out.**

Sky marshal. A man or woman whose job is to prevent
airplane hijacking. They belong to a newly formed group
of U.S. law-enforcement officials. Some work on the
ground at airports, inspecting lists of passengers to alert
airlines against likely suspects, or inspecting baggage
to prevent the smuggling of weapons onto airplanes.
Others are stationed aboard planes in flight, ready to resist hijacking attempts.

Spaghetti western. An Italian motion picture with a chiefly
Italian cast of actors that is like an **American** western
movie. The plots of spaghetti westerns feature adventure
in an outdoor setting, with a great deal of horseback
riding and gunplay.

Unit pricing. The pricing of goods in a way that tells a customer the price per unit of what he is buying. Consumer goods priced in this manner give not only the charge for the item of merchandise but also the price per pound, ounce, count, or other unit of measure. Most packaged or canned goods are not so priced by stores. The item is marked merely with a figure indicating its overall cost. Elsewhere on the label or container there is usually a statement of the weight, count, or liquid measure of the contents. By relating the overall cost to the quantity, unit pricing makes it easier for the customer to compare the values of competing brands, especially when they come in packages or containers of different sizes or shapes. *See also* 36

V

W

Y

Z

ILLUSTRATION CREDITS

The following list credits, by page, the sources of illustrations used in THE NEW BOOK OF KNOWLEDGE ANNUAL. Credits are listed illustration by illustration—left to right, top to bottom. Wherever appropriate, the name of the photographer or artist has been listed with the source, the two being separated by a dash. When two or more illustrations appear on one page, their credits are separated by semicolons.

10 Norman Webster © *Toronto Globe & Mail*
11 G. Sipahioglu—Jocelyne Benzakin
13 Audrey Topping
14 Audrey Topping
15 Audrey Topping
16 UPI; Audrey Topping
17 G. Sipahioglu—Jocelyne Benzakin
18 G. Sipahioglu—Jocelyne Benzakin; Audrey Topping
19 Audrey Topping
20 Audrey Topping
21 G. Sipahioglu—Jocelyne Benzakin
22 Frank Fischbeck, *Life* magazine © Time Inc.; Audrey Topping
23 Audrey Topping; G. Sipahioglu— Jocelyne Benzakin; Lyn-Annan— Photo Trends
24 Audrey Topping
26 Brown Brothers
27 David Krasnor—Photo Researchers
28 McDermott—Photo Researchers; Lyon—Rapho-Guillumette
29 Carew—Monkmeyer
30 Monroe Pinckard—Rapho-Guillumette
31 UPI
32 The Bettman Archive; Culver Pictures
33 Paris Match—Pictorial Parade; Hugh Rogers—Monkmeyer
34 Culver Pictures; Steve Northrup— Camera 5
35 UPI
37 Watson—Monkmeyer
38 Irene Bayer—Monkmeyer
39 Forsyth—Monkmeyer; Sanford— Monkmeyer
40 Forsyth—Monkmeyer
41 Strickler—Monkmeyer
42 George Sottung
44 Fred Ward—Black Star
45 Michael Abramson—Black Star
46 Eyerman—Black Star
47 NASA; UPI
48 Singh—Black Star
49 Wide World; Delassus-Gamma— Photoreporters
50 *London Daily Express*—Pictorial Parade
51 Richard Balagur—Nancy Palmer
52 ©Ian Berry—Magnum
53 *The Times*, London—Pictorial Parade
54 UPI
55 J. P. Laffont-Gamma—Photoreporters
56 AFP—Pictorial Parade
57 Wide World
58 NASA
59 Photoreporters
60 Bill Whiting—Camera 5
61 UPI
62 UPI
63 Photoreporters; Liaison; UPI
64 UPI
65 UPI
66 UPI
67 UPI; Photoreporters
68 USDA; UPI; Photoreporters
69 YAN—Rapho-Guillumette; NASA— Black Star; Richard Balagur—Nancy Palmer; UPI; NASA; Al Satterwhite—Camera 5
70 Bernheim—Rapho-Guillumette

71 Nancy Palmer; Keystone
72 G. Sipahioglu—Liaison
73 Keystone
74 Mohamed Amin—Keystone
75 UPI
76 Pictorial Parade
77 Argus Africa—Photo Trends
78 Bernheim—Rapho-Guillumette; Englebert—De Wys
79 Marc & Evelyne Bernheim—Rapho-Guillumette; Englebert—De Wys
80 Marc & Evelyne Bernheim—Rapho-Guillumette
81 Englebert—De Wys
82 Grant Heilman
83 UPI; Jerry Carlson—Farm Journal
84 Grant Heilman; UPI
85 Grant Heilman; Limousin Breeders Assoc.
87 Ball—Farm Journal
88 Farm Journal
90 UPI; Viking Press
91 Balthazar Korab—William Kessler; Hickey & Roberston, Rice University
92 Pierpont Morgan Library
93 Boston Fine Arts Museum; James Sudler Assoc.; Multiples Inc., NYC
94 White House Historical Association
95 Boston Fine Arts Museum
96 Citizen Exchange Corps
97 Citizen Exchange Corps
98 Citizen Exchange Corps
99 Citizen Exchange Corps
100 Eric Sutherland—Walker Art Center, Minneapolis
101 Parke-Bernet Galleries
102 Arthur Gough
103 Elliott Erwitt—Magnum
104 Edward Weston © Doubleday & Co.; Arthur Freed © Doubleday & Co.
105 Walker Evans—Museum of Modern Art
106 Morley Baer
107 Morley Baer
108 Joseph W. Molitor
109 Bo Parker © ESTO; Ezra Stoller © ESTO
111 Ron Vickers Ltd.
112 *London Daily Express*—Pictorial Parade
113 © HERBLOCK; Mark Godfrey— Black Star
114 Harmit Singh—Black Star
115 Asak—Black Star; Silverstone—Magnum
116 Khoo-APA—Keystone
118 Jones, PJJ—Pictorial Parade
119 Photoreporters; UPI
120 Wright—*Miami News*; Wide World
122 Photoreporters; Amin—Keystone; Photoreporters
123 UPI
124 UPI
125 *Sydney Morning Herald*
127 *Sydney Morning Herald*; Photoreporters
128 Australian News & Information Service
130 UPI
131 UPI
132 UPI; Dennis Brack—Black Star

133 UPI
134 Monroe Pinckard—Rapho-Guillumette
135 Monroe Pinckard—Rapho-Guillumette; National Film Board of Canada
136 UPI
137 UPI
138 UPI
139 UPI
140 UPI
141 UPI
143 Canada Wide—Pictorial Parade
144 Canadian Consulate
145 UPI
146 Ken Regan—Camera 5
147 Fred DeVan—Nancy Palmer; UPI
148 Doug Wilson—Black Star; UPI
149 UPI
151 © 1971 Beaverbrook Newspapers Ltd.; UPI
152 Booth; Ken Regan—Camera 5
153 UPI
154 UPI
156 *The New York Times*
157 Shelton—Monkmeyer; Roberts—Rapho-Guillumette
158 UPI
159 Writers Committee, Great Cities School Improvement Program, Detroit Public Schools. Illus: Ruth Ives. © 1962. Follett Publishing Co.
160 Cowell—Black Star
161 UPI
162 © George Zimbel—Photo Researchers
163 © George Zimbel—Photo Researchers
164 Granitsas—Photo Researchers
165 Granitsas—Photo Researchers
166 Zodiac
168 Martha Swope
169 © William Pierce
170 Sy Friedman—Zodiac
171 William Kaufman—Lincoln Center
172 Warner Bros.
173 Columbia Pictures; National General Pictures, Cinema Center Films
174 Universal Pictures
175 Cinema Center Films
176 Lawrence Fried
177 Fletcher Drake—JFK Center
178 UPI
179 Sahm Doherty—Camera 5
180 Curt Gunther—Camera 5
181 A&M Records
182 New York City Ballet
183 Jack Mitchell
184 Brooklyn Academy of Music
185 CBS NEWS
186 NBC; ABC
187 CBS
188 NET
189 Children's Television Workshop
190 CBS; ABC
191 NBC
192 Yale Joel, *Life* magazine © Time, Inc.
193 Al Satterwhite—Camera 5
194 USDA; Horst Schafer—Photo Trends
195 Horst Schafer—Photo Trends; UPI
197 P. Michael O'Sullivan—Camera 5; Tom McHugh—Photo Researchers
198 Tom McHugh—Photo Researchers; Tim Kantor—Rapho-Guillumette
199 Andrew Sachs—Black Star

200 Syd Greenberg—DPI
201 Alcoa
202 Wide World
203 Keystone; Sovfoto
205 Gamma—Photoreporters
206 Keystone
207 UPI
208 Henri Bureau—Photoreporters; Hardy—Photoreporters
209 Bernard Nagler—Black Star
211 UPI
212 Sovfoto
213 Sovfoto
214 Magnum Photos
215 UPI; Burk Uzzle—Magnum
216 UPI
225 Tandy Leather Co.
226 *Creative Crafts* magazine
227 *Creative Crafts* magazine
228 Camera Press—Jocelyne Benzakin
229 UPI
230 Sergio Larrain—Magnum
231 Francolon—Liaison
232 G. Sipahioglu—Jocelyne Benzakin
233 Eduardo Comesana—Pictorial Parade
234 UPI
235 UPI
236 UPI
237 UPI
238 Wide World
239 Annan—Photo Trends
240 Holt, Rinehart & Winston, Inc.; Y.R. Okamoto
241 Alfred A. Knopf, Inc.; Dennis Stock—Magnum; CBS; Holt, Rinehart & Winston, Inc.
243 W. W. Norton & Company, Inc.; Niki Ekstrom; Harper & Row, Publishers
244 © Karsh, Ottawa—Rapho-Guillumette; Oxford University Press
245 McGraw-Hill, Inc.; Ingrid Froelich—Photoreporters; Hal Malament—Black Star
246 Betsy Byars, *Summer of the Swans,* © 1970, Viking Press
247 Children's Book Council; © 1970 by Arnold Lobel—Harper & Row, Publishers
248 Natalie Babbit, *Knee Knock Rise,* © 1970, Farrar, Straus & Giroux, Inc.
249 Lothrop Lee & Shepard Co.—Hannah Lyons Johnson & Tony Chen
250 The Macmillan Company
251 Illustration from *A Story, A Story* by Gail E. Haley © 1970. Used by permission of Atheneum Publishers, N.Y.
252 *Flip* © 1971 by Youth ways Corporation; *Circus* © 1971 by Circus Enterprises Corporation; *Kids* © 1971 by Kid's Publishers, Inc.
253 *Kids* © 1971 by Kid's Publishers, Inc.
254 Wide World
255 UPI; Wide World
256 UPI
257 UPI
259 *The New York Times;* UPI
260 Baracs—Photoreporters
261 T. Tanuma, *Life* magazine © Time Inc.; Audrey Topping
262 Keystone
263 Israel Gov't Press Office; Oliphant—*Denver Post*
264 Israel Gov't Press Office
265 UPI

266 Keystone
267 Chauvel-Gamma—Photoreporters; UPI
268 UPI
269 UPI; Gamma—Photoreporters
270 Continental Oil Company
272 George Buctel
273 Photoreporters
274 UPI
275 UPI
277 Botti—Photoreporters
278 Anne-Marie Barden
279 Anne-Marie Barden
280 Terence Spencer, *Life* magazine © Time Inc.
281 Vernon Merritt, *Life* magazine © Time Inc.
282 Paolo Koch—Rapho-Guillumette; Charles Moore—Black Star
283 C. Moore—Black Star; Sally Wimer—*Invitation to Snowmobiling* magazine
284 UPI
285 UPI
286 Burchman—Pictorial Parade; Michael Rougier, *Life* © Time Inc.
288 UPI
289 UPI
290 UPI; © Karsh, Ottawa—Rapho-Guillumette; Lee Lockwood—Black Star
291 © Karsh, Ottawa—Rapho-Guillumette; G. Davis—Pictorial Parade
292 © Arnold Newman; The Bettman Archive; R. Cohen, AGIP—Black Star
293 Marie Claire, Paris Match—Black Star
296 Keystone
297 Shelly Rustin—Nancy Palmer; Don Rutledge—Religious News Service
298 Fletcher Drake—Pix; Religious News Service
299 UPI; Wide World
301 Keystone
302 *The Times,* London—Pictorial Parade; Israel Gov't Press Office
303 Agor-Camera Press—Pix
304 UPI
305 Scripps Institution of Oceanography
307 Oak Ridge National Laboratory
308 Original painting by Helmut K. Wimer—The American Museum, Hayden Planetarium
309 UPI
310 Scripps Institution of Oceanography
311 UPI
312 Ontario Science Center
313 Ontario Science Center
314 Ontario Science Center
315 Ontario Science Center
316 UPI
317 NASA
318 NASA
319 NASA
321 NASA
324 UPI
325 UPI
326 *London Daily Express*—Pictorial Parade
327 UPI
329 UPI
330 UPI
331 Heinz Kluetmeier for *Sports Illustrated* © Time Inc.
332 Catherine M. Ursillo; Ken Regan—Camera 5; UPI
333 UPI

334 Tom McLaughlin—Quaker Oats Company; Evelyn M. Shafer
335 UPI
336 UPI
337 UPI
338 UPI
339 UPI
340 M. Tadder—Pictorial Parade
341 *Ski Racing* magazine; UPI
342 UPI; Pictorial Parade
343 Gay Franklin—Camera 5
344 Wide World
345 James Drake for *Sports Illustrated* © Time Inc.
346 UPI
347 Neil Leifer for *Sports Illustrated* © Time Inc.; UPI
348 Neil Leifer for *Sports Illustrated* © Time Inc.
349 UPI
350 Santi Visalli—Photoreporters
351 Ford; General Motors; American Motors; Chrysler Corporation
352 Boeing
353 YAN—Rapho-Guillumette; Photoreporters
354 UPI
355 UPI; D. Hamilton—Auto Train Corp.
356 Pictorial Parade
357 Kevin Egan—Camera 5
358 © Leonard Freed—Magnum
359 *The New York Times;* UPI
360 UPI; Laffont-Gamma—Photoreporters
361 UPI
362 Wessberg—Black Star; UPI
363 UPI
364 Marc & Evelyne Bernheim—Rapho-Guillumette
365 United Nations
366 Frank Fischbeck, *Life* magazine © Time Inc.
367 UPI
368 UPI; Depardon-Gamma—Photoreporters
369 D. Bruce—Photoreporters; UPI; Leonard Freed—Magnum
370 Catherine M. Ursillo; Uzzle—Magnum
371 C. Gunther—Camera 5; B. Whiting—Camera 5
372 UPI
373 Stevenson
374 Carroll—Black Star
375 Michael Abramson—Black Star
376 Charles Moore—Black Star
377 Morton Broffman; Whitney Darrow, Sr.
379 Fred Ward—Black Star
381 UPI
382 Wide World
383 UPI; © HERBLOCK
384 Dennis Brack—Black Star
385 FFA; A. Sacks—CNA
386 John Shearer, *Life* magazine © Time Inc.
387 John Shearer, *Life* magazine © Time Inc.
388 Boys Clubs of America
389 Camp Fire Girls
390 Girl Scouts of America
391 Girl Scouts of America
392 Future Farmers of America
393 4-H Clubs
395 Wide World; UPI
396 UPI

Front cover photo: Childrens Television Workshop
Back cover photos: Curt Gunther—Camera 5; James Drake for *Sports Illustrated* © Time Inc.; Norman Webster © *Toronto Globe & Mail*

The Youthful Consumer by Marylin Bender, pages 37–41, © 1971 by The New York Times Company. Reprinted by permission.